DEVELOPMENTAL PSYCHOLOGY

Achievements and Prospects

Edited by

Mark Bennett

PSYCHOLOGY PRESS
ALERE FLAMMAM
Taylor & Francis Group

USA	Publishing Office:	PSYCHOLOGY PRESS *A member of the Taylor & Francis Group* 325 Chestnut Street Philadelphia, PA 19106 Tel: (215) 625–8900 Fax: (215) 625–2940
	Distribution Center:	PSYCHOLOGY PRESS *A member of the Taylor & Francis Group* 47 Runway Road, Suite G Levittown, PA 19057 Tel: (215) 269–0400 Fax: (215) 269–0363
UK		PSYCHOLOGY PRESS *A member of the Taylor & Francis Group* 1 Gunpowder Square London EC4A 3DE Tel: +44 171 583 0490 Fax: +44 171 583 0581

DEVELOPMENTAL PSYCHOLOGY: Achievements and Prospects

1 2 3 4 5 6 7 8 9 0

Printed by Edwards Brothers, Ann Arbor, MI, 1999.
Cover design by Claire O'Neill.

A CIP catalog record for this book is available from the British Library.
   The paper in this publication meets the requirements of the ANSI Standard Z39.48–1984 (Permanence of Paper).

Library of Congress Cataloging-in-Publication Data
        Developmental psychology : achievements and prospects / edited by
        Mark Bennett.
           p. cm.
        Includes bibliographical references and index.
        ISBN 0-86377-577-2 (case : alk. paper)
        ISBN 0-86377-578-0 (pbk. : alk. paper)
        1. Developmental psychology. I. Bennett, Mark, 1956-
        BF713 .D4646 1999
        155--dc21

                                                                    99-29808
                                                                    CIP
ISBN 0-86377-577-2(case)
ISBN 0-86377-578-0(paper)

For Ann

CONTENTS

14

Playing a Passing Game: Rationalism, Empiricism, and Cognitive Development

James Russell   253

15

Understanding Socialization: From Unidirectional to Bidirectional Conceptions

H. Rudolph Schaffer   272

16

Looking Back and Looking Forward on Intelligence: Toward a Theory of Successful Intelligence

Robert J. Sternberg   289

17 Cognitive Development

CONTRIBUTORS

Mark Bennett, (Editor) Senior Lecturer in psychology at the University of Dundee, Scotland. Previously he has held positions at Durham University and the Roehampton Institute. His main teaching and research interests are in the area of social-cognitive development and he has published widely in this field.

Marc H. Bornstein, Child and Family Research, National Institute of Child Health and Human Development, Bethesda, Maryland, USA

Robbie Case, Institute of Child Study, University of Toronto, Toronto, Ontario, Canada, and Department of Psychology, Stanford University, Stanford, California, USA

Judy Dunn, Social, Genetic and Developmental Psychology Centre, Institute of Psychiatry, Denmark Hill, London, UK

Jacqueline J. Goodnow, School of Behavioural Sciences, Macquarie University, Sydney N.S.W., Australia

Paul L. Harris, Department of Experimental Psychology, University of Oxford, Oxford, UK

Willard W. Hartup, Institute of Child Development, University of Minnesota, Minneapolis, Minnesota, USA

R. Peter Hobson, Developmental Psychopathology Research Unit, Tavistock Clinic, London, and University College, London, UK

Mark H. Johnson, Department of Psychology, Birkbeck College, University of London, London, UK

Frank C. Keil, Department of Psychology, Yale University, New Haven, Connecticut, USA

Katherine Nelson, Graduate School, City University of New York, New York, USA

Josef Perner, Department of Psychology, University of Salzburg, Salzburg, Austria

Robert Plomin, Social, Genetic, and Developmental Psychology Centre, Institute of Psychiatry, Denmark Hill, London, UK

James Russell, Department of Experimental Psychology, University of Cambridge, Cambridge, UK

H. Rudolph Schaffer, Department of Psychology, University of Strathcyde, Glasgow, Scotland, UK

Robert J. Sternberg, Department of Psychology, Yale University, New Haven, Connecticut, USA

James V. Wertsch, Department of Education, Washington University, St. Louis, Missouri, USA

PREFACE

The spectacular specialization of research in developmental psychology, coupled with a corresponding proliferation of journals, has meant that it is virtually impossible to keep up with what is happening in research areas adjacent to one's own, let alone those that are far removed. A sense of frustration at the inevitability of my own ignorance was the starting point for this book.

To attempt to satisfy what I assumed would be a widespread curiousity about research and theoretical developments throughout the field, I invited many of the world's most eminent developmentalists to comment, in a brief and personal way, on what they consider to have been developmental psychology's major achievements. I asked them to identify the major questions guiding research in their specialization, commenting on what is now known, the sorts of methods that have been used, and where the field might be heading. As one would expect of such a distinguished array of contributors, the chapters speak with authority and a willingness to venture challenging views. To a degree, then, my curiousity about "developmental psychology at large" has been satisfied. But above all, it has been sharpened, and that must be the greater compliment to the contributors.

I hope this book will be of interest to various audiences—developmentalists, colleagues in other branches of psychology, and, of course, students of developmental psychology, particularly graduate students and advanced undergraduates. To attempt to orientate readers who are less well acquainted with the field, I introduce the book with some general, stage-setting remarks about developmental psychology's history and principal themes, and broadly situate the succeeding chapters within that context.

It is cliché of book reviews that edited volumes are often curious and idiosyncratic collections of chapters. Essential to the personal character of this volume was the need to avoid constraining contributors with rigid guidelines, and I therefore make no apology in response to charges that the chapters may be idiosyncratic! I would especially like to thank

Alison Mudditt, at Psychology Press, who was quick to recognize the value of a book such as this, and who has been a patient and supportive editor.

Preparing this book has, for the most part, been one of the most enjoyable experiences of my academic life to date. I wish to convey sincere thanks to the contributors, all of whom were happy to forego royalties—which are directed not at my own pockets, I hasten to add, but those of Save the Children, Amnesty International, and the Society for Research in Child Development. Special thanks, too, to Psychology Press for so readily agreeing to enhanced royalties.

Mark Bennett
Dundee, Scotland

CHAPTER 1   Mark Bennett

Introduction

Despite a distinguished prehistory going back as far as Aristotle and Plato, developmental psychology is little more than one hundred years old. It was only in the latter part of the nineteenth century that the scientific study of children's development began in earnest, owing, amongst other influences, to Darwin's theory (which focused attention on the inheritance of adaptive behaviors) and to social changes which saw the introduction of mass education (prompting, for example, a desire to understand children's learning and the need for mental assessment). In my view, it would not be overstating the case to suggest that a profound interest in children's development, both scientific and lay, has been one of the striking features of the twentieth century.

In North America, key figures in the establishment of developmental psychology were G. Stanley Hall (White, 1992) and James Mark Baldwin (Cairns, 1992). Hall's contribution was immense in that he pioneered the scientific study of "the contents of children's minds," founded the Child-Study Association, and played a leading role in establishing the American Psychological Association. Baldwin, however, may be credited with having laid central theoretical foundations for developmental psychology, especially in the study of cognitive development (see chapter by Robbie Case). In Europe, an early pioneer was Alfred Binet, who, although now remembered largely for his work on IQ testing, conducted research on many aspects of children's development, such as perception and memory (Siegler, 1992).

Despite a good deal of early activity, progress was undoubtedly hampered, particularly in North America, by behaviorism's grip on psychol-

1

ogy. From the 1920s through to the 1950s, psychology's focus was upon the functional relations between observable stimuli and behavioral responses; elusive concepts such as development and cognition were widely eschewed. In Europe at this time, however, Jean Piaget was engaged in a prodigious and sustained program of research that sought to understand the development of human cognition as a form of biological adaptation to a complex environment. Piaget more than any single individual has shaped developmental psychology and, indeed, has established what are taken by many to be the sine qua non of an adequate developmental theory: the specification of mechanisms of change and structural and functional explanation. Moreover, the theoretical work created a fertile territory between nativism and environmentalism, namely, constructivism (Beilin, 1992). As such, then, Piaget's work can be seen as having an enduring influence within developmental psychology. Indeed, it has been suggested that "assessing the impact of Piaget on developmental psychology is like assessing the impact of Shakespeare on English literature—impossible. The impact is too monumental to embrace and at the same time too omnipresent to detect" (Beilin, 1992, p. 19).[1] Although Piaget's direct influence on developmental psychology has waned in recent years, his legacy is unmistakable, as several of the chapters of this book note.

During its relatively short life, developmental psychology has become an established discipline, flourishing both theoretically and methodologically, and presenting rich descriptions of development over an extensive range of content areas, as the chapters of this book demonstrate. While its early decades saw the appearance of a number of grand theories, for example, those of Baldwin, Erikson, Vygotsky, Werner, and, of course, preeminently Piaget, more recently there has been a proliferation of short-range theories addressing more circumscribed aspects of development, many of which are dealt with in this volume. Despite this move away from grand theories, it is clear that there have been many enduring themes.

One theme that, inevitably perhaps, has consistently occupied center stage has been concern about the *sources* of development: across a host of areas—personality, intelligence, perception, etc.—there has been controversy about how far development reflects either inherited or environmental factors. As Marc Bornstein notes, such controversy has distant

---

[1]As Beilin notes, this observation was made by an anonymous reviewer of his 1992 paper. I am able to disclose that the reviewer is amongst the contributors of this volume. A clue to his identity is given in my wish "to correct misunderstanding."

roots in philosophy. However, what has happened increasingly is that we have moved away from simple oppositions based on commitment either to the tradition of empiricism or that of nativism toward more complex interactionist accounts exemplified, for example, in *systems models*. Thus, Bornstein comments upon a move toward the use of the concept of *transaction* "that inherited constitution and experienced environment mutually influence one another through time." Similarly, Rudolph Schaffer shows that whereas earlier in the century, under the influence of psychologists like Watson, it was widely accepted that behavioral differences between children were almost entirely the result of socialization factors, more recent research has demonstrated that there exist innate temperamental differences (for example, in irritability, impulsivity, and irregularity) that themselves contribute to creating different social environments for children (notably, in terms of posing different challenges for their parents and caregivers).

Robert Plomin turns our attention to recent research in behavioral genetics. He shows how such research has established that genes influence (although do not determine) many aspects of behavior and, importantly, that they vary in the extent to which their influence is modified by environmental factors. He notes that when considering psychological traits, genes are complexly and multiply related to behavior and that their influence is significantly moderated by many types of environmental factors. Genes also appear to play a role in environment selection. Moreover, children's environments are significantly shaped by parents' behavior, which itself has genetic components. Of special interest to developmentalists is Plomin's discussion of how current research "is moving beyond simply demonstrating genetic influence . . . to ask questions about genetic change and continuity during development." For example, Plomin describes how recent work has shown that the magnitude of genetic influence on cognitive ability changes during development; specifically, and contrary to what might be expected from a commonsense view, genetic influence on cognitive development appears to increase gradually from infancy, through childhood and adolescence, to adulthood.

Katherine Nelson, considering the nature/nurture controversy in the context of language development, makes a more radical case than others and argues that "There is no either/or here, no nature/nurture choice; both are not only necessary but indivisible. It is possible to break the system apart, to examine brain function, for example, but then the system is no longer functioning as a system (i.e., it is no longer active in its environment)." Thus her contention is a fundamental and critical one, namely, that our analytic categories, nature and nurture, are essentially artificial, at least when considering complex phenomena like language.

Despite roots in biology, it is perhaps an irony of developmental psychology's history that it is only quite recently that knowledge of the biological bases of behavior has really proliferated. Of course, this proliferation has been due largely to technological developments, such as DNA chips (see Plomin) and functional magnetic resonance imaging (see Johnson). On the strength of such advances, Mark Johnson makes the case that we now know enough about brain development to be able to assert that a promising future for developmental psychology lies in a closer association with developmental biology. He argues that the dissociation of cognitive development from developmental biology in recent decades has resulted in models that are biologically implausible (in particular, nativist accounts that postulate the existence of particular brain structures responsible, in a largely invariant way, for processing domain-specific information). Although not denying that there is domain-related specialization in cognition, he suggests that this is primarily due to post-natal interactions with the environment. Taking the example of face processing, Johnson proposes a neuroconstructivist account that emphasizes how preexisting brain structures guide orientation to aspects of the environment; importantly, experience then further tunes neural circuits, thereby achieving optimal local functioning by means of gradual specialization. Thus, Johnson argues that "we need theories of the child as an active contributor to its own subsequent brain specialization."

This general notion of the child as playing an active role in its own development is one that has become ever-more prominent during developmental psychology's history. Most significantly perhaps, in terms of influencing the field, is its central part in Piaget's theory, in which the child is seen as actively constructing knowledge of the world. But it is evident elsewhere, too. In the field of socialization, for example, Schaffer notes that whereas once the child was seen as essentially passive, it is now widely accepted that socialization is a two-way street: "Children, . . . by virtue of their individual characteristics, affect how parents behave towards them, and in this way help to determine their own upbringing." Thus, current work on socialization, as Schaffer makes clear, sees reciprocity and mutuality as basic in the parent–child relationship.

Willard Hartup observes that this change in the zeitgeist of developmental psychology, from seeing children as passive recipients to viewing them instead as active agents, has had profound consequences and opened up new areas for research. For example, where once peer relationships were seen as trivial phenomena unworthy of attention, it is now accepted that children actively socialize one another and that the peer group plays a key role in development. Hartup's chapter makes clear that such relationships contribute importantly to children's social skill and self-regulative development. Judy Dunn too discusses how children's relationships with one another contribute to the development of interpersonal understanding.

Another theme that has been central in developmental psychology (particularly during the 1970s and 1980s) is the question of whether development is best conceptualized in terms of discrete, qualitatively distinct stages or as a gradual and continuous process of incremental change. Clearly, the most influential proponent of the stage view has been Piaget, who asserted that cognitive development progressed through an invariant series of stages and that within any particular stage all aspects of thought were interrelated by virtue of the logical structures taken to define that stage. Robbie Case provides a clear statement of the intellectual origins and major features of Piaget's stage conception of cognitive development. He also discusses the various alternatives to Piaget's theory, such as (i) neo-Piagetian theory (which sees conceptual development as a more local process, although nevertheless limited by general constraints); (ii) the view that conceptual development is best understood as the acquisition of expertise (i.e., conceptual development as reflecting novice-to-expert shifts based on the establishment of increasingly elaborated knowledge networks); and (iii) the theory-based knowledge approach (in which developmental differences in thinking reflect changes in children's naive theories about particular domains of knowledge, such as biology, psychology, and mechanics). Proponents of the latter view in particular have emphasized the "modularity of mind": that the mind comprises various "modules," which are specialized for processing different types of information, or "domains." Despite the differences between these approaches, Case identifies various points of convergence, perhaps the most important being that "the notion of a systemwide cognitive structure should be replaced by a notion of structures that are more domain specific."

That cognitive development is likely to be domain specific is the starting point for Frank Keil's chapter. However, Keil notes various problems facing current researchers, such as that we lack any formal specification of the concept of "domain" and thus cannot adequately distinguish between pockets of local expertise (e.g., cartoon superheroes) and universal domains (e.g., folk psychology). To begin to address this, he urges that we examine "how patterns in the world cluster according to lawful regularities, with the broad domains being characterized by much more distinctive and interconnected principles." Clearly the description of the distinctive informational properties of domains would involve a significant extension of most current research programs. However, referring to the Gibsons' work on the relation between the visual system and the structure of the environment, Keil argues for the necessity of looking both at cognizer and cognized, suggesting that "different kinds of cognitive structures optimally resonate with different kinds of real-world relations." Keil also points out that we have typically assumed that, within a domain, children have qualitatively distinct types of representations at different ages. He cautions that we should be open to the possibility that rather than there being a homogeneous architecture underlying cognition, there may be hybrid architectures throughout development. We need, too, to give more attention to implicit nonverbalized knowledge and to guard against the widespread assumption that such knowledge is impoverished by comparison with that which is explicit and verbalizable. Thus, while Keil subscribes to the now-orthodox view that cognitive development is domain specific, he offers many cautions to current researchers.

A further trend within developmental psychology, especially conspicuous in recent years, has been a move toward studying development within its social contexts. Thus, where once it was typical to view the child in a relatively isolated way, many now attempt explicitly to locate development within social contexts, arguing for the indivisibility of child and context. This emphasis on development's social nature is due importantly to the work of Vygotsky, discussed by James Wertsch. An innovative feature of Vygotsky's approach was his proposal that even mental processes, such as thinking and attention, have sociocultural origins; social contexts are seen not merely as influencing overt behavior (as might be expected under folk psychological notions), but as constitutive of the apparently "private" world of mental phenomena. Thus, in a now-classic quote, Vygotsky asserted that:

> Any function in the child's cultural development appears twice, or on two planes. First it appears on the social plane, and then on the psychological plane. First it appears between people as an interpsychological category, and then within the child as an intrapsychological category. This is equally true with regard to voluntary attention, logical memory, the formation of concepts, and the development of volition. (Vygotsky, 1981, p. 163)

For Vygotsky, then, thinking is an activity that is social in origins. It is also social in form since it reflects the conventional tools of a culture (for example, counting and other conceptual systems and, preeminently, language; see Nelson this volume). Vygotsky's focus on the central role of the social context in development has inspired a great deal of research in developmental psychology, for example, Bruner's (1983) work on the way in which adults "scaffold" children's language acquisition, Rogoff's (1990) study of "apprenticeship in thinking," and Wertsch's (1991) analysis of "mediation," that is, the use of cultural tools in thinking. Increasingly, then, within the "sociohistoric" tradition, and elsewhere, we have seen an awareness of the need for development to be understood as contextually embedded. However, as will be noted, this is not to say that all aspects of Vygotsky's work have been comprehensively embraced.

The "socializing" of developmental research is seen clearly in Jacqueline Goodnow's chapter, which looks at the attempt by many researchers to examine development within the key context of the family. Although much progress has occurred in this field, what emerges from Goodnow's discussion, surprisingly perhaps, is the rather partial picture we have of the family's role in children's development. For example, she notes that considerable attention has been directed at: mothers' behavior (with fathers, grandparents, and siblings much neglected until recently); the psychological effects of the *number* of parents in a household (single parent versus dual parent families); and the management of children's transgressions (e.g., punishment versus reasoning). Although not denying the importance of these topics, Goodnow notes many virgin territories for future research on the family, for example, life-span approaches and the family as a "resource" to its members. Although we should not be surprised by how much remains to be done, given the relative recency of work in this field, Goodnow makes the astute observation that "In the course of zooming in on a particular feature of families or a particular aspect of influence, it is easy to lose the rest of the picture, to mistake the part for the whole." Clearly there is an important general lesson here for all areas of research, especially in view of the proliferation of short-range theories: a need to be ever vigilant to the bigger picture of development. As Bornstein implies, it is only too easy to overlook the "unity of development," that is, that there exist intimate connections between the physical, physiological, neurological, perceptual, cognitive, emotional, and social lines of ontogeny.

Concurrent with the increased recognition of the social contexts of development has been a burgeoning of interest in the social *content* of cognition. Thus, whereas early work focused largely on understanding of physical and logical phenomena (especially conservation), research since the 1970s has broadened significantly to address children's understanding of many aspects of the social world (Bennett, 1993): for example, social rules, event structures, personality traits, gender, emotion, economics, social structure, and, most prominently of all, "theories of mind." The chapters by Judy Dunn, Paul Harris, and Josef Perner each look, in very different ways, at the remarkable output of work on children's theories of mind.

Dunn, taking a strongly social orientation to "mindreading," demonstrates that in their early attempts to understand and influence others' minds, children evince considerably greater understanding in the crucible of family life than they do in the context of the laboratory. Dunn discusses the implications of such findings for our understanding of the social origins and functions of mindreading skills. In doing so, she alerts us to the need for caution in interpreting laboratory-based research.

Harris draws attention to the close relationship between communication and social cognition, arguing that "the child's emerging grasp of the mental states of knowing and thinking is initially embedded in the context of communication." Beyond elaborating this thesis, what is valuable about Harris' chapter is that it makes a strong case for the existence of continuities between work conducted in the 1970s, on babies' imitation, intersubjectivity, and joint attention, and work conducted in the 1980s and 1990s on preschoolers' understanding of mental representation. That is, Harris sketches a developmental account that takes us from early joint attention behavior through to that point at which children appreciate that others may hold partial or misleading information about the world.

Perner begins his consideration of theory of mind work by demonstrating the field's indebtedness to analytic philosophers, especially their work on folk psychology. He guides us through analysis of the distinction between the *contents* of mental states and the *functions* they serve and shows how such analysis has helped clarify a variety of persistent problems, such as the form of mental state understanding that might be revealed by the capacity for pretense. Following this conceptual analysis, Perner goes on to provide an overview of some of the major developments in children's theories of mind. In addition, he considers individual differences in this area, commenting upon the role of social and genetic factors in theory of mind development. However, perhaps most exciting, Perner makes the case that research on theory of mind has the potential to provide insights into the development of consciousness.

One theme that has waxed and waned within developmental psychology has been the relation between the normal and abnormal in development. Despite various explorations of their relation in particular areas of developmental psychology, Peter Hobson, a clinician and academic, suggests that the potential for developmental psychopathology to broaden the scope of developmental theories has not yet been fully realized. He argues that the attempt to encompass typical and atypical phenomena in development has revolutionary potential because one may come to see typical development in a new light. He also elaborates the point that "the study of psychopathological conditions enables us to pursue empirical investigations in areas that are otherwise largely inaccessible. In particular, one can see how particular psychological abilities and disabilities that usually develop in tandem can become dissociated in the abnormal case." (Interestingly, Johnson also comments on the possible benefits of studying the abnormal case, although he draws rather different conclusions.) Moreover, Hobson argues that research in developmental psychopathology bears upon our choice among "higher-order theories" about development, such as constructivism and contextualism. Thus, notwithstanding developmental psychology's often-ambivalent attitude toward the issue of pathology, Hobson makes a compelling case for its inclusion in future research programs.

Finally, a recent development in the field, one noted by Bornstein, is an emerging concern about the validity of linear models of development—models that assume, for example, direct cause–effect relationships, that effects are proportional to causes, and that development describes a "line" or specifiable course. Thus, Bornstein points out that research seldom if ever demonstrates that early experiences have direct effects, nor that the extent of an effect is a simple function of the potency of a particular cause. And with respect to the issue of conceptualizations of development as following a clear trajectory, or course, Keil sounds a note of caution. As we have noted, Keil suggests that it may be a mistake to assume that at particular points in development, cognition has particular forms, such that children will think about a given task in a single, age-dependent way. Rather than single architectures underlying cognition, Keil considers the possibility that there may exist hybrid architectures throughout development. Siegler (1997), similarly, has offered an important alternative to the widely held view that there exist one-to-one correspondences between age and characteristic ways of thinking. He argues for a view of cognitive development that takes it that at any given point children have access to *multiple* strategies and that "developmental change involves shifts in the frequency with which children rely on these ways of thinking" (p. 95). Growing recognition of the complexity of development is evident elsewhere, too, for example in formal models of nonlinearity in development (see Thelen & Smith, 1994; van Geert, 1994).

Thus far one might suppose that the chapters of this book present a resolutely positive picture of developmental psychology's achievements and prospects. Charges of complacency would be hard to sustain, however, since all the contributors note the difficulties of their fields. Moreover, it is perfectly clear that there are tensions between the theoretical positions of many of the contributors to this volume. For example, Keil asserts that collaborations with cognitive scientists have been of the utmost importance; Johnson sees such collaborations as having resulted in some seriously counterproductive outcomes. And while Johnson is at pains to identify his brand of connectionism as neither nativist nor empiricist, but as constructivist, Russell asserts that despite their claims, connectionists are in a fundamental sense empiricists since their position "assumes that there is no more in a concept than there is in the experience that gave rise to it." And so on. Elsewhere, too, we find trenchant commentary on broad swathes of inquiry. For example, among other issues, Nelson discusses how under Piaget's influence developmental psychology has "blocked off" language from the study of cognition: because of Piaget's insistence that language was dependent on cognition, language development has been studied as a phenomenon in its own right, and as a consequence we know relatively little about its contribution to cognitive development. Sternberg, similarly, is extremely critical of much of the psychometrically based work on intelligence, especially that which has postulated the existence of *general* intelligence, or *g*. Dismissing a century's efforts, Sternberg argues that *g* does not exist and instead proposes a theory of "successful intelligence," which he argues represents an advance both scientifically and in terms of more fully realizing human potential.

Further criticism, this time of work on cognitive development, comes from Wertsch, who observes that within the field, as within our culture generally, there is a widespread assumption that terms such as "thinking" and "memory" refer to processes located exclusively within individuals. Such an assumption gives an "analytic primacy to individual over social processes" and, argues Wertsch, constrains our understanding of the social dimensions of cognitive development. Wertsch is critical of the pervasive failure of cognitive developmentalists to recognize how the symbolic tools of a culture guide cognition and action. Acknowledgment of the mediation of cognition by "cultural tools," he argues, would bring into focus an appreciation of the links between cognitive development and its cultural, historical, and institutional contexts. Thus, although some aspects of Vygotsky's work have been widely influential (for example, that on the "zone of proximal development"), others are acknowledged but remain to be adequately incorporated into current theoretical and empirical work.

Similar grand-scale injunctions to the discipline come from James Russell. He begins by examining the rationalist and empiricist epistemologies found in developmental psychology and finds both wanting. There are many significant targets along the way: Hume, connectionism, Fodor, and modular nativism. Drawing on Aristotle, Kant, and Quine, Russell drafts the outlines of a different kind of cognitive–developmental psychology from much that we see today, but one which, interestingly, is not far removed from genetic epistemology.

Thus, several chapters present determined criticism. Nevertheless, the overwhelming sense that one gains from this volume is of confidence and optimism. In my view this confidence broadly reflects the character of contemporary developmental psychology. Indeed, it is striking that, unlike some other areas of psychology, for example, social psychology, we have not had a period of "crisis" (see Israel & Tajfel, 1972) in which the fundamental nature and goals of developmental inquiry have been contested. It is striking too that, unlike so many areas within the human sciences (such as geography, sociology, economics, and anthropology), we have not been through a period of self-scrutiny prompted by postmodern critiques (see Doherty, Graham, & Malek, 1993). This is perhaps surprising insofar as there now exist numerous postmodern critiques of the very notion of development itself, that is, arguments to the effect that development is no more than one of modernity's many illusions.[2] (See Chandler, 1997, for a summary of such critiques.) Arguably, given current in-house concerns about the way in which developmental psychology has addressed the concept of development (e.g., Amsel & Renninger, 1997), engaging with our critics may be no bad thing and may serve to prompt clearer and more widespread consideration of how best to draw the conceptual distinction between development and change.

A willingness to engage with those beyond the disciplinary boundaries of developmental psychology has, from its early days, been a hallmark of the discipline and undoubtedly has contributed to its success. As the chapters of this volume attest, developmental psychology's achievements have not occurred in isolation: biology, cognitive science, ethology, evolutionary psychology, linguistics, neuroscience, philosophy, and theory of computation have all played a significant role in the development of developmental psychology. It seems unlikely that there will be any diminution of such productive intellectual alliances. On the contrary: the spectacular expansion of information technologies is likely to enhance such endeavors and may contribute to the further promotion of interdisciplinary developmentalism. And as the chapters of this book affirm, the conceptual and theoretical developments of recent years have provided a renewed clarity to many of developmental psychology's major questions. This, coupled with dramatic technological and methodological advances, gives a compelling quality to Hartup's contention that developmental psychology's "end-of-the-century agenda is as feasible as it is formidable."

---

[2]When I recently mentioned this to a senior and well-known developmentalist, his response was, "Postmodernists? Pah! Someone tell them about the object concept." I relate this anecdote because I think it speaks of developmentalists' conception of the ontological status of their "developables," that is, that they have a self-evident and unproblematic facticity. (However, while there may exist further such examples, which can be well defended against charges that only change—and not develop—has taken place, a great many of the changes that occur during childhood might better be seen as just that. It seems reasonable to suggest that further debate on this matter would benefit the field.)

☐ Acknowledgments

Thanks are conveyed to Martyn Barrett and Fabio Sani for critical comments on an earlier version of this chapter.

☐ References

Amsel, E., & Renninger, A. K. (Eds.). (1997). *Change and development: Issues of theory, method and application.* Mahwah, NJ: Erlbaum.

Beilin, H. (1992). Piaget's enduring contribution to developmental psychology. *Developmental Psychology, 28,* 17–24.

Bennett, M. (Ed.). (1993). *The child as psychologist.* Hemel Hempstead, Hertfordshire, UK: Harvester Wheatsheaf.

Bruner, J. (1983). *Child's talk.* New York: Norton.

Cairns, R. B. (1992). The making of a developmental science: The contribution and intellectual heritage of James Mark Baldwin. *Developmental Psychology, 28,* 191–204.

Chandler, M. J. (1997). Stumping for progress in a post-modern world. In E. Amsel & A. K. Renninger (Eds.), *Change and development: Issues of theory, method and application.* Mahwah, NJ: Erlbaum.

Doherty, J. M., Graham, E., & Malek, M. (Eds.). (1993). *Postmodernism and the social sciences.* London: Macmillan.

Israel, J., & Tajfel, H. (Eds.). (1972). *The context of social psychology: A critical assessment.* London: Academic Press.

Rogoff, B. (1990). *Apprenticeship in thinking: Cognitive development in social context.* New York: Oxford University Press.

Siegler, R. S. (1992). The other Alfred Binet. *Developmental Psychology, 28,* 179–190.

Siegler, R. S. (1997). Concepts and methods for studying cognitive change. In E. Amsel & A. K. Renninger (Eds.), *Change and development: Issues of theory, method and application.* Mahwah, NJ: Erlbaum.

Thelen, E., & Smith, L. B. (1994). *A dynamic systems approach to the development of cognition and action.* Cambridge, MA: MIT Press.

van Geert, P. (1994). *Dynamic systems of development: Change between complexity and chaos.* Hemel Hempstead, Hertfordshire, UK: Harvester Wheatsheaf.

Vygotsky, L. S. (1981). The genesis of higher mental functions. In J. V. Wertsch (Ed.), *The concept of activity in Soviet psychology.* Armonk, NY: M.E. Sharpe.

Wertsch, J. V. (1991). *Voices of the mind: A sociocultural approach to mediated action.* Cambridge, MA: Harvard University Press.

White, S. H. (1992). G. Stanley Hall: From philosophy to developmental psychology. *Developmental Psychology, 28,* 25–34.

Marc H. Bornstein[1]

Human Infancy: Past, Present, Future

☐ Why Infancy?

Infancy is the phase in the human life cycle that extends from birth roughly to the emergence of language; the term "infant" derives from the Latin *in* + *fans*, literally "nonspeaker." Infancy encompasses only a very small percentage of the average person's life expectancy. Why, then, is infancy so special? Infants attract attention to themselves, and they pose compelling, abiding, and thought-provoking questions.

Infancy achieved recognition as an independent and significant stage of life in pre-Classical times. When the Romans depicted periods in the life cycle of a typical man on "biographical" sarcophagi, they included images of infancy. Indeed, artists everywhere and throughout the ages have represented infancy as typically the first or second age in the life span (Bornstein, 1999). Iconographically, infants symbolize origins and beginnings.

Infancy is about change most noticeably, and the pervasiveness, rapidity, and clarity of developmental change in infancy impel irresistible fascination: the shape and capacity of the body and muscles, the complexity of the nervous system, the advent of sensory and perceptual capacities, the ability to understand and master objects in the world, the acquisition of communicative competencies, the emergence of characteristic personal

---

[1]This chapter summarizes selected aspects of my research, and portions of the text have appeared in previous scientific publications. I thank J. Lampard and B. Wright for comments and assistance.

and social styles, and the formation of social bonds. At no other time does development occur in so many different aspects of life so quickly and so thoroughgoingly. Thus, for everyone who comes into contact with them, infants provoke endless curiosity, engender compelling challenges, and dispense lots of plain fun. *What can infants do? What accounts for the striking developments that occur in infancy? How will my baby develop?*

Infants are of interest to people in different walks of life for many reasons: to parents for their personal and future investment, to philosophers and psychologists for answers to the imponderable questions they pose, and to practitioners for the magnificent potential locked inside each baby. Politicians kiss babies before elections to show how human and caring they really are!

Philosophy and psychological science have been attracted to infancy by the opportunities infants afford to understand the origins of adult life. Studying infants means human beings studying themselves from as early in life as is normally accessible to observation; paradoxically, the details of that time are lost to us, although we were all once infants. *How do infants see, hear, and feel? What do infants know and understand?* Considering the diversity of the people we know and the range of tendencies and capacities they exhibit, we naturally wonder how they started out and how they got to be who they are. *How is who we are a reflection of our genetic endowment, and how a shaping by the experiences we have had?* Some contend that infancy is part of a continuous lifeline, whereas others describe a major discontinuity between infancy and succeeding developmental periods. Some contend that infancy and what happens to us in infancy are ephemeral, others that infant experiences extend lifelong. *What is the significance of experiences and activities in infancy for the life course?*

Practitioners attend to infancy out of the need to respond to social, medical, and biological problems. Twentieth-century advances in obstetric technologies have led to the survival of greater numbers of infants born preterm. *What quality of life can "preemies" expect?* Some babies develop extremely well, whereas others become casualties. *What accounts for the differences?* Large numbers of infants are born to mothers or fathers who abuse illicit substances. *Are such infants neurologically compromised by virtue of damage done to their brains in the months before they are born? Do these infants possess the capacity and plasticity to adapt successfully to life?* Understanding infancy can promote the development of children whose potential appears to have been compromised. *What can be done to enhance the chances that infants will live, thrive, and actualize their fullest potential?* These questions motivate professionals to attend to and study infants, but these rationales are by no means mutually exclusive, the province of one group.

My goal in this chapter is to overview some prominent but everyday theoretical, empirical, and practical issues that conspire to make infancy so perennially fascinating a focus of interest to parent, philosopher, psychologist, and professional practitioner. Infancy studies have been marked by great strides of methodology and knowledge building. Although speculation about infants may be as old as time, scientific attention to infants really began with Darwin (1877) near the start of the twentieth century, and surprisingly infancy studies (meaning close observation and experimentation) are only approximately a half-century old. Nonetheless, in this brief period our understanding of our own infancies has undergone a revolution, and infancy research has moved well beyond its own infancy into the maturity of a sophisticated science with sophisticated scientists attacking sophisticated scientific problems from the philosophical and descriptive to the methodological and explanatory. Indeed, infancy research is one of the unmitigated successes of scientific investigation in the twentieth century.

Although philosophers, psychologists, and practitioners have appropriated infants to their purview, the story of infancy has to begin with parents. Parents are heavily invested in infants, their survival, and their socialization and education. Every parent is fascinated by the dramatic ways in which their helpless and apparently disorganized newborn baby transforms into the remarkably competent and curious, frustrating, and frustrated child.

☐ Parents and Infants

Each day more than three-quarters-of-a-million adults around the world experience the joys and heartaches, challenges and rewards of becoming parents to a newborn (Population Reference Bureau, 1993). Although Darwin (1877) wrote down and published observations of his firstborn son, Doddy, every parent who has not written down her or his observations has surely made extensive mental notes.[2] Parents playing with their infants are the first philosophers of infancy (asking themselves es-

---

[2]The first-ever reports of children were diary descriptions of infants in their natural settings written by parents, so-called baby biographies (Wallace, Franklin, & Keegan, 1994). Darwin published observations he had made in the early 1840s on his firstborn son William Erasmus, nicknamed "Doddy." Darwin's (1877) "A Biographical Sketch of an Infant" gave great impetus to infancy studies (Dixon & Lerner, 1999): In succeeding years, baby biographies grew in popularity around the world—whether they were scientific documents, parents' private records, or illustrations of educational practices—and they continue to appear today (e.g., Mendelson, 1990; Stern, 1990). Perhaps the most influential of the modern baby biographers was Piaget (1952), whose writings and theorizing refer chiefly to observations of his own young children, Jacqueline, Lucienne, and Laurent. Early observations of infancy heightened awareness in parents, provoked formal studies, and stimulated progress in how to guide infant development.

sentially epistemological questions), the first scientists of infancy (tinkering to elicit this or that reaction), and the first practitioners of infancy (making sure about wellness and ministering to illness).

Infants do not develop in a vacuum; their arrival and presence profoundly shape, just as they themselves are shaped by, family members and other people and institutions with whom their families come into contact. (See also Schaffer, this volume.) Nothing rivets the attention or stirs the emotions of adults more than a newborn. Infants are compelling and powerful stimuli in their specific physiognomy (as Lorenz, 1935/1970, observed) as well as by dint of their general being; indeed, the field of child development has identified and labeled the phenomenon "infant effects" (Bell, 1968; Bell & Harper, 1977). By their very coming into existence, infants forever alter the sleeping, eating, and working habits of their parents; they change who parents are and how parents define themselves (Bornstein, 1995a). Infancy is a phase of the life cycle when human caregiving occurs at its most intense levels and could exert its most salient influences. Infants are thought to be particularly susceptible and responsive to external experiences: The infant is most dependent on caregiving, and the human being's ability to cope alone is minimal. The sheer amount of interaction between parent and child is also greatest in infancy; parents spend more than twice as much time with their infants as they do with their children in middle childhood (Barnard & Martell, 1995; Collins, Harris, & Susman, 1995). Moreover, parenting responsibilities are also greatest then; parenting infants is a 168-hour-a-week job just because the human infant is totally dependent on parents for survival. Infants engender responsibility and make undeniable demands; infants are also fun to observe, to talk to, and to play with; infants do not know how to be agonistic, deceiving, or malicious (Papoušek & Papoušek, 1995). In the last analysis, it is the special and enduring task of parents to enculturate children, that is, to prepare them for the physical, economic, and psychosocial situations that are characteristic of the environment and culture in which they are to survive and thrive (Bornstein, 1991; Bugental & Goodnow, 1998; Cole, 1999).

☐ Philosophers, Psychologists, and Infants

The Origins of Knowledge and Character

Observing the constructs, structures, or functions and the dramatic developments in each that hallmark infancy has motivated scholars of diverse stripes to ask about the nature, sources, and consequences of this initial phase of life, and their attempts at answers have inevitably and invariably led to speculations about the roles of heredity and experience—the classic *nature/nurture* controversy (Dixon & Lerner, 1999). In *The Laws*, Plato (*ca* 355 BC/1970) theorized about the significance of infancy in just these respects. The debate first starkly contrasted schools of nativist and empiricist philosophies, both of which were interested in epistemology, understanding where knowledge comes from and how it grows. Empiricism was fostered by two separate but coordinated views. One derived from John Locke (1632–1704) who reputedly described the mind of the infant as a "tabula rasa," and a slightly different view was attributed to William James (1842–1910) who asserted that the world of the infant is a "blooming, buzzing confusion" out of which infants' experiences help them to organize and to create mental order. Empiricism takes an inherently developmental (discontinuous) stance because it contrasts the naiveté of infancy with the sophistication of maturity. By contrast, nativism viewed the empiricist belief that human beings begin life "empty headed" as both theologically and philosophically intolerable and logically indefensible: God would not create "in His image" mindless creatures with no awareness of good and evil, but rather that knowledge is inherent in us, and (anyway) it could not be learned in so short a span of time as childhood. Thus, the likes of Rene Descartes (1596–1650) and Immanuel Kant (1724–1804) proposed that infants are endowed at birth with "innate ideas" that assist in understanding the nature of the world. According to nativists, infants and adults share many of the same capacities, and so nativism is not particularly developmental (it is continuous), although it does acknowledge that certain abilities may take time to emerge or mature.

The nature/nurture debate is centuries old, but its central tenets have remained elemental to thinking about infancy through to the close of the twentieth century. Two prominent theorists give us a flavor of how these contrasting views of infancy and human nature have found expression in modern times. The intellectual founder of the nativist movement in America, maturationism, was the psychologist–pediatrician Gesell, who wrote about infancy that:

> the original impulse to growth . . . is endogenous rather than exogenous. The so-called environment, whether internal or external, does not generate the progression of development. Environmental factors support, inflect, and specify, but they do not engender the basic forms and sequences of ontogenesis. (1954, p. 354)

America's premier empiricist, and Gesell's contemporary, emphasized the plasticity of human beings from infancy. Watson wrote:

> Give me a dozen healthy infants, well-formed, and my own specified world to bring them up in, and I'll guarantee to take any one at random

and train him to become any type of specialist I might select—doctor, law-yer, artist, merchant-chief and yes, even beggarman and thief, regardless of his talents, penchants, tendencies, abilities, vocations, race of his ances-tors. (1924/1970, p. 104)

The pages of today's premier scientific journals and handbooks devoted to infancy studies and child development regularly echo these soundings (Scarr & Kidd, 1983; Spelke & Newport, 1998).

Continuity or Discontinuity From Infancy?

Beyond these compelling questions of the origins of knowledge and character, debate has also raged concerning the significance of infancy in human development generally (Bornstein & Kessen, 1979; Bornstein & Lamb, 1992). Proponents of one view have asserted that the behavior patterns and experiences manifest or developing in infancy are crucial to the balance of the life span: Intellectual predilections, emotional tenden-cies, and social orientations present at the start establish long-lasting pat-terns. Folk wisdom and poetry, for example, express the conviction that infancy and experiences in early life are formative in development:

> The childhood shows the man,
> As the morning shows the day.
> —J. Milton, 1671, *Paradise Regained*, Book IV, line 220.

> 'Tis education forms the common mind:
> Just as the twig is bent, the tree's inclined.
> —A. Pope, 1734, *Moral Essays*, line 149.

Plato held this view, as have diverse schools of psychology, including psychoanalysis, learning theory, and ethology. Freud (1920) and Erikson (1963), for example, threw intense focus on infancy by suggesting that the ways babies are treated establish their personality traits and interper-sonal patterns. Similarly, Watson (1924/1970), Hebb (1949), and Dollard and Miller (1950), who dominated developmental psychology in the middle of the twentieth century, stressed the salience of infant experi-ences because they are first, have no competing propensities to replace, and so yield to easy and rapid learning. An additional perspective on the far-reaching portentousness of infancy was offered by students of mental development. Most notably, Piaget (1952) theorized that higher intellec-tual capacities build on simple developments that take place very early in life. Moreover, early behavior patterns were believed to establish more complex behavior patterns. Ethologists like Lorenz (1935/1970) and Tin-bergen (1951, 1963) and other students of animal behavior, as well as embryologists, such as Coghill (1929) studying prenatal physiology, like-wise emphasized the special role of early experiences. They even con-tended that there are predetermined "sensitive periods" in infancy during which development is maximally susceptible to influence by spe-cific types of experiences (Bornstein, 1989a). During such periods, lessons are learned more easily and sustain themselves with greater en-durance than at other times.

Although these diverse schools independently proclaimed the theoret-ical and empirical importance of infancy and early experiences for later development, popular commitment and manifest understanding of the proposition only developed as a result of some dramatic empirical obser-vations published around the middle of the twentieth century. At that time, reports that children who were reared in impersonal institutions emerged as psychologically stunted led to widespread belief that children need close relationships in infancy and that, if they were denied such re-lationships, children would not develop into psychologically healthy in-dividuals (Bowlby, 1969, 1973).

In overview, the rationales that underpin the "infancy-is-important" position are commonsensical: The immature nervous system is thought to be especially plastic to experience; neoteny (the prolongation of in-fancy, especially in human beings) is thought to have enormous adaptive significance (Bjorklund, 1997; Gould, 1977); and the infant is thought to possess an extraordinary facility for learning and to possess few competing responses. All of these factors argued convincingly that expe-riences in infancy should instrumentally influence the course of subse-quent development.

By the early 1960s consensus reigned that infancy occupied a special place in development. Two related trends then emerged: a massive in-crease in the amount of research on infancy and the first attempts to en-gineer compensatory experiences for deprived children. By capitalizing on the special sensitivity of infants, social science proposed to "immu-nize" children against the debilitating effects of deprivation. More than anything else, the apparent failure of these interventions triggered a de-cline of confidence in the notion that infant experiences were especially influential after all. Scholars now agree that this social engineering fail-ure was more apparent than real. Studies that reached this conclusion typically found that the effects of educational interventions on IQ scores were short-lived (Jensen, 1969). However, recent evidence suggests that the timing of interventions, the nature of interventions, the selection of outcome variables, as well as myriad other factors all play contributing roles in child development (Bornstein, 1989b, 1995b; Consortium for Longitudinal Studies, 1983). This conclusion emerged from long-term follow-up studies of children who, as infants, had either been enrolled in special enrichment programs or assigned to control groups. The out-comes measured in these studies, for example, involved later school competence, and the results were impressive: Children in experimental groups were less likely to be held back in school than controls, and they were less likely to need special education classes (Zigler & Finn-Steven-son, 1999).

Nonetheless, some philosophers, psychologists, and social critics have propounded the view that experiences in infancy are peripheral or ephemeral, in the sense that they exert little or no enduring effect on de-velopment (Kagan, 1998; Kagan, Kearsley, & Zelazo, 1978; Lewis, 1997). Instead, these individuals attribute the engine and controls of develop-ment to genetics, biology, and maturation or to contemporaneous context. Gesell (1954), as noted, contended that, like anatomy, the psy-chology and behavior of individuals unfold on the basis of a maturing bi-ological program virtually undeflected by experience. Similarly, the embryologist Waddington (1962, 1972) argued, on principles of growth such as canalization, that early experiences do not (and should not) exert long-term predictive significance: For its basics, nature has not left human development to the whims of individual experience. Opponents to the emphasis on early experiences have pointed to research indicating that major differences in rearing environments have little apparent ef-fect on the way children develop. For example, children reared in (ade-quate quality) daycare and homecare demonstrate remarkably similar long-term outcomes (Lamb, 1998), and even impoverishment (of, say, a rural Guatemalan environment or a Romanian orphanage) reportedly does not retard development or do so immutably (Clarke & Clarke, 1976; Kagan & Klein, 1973; Rutter & English and Romanian Adoptees Study Team, 1998). Some human development is obviously malleable, and plasticity of brain and behavior remains a significant feature of human adaptation long after infancy (Nelson & Bloom, 1997). Thus, even if conditions during infancy will not support development, their in-fluences can often be counterbalanced or reversed by compensating later experiences.

As a consequence, claims against continuity in development, and that behavior patterns emergent in infancy are unlikely to have predictable long-term consequences, attract attention from time to time. Such con-clusions might be premature because notions about how experiences in infancy influence later development are often oversimplified. One diffi-culty lies in an overreliance on linear models of development that hold that early experiences have direct short- and long-term effects; unfortu-nately, simple linear relations are almost never empirically substanti-ated, and they may result in overly simplistic formulations. In practice, the long-term significance of infancy appears to vary depending on domain or circumstances in ways that are much more nuanced and complex than facile and extreme assertions or conclusions would dictate. Although not all infant experiences are critical for later development, and single events are rarely formative, on their face some infant experiences have demonstrable long-lasting effects (language exposure), and some critical events in infancy can shape a person's future deflecting it in favorable (bilingual exposure) or unfavorable (accident or illness) directions. Other single events (divorce) become critical because they establish new contexts that persist through childhood and into maturity. Infancy is manifestly important to those interested in the balance of the life span, even if the effects of experiences in infancy are neither obvious nor direct.

Contemporary Theoretical Orientations to Infancy

Transaction, Systems, and Context

Nature and nurture have persisted as central themes of infancy studies (Plomin & McClearn, 1993), even though more contemporary formulations such as *transaction*—that inherited constitution and experienced environment mutually influence one another through time (Sameroff, 1983)—are supplanting them. In essence, neither genetic or biological predispositions nor parent- or environment-provided experiences alone determine the course, direction, termination, or final resting level of development. Rather, multiple influences codetermine ontogenesis, and it is impossible to separate them or their mutual involvement through time. Infant developmentalists are interested in learning *which* experiences affect *what* aspects of development *when* and *how*, the *ways* in which individual infants are so affected, as well as the *ways* individual infants affect aspects of their own development.

Contemporary developmental scientists also embrace *systems models* and *contextual perspectives* as unifying conceptions of a psychology of infancy. Multiple antecedent forces distal to the infant (environment, experience) as well as multiple forces proximal to the infant (genetics, biology) mutually influence the origins, status, and growth of every developmental construct, structure, and function in the infant. Not only do these many tributaries contribute to the flow of development, but also in turn the development of every construct, structure, and function affects all other facets of the maturing, growing, thinking, speaking, feeling, sensing, and interacting child (Fischer & Bidell, 1998; Thelen & Smith, 1998). The systems perspective underscores the proposition that multiple developmental pathways lead to and from every developmental event. For example, the relevant antecedents of the infant's achieving object permanence include, not just cognition, but also motor maturity, spatial understanding, problem solving ability, memory for objects and location, representational and causal knowledge, previous familiarity with similar tasks, and the interactions and integration of all these different knowledge subsystems. Similarly, developmental change is dynamic and thoroughgoing and reverberates at many levels through time. Achieving self-produced locomotion in infancy portends consequences in multiple component processes as far flung as visual-vestibular adaptation, visual attention to changes in the environment, the differentiation of emotions, social referencing, as well as in new-found adult fears (Bertenthal & Clifton, 1998; McCune, 1992; Thelen & Smith, 1998).

The *contextual perspective* in infancy acknowledges that all aspects of infant life and development in infancy are mutually embedded insofar as they exist at many levels—"the inner-biological, individual-psychological, dyadic, social network, community, societal, cultural, outer-ecological, and historical" (Dixon & Lerner, 1999). At a given point in infancy, influences of any and all of these levels directly contribute to or interact with the others to affect the emerging status and development of every construct, structure, and function in the child (Bronfenbrenner & Morris, 1998; Magnusson & Stattin, 1998).

Scientific Studies of Infancy

The Questions Asked in Infancy Studies.
In their relatively brief history, scientific studies of human infancy have tended to focus on narrow, tractable, and testable problems more than grand philosophical conundra, even if in doing the former they have had the latter in mind. Infancy research normally concerns itself with evaluating the nature and status of a construct, structure, or function in early life, with attempting to specify when and how it emerges and the course of its initial development, and with identifying the consequences its development has. *What is a social smile? When do infants first smile socially? How does smiling change in infancy? What influences some infants to smile more and others less? What implications has infant smiling for child development?* Two general classes of scientific question are posed. One asks about the *developmental function,* which describes (and perhaps explains) the species-typical emergence and growth of a construct, structure, or function in infants generally. *What are the sources, characteristics, rates of change, and so forth of the normative growth of smiling in infants?* The other class focuses on *individual variation,* which describes (and perhaps explains) differences in constructs, structures, or functions among infants. *What is the scope of individual variation in infant smiling? Do differences in smiling among infants re-*

main ordered in the course of development? Answers to questions about the developmental function and individual variation are also crucial to understanding infancy and development in infancy (Colombo & Fagen, 1990; Oyama, 1985).

The Several Challenges to Infancy Studies.   Despite the keen observations of parents and the seminal thinking of philosophers, we remain grossly ignorant about many aspects of infancy. To address questions to infants is not easy, and what we now know in answer to them has been hard won. In large part, the impediments to infancy studies are attributable to the enormous practical and logistical challenges infants commonly present. Perhaps the major quandary faced by students of infancy is that, at base, they are in a one-way conversation trying to communicate with a mute partner who does not even necessarily know she or he is a partner. Researchers are typically about the business of determining what is inside the baby's head, what infants sense and know and feel about the people and things around them. Because they cannot straightforwardly ask them, however, researchers can only make inferences about infants' capacities from physiological measurements or behavioral responses. First, researchers confront the fact that infants are unable either to grasp or to answer research questions unambiguously and reliably. We can question and test older children and adults verbally, but not infants. In addition, infants are notoriously uncooperative, because unlike children and adults they are not (necessarily) motivated to perform for researchers. Other not-insignificant problems that vex scientific investigators are infants' fleeting attention spans, their limited response repertoires, the variability inherent in most of their behaviors, and their seemingly strict dependency on state. Researchers must also assiduously resist reaching conclusions about the absence of capabilities in infancy based only on the failure of infants to behave in a desired way; even if they do not or cannot show it, babies may still sense, know, and feel.

Beyond the logistical problems infants present to research lie significant and imposing theoretical ones. Infants often make it difficult to tell whether fundamental development has occurred in an underlying construct (attachment, imitation, fear), or whether there is simply some superficial change in the way they express an unchanging construct. Fear may look the same in the faces of 6-month-olds and 18-month-olds, and thus the same observational and scoring techniques can assess fear at these two ages. But, 6-month-olds may express affection for their parents by crying at their departure, whereas 18-month-olds signal attachment by talking. These developmental changes do not necessarily mean that an underlying construct has changed; they may simply indicate that a set of different age-appropriate means has been found to mediate emotional relationships.

To engage and learn from infants, researchers have designed innovative and ingenious procedures. Their techniques range from biographical and case descriptions (where, as we learned, infancy studies began), through naturalistic or structured observations, to recording psychophysiology and behavior in increasingly experimental ways. Studies of infants are carried out in homes and on playgrounds, in laboratories and around fields. In this regard, consider the remarkable success of *habituation*, a nonverbal technique used to ask questions of and obtain answers from young babies (Bornstein, 1985; Fantz, 1964). Imagine a baby sitting in an infant seat opposite to a visual panel on which we project an image. When a visual image first appears, a baby will normally and naturally orient and attend to it; after all, it is new and novel. If, however, the same image is presented repeatedly, the baby's response to it—often the baby's visual attention is measured—wanes. This decrement in attention indicates habituation. Simply put, the stimulus on later exposures is not new and novel as it was on earlier exposures; habituation reflects an elementary kind of learning. Like many simple phenomena, habituation is deceptively powerful, and it has been employed for over 30 years to reveal a variety of capacities in infants. For example, habituation has been used to investigate *detection* and *discrimination* abilities: When habituation to one stimulus is followed by a test with a second stimulus, recovery of looking or "dishabituation" to the test stimulus indicates detection and discrimination between the two stimuli. The study of visual acuity and pattern, face, and color perception has prospered in this way (Bornstein & Arterberry, 1999; Bornstein & Lamb, 1992; Kellman & Arterberry, 1998). At the same time, people frequently treat discriminable properties, objects, or events in the environment as effectively similar; that is, they *categorize*: The generalization of habituation to physically different, perceptually discriminable stimuli is taken to index such perceptual organization in the infant. A surprising understanding of speech perception and cognition in babies has been achieved following this logic (Aslin, Jusczyk, & Pisoni, 1998). Habituation lends itself to the study of *memory*: By habituating infants and testing them immediately afterward with the same stimulus, it is possible to study infant short-term recognition, as it is possible to institute a delay between habituation and test to study infant long-term recognition. Not only have insights into infants' memory for faces and persons been gained via habituation (Nelson, 1995), but the effects of age, stimulus, and interference on infants' memory have all been investigated in this way. In studies of *concept formation*, infants are habituated to a variety of stimuli from a given class and are subsequently tested for generalization of habituation to a novel member of that class versus dishabituation to a novel stimulus from a different class. Thus, links between rudimentary sensory/perceptual capacities and more mature mental abilities have been forged. It is unsurprising that some infants are fast but others are slow in habituating; habituation is also a moderately stable individual differences characteristic in infants. Remarkably, the individual differences aspect of habituation performance has proved predictive of later development: Longitudinal research indicates that children who habituate more efficiently in infancy possess more vocabulary, play in more sophisticated ways, and score higher on intelligence tests in later childhood (Bornstein, 1985, 1998). Thus, despite formidable methodological and theoretical challenges, much has been learned about infancy.

The "Competent" Infant.   Infancy is characterized by remarkable capacities and extraordinary changes, many of which are evident even on casual observation because of their magnitude, celerity, and scope. Still others are hidden to untutored observation and remained so for centuries. In the twentieth century new methods (like habituation) have led to startling revelations about infants as well as to some startling claims. The twentieth century, unlike any preceding, has witnessed the advent of a new and revolutionary conception of human infancy, and enough "fact" is known today to permit the compilation of volumes about infants that supplant outmoded conceptions (Ames, Ilg, & Haber, 1982; Arlitt, 1946; Bornstein & Lamb, 1992; Bower, 1977, 1982; Bremner, 1994; Cairns, 1998; Cramer, 1992; Fogel, 1984; Frank, 1966; Kagan et al., 1978; McCall, 1979; Richards, 1980; Rosenblith & Sims-Knight, 1985; Sherrod, Vietze, & Friedman, 1978; Smart & Smart, 1978; Stone, Smith, & Murphy, 1973; Willemsen, 1979).

In the physical, neurological, and psychomotor domains of growth, for example, in the first year after birth children's weight triples, the nervous system overproliferates and then prunes itself with sophisticated adaptation, and babies transform from immature beings unable to move their limbs in a coordinated manner to ones who can purposefully control the complicated sequences of muscle contractions and flections necessary to walk, to reach, and to grasp (Bertenthal & Clifton, 1998; Gottlieb, Wahlsten, & Lickliter, 1998; Johnson, 1999). From birth, all the sensory channels (vision, hearing, touch, taste, and smell) function at a high level (Aslin et al., 1998; Bornstein & Arterberry, 1999); indeed, research into prenatal development confirms that fetuses are capable of perceiving and learning in multiple modalities (Lecanuet, Fifer, Krasnegor, & Smotherman, 1995). But beyond the simple registration of experience, newborns naturally seek out information in the environment (even if they do not make fine differentiations): Thus, infants not only look at, but also systematically explore, perceptual patterns as if trying to learn about them (Granrud, 1993; Haith, 1980). As the ability to take in information improves, the capacities to attribute meaning to that information and to make sense of the world advance (Haith & Benson, 1998). Being able to see does not necessarily mean that babies understand, but when infants see and then recognize objects, and they consistently observe the manner in which objects behave in relation to one another, they start to learn the laws that govern activity in the physical world. Cognitive development in infancy is also hallmarked by infants' growing realizations that objects have an independent and permanent existence and that acting on objects yields predictable but differing effects depending on whether the object is a table, a rattle, or a cat.

The growth of a rich cognitive repertoire in infancy has been understood qualitatively by emphasizing the changing ways in which infants actively attempt to interpret or make sense of their experiences as well as by quantitative approaches that address what infants know and how they get to know it. Fresh evidence indicates that infants fill in missing parts of figures, integrate information over space and time, form categories and concepts, abstract prototypes, match across modalities, distinguish the behavior of animates from inanimates, discriminate small numerosities, imitate extensively, and retain memories over days and months (Bornstein, 1984; Quinn & Eimas, 1996; Rovee-Collier, 1997). All these understandings in turn make it possible for the infant to act with intentionality, a critical feature of intelligent behavior.

Even early in infancy, emotions and affects appear to function communicatively; they permit infants to read others' appraisals and intentions, and they enable infants to project their own appraisals and intentions to others (Saarni, Mumme, & Campos, 1998; Thompson, 1998). Emotions also play a major role in organizing behavior; individual differences in emotionality construct the core of temperament, a constitutionally-based source of individual differences in personality. Temperamental variation is a self-evident characteristic of young infants, and these individual differences are significant because of their potential for influencing infants' cognitive and social interactions (Rothbart & Bates, 1998; Sanson & Rothbart, 1995). Infants affect their social environment; for example, their cries are extremely potent, eliciting irresistible and prompt responses from most people who hear them (Bornstein et al., 1992). At first, infants probably do not understand the potential meaning of signals to which adults readily attach so much communicative, emotional, and social significance, but later infants learn that their cries predictably affect others and eventually they may cry in order to exert a desired effect. Infancy witnesses the dawning of social awareness and steady growth in responsibility for the child's maintaining sequences of social interaction. Another major step in socioemotional development is taken with the formation of life-long attachments, infants' enduring relationships with specific individuals, especially parents (Harwood, Miller, & Irizarry, 1995; Lamb, Hwang, Ketterlinus, & Fracasso, 1999). Interactions with others affect the development of an infant's characteristic social style, and that style is in turn believed to influence later interactions and experiences.

Infancy may end when language begins, but it is evident that language does not emerge suddenly and full blown late in the second year of life. Rather, the acquisition of language reflects multiple processes: the segmentation, prediction, and comprehension of visual and auditory information; the development of concepts and their symbolic representation; the formation of social relationships and motivations and recognition of the reciprocal basis of social interaction; as well as the internalization of elementary rules of turn-taking and communication (Bloom, 1998; Bornstein & Lamb, 1992). The comprehension and production of speech rank among the major achievements of the infancy period, but the motivations to acquire language and to communicate are more than just passingly social (Uzgiris, 1979). All of the diverse and dynamic aspects of development interrelate.

Infancy studies have afforded a clear appreciation of the unity of development, of the fact that physical, physiological, neurological, perceptual, cognitive, emotional, and social lines of ontogeny parallel and intimately relate to one another. However, beyond the rudimentary, the feats of infant development are still poorly understood: Precious little is known about the factors that underlie infant development, propel developmental change, or account for individual variation in development. When seeking to determine the nature of any one construct, structure, or function, or what factors account for its status, for its change, or for changes it initiates, it has been too easy to overlook the contributions and the dynamics of related systems.

☐ Practititioners and Infants

Appreciating babies as human beings and the general desire to improve the lives of babies (those who are normal and certainly those whose development may be compromised) have motivated dedicated efforts on the part of practitioners (Leach, 1983, 1989; Spock, 1946). There is a subspecialty of infant psychiatry (Minde & Minde, 1986). Dramatic advances in the design of incubators and respirators in the middle of the twentieth century have made it possible to keep alive preterm babies who would formerly have met an early demise. Other political, social, and economic forces also conspired to focus interest on practical aspects of infancy. The 1960s witnessed the beginning of the "War on Poverty" in the United States and the concomitant introduction of interventions designed to provide infants from deprived and underprivileged backgrounds with a "Head Start" so as to prevent later school failure (Zigler & Finn-Stevenson, 1999). It was only in the 1980s that infants receiving cardiac surgery were compared in an anesthesia regimen that included an analgesic (fentanyl, to kill pain) versus the standard practice (which were drugs that rendered infants unconscious, but did not include an analgesic). The outcomes were dramatically in favor of the benefits of using an analgesic. The prevailing belief was that the nervous system of infants was not mature enough for infants to "experience" pain, and so analgesics were not used. In the last 15 years, this opinion has turned around completely. Indeed, the prevailing view is now that, if anything, younger infants feel "more pain" than older infants (Anand, Sippell, & Aynsley-Green, 1987). In modern times, the literature designed to help parents enrich their infant's development has proliferated (Better Homes & Gardens, 1963; Connor, 1997; Jackson & Jackson, 1978); and where infants would formerly have played contentedly with rattles, mirrors, or even scraps of paper, parents now shower infants with "creative playthings"—mobiles, busy boxes, bull's-eyes and star patterns taken directly from the laboratory, and even crib bumpers filled with goldfish!—in hopes of fostering or optimizing development (Bornstein, 1990; Millêtre, 1994). Today, advice on parenting infants can be found in massive professional compendia, in classic "how to" books, as well as in uncountable popular periodicals that overflow the world's drug store and airport magazine racks. Babies are big business.

Happily, the twenty-first century is heralding a convergence of applied, scientific, and theoretical concerns. For example, the Infant Health and Development Program (1990) conducted an intervention with preterm infants designed to provide at-risk babies with sound and up-to-date compensatory experience. Infants were given high quality pediatric care, their homes were visited by trained caseworkers, and their parents were afforded instruction and opportunities in how to care for and enhance the development of their babies. Children in a control group received only pediatric care. Normally, infants born preterm present a variety of neurological and sensorimotor feeding and sleep dysfunctions, and they experience numerous problems making their day-to-day care more difficult. In this study, infants receiving intervention had significantly higher mean IQ scores than the control group at 3 years, and their mothers reported significantly fewer behavioral problems than did mothers of control-group infants.

In the past, many people believed that only full-time mothers could provide young children with the care they needed to thrive, beliefs that were fostered by an extensive literature on the adverse effects of maternal deprivation (Rutter, 1995). Contemporary social critics have argued, however, that high quality daycare can adequately substitute for home-care and thus relieve employed parents of full-time childcare responsibilities (Lamb, 1998). For example, the quality of children's emotional attachments appears to depend not on the absolute amount of time that parents spend with infants, but on the quality of parents' interactions with them. These developments in turn raise critical, as-yet-unanswered, applied and practical questions: *What precisely constitute quality interactions for infants? What are the long-term effects of nonparental infant daycare? What consequences (if any) would arise if fathers rather than mothers assumed responsibility for infant care?*

☐ Conclusions

What has Been Learned From and About Infants?

Parents, philosophers, psychologists, and practitioners all accord overwhelming significance to infancy. Because of the nature and structure of infants themselves, as well as the range, the magnitude, and the implications of developmental changes that occur to them, infancy is an unquestionably fascinating and appealing phase of the life cycle. Some of the key issues in developmental study, the transactions of nature and nurture, for example, are rendered in sharp relief when addressed in the context of infants. Babies tell us about life generally as well as about the beginnings of life specifically.

As a professional who has spent most of his career studying infants, I regard infancy as extremely important, and I would assert that infancy has a uniquely formative, but not determinative, significance in ontogeny. Infancy predicts future development in varying ways and in varying degrees across varying domains. But patterns of infant development are inherently complex: Not all infant experiences are equivalently meaningful, and certain domains of development are more susceptible to the effects of early experience than are others. Thus, interactions and interventions with infants are valuable in their own right, because they improve current conditions and hold out the opportunity to improve long-term outcomes. "Some aspects of childhood are not specific preparations for adulthood. Rather, they are designed by evolution to adapt the child to its current environment but not necessarily to a future one"

(Bjorklund, 1997, p. 153). Certainly, later experiences also interact with the effects of earlier ones to shape the complete developmental course.

This chapter reasserts a basic coherence of infant development amidst its superficial chaos, species-typical universals in infancy amidst a plethora of behaviors that are environmentally and culturally conditioned, and a special place for infancy in the continuity that is also human development. By studying infancy we learn about processes and experiences that in one or another way have lifelong implications. Our infancy is the first extrauterine phase of our lives, and the characteristics we develop and acquire in infancy are fundamental; at minimum, some will endure, and others will serve as the foundation that later experiences build on or modify. Infancy is only one phase in the life span, however, and so our cognitive competencies and social styles will be shaped by our experiences and by developments after infancy. The start does not fix the course or outcome of development, but it makes sense that infant starts exert an impact on the route followed and terminus reached in the rest of the life cycle.

☐ References

Ames, L. B., Ilg, F. L., & Haber, C. C. (1982). *Your one-year-old: The fun-loving, fussy 12- to 24-month old*. New York: Dell.

Anand, K. J. S., Sippell, W. G., & Aynsley-Green, A. (1987). A randomized trial of fentanyl anesthesia undergoing surgery: Effect on the stress response. *Lancet, 1,* 243–248.

Arlitt, A. H. (1946). *Psychology of infancy and early childhood*. New York: McGraw-Hill.

Aslin, R. N., Jusczyk, P. W., & Pisoni, D. B. (1998). Speech and auditory processing during infancy: Constraints on and precursors to language. In D. Kuhn & R. S. Siegler (Ed.), *Handbook of child psychology: Vol. 2. Cognition, perception, and language* (5th ed., pp. 147–198). New York: Wiley.

Barnard, K. E., & Martell, L. K. (1995). Mothering. In M. H. Bornstein (Ed.), *Handbook of parenting* (Vol. 3, pp. 3–26). Mahwah, NJ: Erlbaum.

Bell, R. Q. (1968). A reinterpretation of the direction of effects in studies of socialization. *Psychological Review, 75,* 81–95.

Bell, R. Q., & Harper, L. (1977). *Child effects on adults*. Hillsdale, NJ: Erlbaum.

Bertenthal, B. I., & Clifton, R. K. (1998). Perception and action. In D. Kuhn & R. S. Siegler (Ed.) & W. Damon (Series Ed.), *Handbook of child psychology: Vol. 2. Cognition, perception, and language* (5th ed., pp. 51–102). New York: Wiley.

Better Homes & Gardens. (1963). *Baby book*. New York: Bantam Books.

Bjorklund, D. F. (1997). The role of immaturity in human development. *Psychological Bulletin, 122,* 153–169.

Bloom, L. (1998). Language acquisition in its developmental context. In D. Kuhn & R. S. Siegler (Ed.) & W. Damon (Series Ed.), *Handbook of child psychology: Vol. 2. Cognition, perception, and language* (5th ed., pp. 309–370). New York: Wiley.

Bornstein, M. H. (1984). A descriptive taxonomy of psychological categories used by infants. In C. Sophian (Ed.), *Origins of cognitive skills* (pp. 313–338). Hillsdale, NJ: Erlbaum.

Bornstein, M. H. (1985). Habituation of attention as a measure of visual information processing in human infants: Summary, systematization, and synthesis. In G. Gottlieb & N. A. Krasnegor (Eds.), *Measurement of audition and vision in the first year of postnatal life: A methodological overview* (pp. 253–300). Norwood, NJ: Ablex.

Bornstein, M. H. (1989a). Sensitive periods in development: Structural characteristics and causal interpretations. *Psychological Bulletin, 105,* 179–197.

Bornstein, M. H. (1989b). Between caretakers and their young: Two modes of interaction and their consequences for cognitive growth. In M. H. Bornstein & J. S. Bruner (Eds.), *Interaction in human development* (pp. 197–214). Hillsdale, NJ: Erlbaum.

Bornstein, M. H. (1990). *Wide world.* Osaka: Senshukai.

Bornstein, M. H. (Ed.). (1991). *Cultural approaches to parenting.* Hillsdale, NJ: Erlbaum.

Bornstein, M. H. (Ed.). (1995a). *Handbook of parenting. Vol. 1: Children and parenting. Vol. 2: Biology and ecology of parenting. Vol. 3: Status and social conditions of parenting. Vol. 4: Applied and practical parenting.* Mahwah, NJ: Erlbaum.

Bornstein, M. H. (1995b). Parenting infants. In M. H. Bornstein (Ed.), *Handbook of parenting* (Vol. 1, pp. 3–39). Mahwah, NJ: Erlbaum.

Bornstein, M. H. (1998). Stability in mental development from early life: Methods, measures, models, meanings and myths. In F. Simion & G. Butterworth (Eds.), *The development of sensory, motor and cognitive capacities in early infancy: From perception to cognition* (pp. 301–332). Hove, England: Psychology Press.

Bornstein, M. H. (1999). *Infancy as a stage of life.* National Institute of Child Health and Human Development. Manuscript in preparation.

Bornstein, M. H., & Arterberry, M. (1999). Perceptual development. In M. H. Bornstein & M. E. Lamb (Eds.), *Developmental psychology: An advanced textbook* (4th ed., pp. 231–274). Mahwah, NJ: Erlbaum.

Bornstein, M. H., & Kessen, W. (Eds.). (1979). *Psychological development from infancy: Image to intention.* Hillsdale, NJ: Erlbaum.

Bornstein, M. H., & Lamb, M. E. (1992). *Development in infancy: An introduction* (3rd ed.). New York: McGraw-Hill.

Bornstein, M. H., Tamis-LeMonda, C. S., Tal, J., Ludemann, P., Toda, S., Rahn, C. W., Pêcheux, M.-G., Azuma, H., & Vardi, D. (1992). Maternal responsiveness to infants in three societies: The United States, France, and Japan. *Child Development, 63,* 808–821.

Bower, T. G. R. (1977). *A primer of infant development.* San Francisco: W. H. Freeman.

Bower, T. G. R. (1982). *Development in infancy.* San Francisco: W. H. Freeman.

Bowlby, J. (1969). *Attachment and loss (Vol. 1) attachment.* New York: Basic Books.

Bowlby, J. (1973). *Attachment and loss (Vol. 2) separation.* New York: Basic Books.

Bremner, J. G. (1994). *Infancy.* London, UK: Blackwell.

Bronfenbrenner, U., & Morris, P. A. (1998). The ecology of developmental processes. In R. M. Lerner (Ed.) & W. Damon (Series Ed.), *Handbook of child psychology: Vol. 1. Theoretical models of human development* (5th ed., pp. 993–1028). New York: Wiley.

Bugental, D. B., & Goodnow, J. J. (1998). Socialization processes. In N. Eisenberg (Ed.) & W. Damon (Series Ed.), *Handbook of child psychology: Vol. 3. Social, emotional, and personality development* (5th ed., pp. 389–462). New York: Wiley.

Cairns, R. B. (1998). The making of developmental psychology. In R. M. Lerner (Ed.) & W. Damon (Series Ed.), *Handbook of child psychology: Vol. 1. Theoretical models of human development* (5th ed., pp. 25–105). New York: Wiley.

Clarke, A. M., & Clarke, A. D. B. (Eds.). (1976). *Early experience: Myth and evidence.* New York: Free Press.

Coghill, G. E. (1929). *Anatomy and the problem of behavior.* Cambridge, UK: Cambridge University Press.

Cole, M. (1999). Culture in development. In M. H. Bornstein & M. E. Lamb (Eds.), *Developmental psychology: An advanced textbook* (4th ed., pp. 731–789). Mahwah, NJ: Erlbaum.

Collins, W. A., Harris, M. L., & Susman, A. (1995). Parenting during middle childhood. In M. H. Bornstein (Ed.), *Handbook of parenting* (Vol. 1, pp. 65–89). Mahwah, NJ: Erlbaum.

Colombo, J., & Fagen, J. (Eds.). (1990). *Individual difference in infancy: Reliability, stability, prediction.* Hillsdale, NJ: Erlbaum.

Connor, B. (1997). *The Parent's Journal guide to raising great kids.* New York: Bantam Books.

Consortium for Longitudinal Studies. (1983). *As the twig is bent: Lasting effects of preschool programs.* Hillsdale, NJ: Erlbaum.

Cramer, B. G. (1992). *The importance of being baby* (G. Gill, trans.). New York: Addison-Wesley.

Darwin, C. R. (1877). A biographical sketch of an infant. *Mind, 2,* 286–294.

Dixon, R. A., & Lerner, R. M. (1999). History and systems in developmental psychology. In M. H. Bornstein & M. E. Lamb (Eds.), *Developmental psychology: An advanced textbook* (5th ed., pp. 3–45). Mahwah, NJ: Erlbaum.

Dollard, J., & Miller, N. (1950). *Personality and psychotherapy.* New York: McGraw-Hill.

Erikson, E. H. (1963). *Childhood and society.* New York: W. W. Norton.

Fantz, R. L. (1964). Visual experience in infants: Decreased attention to familiar patterns relative to novel ones. *Science, 146,* 668–670.

Fischer, K. W., & Bidell, T. R. (1998). Dynamic development of psychological structures in action and thought. In R. M. Lerner (Ed.) & W. Damon (Series Ed.), *Handbook of child psychology: Vol. 1. Theoretical models of human development* (5th ed., pp. 467–561). New York: Wiley.

Fogel, A. (1984). *Infancy: Infant, family, and society.* New York: West Publishing.

Frank, L. K. (1966). *On the importance of infancy.* New York: Random House.

Freud, S. (1920). *Introductory lectures on psychoanalysis* (J. Strachey, Trans.). New York: W. W. Norton.

Gesell, A. L. (1954). The ontogenesis of infant behavior. In L. Carmichael (Ed.), *Manual of child psychology* (2nd ed., pp. 335–373). New York: Wiley.

Gottlieb, D., Wahlsten, D., & Lickliter, R. (1998). The significance of biology for human development: A developmental psychobiological systems view. In R. M. Lerner (Ed.) & W. Damon (Series Ed.), *Handbook of child psychology: Vol. 1. Theoretical models of human development* (5th ed., pp. 233–273). New York: Wiley.

Gould, S. J. (1977). *Ontogeny and phylogeny.* Cambridge, MA: Harvard University Press.

Granrud, C. (Ed.). (1993). *Visual perception and cognition in infancy.* Hillsdale, NJ: Erlbaum.

Haith, M. M. (1980). *Rules that babies look by: The organization of newborn visual activity.* Hillsdale, NJ: Erlbaum.

Haith, M. M., & Benson, J. B. (1998). Infant cognition. In D. Kuhn & R. S. Siegler (Ed.) & W. Damon (Series Ed.), *Handbook of child psychology: Vol. 2. Cognition, perception, and language* (5th ed., pp. 199–254). New York: Wiley.

Harwood, R. L., Miller, J. G., & Irizarry, N. L. (1995). *Culture and attachment: Perceptions of the child in context.* New York: Guilford.

Hebb, D. O. (1949). *The organization of behavior.* New York: Wiley.

Infant Health and Development Program. (1990). Enhancing the outcomes of low birth-weight, premature infants: A multisite, randomized trial. *Journal of the American Medical Association, 263,* 3035–3042.

Jackson, J. F., & Jackson, J. H. (1978). *Infant culture: The first year of life—What your baby can see, hear, feel, taste, and learn.* New York: Thomas Y. Crowell.

Jensen, A. (1969). How much can we boost IQ and scholastic achievement? *Harvard Educational Review, 39,* 1–123.

Johnson, M. H. (1999). Developmental neuroscience. In M. H. Bornstein & M. E. Lamb (Eds.), *Developmental psychology: An advanced textbook* (4th ed., pp. 199–230). Mahwah, NJ: Erlbaum.

Kagan, J. (1998). *Three seductive ideas.* Cambridge, MA: Harvard University Press.

Kagan, J., Kearsley, R. B., & Zelazo, P. R. (1978). *Infancy: Its place in human development.* Cambridge, MA: Harvard University Press.

Kagan, J., & Klein, R. (1973). Cross-cultural perspectives on early development. *American Psychologist, 28,* 947–961.

Kellman, P. J., & Arterberry, M. E. (1998). *The cradle of knowledge: Development of perception in infancy.* Cambridge, MA: MIT Press.

Lamb, M. E. (1998). Nonparental child care: Context, quality, correlates, and consequences. In I. E. Sigel & K. A. Renninger (Eds.) & W. Damon (Series Ed.), *Handbook of child psychology: Vol. 4. Child psychology in practice* (5th ed., pp. 73–133). New York: Wiley.

Lamb, M. E., Hwang, C. P., Ketterlinus, R. D., & Fracasso, M. (1999). Parent-child relationships: Development in the context of the family. In M. H. Bornstein & M. E. Lamb (Eds.), *Developmental psychology: An advanced textbook* (4th ed., pp. 411–450). Mahwah, NJ: Erlbaum.

Leach, P. (1983). *Babyhood.* New York: Knopf.

Leach, P. (1989). *Your baby & child.* New York: Knopf.

Lecanuet, J.-P., Fifer, W. P., Krasnegor, N. A., & Smotherman, W. P. (1995). *Fetal development: A psychobiological perspective.* Hillsdale, NJ: Erlbaum.

Lewis, M. (1997). *Altering fate: Why the past does not predict the future.* New York: Guilford Press.

Lorenz, K. (1935/1970). *Studies in animal and human behavior* (R. Martin, Trans.). London: Methuen.

Magnusson, D., & Stattin, H. (1998). Person-context interaction theories. In R. M. Lerner (Ed.) & W. Damon (Series Ed.), *Handbook of child psychology: Vol. 1. Theoretical models of human development* (5th ed., pp. 685–759). New York: Wiley.

McCall, R. B. (1979). *Infants.* New York: Vintage Books.

McCune, L. (1992). First words: A dynamic systems view. In C. A. Ferguson, L. Menn, & C. Stoel-Gammon (Eds.), *Phonological development: Models, research, implications* (pp. 313–336). Timonium, MD: York Press.

Mendelson, M. J. (1990). *Becoming a brother: A child learns about life, family, and self.* Cambridge, MA: MIT Press.

Millêtre, B. (1994). *Bébé s'éveille: Le vrai premier livre de bébé.* Paris: Librarie GRUND.

Minde, K., & Minde, R. (1986). *Infant psychiatry: An introductory textbook.* Beverly Hills, CA: Sage.

Nelson, C. A. (1995). The ontogeny of human memory: A cognitive neuroscience perspective. *Developmental Psychology, 31,* 723–738.

Nelson, C. A., & Bloom, F. E. (1997). Child development and neuroscience. *Child Development, 68,* 970–987.

Oyama, S. (1985). *The ontogeny of information.* Cambridge: Cambridge University Press.

Papoušek, H., & Papoušek, M. (1995). Intuitive parenting. In M. H. Bornstein (Ed.), *Handbook of parenting* (Vol. 2, pp. 117–136). Mahwah, NJ: Erlbaum.

Piaget, J. (1952). *The origins of intelligence in children.* New York: Norton.

Plato. (1970). *The laws* (T. J. Saunders, Trans.). New York: Penguin Books.

Plomin, R., & McClearn, G. E. (Eds.). (1993). *Nature, nurture, and psychology.* Washington, DC: American Psychological Association.

Population Reference Bureau. (1993). *1993 World population data sheet.* Washington, DC: Population Reference Bureau, Inc.

Quinn, P. C., & Eimas, P. D. (1996). Perceptual organization and categorization in young infants. In C. Rovee-Collier & L. P. Lipsett (Eds.), *Advances in infancy research* (Vol. 10, pp. 1–36). Norwood, NJ: Ablex.

Richards, M. (1980). *Infancy: World of the newborn*. New York: Harper & Row.

Rosenblith, J. F., & Sims-Knight, J. E. (1985). *In the beginning: Development in the first two years of life*. Monterey, CA: Brooks/Cole Publishing.

Rothbart, M. K., & Bates, J. E. (1998). Temperament. In N. Eisenberg (Ed.) & W. Damon (Series Ed.), *Handbook of child psychology: Vol. 3. Social, emotional, and personality development* (5th ed., pp. 105–176). New York: Wiley.

Rovee-Collier, C. (1997). Dissociations in infant memory: Rethinking the development of implicit and explicit memory. *Psychological Review, 104*, 467–498.

Rutter, M. (1995). Maternal deprivation. In M. H. Bornstein (Ed.), *Handbook of parenting* (Vol. 4, pp. 3–31). Mahwah, NJ: Erlbaum.

Rutter, M., & English and Romanian Adoptees (ERA) Study Team. (1998). Developmental catch-up, and deficit, following adoption after severe global early privation. *Journal of Child Psychology and Psychiatry, 39*, 465–473.

Saarni, C., Mumme, D. L., & Campos, J. J. (1998). Emotional development: Action, communication, and understanding. In N. Eisenberg (Ed.) & W. Damon (Series Ed.), *Handbook of child psychology: Vol. 3. Social, emotional, and personality development* (5th ed., pp. 237–309). New York: Wiley.

Sameroff, A. J. (1983). Developmental systems: Contexts and evolution. In W. Kessen (Ed.) & P. H. Mussen (Series Ed.), *Handbook of child psychology: Vol. 1. History, theory, and methods* (pp. 237–294). New York: Wiley.

Sanson, A., & Rothbart, M. K. (1995). Child temperament and parenting. In M. H. Bornstein (Ed.), *Handbook of parenting* (Vol. 4, pp. 299–321). Mahwah, NJ: Erlbaum.

Scarr, S., & Kidd, K. K. (1983). Developmental behavior genetics. In M. M. Haith & J. J. Campos (Eds.) & P. H. Mussen (Series Ed.), *Handbook of child psychology: Vol. 2. Infancy and developmental psychobiology* (pp. 345–433). New York: Wiley.

Sherrod, K., Vietze, P., & Friedman, S. (1978). *Infancy*. Monterey, CA: Brooks/Cole.

Smart, M. S., & Smart, R. C. (1978). *Infants: Development and relationships*. New York: Macmillan.

Spelke, E. S., & Newport, E. L. (1998). Nativism, empiricism, and the development of knowledge. In R. M. Lerner (Ed.) & W. Damon (Series Ed.), *Handbook of child psychology: Vol. 1. Theoretical models of human development* (5th ed., pp. 275–340). New York: Wiley.

Spock, B. (1946). *Baby and child care*. New York: Pocket Books.

Stern, D. N. (1990). *Diary of a baby*. New York: Basic Books.

Stone, J., Smith, H., & Murphy, L. (Eds.). (1973). *The competent infant*. New York: Basic Books.

Thelen, E., & Smith, L. B. (1998). Dynamic systems theories. In R. M. Lerner (Ed.) & W. Damon (Series Ed.), *Handbook of child psychology: Vol. 1. Theoretical models of human development* (5th ed., pp. 563–634). New York: Wiley.

Thompson, R. A. (1998). Early sociopersonality development. In N. Eisenberg (Ed.) & W. Damon (Series Ed.), *Handbook of child psychology: Vol. 3. Social, emotional, and personality development* (5th ed., pp. 25–104). New York: Wiley.

Tinbergen, N. (1951). *The study of instinct*. Oxford, UK: Oxford University Press.

Tinbergen, N. (1963). On aims and methods of ethology. *Zeitschrif Tier psychologie, 20*, 410–433.

Uzgiris, I. C. (Ed.). (1979). *Social interaction and communication during infancy*. San Francisco: Jossey-Bass.

Waddington, C. H. (1962). *New patterns in genetics and development.* New York: Columbia University Press.

Waddington, C. H. (1972). Form and information. In C. H. Waddington (Ed.), *Towards a theoretical biology* (Vol. 4, pp. 109–145). Edinburgh: Edinburgh University Press.

Wallace, D. B., Franklin, M. B., & Keegan, R. T. (1994). The observing eye: A century of baby diaries. *Human Development, 37,* 1–29.

Watson, J. B. (1924/1970). *Behaviorism.* New York: Norton.

Willemsen, E. (1979). *Understanding infancy.* San Francisco: W. H. Freeman.

Zigler, E., & Finn-Stevenson, M. (1999). Applied developmental psychology. In M. H. Bornstein & M. E. Lamb (Eds.), *Developmental psychology: An advanced textbook* (4th ed., pp. 555–598). Mahwah, NJ: Erlbaum.

3

CHAPTER   Robbie Case

Conceptual Development

☐ Introduction

Throughout this century research in cognitive development has been conducted within three different theoretical frameworks, each with its own pioneers, its own epistemology, and its own tradition of progressive inquiry. In the present chapter I describe these three traditions and the dialogue that has taken place between them. I conclude with a brief description of a new line of work in which an attempt has been made to construct a theoretical framework in which the assumptions of the three traditions are integrated.

☐ The Empiricist Tradition

According to the empiricist view, knowledge of the world is acquired by a process in which the sensory organs detect stimuli in the external world, and the mind detects the customary patterns or "conjunctions" in these stimuli. Early attempts to apply this perspective were designed to show that laws of learning in young children were identical to those in lower species (Thorndike, 1914; Watson, 1914). Later work was aimed at showing the changes that took place in children's capability for learning at older ages (Kendler & Kendler, 1962). The paradigm that was used most extensively for this purpose was one in which children were presented with pairs of sensory stimuli that varied along a number of di-

36

mensions (e.g., form, color, pattern) and were asked to figure out which stimulus feature was associated with receipt of a small reward. On each trial children were allowed one guess as to which stimulus would be rewarded. When they had succeeded in picking the correct stimulus on some predetermined number of trials, they were said to have acquired the concept. At that point, a different feature was selected, and a fresh sequence of experimental trials was initiated.

The results that were obtained from these studies were as follows. Preschool children could learn to select a stimulus on the basis of its shape, color, or pattern by the age of 3 to 4 years. They could also learn to change the basis for their selection when the criterion was changed. However, they performed both tasks in a rather slow and laborious manner, with the result that their learning curves looked much like those exhibited by other primates (Kendler, Kendler, & Wells, 1960). By the age of 5 to 6 years, children's original learning became much more rapid. They also became capable of relearning much more rapidly, typically within one or two trials (Kendler & Kendler, 1962). However, this was true only if the new criterion was one that required attention to the same general stimulus dimension (e.g., square shape rather than circular shape). If they were required to shift to a different dimension (e.g., size) as well as a different attribute (small), they still had difficulties, particularly if the new dimension was less salient than the old. The capability for shifting dimensions as well as attributes did not emerge until the age of 7 to 10 years of age (Mumbauer & Odom, 1967; Osler & Kovsky, 1966).

When these phenomena were first observed, the change in children's learning on such tasks was hypothesized to be part of a larger pattern, which White (1967) referred to as the "5 to 7 shift." In keeping with the learning theories of the time, Kendler & Kendler (1962) proposed that the shift was caused by a switch in the underlying mechanism of processing. The notion was that children under the age of 5, similar to other primates, process the world primarily in terms of its physical features, and that they make decisions on the basis of some sort of association strength: Each separate "correct" object (e.g., large circle, small circle, black circle, white circle) has to be associated with the presence of a reward, while each incorrect one has to be associated with the absence of a reward. On any trial, the object that has most often been associated with a reward is the one that is chosen. After this age, however, children begin to covertly label each physical object using verbal labels (e.g., circle). As a consequence, they are capable of much more rapid initial learning, because only one association need be learned (circle–reward). Children are also capable of much more rapid relearning, since all they have to do is substitute one word for another, not learn a whole new set of associations. This same change, that is, the change from unmediated to verbally mediated learning, was believed to have a wide variety of other consequences for children's cognition, especially the sort that is required in school (Kendler & Kendler, 1967; Rohwer, 1970).

As the century unfolded, the notion of a one-time shift from preverbal to verbal mediation was abandoned, because it did not fit the overall pattern that emerged as further training and transfer studies were conducted (see Stevenson, 1972, chapter 9 for a review). Although the phenomena were more complex than originally imagined, however, they were very robust, and subsequent theorists have felt obliged to address them, albeit in a different fashion.

☐ The Rationalist Tradition

The second theoretical tradition in which children's conceptual structures have been studied is one that drew its inspiration from Continental rationalism rather than British Empiricism. In reaction to British empiricists, philosophers such as Kant (1961) suggested that knowledge is acquired by a process in which order is imposed by the human mind on the data that the senses provide, not merely detected in these data. Examples of concepts that played this foundational role in Kant's system were space, time, causality, and number. Without some preexisting concept in each of these categories, Kant argued that it would be impossible to make any sense of the data of sensory experience: to see events as taking place in space, for example, as unfolding through time, or as exerting a causal influence on each other. For this reason he believed that these categories must exist in some a priori form rather than being induced from experience.

Developmental psychologists who were influenced by Kant's view tended to see the study of children's cognitive development in a different fashion from those who were influenced by empiricists. They thought that one should begin by exploring the foundational concepts with which children come equipped at birth, then go on to document any change that may take place in these concepts with age, not look at their increasing ability to associate stimuli with each other. The first developmental theorist to apply this approach was Baldwin (1968). According to Baldwin, children's conceptual categories or "schemata" progress through a sequence of four universal stages, which he termed the stages of "sensorimotor," "quasilogical," "logical," and "hyperlogical" thought. In any given stage, Baldwin believed that new experience is "assimilated" to the existing set of schemata, much in the manner that the body assimilates food. He saw transition from one form of thought to the next as driven by "accommodation," a process by which existing schemata are broken down and then reorganized into new and more adaptive patterns.

There was one interesting respect in which Baldwin attempted to go beyond Kant, which had a major impact on subsequent theorists. Baldwin saw children's conceptual understanding in each of Kant's categories as something that they construct, not something that is inborn. The only primitive elements with which he saw children being endowed at birth were entities that he called "circular reactions," that is, feedback mechanisms through which the infant learns to repeat movements that have positive consequences. He believed that these circular reactions led to the formation of habits. Although habits have great functional value—freeing up attention to deal with other matters—they also have their limitations. Old habits do not always work in new situations. As children encountered the limitations of their existing habits, Baldwin found that they renewed their interest in situations in which they appeared to have lost interest and actively experimented with new approaches. At certain points in their development, this experimentation led only to frustration. At others it seemed to lead to a sudden restructuring of their activity. To account for this (informal) observation, he proposed that the attempt to "accommodate" to a new situation often required change of a biological nature: one which increased the overall degree of integration of the child's cortex, and by this means also increased the span and power of their attention (and hence their ability to deal with complexity).

Baldwin called for subsequent generations of biologists to explore these changes in attentional capacity and to chart the process by which lower-order schemata are broken up and are assembled into higher-order schemata in each of the categories that Kant had outlined. The name that he proposed for this effort was "genetic epistemology."

It was Piaget's (1960, 1970) acceptance of Baldwin's challenge, and his reworking of Baldwin's theory, that led to the classic "constructivist" view of cognitive development that is associated with this tradition. The most important feature that Piaget added to Baldwin's theory was the notion of a "logical structure": that is, a coherent set of logical operations that can be applied to any domain of human activity, and to which any cognitive task in the domain must ultimately be assimilated. Piaget hypothesized that the form of children's structures is different at different stages of their development and that it is this difference that gives the thought of young children its unique character. To highlight the importance of these structures, he relabeled Baldwin's second and third stages of development, calling them the stages of "preoperational" and "operational" thought, respectively. He also divided the stage of operational thought into the "concrete" and "formal" periods and added additional substages to each. Finally, he made a number of other adjustments that were necessary to give his system coherence, such as increasing the emphasis on reflexive abstraction as the underlying developmental mechanism and decreasing the emphasis on increased attentional power and cortical coordination.

Together with his collaborators at the University of Geneva, Piaget also conducted a vast number of empirical studies: ones that were designed to reveal the details of children's conceptual understanding in each of Kant's categories, and the process by which this understanding is arrived at. His basic procedure was to present children with a wide variety of simple problems or tasks in order to see how they would respond to these problems, and then to interview them in order to determine the reasoning on which these responses were based. A final step was to look for a common pattern in children's reasoning at different ages and to treat this pattern as a clue regarding the underlying logical structure that was present.

As Piaget modeled these structures he devised a number of tasks that he hoped would document their existence more directly (Inhelder & Piaget, 1958, 1964). Two of the most famous of these were conservation (a task based on early work on "suggestion" by Binet, 1900) and class inclusion. As it happens, the class inclusion task is similar in certain respects to the concept learning task investigated by empiricists. Children see, for example, 9 squares, 5 of which are red. They are then asked, "Are there more red squares or squares?" Similar to the concept learning task, this task presents children with a simple set of shapes that can be classified in a number of different ways (by shape, color, etc.). It also requires them to overcome their "natural" or "habitual" way of classifying a set of stimuli (red versus white) and to sustain a focus on subordinate stimulus values, without losing sight of a superordinate classification. Finally, like the concept learning task, this task is passed for the first time during the same general age range: 7 to 10 years.

Although the tasks and the age of passing are similar, however, the form of interpretation that the two groups of theorists developed to explain the developmental change was quite different. For early learning theorists, the switch to a new form of response was seen as the result of applying a learned set of labels to stimuli and forming associations among these labels rather than among the primary stimuli themselves. For Piaget and those who followed him, the switch was seen as the result of acquiring a new logical structure, one in which superordinate and subordinate categories were differentiated and integrated. This structure, in turn, was seen as emerging from an internal process of reflection, not from a process in which empirical experience and the associations to which this leads played a major role.

☐ The Sociohistoric Tradition

The third major tradition in the study of cognitive development is the sociohistoric tradition. (See also Wertsch, this volume.) According to the sociohistoric view, conceptual knowledge does not have its primary origin in the structure of the objective world (as empiricist philosophers suggested). Nor does it have its origin in the structure of the subject and his spontaneous cogitation (as rationalist philosophers suggested). It does not even have its primary origin in the interaction between the structure of the subject and the structure of the objective world (as Baldwin and Piaget maintained). Rather, it has its primary origin in the social and material history of the culture of which the subject is a part and the tools, concepts, and symbol systems that the culture has developed for interacting with its environment.

Developmental psychologists who accepted the sociohistoric perspective viewed the study of children's conceptual understanding in a different fashion from empiricists or rationalists. They believed that one should begin the study of children's thought by analyzing the social, cultural, and physical contexts in which children find themselves, and the social, linguistic, and material tools that their culture provides them for coping with these contexts. One should then proceed to examine the way in which these intellectual and physical tools are passed on from one generation to the next.

The best known of the early sociohistoric theories was that of Vygotsky (1962). According to Vygotsky, children's thought must be seen in a context that includes both its biological and its cultural evolution. Three of the most important features of human beings as a species are (1) that they have developed language, (2) that they fashion their own tools, and (3) that they transmit the discoveries and inventions of one generation to the next via institutions such as schooling. From the perspective of Vygotsky's theory, the most important milestone in children's early development is the acquisition of language. Children first master language for social (interpersonal) purposes. Next, they internalize this language and use it for intrapersonal (self-regulatory) purposes. Finally, as this change takes place, their culture recognizes their new capabilities and begins an initiation process that includes an introduction to the forms of social practice in which they will have to engage as adults. In modern literate societies this initiation process normally includes the teaching of such skills as reading, writing, and arithmetic in primary school, followed by such subjects as science and formal mathematics in secondary school. Followers of Vygotsky often saw the acquisition of the first set of skills as being causally related to the appearance of the concrete logical competencies that children develop in middle childhood, and the second set as being causally linked to the emergence of the more formal competencies that appear in adolescence.

Early research in the sociohistoric tradition led to a number of interesting new findings. One of the most provocative was that adults in a traditional agricultural society, especially ones who have not attended school, tend to perform at a much lower level than adults who have attended school on tests of mnemonic and formal logical capabilities such as syllogisms (Vygotsky, 1962; Luria, 1966). To Vygotsky, this finding indicated that modern schooling, not some universal process of reflexive abstraction, is the major instrument of high level cognitive growth.

This inference has not gone unchallenged in recent years. Nevertheless, the datum is an important one, and has led to follow-up studies that have continued to this day (Cole, 1996). In most of the early studies, strong schooling effects were found, not just on the sort of tasks that Vygotsky and his followers had used, but also on tasks that had been used in the other two traditions as well (Cole, Gay, Glick, & Sharp, 1971; Goodnow, 1962; Greenfield, Reich, & Oliver, 1966). Although the results differed somewhat from study to study, the general pattern was that children moved through the 5 to 7 shift at a considerably later age if they did not attend school; very often, too, they failed to show the teenage shift to a more abstract or "formal" type of response. The shift that they showed in this latter period was one that could only be understood by studying their culture, their beliefs, and socialization practices (Greenfield, 1966).

As this tradition developed, ethnographic and historical methods were utilized with increasing frequency in order to place children's reasoning in context. Use of these methods further differentiated this tradition from the others. If the empiricist tradition took physics as its model of a well-developed science, and the second tradition took evolutionary biology as its model, then the third tradition increasingly turned to anthropology for methodological guidance.

☐ Dialogue Between the Empiricist and Rationalist Traditions

Until the late 1950s, North American psychology was dominated by empiricism of a rather extreme form: namely, the school of "logical positivism." Although the influence of this school was rather short-lived in philosophy, and much weaker from the start in Europe than in North America, its influence on American psychology lasted much longer and served to justify the radical behaviorism that developed on that continent. During the late 1950s and early 1960s, however, North American behaviorism began to come under fire from within North America as well as outside it. The most common criticism was that behaviorism failed to do justice to the organization of human behavior and the complex inner processes that are responsible for generating it (Bruner, Goodnow, & Austin, 1956; Chomsky, 1957; Miller, Galanter, & Pribram, 1960; Newell, Shaw, & Simon, 1958). At the same time as this criticism was being voiced, computers were emerging as a new economic force, and a new discipline was being created whose province was the design of software for them. Eventually, investigators from the newly formed discipline of computer science joined hands with psychologists, linguists, and other social scientists in an effort to describe the cognitive processes that are necessary to generate and control complex human behavior. This event became known as the "cognitive revolution" and the new discipline became known as "cognitive science" (Gardner, 1985).

Interestingly, although theories of learning underwent a profound transformation at this time, the underlying epistemology on which they were based changed relatively little. By and large, North American investigators still presumed that the ultimate locus of knowledge was the empirical world, and that the acquisition of knowledge by psychologists should follow the canons of experimental physics. In the field of cognitive development, the result was an interesting ambivalence. On the one hand, there was a great surge of interest in the sort of work that Piaget had pioneered: On the other hand, Piaget's theory was often read with empiricist glasses. Thus, many American investigators found the manner in which his theory had been formulated was excessively abstract, vague, and difficult to operationalize (Brainerd, 1976; Flavell, 1963). They also found it too impregnated with general philosophical arguments and hence difficult to verify or falsify. They had problems with the substance of the theory as well: in particular, they thought that the general logical structures Piaget hypothesized probably did not exist, and that such cognitive structures as did exist were more likely to be the result of empirical learning than "reflexive abstraction." Finally, they viewed Piaget's method of interviewing children as too clinical and subjective and his methods of sampling and data analysis as too unsystematic.

☐ New Models of Children's Conceptual Understanding

Several different lines of inquiry have been pursued in the last two decades in response to the empiricist critique. The first of these to be considered below (often referred to as neo-Piagetian theory) had its origins in an attempt to integrate the core assumptions of the empiricist and rationalist traditions. The other three positions to be outlined had their origins in attempts to preserve the core assumptions of one of the three classic traditions (i.e., empiricist, rationalist, and sociohistoric) but to develop a theory that would overcome problems with which that view had been associated.

Conceptual Development as a Local Process Limited by General Constraints

The first line of theoretical inquiry to emerge was one that became known as "neo-Piagetian" theory. This theoretical enterprise involved a direct attempt to build a bridge between the assumptions and methods that had underpinned Piaget's research program and the assumptions and methods of empiricism. Neo-Piagetians accepted Piaget's position that children construct their own understanding of the world and that reflexive abstraction plays an important role in this process. They also accepted Piaget's contention that development is a very general process in which changes that cannot be tied to any form of specific external stimulation play an important role. Finally, they accepted the implicit methodological canons underlying Piaget's research including (1) the notion that misleading tasks provide a particularly important window on children's conceptual understanding, and (2) the notion that the best way to develop a balanced view of children's intellectual capabilities is to examine their cognition on a broad spectrum of tasks that span all the major categories of human understanding.

At the same time, neo-Piagetians also agreed with empiricists that much of children's knowledge of the world is acquired in a more piecemeal fashion than Piaget had indicated, and that local task factors, specific experience, and associative processes play a crucial role in this process. They also accepted the notion that one must examine and explain children's performance in specific contexts in great detail, and model the process of learning. Finally, they accepted the necessity of defining their constructs and task situations in operational terms. The notion of a scheme, for example, was defined in the first neo-Piagetian system as an ordered pair of responses, s-r (Pascual-Leone, 1970).

Different neo-Piagetian theorists proposed somewhat different views of the general architecture of the cognitive system and the way in which that system develops. Nevertheless, there was a core set of propositions to that most neo-Piagetians subscribed that included the following: Children's cognitive development does show a general pattern of growth across many different domains; however, this is not because of the existence of systemwide logicomathematical structures. Rather, it is because the local structures that children construct are all subject to a common, systemwide constraint in attentional capacity, and this constraint gradually lifts with age. Different theorists focused on different aspects of children's capacity, such as their short-term memory, their working memory, or their information processing speed (Biggs & Collis, 1982; Case, 1985; Demetriou, Efklides, & Platsidou, 1993; Fischer, 1980; Halford, 1982, 1993; Pascual-Leone, 1970). They also used different metrics for calibrating the load that any given task places on children's information processing capacity. Several of them also returned to Baldwin's notion regarding the neurological bases of these changes (Case, 1992; Fischer, 1997; Pascual-Leone, Hamstra, Benson, Khan, Englund, 1990). Finally, and most recently, several of them used mathematical techniques drawn from dynamic systems theory to model the sudden transitions that could take place as neurological and task-specific variables reached critical levels (Case, 1996; van der Maas & Molenaar, 1992).

Regardless of the specifics of their theories, there was general agreement with regard to the steps that needed to be taken in examining children's responses to classic developmental tasks. Among these were (1) that a far more detailed analysis of specific task requirements was necessary than Piaget had attempted, (2) that these specific requirements had to be related to children's more general information-processing capacities—not just to their logical competencies, and (3) that revolutionary as well as continuous change in children's capabilities had to be accounted for.

In support of this analysis, neo-Piagetian theorists gathered several new kinds of data. Among the most important were those that demonstrate the following: (1) Tests of children's information processing capacity do reveal an increase with age (Case, 1972b; Pascual-Leone, 1970). (2) Subjects whose information processing capacity develops in an unusually rapid or slow manner show a corresponding acceleration or delay in acquiring new conceptual understandings of the sort studied by Piaget (Case, 1985; Crammond, 1992). (3) Finally, the age at which conceptual tasks are passed can be reduced by two years, by training studies that chunk two task-relevant (i.e., not misleading) schemes together (Case, 1972a). Conversely, it can be increased by two years by task modifications that increase the number of schemes that must be coordinated in order to arrive at a successful task solution (Case, 1972b; Pascual-Leone & Smith, 1969).

Conceptual Development as a Sequence of Theoretical Revolutions

In contrast to the first line of work, which attempted to integrate the assumptions of the empiricist and rationalist traditions, the second line of work stayed more squarely within the rationalist tradition itself. Rather than turning to information processing theory for inspiration, theorists who took this second direction turned to two other sources: Chomsky's work on the acquisition of the structures of natural language and Kuhn's (1962) work on theory change in science. According to Chomsky (1957), the reason that children come to understand and speak language as rapidly as they do is that they have an innate language acquisition device: one that is modular in nature, and that sensitizes them to the features in their environment that are relevant. According to Kuhn, progress in science does not take place evenly. Rather it takes place in spurts: ones in which relatively short periods of revolutionary change are punctuated by long periods of "problem solving" within the general paradigm that any new theory affords.

Putting these two notions together, investigators in this second group suggested that the mind is best conceived as a loosely connected set of modules, each of which is specialized for executing its own particular function in the same way as is the system for natural language (Carey, 1985; Fodor, 1982; Gardner, 1985). At birth, children possess "naive theories" of the world (Spelke, 1988). As they grow older, they rework these theories several times. Such reworkings were seen as taking place in one of two fashions: Existing concepts can be related in new ways as children encounter more experience with the world or more experience in trying to understand adult explanations. (This sort of change is analogous to the sort that occurs during stable periods in science, when new data are being gathered, and the problems with the existing theoretical structure are being worked out.) Alternatively, existing conceptual structures can be radically restructured. This corresponds to the change that takes place during scientific revolutions.

As was the case with neo-Piagetian theory, there was a good deal of variety among theory theorists, and the position itself continued to evolve in response to this diversity on the one hand and to new data on the other. Among the most interesting data that emerged were those that showed how children's responses to a wide variety of novel tasks changed in sequence, when their underlying theory of the domain was undergoing restructuring. Such a pattern was shown for tasks having to do with biological life (Carey, 1985, 1988; Keil, 1994), as well as tasks having to do with the understanding of mental phenomena (see Perner, this volume). Although this pattern was similar to the pattern that Piaget had found in many respects, it was a good deal more domain specific and was interpreted in terms of a revolutionary change in the content of children's beliefs, not a revolutionary change in their logical structures.

Conceptual Development as the Acquisition of Expertise

A third view of conceptual structures that has been proposed in the post-Piagetian era has its origins in the empiricist tradition in work on expert systems. Early studies of chess experts revealed—somewhat to everyone's surprise—that these individuals do not appear to have a set of general problem-solving heuristics that are more powerful than those of novices. Nor do they appear to have a larger memory capacity. To be sure, they can perform powerful feats of memory. For example, if presented with a chess board for only a few seconds, they can reproduce the entire configuration of pieces without error. However, this is true only if the pieces are placed in the sort of configuration that they might typically assume in a real chess game. If the pieces are placed on the board randomly, the ability of experts to remember their position is no better than that of novices (DeGroot, 1966). This study, and others like it, convinced many investigators that the main thing that distinguishes chess experts from others—other than a love of, or talent for, the game—is that they possess a huge repertoire of chess patterns that they can recognize (e.g., presence of an open file) and good moves that they can make in response to these patterns (e.g., move a rook to this file). This notion of expertise fits well with attempts to simulate the performance of chess experts on a computer. With about 10,000 patterns of the above sort, computer programs were created that did a very good job of simulating expert performance: beating human novices in the same general fashion, and in the same number of moves, as would a real expert, and losing to "grand masters" in a similar fashion as well.

This early work on expertise was soon extended to domains of knowledge that were less perceptually based, such as medicine and physics. Studies in these domains also found that the distinguishing feature of experts was the vast network of specific knowledge that they possessed, not a more powerful set of general heuristics or strategies. Equipped with this specific knowledge, experts would classify new problems in a different fashion from novices, typically according to the deep "principles" that they embodied, rather than with regard to their superficial features (Chi & Rees, 1983). Once the problems were classified in this fashion, experts were able to solve them with less effort and less elaborate problem solving processes than were novices. Once again, attempts to create expert systems on a computer were more successful when they built a huge repertoire of specific knowledge, and a powerful way of representing that knowledge, than when they tried endowing the system with more powerful problem solving strategies.

As Hayes (1985) pointed out, a repertoire of the magnitude required by these simulations takes many years for humans to acquire. Indeed, his review of the literature suggested that even in the extreme case of "child prodigies," one never finds a lasting contribution to a field being made until at least 10 years of study have been logged, with a daily investment on the order of 8 to 10 hours. Needless to say, one of the obvious things that distinguishes 10-year-olds from newborns is that they have had 10 additional years of experience. It was not long, therefore, before developmentalists in the empiricist tradition began to view the work on expert systems as providing a model for children's intellectual development. According to their view, extremely young children are best viewed as "universal novices," while adults are best viewed as individuals who have become expert in the wide range of problems that daily life (or school) presents.

In an early series of studies designed to demonstrate this point, Chi and her colleagues modeled children's knowledge networks about a particular class of objects (dinosaurs) in terms of the features of each dinosaur that they were aware of and could talk about (has sharp teeth, eats meat, is large, etc.). She then showed that as children's knowledge of dinosaurs increases, the knowledge network that they possess becomes increasingly coherent, in the sense that local groups of dinosaurs acquire more and more internal connecting links, which serve to distinguish them from other groups (Chi & Koeske, 1983). Finally, she showed that 6-year-olds with a lot of dinosaur experience (and coherent knowledge networks) tend to sort dinosaurs in the classic hierarchical fashion that is normally not seen until the age of 7 years (after the 5 to 7 shift), while 7-year-old children with the same IQ who have had little experience (and whose knowledge networks are not well differentiated) tend to sort dinosaurs in the syncretic and error-prone fashion that is normally typical of children who are 5 years of age or younger (Chi, Hutchinson, & Robin, 1989). Chi's interpretation of Piaget's findings on classification and class inclusion, therefore, was that the performance typically displayed by young children often results from an immature knowledge network, not from the absence of some powerful general logic that specifies how classes and subclasses are related or some powerful general "processing capacity." Indeed, Chi (1976) suggested that the age-related growth of processing capacity itself might just be an epiphenomenon. The real source of growth, she proposed, might be the acquisition of a huge knowledge network, one that is in turn acquired through the accumulation of a vast amount of specific experience.

Conceptual Development as Initiation Into a Community of Praxis

The fourth line of inquiry in the post-Piagetian era had its roots in the sociohistoric tradition. The general starting point from which this work took off was Vygotsky and Luria's demonstration that the performance of adults in a traditional agricultural setting, on a set of mnemonic and logical tasks, is a function of their degree of exposure to modern schooling. Several important questions were raised by this finding. First, how general is this effect? Is it one that applies across the board and produces a change in the full range of intellectual performance of which individuals in the culture are capable, or is it restricted to school-type tasks? Second, what aspect of schooling is responsible for producing this effect? Is it the acquisition of new symbol systems, such as those involved in literacy and numeracy? (Olson, 1977). Is it exposure to the new form of instruction, one that originally evolved to teach these systems, and that did so in a "decontextualized" context (Greenfield & Bruner, 1966)? Is it the mastery of the formal systems of Western thought, the ones that the new symbolic systems were designed to represent and that evolved with them?

A good deal of work has been devoted to pursuing these questions since Vygotsky's early studies. Because much of this work is summarized in the chapter by Wertsch, I shall only mention some of the highlights here. Early work in the sociohistoric tradition accepted Vygotsky's notion that children's conceptual development depends on the acquisition of an intellectual and physical technology, one that is normally acquired in school and that depends on the acquisition of literacy and numeracy. Recent work in this tradition has continued the emphasis on the importance of mastering the intellectual technology that one's culture provides. However, it has painted a picture that is a good deal more complex and context specific. Not only is there no formal structure that applies across all contexts, but literate structures are not necessarily superior to other structures and may in fact lead to practices that are less rather than more sophisticated. The same holds for the institutions with which literacy has been associated, namely, schools and the historical practices that have developed within them. Although they may offer certain advantages, they may also offer certain disadvantages that are equally important to understand. Finally, a similarly differentiated picture has evolved in regard to the benefits of group versus individual practice in instruction. Although the creation of a "classroom community" does appear to have certain benefits, these benefits are not distributed equally and appear to be stronger in general developmental competencies than in specific, well-defined skills (Damon, 1996).

☐ Comparison of Current Views and Abstraction of Common Principles

To say that large differences still separate the different traditions would be correct. However, to say that the process of dialogue has had no effect would not be. If one looks at the general structure of the new theories in each tradition and compares them with their predecessors, one sees a number of important points of convergence. In contrast to the state of affairs that were present 20 years earlier, contemporary theorists in each school now agree (1) that the notion of a systemwide cognitive structure should be replaced by a notion of structures that are more domain specific, (2) that children's cognitive structures should not be modeled as systems of logical operations, but as systems for making meaning, each with its own distinctive conceptual and/or symbolic content (Note: this is a move that Piaget also made in his later years [Piaget & Garcia, 1991]), and (3) that children's physical and/or social experience should be assigned a much more central role in explaining the process of structural change than Piaget's early theory gave it.

For theorists in the empiricist tradition, the move to this middle ground has meant a move away from an atomistic view of knowledge and toward a view where broad structural or disciplinary coherencies or both are given more emphasis. For theorists in the rationalist tradition, the move to this middle ground has meant a move away from analyses that are systemwide and toward a detailed consideration of factors that are domain specific. For theorists in the sociohistoric tradition, the new position has entailed a similar movement: away from a general and unilinear model of social, economic, and intellectual change and toward a model in which all three of these variables are viewed in terms that are more particular.

Given the trend toward greater convergence, it seems possible that we may see a greater convergence still in the years to come. This is the direction that I have pursued in my own work. Starting with a point of view that was generally classified as "neo-Piagetian," I have attempted to show how one needs some sort of notion of general cognitive structures (which until then had been missing from neo-Piagetian theory) if one is to explain the full pattern of children's cognitive development and its strong responsiveness to education. However, the structures one must postulate must be (1) less based on "logic" and more on semantic meaning, (2) less based on systemwide analyses of children's performance and more on analyses that are "modular," and (3) less focused on universal operations and more on symbols and forms of representation that are cultural constructions.

Readers who are interested in this particular form of synthesis are referred to our recent monograph (Case & Okamoto, 1996). The general points with which I would like to end, however, are ones that transcend this or any other particular attempt at synthesis. Stated in their simplest form, they follow: (1) Piaget's contribution to the rationalist tradition was so monumental that it temporarily obscured the important contributions that had been made in that tradition in the past, as well as contemporary and previous contributions that were being made in other traditions; (2) in the post-Piagetian era, there has been a reflowering of interest in these other traditions, as well as a renewed interest within the rationalist tradition in certain ideas that Piaget had inherited but deemphasized. The current era is thus a particularly lively one, characterized by exciting developments within each of these traditions on its own, as well as increased interest in drawing all three traditions together, in order to forge a vision of children's conceptual growth that is multidimensional and yet coherent. Two final developments that appear promising, but that are unfortunately beyond the purview of the present chapter, are the potential for the integration of neuropsychological and developmental perspectives and the incorporation of elements from dynamic systems theory (e.g., substituting "attractor states" for stages) into developmental theory (Van Geert, 1994).

☐ References

Baldwin, J. M. (1968). *The development of the child and of the race.* New York: Augustus M. Kelly. (Original work published 1894)

Binet, A. (1900). *La suggestibilite.* Paris: Schleicher et Frères.

Biggs, J., & Collis, K. (1982). *Evaluating the quality of learning: The SOLO taxonomy.* New York: Academic.

Brainerd, C. J. (1976). Stage, structure, and developmental theory. In G. Steiner (Ed.), *The psychology of the twentieth century.* Munich: Kindler.

Bruner, J. S., Goodnow, J. J., & Austin, G. A. (1956). *A study in thinking.* New York: Wiley.

Carey, S. (1985). *Conceptual change in childhood.* Cambridge, MA: MIT Press.

Carey, S. (1988). Reorganization of knowledge in the course of acquisition. In S. Strauss (Ed.), *Ontogeny, phylogeny, and historical development* (pp. 1–27). New York: Ablex.

Case, R. (1972a). Learning and development: A neo-Piagetian interpretation. *Human Development, 15,* 339–358.

Case, R. (1972b). Validation of a neo-Piagetian capacity construct. *Journal of Experimental Child Psychology, 14,* 287–302.

Case, R. (1985). *Intellectual development: Birth to adulthood.* New York: Academic Press.

Case, R. (1992). The role of the frontal lobes in the regulation of cognitive development. *Brain and Cognition, 20,* 51–73.

Case, R. (1996). Modelling the dynamic interplay between general and specific change in children's conceptual understanding. In R. Case & Y. Okamoto. The role of central conceptual structures in the development of children's thought. *Monographs of the Society for Research in Child Development, 61* (Serial No. 246, pp. 156–188). Chicago: University of Chicago Press.

Case, R. (1997). The development of conceptual structures. In D. Kuhn & R. S. Siegler (Eds.), *Handbook of child psychology: Cognitive, perceptual, and neurological development* (4th ed., vol. 2, pp. 745–800). New York: Wiley.

Case, R., & Okamoto, Y. (1996). The role of central conceptual structures in the development of children's thought. *Monographs of the Society for Research in Child Development, 61* (Serial No. 246). Chicago: University of Chicago Press.

Chi, M. T. H. (1976). Short-term memory limitations in children: Capacity or processing deficits? *Memory & Cognition, 4,* 559–572.

Chi, M. T. H., Hutchinson, J. E., & Robin, A. F. (1989). How inferences about novel domain-related concepts can be constrained by structured knowledge. *Merrill-Palmer Quarterly, 35,* 27–62.

Chi, M. T. H., & Koeske, R. D. (1983). Network representation of a child's dinosaur knowledge. *Developmental Psychology, 19,* 29–39.

Chi, M. T. H., & Rees, E. (1983). A learning framework for development. In M. T. H. Chi (Ed.), *Trends in memory development.* Basel: Karger.

Chomsky, N. (1957). *Syntactic structures.* The Hague: Mouton.

Cole, M. (1996). *Cultural psychology.* Cambridge, MA.: Harvard University Press.

Cole, M., Gay, J., Glick, J. A., & Sharp, D. D. (1971). *The cultural context of learning and thinking.* New York: Basic Books.

Crammond, J. (1992). Analyzing the basic developmental processes of children with different types of learning disability. In R. Case (Ed.), *The mind's staircase: Exploring the conceptual underpinnings of children's thought and knowledge* (pp. 285–302). Hillsdale, NJ: Erlbaum.

Damon, W. (1996). Nature, second nature and individual development: An ethnographic opportunity. In R. Jessor & A. Colby (Eds.), *Ethnography and human development.* Chicago: University of Chicago Press.

DeGroot, A. (1966). Perception and memory versus thought: Some old ideas and recent findings. In B. Kleinmuntz (Ed.), *Problem solving.* New York: Wiley.

Demetriou, A., Efklides, A., & Platsidou, M. (1993). The architecture and dynamics of the developing mind. *Monographs of the Society for Research in Child Development, 58,* 5–6.

Fischer, K. W. (1980). A theory of cognitive development: The control and construction of hierarchies of skills. *Psychological Review, 87,* 477–531.

Flavell, J. H. (1963). *The developmental psychology of Jean Piaget.* Princeton, NJ: Van Nostrand.

Fodor, J. (1982). *The modularity of mind.* Cambridge, MA: MIT Press.

Gardner, H. (1985). *The mind's new science: A history of the cognitive revolution.* New York: Basic Books.

Goodnow, J. J. (1962). A test of milieu differences with some of Piaget's tasks. *Psychological Monographs, 36*(555).

Greenfield, P. M. (1966). On culture and conservation. In J. S. Bruner, R. R. Oliver, & P. M. Greenfield, *Studies in cognitive growth* (pp. 225–256) New York: Wiley.

Greenfield, P. M., & Bruner, J. S. (1966). Culture and cognitive growth. *International Journal of Psychology, 1,* 89.

Greenfield, P. M., Reich, L. M., & Oliver, R. R. (1966). On culture and equivalence II. In J. S. Bruner, R. R. Oliver, & P. M. Greenfield (Eds.), *Studies in cognitive growth* (pp. 270–319). New York: Wiley.

Halford, G. S. (1982). *The development of thought.* Hillsdale, NJ: Erlbaum.

Halford, G. S. (1993). *Children's understanding: The development of mental models.* Hillsdale, NJ: Erlbaum.

Hayes, J. R. (1985). Three problems in teaching general skills. In S. Chipman, J. Segal, & R. Glaser (Eds.), *Thinking and learning skills* (Vol. 2). Hillsdale, NJ: Erlbaum.

Inhelder, B., & Piaget, J. (1958). *The growth of logical thinking from childhood to adolescence.* New York: Basic Books.

Inhelder, B., & Piaget, J. (1964). *The early growth of logic in the child.* London: Routledge & Kegan Paul.

Kant, I. (1961). Critique of pure reason. New York: Doubleday Anchor. (Original work published 1796)

Keil, F. C. (1994). The birth and nurturance of concepts by domains: The origins of concepts of living things. In L. A. Hirschfeld & S. A. Gelman (Eds.), *Mapping the mind: Domain specificity in cognition and culture* (pp. 234–254). New York: Cambridge University Press.

Kendler, H. H., & Kendler, T. S. (1962).Vertical and horizontal processes in problem solving. *Psychological Review, 69,* 1–16.

Kendler, T. S., & Kendler, H. H. (1967). Experimental analysis of inferential behavior in children. In L. P. Lipsitt & C. C. Spiker (Eds.), *Advances in children's development and behavior.* New York: Academic Press. *Psychological Review, 99,* 22–44.

Kendler, T. S., Kendler, H. H., & Wells, D. (1960). Reversal and nonreversal shifts in nursery school children. *Journal of Comparative and Physiological Psychology, 53,* 83–88.

Kuhn, T. S. (1962). *The structure of scientific revolutions.* Chicago: University of Chicago Press.

Luria, A. R. (1966). *Higher cortical functions in man.* New York: Basic Books.

Miller, G. A., Galanter, E., & Pribram, K. H. (1960). *Plans and the structure of behavior.* New York: Holt, Rinehart, & Winston.

Mumbauer, C. C., & Odom, R. D. (1967). Variables affecting the performance of preschool children in intradimensional, reversal and extradimensional shifts. *Journal of Experimental Psychology, 75,* 180–187.

Newell, A., Shaw, J. C., & Simon, H. A. (1958). Elements of a theory of human problem solving. *Psychological Review, 65,* 151–166.

Olson, D. R. (1977). From utterance to text. *Harvard Educational Review, 47,* 257–281.

Osler, S. F., & Kovsky, E. (1966). Structure and strategy in concept attainment. *Journal of Experimental Child Psychology, 4,* 198–209.

Pascual-Leone, J. (1970). A mathematical model for the transition rule in Piaget's development stages. *Acta Psychologica, 32,* 301–345.

Pascual-Leone, J., Hamstra, N., Benson, N., Khan, I., & Englund, R. (1990). *The P300 event-related potential and mental capacity.* Paper presented at the Fourth International Evoked Potentials Symposium, Toronto. (Available in conference proceedings.)

Pascual-Leone, J., & Smith, J. (1969). The encoding and decoding of symbols by children. A new experimental paradigm and a neo-Piagetian theory. *Journal of Experimental Child Psychology, 8,* 328–355.

Piaget, J. (1960). *The psychology of intelligence.* Totowa, NJ: Littlefield Adams.

Piaget, J. (1970). Piaget's theory. In P. H. Mussen (Ed.), *Handbook of child development* (pp. 703–732). New York: Wiley.

Piaget, J., & Garcia, R. (1991). *Toward a logic of meanings.* Hillsdale, NJ: Erlbaum.

Rohwer, W. D. (1970). Implications of cognitive development for education. In P. H. Mussen (Ed.), *Handbook of child psychology.* New York: Wiley.

Spelke, E. S. (1988). The origins of physical knowledge. In L. Weiskrantz (Ed.), *Thought without language*. Oxford, UK: Oxford University Press.

Stevenson, H. W. (1972). *Children's learning*. New York: Appleton Century Crofts.

Thorndike, E. L. (1914). *Educational Psychology* (Vol. III). New York: Teachers College Press, Columbia University.

Thorndike, E. L. (1925). *The measurement of intelligence*. New York: Teacher's College Press, Columbia University.

van der Maas, H. L. J., & Molenaar, P. C. M. (1992). Stagewise cognitive development: An application of catastrophe theory. *Psychological Review, 99*, 395–417.

Van Geert, P. (1994). *Dynamic systems of development: Change between complexity and chaos*. Hemel Hempstead, Hertfordshire: Harvester Wheatsheaf.

Vygotsky, L. S. (1962). *Thought and language* (E. Hanfmann & G. Vaker, Trans.). Cambridge, MA: MIT Press. (Original work published 1934)

Watson, J. S. (1914). *Behavior, an introduction to comparative psychology*. New York: Holt Rinehart Winston.

White, S. H. (1967). Some general outlines of the matrix of developmental changes between five and seven years. *Bulletin of the Orton Society, 20*, 41–57.

CHAPTER   Judy Dunn

Mindreading and Social Relationships

☐ Introduction

When do children begin to understand why people behave the way they do? When do they grasp that how others feel and think affects how they will behave? How does this growth in understanding affect their close relationships? Clearly, what children understand about why people behave the way they do and how far they understand other people's feelings and intentions carry profound implications for their own social lives. And children's understanding of their social world appears—in commonsense terms—likely to be linked to their own social experiences. Do such social experiences then explain individual differences in children's sophistication in understanding others?

These issues are central to both cognitive and social development, yet until the last few years they have been relatively little studied. Piaget's investigations of children's understanding of the mind began in the 1920s and are described in his first books (e.g., Piaget, 1926, 1928, 1929). After this seminal work, he turned his attention chiefly to children's understanding of physical phenomena, and this set an important direction for the cognitive developmentalists who followed him; it was not until the mid-1980s that interest in children's grasp of mental life

The research in this chapter conducted by Dunn and colleagues is supported by grants from the National Institutes of Health (HD 23158) and the ERSC.

began to revive, and over the last decade there has been a great burst of attention from developmental psychologists to children's understanding of mind (see also chapters by Harris and Perner). Young children's grasp of the links between what people desire, think, or believe, and their actions has now come to dominate much of cognitive developmental psychology to a striking extent. The focus has been chiefly upon the normative developmental changes in this understanding over the early years. We have learned a great deal about preschool children's growing ability to distinguish thoughts and things, their increasing interest in talking about thinking and knowing, their curiosity about why people behave the way they do, and their ability to play with hypothetical events and to share imaginary narratives in pretend play (see Astington, 1993, for a lucid summary). Yet there is a paradox here. What we have *not* learned about—until very recently—is how these developments in cognition are linked to children's real-life social experiences and why some children appear to be sophisticated manipulators of others' feelings and beliefs, and other children are much less so.

Why should this be so? Until quite recently, cognitive and socioemotional development were studied as separate domains (Dunn, 1996). The mapping of children's discovery of the mind, which has proved so exciting, did not include a focus on the role of social experience in influencing the development of understanding, and little attention was devoted to individual differences in mindreading and their possible links with social relations. That divide between a focus on cognitive and on social development has, however, now begun to be bridged, and the results have exciting implications for both domains. Two general lessons have become apparent from this research that begin to "bridge the gap," and it is these lessons that are the key themes for this chapter. The focus here is not, then, on these recent achievements in research on age changes in children's mindreading abilities over the early years (see Perner, this volume, for such an account) but, rather, on the links between children's growing understanding of mental life and their social relationships.

☐ Lessons About the Nature of Children's Understanding

The first lesson from research that crosses the divide between cognitive and social development is that we can learn about the *nature* of children's understanding from research that examines children's behavior and understanding in real-life social settings, and that this research highlights the capacities that even young children can show in the domain of understanding other people's feelings, beliefs, and intentions. If children are observed as they share pretend games with their friends or siblings, as they argue with family members, as they tell the story to their parents of "what happened" to them, many aspects of their behavior and talk with these familiar others appear to reflect considerable understanding of people's desires, intentions, plans, and beliefs. There is a major tension here in current cognitive developmental research (Russell, 1998) as the naturalistic data suggest this understanding of mental states is evident at considerably younger ages than would be expected on the basis of the standard experimental assessments of their understanding of the connections between what people believe or think and their actions (the "false belief" paradigm; see Perner and, for example, Bartsch & Wellman, 1989). Two brief examples from naturalistic research will serve to illustrate this point: children's talk about the mind, and their attempts at deception, within the setting of their family lives.

Talk About the Mind

Children show a rapidly increasing interest in inner states, including feelings, wants, and mental states, during the second and third years (Bartsch & Wellman, 1995; Brown, Donelan McCall, & Dunn, 1996). Bartsch and Wellman's meticulous analyses of a large data set of children's talk (the Child Language Data Exchange System [CHILDES], MacWhinney & Snow, 1985), for instance, make clear that children start talking about thinking around their third birthday and that they make explicit contrasts between thought and reality ("I thought so, 'cept they weren't") at an age when most of them would clearly fail the formal mindreading assessment, the false belief task. They also distinguish between their own mental states and those of others at a surprisingly young age. As one 3-year-old in a study of ours commented (quite accurately) to her 4-month-old baby sibling, "You don't remember Judy, I do!" Our studies showed that questions to parents about other people's feelings and wants, and about why they act the way they do, which increase in frequency so markedly over the third year (Dunn, 1988), are often focused on hurt or upset: "What's that frighten you, Mum?" "Why are you upset?" Our observers were also asked about their likes and dislikes: "Do you like monsters?" "Do you get cross?" "Want a little bit of biscuit?" This issue of *emotion* featuring so prominently in children's first essays into talking about people's behavior is one that will prove a recurrent theme.

Deception

The second example where naturalistic data differ in import from the findings of much experimental work is deception. Children's first essays into deception have been a focus of particular interest to theory of mind researchers, since intentional deception involves an attempt to manipulate what another person thinks or believes. In experimental research on children's understanding of deception, the findings, and the developmental accounts that are generated from them, vary very much across studies (Chandler, Fritz, & Hala, 1989; Sodian, 1991; Strichartz & Burton, 1990). Some report that 4-year-olds are unable to deceive successfully. Yet, in contrast, within their family worlds children as young as two years of age frequently appear to try to deceive their parents to get out of trouble, to shift blame for misdeeds onto a sibling, or to give false excuses for wrongdoing (Dunn, 1988). A recent systematic study of naturally occurring incidents in which children apparently tried to deceive other people at home (Newton, 1994) documented several different kinds of deception shown by 3- and 4-year-olds. These included not only the false excuses to avoid punishment or disapproval, but also incidents of "bravado" in which the children concealed or denied their own emotional state by denying that a punishment hurt, for instance. That is, at 3 years old they were already engaging in "impression management"! It is of special interest that the 3-year-olds in Newton's work were observed to be attempting all the types of deception shown by the older children, although the frequency of these attempts increased with age. They were already trying to manipulate what other family members thought or expected. A second point of importance in this research is the evidence that even children who failed the standard "theory of mind" tests were observed to try to deceive others in the daily dramas of family life.

Emotion, Social Context, and Understanding

Why is there a discrepancy between conclusions about children's capacities from naturalistic and experimental studies? Newton (1994), in his study of deception, documented the circumstances in which these incidents occurred and emphasized that these happened "in situations of conflict when the child is in an emotionally charged state of opposition to parental control." Clearly, these situations are very different from the usual experimental setups in which deception and other aspects of mind-reading have been studied, different both in terms of the familiarity of the people involved and the emotional salience of the interactions for the children. And the significance of the emotional and pragmatic context in which children display these early powers of understanding others is evident again when we consider the other examples of early mindreading reported from naturalistic studies, which include evidence of teasing, comforting or joking, all of which indicate some grasp of others' inner states and involve interactive situations that are "highly colored" in terms of the interactants' feelings. They are situations in which children and their interlocutors are feeling frustration, emotion, desire: rarely are these interactions affectively neutral. There is now growing evidence that the early stages of developing understanding of other people's feelings and mental states are especially clear in these emotionally vivid interactions with highly familiar others (Reddy, 1991). A general message, then, is that we should pay attention to such emotional and pragmatic issues, if we are not to misrepresent children's mindreading capacities.

☐ Social Processes Implicated

The second lesson from recent research that bridges the divide between studies of cognitive and social development is that social and emotional processes may well be implicated in the *development* of mindreading, as well as important in revealing the earliest stages of children's understanding. It is increasingly clear, for example, that to understand *individual differences* in children's abilities to understand mental states and their links to human action, children's social experiences must be examined, and interest in understanding the antecedents and sequelae of these individual differences has grown rapidly in the last few years. Several kinds of interactive events not only reveal children's mindreading abilities vividly, but also suggest processes that may be implicated in their development, and these are currently under active scrutiny by researchers. They include children's experiences of sharing and negotiating *a pretend world* with another person in joint play, *conversations about inner states*, which include arguments and conflict with others in which children are faced with another's point of view, and joint *narratives and causal discourse* about the social world.

Joint Pretend

At least four independent studies have now shown that individual differences in children's experiences of sharing a pretend world with another child are linked to early success on mindreading and emotion understanding tasks (Astington & Jenkins, 1995; Dunn & Cutting, in press; Hughes & Dunn, in press; Youngblade & Dunn, 1995), paralleling the finding that 4-year-olds who were particularly inclined to engage in pretense were accelerated in their development of knowledge about the mind (Taylor & Carlson, 1997). Clearly, this sharing of a make-believe world with another person, in which roles are taken up and a story line jointly elaborated, should be much helped by children's ability to take account of their partner's thoughts; in turn, it is plausible that the experience of collaborating on developing a pretend narrative will foster the growth of such abilities. However, we should of course be extremely cautious about making inferences about the direction of effects from these correlational data. The correlations are found *both* between early social processes (the experience of joint pretend play as 2- and 3-year-olds) and later cognitive task performance (Youngblade & Dunn, 1995), and also between cognitive task performance as 3- to 4-year-olds and later pretend play with a friend as 6- to 7-year-olds (Maguire & Dunn, 1997). While it could be that sharing a pretend world fosters the understanding of the mind, it may also be that children who are good at understanding emotions and other minds make better play companions.

A general point of much importance is that these studies show us that children begin to play with multiple, hypothetical realities and to "decouple" reality from fantasy not as solitary cognitive enterprises but through negotiating social interactions in which these cognitive states are shared with another person. Note that these findings fit well with the theoretical argument that simulation or role-taking plays a key part in the development of children's understanding of mind (Harris, 1991). It is notable too that when children are engaged in shared pretend play they are especially likely to talk about inner states (see, for example, Hughes & Dunn, 1997), and such conversations may play a key role in explaining the link between pretend play experiences and cognitive performance, the topic to which we turn next.

Conversations About Inner States

Children who frequently participate in conversations in which mental states or feelings are referred to and discussed are much more successful on later assessments of mindreading and emotion understanding. This has been established from a series of recent studies linking participation in such discourse with later differences in the maturity of children's mindreading and emotion understanding (Brown et al., 1996; Dunn, Brown, & Beardsall, 1991; Dunn, Brown, Slomkowski, Tesla, & Youngblade, 1991; Hughes & Dunn, 1998). Moreover, experimental studies employing theory of mind tasks show that the success of the children is enhanced if they are given the opportunity to engage in conversations about the behavior of the protagonists in the task scenarios (Appleton & Reddy, 1996). These findings on conversations about inner states raise a series of further questions. What precipitates such conversations in real-life settings? Is it the "content" of the talks that is important in relation to the development of cognitive skills, or do the pragmatics also matter? Are conversational narratives important? They have been highlighted by Bruner (1990) and Feldman (1992) as of major significance in the development of understanding. What about the particular social partner with whom the child is conversing? Are mothers of special significance? What about children's communication with other children, which is seen by Piaget to be of particular importance in the growth of social understanding?

On each of these issues, the evidence is growing. As regards the precipitation of conversations about inner states, it is now evident that children's own emotional state is important in the initiation of the talk about inner states during the second and third year. In one of our studies the mothers were more than twice as likely to talk about feelings with their children when the children were upset or angry than when they were happy or expressing neutral emotions (Dunn & Brown, 1994). The children themselves were more likely to engage in causal talk about feelings when they were angry or upset, and the frequency of such causal talk was correlated over time with their performance on emotion understanding tasks (Dunn & Brown, 1993). Moreover, the children's conflict management style, or specifically the extent to which they took account of their antagonist's point of view, was linked to their social understanding as assessed in task situations (Dunn & Herrera, 1997; Slomkowski & Dunn, 1992). Recall Newton's findings on conflict as the setting for early attempts to deceive others. Again we are reminded that the emotional context may be key to what is learned in particular interactions. It is a point made in the research on disputes and conflict by Stein and her colleagues (Stein & Miller, 1993), in which the significance of argumentative interactions between mothers and their children and between siblings and friends in the development of understanding is highlighted.

Such findings raise the issue of whether it is the emotional salience of the disputes, or the "meeting of minds" when children are confronted with their opponents' point of view, that is key to conflict as a formative context. Or are both important? The evidence from these and other studies suggests that what is important is not simply the child's exposure to new information or another person's point of view. Rather, the quality of the relationship between the child and interlocutor, which is reflected in the emotions and pragmatics of their exchanges, is an important contributor. This claim goes further than the argument that conversation is important in the growth of social understanding because it highlights differences between partners in conversation in terms of their information and attitudes (Harris, 1996). My own view is that both the pragmatics (what the interlocutors are trying to do in such talk) and their affect are key features (cf. Bruner's emphasis on the significance of "contexts of practice" for children's acquisition of language, Bruner, 1983).

Narratives

One aspect of communicative exchanges that has been a focus of particular attention in relation to the development of mindreading is narrative. Narrative has been seen Bruner (1990) and Feldman (1992) as a key process through which the development of mind and understanding is fostered. They have argued that patterns of narrative scaffold the kind of metacognition about intentions that lies at the core of theories of mind, that we account for our own actions and those of others principally in terns of narrative stories, and that narrative images generate our sense of self within a particular culture. In our own research we examined the frequency of children's unsolicited narratives about the past and found that the increase in such narratives over the second, third, and fourth years of age paralleled the changes in children's references to psychological issues more broadly. Brown's (1995) study of these narratives made two points relevant to the development of mindreading.

The first concerned emotion, which figures importantly in the early narratives, as it did in the initiation of talk about inner states. The children showed their most sophisticated language skills (sequencing events causally and temporally, referring to inner states, for instance) when they reported stories involving fear, anger, and distress. It was the emotional events they experienced, and particularly the negative experiences, that prompted the children to tell coherent stories about the past. The second point concerned the pragmatic context of the children's early narratives. Brown showed that this sophisticated narrative talk predominated in *instrumental* moves when children were trying to influence someone's behavior. The importance of this evidence, she argued, is that within families (and between friends) discussions frequently center on whose rights were violated in a transgression or who was responsible for an accident. Such discourse often focuses on the recent past, which was experienced from different and competing perspectives. There is a great pressure then in such disputes for children to be able to construct their own compelling accounts of what happened. The urgency with which children wish to have their own needs met and their own points of view appreciated in these conversations may well contribute to the development of their communicative competence (see Mannle and Tomasello's (1987) concept of "communication pressure"). Here, as in the consideration of deception, we come back to that central point: We should not lose sight of the *emotional* context in which children begin to understand others and their own relationship goals.

The Significance of Different Emotional Relationships

An important general issue concerning social processes cuts across these different kinds of interactive events. This has been highlighted by research on children studied in their various relationships, with their mothers, siblings, and friends. We have learned from these studies that children use their powers of understanding quite differently in their different relationships, depending on the quality of the relationship and on the pragmatics of the particular interaction. There was, for example, no significant correlation between children's propensity to take account of their mothers' feelings or intentions when in conflict with them and to do so when in conflict with their siblings or friends. The same child behaved very differently in disputes with friend, with mother, and with sibling. Some children reasoned and negotiated with their mothers but not with their siblings or friends; others negotiated with friends but rarely did so with their mothers (Slomkowski & Dunn, 1992). A similar pattern of findings came from the observations of children engaged in pretend play: Individual differences in their engagement in pretend play with their mothers, siblings, and friends were not correlated (Youngblade & Dunn, 1995). Some engaged in role play with their friends, but not with their mothers or siblings; some did so with their mothers, but not their siblings; and so on. And there were not significant correlations between children's discussion of mental states with their mothers, siblings, and friends (Brown et al., 1996). As we noted above, children's management of conflict, their pretend play, and their discourse about inner states were each related to their performance on standard mindreading tasks and emotion understanding tasks, yet the *use* of this understanding in real-life interaction was influenced by the emotional dynamics of the particular relationship. Whether children used their understanding of other people's inner states depended on the quality of their relationship with the other. Relationship quality, we are reminded, depends on both partners and is unlikely to be linked simply to the sociocognitive skills of either partner. And different kinds of social relationship may play rather different roles in influencing the development of social understanding. Of special interest here are the recent findings on the significance of child–child relationships and studies linking mind-reading with earlier attachment relationships.

The Significance of Children's Relationships With Other Children

My first interest in the early development of social understanding was catalyzed by observations of toddlers in their second year acting in a strikingly sophisticated way to *tease* their older siblings or to aid them in battles with their parents, or to provide comfort to them or to exacerbate their distress. It appeared that in the context of that emotionally unin-hibited relationship with a familiar other child, the toddlers showed con-siderable powers of understanding the other child's inner states (Dunn, 1988). But sibling relationships differ greatly in quality, and of course some children do not have brothers and sisters. What are the implica-tions of individual differences in experiences with siblings or relations with peers for the development of social understanding?

Consider these recent findings from our longitudinal study of children in Pennsylvania. First, individual differences in children's success on mindreading tasks were related to their earlier experiences of coopera-tive play with their older siblings (Dunn, Brown, Slomkowski et al., 1991). Second, talk about feelings with siblings quadrupled in frequency between 33 and 47 months, while such talk with mothers declined in frequency over the same period. Third, when talking with their friends or siblings, children discussed mental states notably more frequently than when talking with their mothers (Brown et al., 1996). And in such conversations with their siblings or friends, children were more likely to discuss *shared* ideas and thoughts (as contrasted with their own thoughts) than when talking with their mothers. Moreover, the length and quality of their friendships were linked positively to their talk about inner states.

Third, children with siblings were reported to be more successful on mindreading tasks than those without siblings (Perner, Ruffman, & Leekham, 1994). And, fourth, in a study of children in Crete the number of siblings and kin with whom children interacted was correlated with their success on such mindreading tasks (Lewis, Freeman, Kyriakidou, Maridaki-Kassotaki, & Berridge, 1996).

It appears that these interactions between children may have real po-tential as influences on children's ability to understand others. Yet they are very different in terms of demands, rewards, and challenges from those of communicating with parents or teachers. The striking increase in child–child conversations that takes place over this relatively short period between 2 years old and 4 years reflects the rapid growth of children's capacity to communicate with a partner who does not make the "allowances" of a parent or teacher who is motivated to respond sensitively to a relatively inexperienced conversationalist, but who may share interests and fantasies more closely than an adult partner. The suggestion that such child–child interactions may be fostering understanding is not one that fits with a conventional Vygotskian account of cognitive development through the experiences of children as apprentices to expert, didactic adults. It should make us rethink that conventional view; and we should remember that from very early childhood onward in most cultures, children spend much more time communicating with other children than they do with adults.

The Significance of Attachment Quality

Within a rather different framework, that of attachment theory, recent work has begun to highlight interesting connections between children's early attachment relationships and their mindreading abilities. Since Bretherton's (1985) seminal writing on the possible links between security of attachment and the acquisition of a theory of mind, researchers have been intrigued by the notion that securely attached children might be better able to reflect on metacognitive issues (Main, 1991). Now there are studies that indicate security of attachment to mothers is indeed related concurrently to competence on theory of mind tasks (Fonagy, Redfern, & Charman, 1997) and also over time. Thus Meins and her colleagues found children who were securely attached in infancy performed better on theory of mind tasks at 4 years and on some assessments of "mentalizing" abilities at 5 years (Meins, Fernyhough, Russell, & Clarke-Carter, 1997). Their interpretation of the processes at work here was that the mothers of the securely attached children were more likely "to treat their children as individuals with minds," showing sensitivity to their current levels of understanding and using mental state terms in their interactions with them, which is a propensity that Meins referred to as "mind-mindedness" (Meins, 1997). The exciting challenge that such work poses is to move toward specifying the social processes implicated and to tackle the intractable questions of direction of effects in links between attachment quality and individual characteristics of children, both social and cognitive.

☐ Questions and Challenges

The recent attempts to bridge the divide between research on social and on cognitive development, in relation to the growth of children's understanding of mental life, have clearly been instructive. We have learned that we should pay close attention to the significance of emotional context in the way children *use* their understanding, to their interactional goals, to their understanding as it is revealed in their various close relationships, to the development of individual differences in understanding and their antecedents in social experience, and to the social processes implicated in both child–child and child–parent close relationships. We need to tackle that intractable question of how cognitive change and affect are linked. At a methodological level, we need to include both experimental and naturalistic strategies; both are useful. But the research has also raised a host of more specific developmental questions that need to be tackled; in this last section four sets of questions raised by this recent research that present key challenges are outlined.

Differentiation of Understanding

How is children's growing ability to understand mental life related to other aspects of their cognitive development? To what extent should understanding other people's beliefs, thoughts, and emotions be differentiated? Does understanding of mind rather reflect some domain-general understanding? In focusing on children's discovery of the mind are we in fact learning about one aspect of more general cognitive development?

A central issue raised by these questions, which is currently a topic of much controversy, concerns modularity of brain function. Moore (1996) has argued that mindreading is, in terms of adaptive function, domain general, but suggests that differentiation of aspects of understanding of mind and emotion may take place developmentally. As a parallel, he cites Karmiloff-Smith's (1992) account in which modularity in adult information processing arises through domain general cognitive mechanisms working within particular and differentiated environments. This brings us to the exciting questions of how far (and when, developmentally) emotion understanding and theory of mind may be differentiated. Intriguing lines of research are developing here. First consider one general developmental account suggested by the evidence on children's talk about the mind (Bartsch & Wellman, 1995). Very young children explain people's actions at first in terms of emotions and desires. Through their social experiences, so the account goes, they come to incorporate the notion of belief in their understanding of why people behave the way they do. Bartsch and Estes (1996) have pointed out that one implication of this is that an understanding of cognitive states arises from an earlier understanding of emotional states. They argue that this has wide implications for our understanding of development:

> A comprehensive account of metacognition will have to be anchored in a much broader understanding of development and will require a better understanding of the relationship between cognitive and noncognitive psychological phenomena. (p. 299)

Second, there are findings from longitudinal research that indicate that the sequelae of children's early success on mindreading tasks may be *different* from those of their success on emotion understanding assessments (Dunn, 1995). Early understanding of emotions was associated with later positive relations with peers, sophisticated understanding of feelings, and moral sensibility. Early mindreading skills, in contrast, were associated with a high degree of connected communication between friends, with sophisticated and frequent role play with friends, and with an increased sensitivity to criticism. Third, the research within an attachment framework suggests that differences in security of attachment in infancy and toddlerhood may be related to some aspects of mindreading but not others (e.g., Meins et al., 1997).

Links Between Emotion and Social Understanding

A second set of challenging questions relates to the links between emotion and social understanding. We have seen that the emotional context is key to the use children make of their social understanding in early childhood. But do these patterns change as children grow up? As children's powers of metacognition develop, do they become less at the mercy of their own feelings? Some of the literature on children's handling of conflict suggests this may be so (Dunn & Herrera, 1997); however, we know little about the issue in general. Does the significance of heightened emotions for what children learn from particular interactions change as they grow up? We are especially ignorant about the developmental changes in children beyond 5 years of age: the preoccupation of cognitive developmental psychologists with the *initial* stages of children's discovery of the mind means we know remarkably little about the developmental changes in understanding and emotions in older children.

Learning About Normal Development From Children at the Extremes

Do links between mindreading and socioemotional development differ for children within the normal range of individual differences and those at the extremes? The increase in studies of individual differences in mindreading has been very important in highlighting the significance of social experiences in the growth of understanding. But with the notable exception of research on autism, most of these studies have focused on normal children.We do need to know whether the nature and patterns of early connections between understanding, social relationships, and emotional experiences differ for children with language problems, disabilities, anxiety problems, or early signs of conduct problems. In all of these groups, children in middle childhood are at risk for both problems in close relationships and in social understanding (see, for example, Dodge, 1991), but little is known about the early development of these links. In the case of children considered "hard to manage" a promising start has been made, which suggests there are both interesting differences in the children's understanding of mind from that of children within the normal range and connections between these cognitive abilities and their antisocial behavior (Hughes, Dunn, & White, 1998). For example, Hughes' research showed that among the hard-to-manage children, false belief tasks that involved a *nasty* surprise were passed with more success than those that involved a *nice* surprise; among the control children no such distinction was found. And the hard-to-manage children whose behavior involved aggression were particularly poor at the executive function tasks that involved planning, while those whose antisocial behavior involved much teasing were better at deception tasks than the other children.

We need, too, to learn more about the significance of cultural and class differences in children's developing mindreading abilities. Provocative recent findings from a socially deprived London sample indicate that social class and parental educational levels can play a major role in contributing to individual differences in mindreading (Cutting & Dunn, in press); the challenge here is to delineate the social processes that are implicated at a more proximal level in explaining these connections.

☐ Conclusions

In summary the challenges and opportunities for understanding the links between children's discovery of the mind and their social relationships are many. Through the new enthusiasm for mapping children's growing understanding of mental life, we have also been given key sign-posts for clarifying the ways this understanding is—or is not—linked to and affected by their social relationships. The research on children within their own world has spotlighted the emotional power of the interactions in which children's understanding of others is fostered; we are reminded that we cannot ignore, and must try to understand, the mutual influence of social and cognitive change in children.

☐ References

Appleton, M., & Reddy, V. (1996). Teaching 3-year-olds to pass false-belief tests: A conversational approach. *Social Development, 5,* 275–291.

Astington, J. W. (1993). *The child's discovery of the mind.* Cambridge, MA: Harvard University Press.

Astington, J. W., & Jenkins, J. M. (1995). Theory of mind development and social understanding. *Cognition and Emotion, 9,* 151–165.

Bartsch, K., & Estes, D. (1996). Individual differences in children's developing theory of mind and implications for metacognition. *Learning and Individual Differences, 8*(4), 281–304.

Bartsch, K., & Wellman, H. (1989). Young children's attribution of action to beliefs and desires. *Child Development, 60,* 946–964.

Bartsch, K., & Wellman, H. M. (1995). *Children talk about the mind.* Oxford, UK: Oxford University Press.

Bretherton, I. (1985). Attachment theory: Retrospect and prospect. In I. Bretherton & E. Waters (Eds.), *Monographs of the Society for Research in Child Development* (50, Serial No. 209).

Brown, J. R. (1995). *What happened?: Emotional experience and children's talk about the past.* Unpublished manuscript.

Brown, J. R., Donelan McCall, N., & Dunn, J. (1996). Why talk about mental states? The significance of children's conversations with friends, siblings, and mothers. *Child Development, 67*(3), 836–849.

Bruner, J. (1983). *Child's talk.* Oxford, UK: Oxford University Press.

Bruner, J. (1990). *Acts of meaning.* Cambridge, MA: Harvard University Press.

Chandler, M., Fritz, A. S., & Hala, S. (1989). Small-scale deceit: Deception as a marker of two-, three- and four-year-olds' theories of mind. *Child Development, 60,* 1263–1277.

Cutting, A., & Dunn, J. (in press). Theory of mind, emotion understanding, language and family background: Individual differences and inter-relations. *Child Development.*

Dodge, K. A. (1991). Emotion and social information processing. In J. Garber & K. Dodge (Eds.), *Emotion regulation* (pp. 159–181). Cambridge, UK: Cambridge University Press.

Dunn, J. (1988). *The beginnings of social understanding* (1st ed.). Cambridge, MA: Harvard University Press.

Dunn, J. (1995). Children as psychologists: The later correlates of individual differences in understanding of emotions and other minds. *Cognition and Emotion, 9*(2–3), 187–201.

Dunn, J. (1996). The Emanuel Miller Memorial Lecture 1995: Children's relationships: Bridging the divide between cognitive and social development. *Journal of Child Psychology and Psychiatry and Allied Disciplines, 37*(5), 507–518.

Dunn, J., & Brown, J. R. (1993). Early conversations about causality: Content, pragmatics and developmental change. *British Journal of Developmental Psychology, 11*(2), 107–123.

Dunn, J., & Brown, J. (1994). Affect expression in the family, children's understanding of emotions, and their interactions with others. Special Issue: Children's emotions and social competence. *Merrill Palmer Quarterly, 40*(1), 120–137.

Dunn, J., Brown, J., & Beardsall, L. (1991). Family talk about feeling states and children's later understanding of others' emotions. *Developmental Psychology, 27* (3), 448–455.

Dunn, J., Brown, J., Slomkowski, C., Tesla, C., & Youngblade, L. (1991). Young children's understanding of other people's feelings and beliefs: Individual differences and their antecedents. *Child Development, 62*(6), 1352–1366.

Dunn, J., & Cutting, A. (in press). Understanding others, and individual differences in friendship interactions in young children. *Social Development.*

Dunn, J., & Herrera, C. (1997). Conflict resolution with friends, siblings, and mothers: A developmental perspective. *Aggressive Behavior, 23,* 343–357.

Feldman, C. F. (1992). The theory of theory of mind. *Human Development, 35,* 107–117.

Fonagy, P., Redfern, S., & Charman, A. (1997). The relationship between belief-desire reasoning and projective measure of attachment security. *British Journal of Developmental Psychology, 15,* 51–61.

Harris, P. L. (1991). The work of the imagination. In A. Whiten (Ed.), *Natural theories of mind: The evolution, development, and simulation of everyday mindreading* (pp. 283–304). Oxford, UK: Blackwell.

Harris, P. L. (1996). Desires, beliefs and language. In P. Carruthers & P. K. Smith (Eds.), *Theories of theories of mind* (pp. 200–220). Cambridge, UK: Cambridge University Press.

Hughes, C., & Dunn, J. (1997). "Pretend you didn't know": Preschoolers' talk about mental states in pretend play. *Cognitive Development, 12,* 477–499.

Hughes, C., & Dunn, J. (1998). Theory of mind and emotion understanding: Longitudinal associations with mental state talk between young friends. *Developmental Psychology, 34* 1026–1037.

Hughes, C., Dunn, J., & White, A. (1998). Trick or treat?: Patterns of cognitive performance and executive function among "hard to manage" preschoolers. *Journal of Child Psychology and Psychiatry, 39*(7), 981–994.

Karmiloff-Smith, A. (1992). *Beyond modularity: A developmental perspective on cognitive science.* Cambridge, MA: MIT Press.

Lewis, C., Freeman, N. H., Kyriakidou, C., Maridaki-Kassotaki, K., & Berridge, D. M. (1996). Social influences on false belief access: Specific sibling influences or general apprenticeship? *Child Development, 67,* 2930–2947.

MacWhinney, B., & Snow, C. E. (1985). The child language data exchange system. *Journal of Child Language, 12,* 271–295.

Maguire, M., & Dunn, J. (1997). Friendships in early childhood, and social understanding. *International Journal of Behavioral Development, 21*(4), 669–686.

Main, M. (1991). Metacognitive knowledge, metacognitive monitoring, and singular (coherent) vs. multiple (incoherent) models of attachment: Findings and directions for future research. In C. M. Parker, J. Stevenson-Hinde, & P. Morris (Eds.), *Attachment across the life cycle.* London: Routledge.

Mannle, S., & Tomasello, M. (1987). Fathers, siblings and the bridge hypothesis. In K. E. Nelson & A. van Kleeck (Eds.), *Children's language* (Vol. 6, pp. 23–41). Hillsdale, NJ: Erlbaum.

Meins, E. (1997). *Security of attachment and the social development of cognition.* Hove, UK: Psychology Press.

Meins, E., Fernyhough, C., Russell, J. T., & Clarke-Carter, D. (1997). Security of attachment as a predictor of symbolic and mentalising abilities: A longitudinal study. *Social Development, 7,* 1–24.

Moore, C. (1996). Evolution and the modularity of mindreading. *Cognitive Development, 11,* 605–621.

Newton, P. (1994). *Preschool prevarication: An investigation of the cognitive prerequisites for deception.* Unpublished doctoral dissertation, Portsmouth University, United Kingdom.

Perner, J., Ruffman, T., & Leekham, S. R. (1994). Theory of mind is contagious: You catch it from your sibs. *Child Development, 65,* 1228–1238.

Piaget, J. (1926). *The language and thought of the child.* London: Kegan Paul.

Piaget, J. (1928). *Judgement and reasoning in the child.* London: Kegan Paul.

Piaget, J. (1929). *The child's conception of the world.* London: Kegan Paul.

Reddy, V. (1991). Playing with others' expectations: Teasing and mucking about in the first year. In A. Whiten (Ed.), *Natural theories of mind.* Oxford, UK: Blackwell.

Russell, J. (1998). Review of Bartsch and Wellman (1995). *Journal of Child Psychology and Psychiatry, 39,* 602.

Slomkowski, C. L., & Dunn, J. (1992). Arguments and relationships within the family: Differences in young children's disputes with mother and sibling. *Developmental Psychology, 28*(5), 919–924.

Sodian, B. (1991). The development of deception in children. *British Journal of Developmental Psychology, 9,* 173–188.

Stein, N., & Miller, C. (1993). The development of memory and reasoning skill in argumentative contexts: Evaluating, explaining, and generating evidence. In R. Glaser (Ed.), *Advances in instructional psychology* (Vol. 4, pp. 284–334). Hillsdale, NJ: Erlbaum.

Strichartz, A. F., & Burton, R. V. (1990). Lies and the truth: A study of the development of the concept. *Child Development, 61,* 211–220.

Taylor, M., & Carlson, S. (1997). The relation between individual differences in fantasy and theory of mind. *Child Development, 68,* 436–455.

Youngblade, L. M., & Dunn, J. (1995). Individual differences in young children's pretend play with mother and sibling: Links to relationships and understanding of other people's feelings and beliefs. *Child Development, 66*(5), 1472–1492.

5

CHAPTER   Jacqueline J. Goodnow

Families and Development

☐ Introduction

This chapter emphasizes two great challenges that mark research on the links between families and development. One is the challenge of going beyond the simple assertion that families matter. We need to move on to the specifics of what matters and how any effects come about. The other is the challenge of rising above the specifics. In the course of zooming in on a particular feature of families or a particular aspect of influence, it is easy to lose the rest of the picture, to mistake the part for the whole. The task is then one of rescuing the missing parts from their invisibility and of putting all the pieces together.

Reflecting the title of this book, each section of the chapter selects some particular "achievements and prospects." The former are described in terms of changes in approach to a series of issues. The latter are described in terms of questions that now stand out as in need of further exploration. For reasons of space, I have been highly selective with regard to both changes and questions. With regret, I have for the same reason imposed severe limits on the references, giving preference to sources that will provide a large amount of follow-up material (e.g., review chapters) or that may fall outside what most developmental texts cover.

The first section of the chapter raises two changes that pervade all areas of research on the topic of families and development. These changes have to do with recognizing diversity within family forms and family effects, and with extending the focus beyond childhood and adolescence.

The sections that follow take up in turn three specific areas of research. The first of these focuses on what are regarded as the significant features of families: the features that make a difference. The second considers the several ways in which families are seen as making a difference and as themselves changed by the people within them (influences are not one-way). The third asks about ways to combine the influence of families with other aspects of experience: with features such as the nature of a neighborhood, the quality of schools, or the customs or traditions of a cultural group. A brief final comment then asks why, in the face of so many contributing factors, family events and family influences are still of major importance.

☐ Life-Span Effects and Diversity in Family Forms

Interest in the topic of families and development has a double basis. One basis is a conceptual interest in why people turn out the way that they do and how both similarities and differences occur. A further basis lies in the hope that changing families will be a way of changing children's lives and perhaps the state of society, which is possibly an easier route than changing the nature of schools, workplaces, or social policies.

That double basis gives a particular relevance to the two changes noted in this section: the recognition of diversity and of life-span effects.

The Recognition of Diversity

It is temptingly easy to regard what we are used to as best or as part of some natural order and to advocate that way of living for all people. Other ways of living seem readily to be perceived as "deprived," "unstimulating," "weird," or at best "exotic." We have, however, come to recognize that families may take many forms and children may grow up to be reasonable human beings in a variety of family environments. They may acquire different values and different skills in various environments, but they may well become competent, confident, and reasonably disposed toward others under a variety of circumstances.

In a related fashion, we have also come to recognize that the results of research based on one social group may not generalize to others. Just as we had to learn that research based on all-male samples did not necessarily apply to both males and females, so now we need to keep in mind that results and conclusions based on accessible "mainstream" samples do not necessarily apply to families in other ethnic, economic, or cultural groups. An "authoritarian" style of parenting, for example, has been found to have negative effects among middle-class "Anglo" groups in the United States (it is also a minority pattern in these samples). However, the same results have not been found in African-American samples (Steinberg, Darling, & Fletcher, 1995; see also Parke & Buriel, 1997, for a general discussion of variations by ethnicity).

The recognition of diversity has not come easily, and it is still fragile, in large part because it runs counter to some of our usual ways of thinking. What has brought it about and might help sustain it?

One contributing factor has been an increase in the number of psychologists with first-hand experience of family patterns that are non-Anglo or non-middle class. Another has been increasing exposure to studies by researchers in other social sciences. (Psychologists are far from being the only researchers interested in family forms and family effects, and we benefit greatly from considering how researchers in other areas approach similar questions.)

Research in the field of family history, for example, has made us aware of changes in what is regarded as best or as normal. Within the Western world, for instance, we are currently experiencing what has been called a "postfamilist" period. After the war of 1939–1945, there was a dramatic rise in the number of people who married, in the percentage of marriages that resulted in children, and in the ideology of a single breadwinner with a wife and children safe in their own home. For many people, the memory of that period helps fuel a nostalgia for times past and the sense that family life is changing in ways never seen before, with inevitable damage to children. The reality, as family historians point out, is that "the good old days" were not always good for all members of the family, that change is constant, and that change occurs with shifts not only in psychological knowledge but also with social and economic circumstances.

For a further example, I shall turn to anthropology. The example concerns the nature of "cosleeping." In Japan, young children routinely sleep either in the same bed as a parent or in the same room (with young meaning up to approximately the age of 10 or 11). Most Europeans and North cultural Americans would find that family pattern strange, even threatening to healthy development. In turn, most Japanese regard as cruel the practice of having young children sleep alone (Shweder, Arnett Jensen, & Goldstein, 1995). The Japanese can hardly be dismissed as a "primitive society." Nor does it make sense to conclude that the whole nation is marked by pathology, any more than we would conclude that everyone in our own society is damaged by enforced separateness. The more reasonable conclusion is that the practice of cosleeping simply represents one of the ways in which the Japanese, along with people in many other societies, express the higher value they place on interconnectedness between people than on separateness and the privacy of "the sacred couple."

At this point, we hardly need more examples of diversity. We still need to know more, however, about how different family patterns come into being and are maintained. We also need to ask what results, processes, or recommendations might generalize across groups, and to avoid equating the recognition of diversity with the notion that all family circumstances are of equal benefit. We all need conditions that help us survive, cope with change, recover from difficulties and disappointments, live on reasonable terms with others, and establish rewarding relationships with others. In any social group, conditions that make it difficult to achieve the skills and values needed to attain those goals are a disadvantage, even though the particular values and skills that people need to develop may vary from one situation to another.

Extending the Focus Beyond Childhood and Adolescence

It is easy to think of families as influencing development only in childhood or adolescence. Into that tendency goes the popular belief that most personalities or life courses are set by the time we are, say, 20, the belief that "as the twig is bent, so grows the tree," and a backlog of research documenting the long-term effects of some early experiences.

What has happened to change or challenge that view? Relevant are shifts in our views about the course of development and about the nature of family influence.

Increasingly, we have come to recognize that development occurs throughout the life span, even though changes during childhood and adolescence may be especially visible. At age 40, we are not identical with what we were at age 20. Most of our physical growth and much of our logical capacity may be established by the age of 20, but changes continue in our sense of identity, our sense of what is possible, many of our interpersonal skills, the kinds of relationships we seek, and the ways in which we use our capacity to think.

Increasingly also, we have come to think of development as a set of pathways, with more than one road leading to the same end point and, within any path, branches or forks at various points along the road. Some branches may be more open to us than others. Some turnings start us on a slope or a trajectory that makes a next set of choices almost preset. Some turnings close off later options. Others allow for recovery or offer second chances. In all cases, however, the options and the turnings do not stop at adolescence.

The third background shift has been an increasing tendency to think of family influences not only in terms of face-to-face interactions but also in terms of resources (and demands on these resources). When psychologists look at family life and its effects, they tend to work from the face-to-face interactions that occur between people. When they want to account for differences in achievement, well-being, or brushes with the law, for example, they tend to start from features such as styles of child-rearing, the way family differences are resolved, or the quality of family relationships.

Families also, however, provide emotional and material resources and these can be readily recognized as making a difference throughout life. Parents, for example, often provide for their adult children emotional and material resources that alter the ease or difficulty with which younger family members can take advantage of opportunities, can stay on an educational track, leave home or stay until an opportune time, manage financially, combine paid work with parenting, or recover from loss or disappointment. In turn, the directions that children's lives take can influence the resources that they can offer to their siblings or their parents and the pattern of development for these family members.

Once more, several questions now stand out as in need of further exploration. When, for example, do parents in various social groups see their influence and their responsibility as ending? What conditions influence the willingness of family members to accept various resources at various times? What are the particular contributions of siblings over the life course? What resources matter other than material goods or money? Material and financial resources are the easiest to study. We need to know more, however, about the contributions of other resources: the provision, for example, of another perspective on a problem, a sounding board, or an ability to see the funny side of events.

The questions are several. What is clear, however, is that focusing only on childhood and adolescence leaves us with a restricted view of the length of time over which family members contribute to each others' development.

☐ The Significant Features of Families

I have already noted that family research always carries the danger of mistaking the part for the whole, of concentrating on one aspect and forgetting the rest of the frame. Research on the significant features of families illustrates especially well that danger, together with several ways of recovering from it. The strongest examples are the tendency to focus only on parents, and on that easily measurable feature: the number of resident parents in a household.

The Focus on Parents

Psychology contains a long-standing interest in the impact of parents on development, often narrowed down to the impact of what mothers do in their face-to-face interactions with children and, a still tighter focus, to the way mothers handle moments of control or rule violation. We have learned a great deal about how to specify these interactions, especially along the dimensions of responsiveness and the restrictiveness of control (Maccoby and Martin, 1983, provide a thorough review). Along the way, however, we have also come to recognize that these interactions are only part of the picture. We began first to rescue fathers from their invisibility, then grandparents, and then siblings.

I shall take siblings as an example of what the richer picture has brought to light (Dunn, 1988, is a prime source). Siblings, we have come to realize, are in many societies major caregivers for younger children, often expected to look after them for much of the day. Siblings are also often regarded as the main sources of a young child's acquisition of language patterns. (For example, home languages may be difficult to sustain among younger children if the older siblings have already switched to the school language.) Siblings also often serve as guides to a new world, as sparring partners (unlike friends, they cannot just drop you completely if you behave badly), and as possible models (one option is to be an understudy, another is to work at being a different character within the family play). These are sources of influence that we would overlook if we focused only on parents.

Psychologists, I need to add, are not the only family researchers to suffer from tunnel vision when it comes to identifying family features. In much of sociology and economics, for example, it has been customary to consider only the father's education and only the father's paid work, taking these as measures of "the family's socioeconomic status" or "the family income." Slowly the recognition has arisen that the mother's education may be especially relevant to what happens with children and adolescents, and that thinking in terms of "the family income" ignores both the work that women do and the internal management of money. If little is spent on children's needs, for example, what does it matter if the total income is large or small? If the management or the decision-making is all in the hands of one person, what does this do to the models of power presented to children?

Focus on the Number of Parents

One of the major changes since the familist 1950s has been the increase in many countries of families with one resident parent. These are the families once referred to as "broken," on the assumption that they could only have started as a two-parent pattern. Currently, these families more often attract such labels as one-parent families, families with one resident parent, or, a term that reflects the composition of many of these families, mother-headed families.

There is by now a massive set of studies correlating the number of resident parents with child outcomes in the form of school achievement or well-being. As usually happens, the correlations do not give us the dynamics of what is happening. We have come to realize, for example, that beyond the fact that only one parent is resident in the household, we need to know:

- If the cause was divorce or separation, what was the state of affairs before this took place?
- What is the nonresident parent contributing? How is this contribution being represented or interpreted to children?
- Are there other adults in the house or readily available? The presence of one other involved adult, parent or not, can make a large difference to the resources available to parent and child and to their sense of isolation or support.
- Is the significant feature the lower income that often goes with mother-headed families, especially after divorce?
- What is the community view of the family? There is a world of difference, for example, between being regarded as the lone parent in a "broken" family instead of being a respected war widow or one of a community in which mother-headed families are far from unusual.

In effect, the easily measurable feature (the number of resident parents) turns out to be only part of the picture, and it may become a misleading part if we look no further.

Steps Toward a Richer Picture

One step consists of bringing together the features of families and the kinds of situations that family members face. Families operating in neighbourhoods marked by little social support, frequent discrimination, or high rates of violence, for example, need different resources from those needed in less demanding situations (e.g., Garborino, Dubrow,

Kostelny, & Pardo, 1992; see also Werner & Smith, 1982). A strong sense of family unity, a pride in one's tradition, the presence of paths out of an area for oneself or for one's children: these now matter more than ever.

A further solution consists of looking more within the family, asking how various members interlock or are interconnected. Within psychology, an approach that does so views families as "systems" (for one example, see Reiss, 1989).

In one version of this approach, a family is seen as a set of interconnecting relationships. There are relationships between parents, between parents and children (mothers, fathers, sons, daughters), between siblings, and possibly between grandparents and both younger generations. We may then ask how the sweetness, sourness, or availability of one relationship affects the development of others.

In a second version of a systems approach, a family is seen as a dynamic unit that always seeks some kind of equilibrium. Changes alter that equilibrium for a while. After a death, a divorce, or an older sibling leaving home, for example, there is a temporary loss of equilibrium, a gap in the system. At the same time, the change opens up new roles, new positions, new possible alliances. As these are taken up, the gaps slowly become filled. The system readjusts into a different pattern and settles into a different equilibrium. The impact on development then comes about by way of the shifting demands and opportunities in the course of gaps being created and the subsequent search for ways to cope with gaps, either by looking for a candidate willing and able to step in, by redistributing what was done before among several people, or by reconsidering what is really needed.

☐ The Nature of Influence

This section notes first a general feature to the main sources of data on the nature of influence. This is the greater frequency of concern with compliance and continuity than with negotiation and change. Noted also is a contrast between two major sources of data: between analyses that focus on moments of transgression and analyses that focus on everyday routines or practices.

The rest of the section then takes up several of the steps forward that have occurred over the last few decades, together with the challenges that remain. These steps and challenges have to do with (a) two-way influences (from parents to children and from children to parents), (b) the significance of people's interpretations of what occurs, and (c) the question of how and when the effects of early events carried forward influence later behaviors.

The emphasis throughout is on direct influence. Influence can come about through the management of what people know or experience. Children, parents, and siblings do keep information from each other. They also try to steer each other toward or away from various kinds of encounters or commitments. These forms of influence, however, are deferred until the next section.

Some Features of the Main Sources of Data

Focus: Compliance and Continuity Across Generations

Reading research on families and development for the first time may easily leave the impression that researchers and parents are preoccupied with issues of replication. Terms such as socialization, cultural transmission, or internalization all appear to carry as their first implication the importance of compliance and of repetition from one generation to another. Far less prominent are comments on the importance of change as well as continuity, on the inevitability of change or transformation, or on the extent to which change may be welcomed by parents (cf. Goodnow, 1994, 1996).

Within developmental psychology, for example, there is a large body of research concerned with how parents act or could act in order to have children who do what they are told, follow rules even in the absence of supervision, and develop a monitoring conscience. In contrast, there is far less research on topics such as the development of empathy, sympathy, involvement, or solidarity with the family. Small also in comparison is the amount of research on the ways in which family members negotiate or compromise in the face of differences, or on the ways in which parents change in response to the influence of their children.

Focus: Occasions of Transgression or Everyday Routines

Within developmental psychology, analyses of influence draw heavily on occasions of transgression. There is, for example, study after study of the strategies that parents use or might use on these occasions: strategies ranging from physical punishment to various kinds of reasoning.

In contrast, anthropology and sociology contain a greater attention to everyday routines or practices. These may be of many kinds: ways of greeting one another, ways of preparing or eating food, ways of dressing, ways of marking the differences between males and females, the arrangement of spaces for sleeping or for various kinds of activity, or the everyday divisions of labor between parents and children or between males and females. When the same practices are followed by most or all members of a group, the term "cultural practices" tends to be used. The process of becoming a member of a group can then be seen as one of coming to observe its practices and coming to feel that they are part of a natural or moral order, or part of what defines one's identity in relation to others. Rejecting a practice (e.g., refusing to go along with an accepted routine) may also come to be a way by which one redefines one's relationship to others in a group (Goodnow, Miller, and Kessel, 1995, provide examples and a summary of these arguments).

The step now being taken is one of considering family patterns in terms of the practices they contain. Families often have routine ways of greeting one another, of eating separately or together, and of celebrating occasions such as birthdays (e.g., Fiese, 1992). They also contain everyday divisions or patterns of household work (e.g., Berk, 1985; Goodnow, 1996). Moreover, these routines often come to be experienced as part of a natural or moral order, part of what defines membership in the family. Now we need to ask more closely about the effects of family practices, the ways in which effects come about, and the specific ways in which what emerges from practices differs from the effects of special moments such as occasions of rule violation. One possibility, for example, is that everyday cultural practices are especially likely to give rise to the sense that a particular way of doing things is beyond question, perhaps because they are usually accompanied by little comment or explanation. Whether that is in fact the case is a question that now needs to be explored.

One-Way and Two-Way Effects

Since the 1960s, it has been customary to say that children and parents influence one another. The specifics of two-way effects or processes within families, however, still need a great deal of further exploration. Most of what we know comes from analyses of parents and children in teaching–learning situations, with an emphasis on the way parents adjust from moment to moment the help they provide in the light of a child's changing competence on a task.

To extend those analyses, I choose two approaches that point to less well traveled paths. One is described by Collins and Luebker (1994). (See also Collins, Gleason, and Sesma, 1997, for the embedding of this proposal in a general view of linked relationships within and outside the family.) Adolescence, these researchers propose, is a period over which the viewpoints of parents and adolescents may diverge from one another and then come together again, with a change on both sides. Here then is an opportunity to ask, in longitudinal fashion, about the areas where family members are more versus less willing to change their views, to "stretch" their expectations, and the steps by which they do so.

The second study comes from Kuczynski and his colleagues (for a recent review that covers these studies and Kuczynski's general interest in both "resistance and conformity", see Kuczynski and Hildebrandt, 1997). In the course of studying the usual topic of children complying with their parents' directives, Kuczynski and his colleagues came to stand the problem on its head. Parents, these researchers realized, were also teaching their children how to say "no" in acceptable ways and how to negotiate: to recognize when it was possible to negotiate and what were the acceptable and unacceptable ways to do so. The response of "Later, okay?" for example, is far more acceptable to most parents than is a defiant "No." We could now well benefit by asking what parents regard as nonnegotiable areas, how they signal to their children that a bottom line has been reached, and what they regard as acceptable ways to negotiate or compromise at different ages.

The Significance of Interpretations

The effect of any action depends on the way it is interpreted. The actions of parents or siblings are given meaning by children; they are perceived, for example, as strange or natural, fair or unfair, kind or unkind, or appropriate or out of proportion. The actions of children are also given meaning by parents; they are perceived, for example, as on time or delayed, as amusing or as a threat to parents' sense of control, as a phase or as indicative of a long-lasting disposition.

The challenge is now to find ways to specify this meaning-giving process. One way to do so is to ask what ready-made interpretations are available within a family or a culture. How far, for example, do family narratives, family explanations, or family comparisons (e.g., "just like her grandmother") promote particular ways of interpreting events?

A second way to do so is to borrow from cognitive-style analyses of social learning. This type of theory regards people as observing others in order to see what is possible, what is difficult, or what is likely to happen if they themselves attempt a particular action. We know relatively little about the ways in which children see others in the family as points of social comparison. A basis for research in this direction, however, is available in studies of the way children in the early years of school overtly or covertly check to see how well others are doing (e.g., Ruble, 1983), and of the way that adults in close relationships respond, positively or with chagrin, to being outperformed by one another (e.g., Beach et al. 1998).

A third way borrows again from research on cognition but places its emphasis on a stepwise breakdown. An example is the breakdown proposed by Grusec and Goodnow (1994) for children responding to a parental message. In a first step, children hear a parental message, either accurately or inaccurately. In a second, the perceived message is accepted, rejected, or transformed. In a third, an accepted message may come to be seen as part of oneself, even as generated by oneself rather than being taken over from someone else.

One advantage to this model is that it provides several bases to an outcome such as a lack of congruence between the positions of two generations. Children may perceive accurately but not accept the message. They can also think they are in agreement with their parents when in fact they are not.

A second advantage is that each step in the process is seen as differentially influenced by particular conditions. Seen as especially relevant to the first step, for example, are the clarity of the parent's message and the extent to which an action so floods a child with emotion that accurate interpretation is difficult. Especially relevant to the second step are the warmth of the relationship between the two family members and the extent to which accepting the other's position is seen as involving benefit or sacrifice. Especially relevant to the third are conditions such as the degree of overt pressure or reward for following a particular course of action (the stronger the pressure or the use of external rewards, the less likely the sense of a position being seen as self-generated). A parent's harsh or rigid position may, for example, be easily read by children but seldom accepted as reasonable or as self-generated.

Once again, the need is for further data related to the several possibilities suggested. Needed also are ways of bringing together these relatively discrete models for the ways in which family members interpret each other's actions. What has been achieved, however, is a move beyond a tempting but misleadingly simple picture (one parental action, one effect) in favor of a picture that is not only richer but also treats both parties to an interaction as actively contributing to its outcome.

How Are Effects Carried Forward?

One of the reasons for giving families a special place among influences on development is the proposal that early experiences have lasting effects. Early difficulties and early attachments are seen as often influencing the way that people act, think, or feel for some time afterward. Assuming for the moment that the evidence for lasting effects is sound, the critical questions then become: How do lasting effects come about? What moderates the strength or the staying power of effects?

Questions about the bases to any long-term effects have been prominent in the developmental literature since the first impact of psychoanalysis (ethology added further arguments, with its accounts of imprinting). In psychoanalytic accounts, early experiences may exert lasting influences by several routes. They may alter the structure of personality, for example, by establishing a harsh or a weak superego. They may alter the reserves of emotional and physical energy available to meet new problems. (Unresolved crises tie up reserves in much the way that an army needs to leave troops behind to take care of an occupied but unpacified territory.) The way in which one crisis or challenge is dealt with may also alter the methods and the confidence that people bring to the next developmental task.

Currently, questions about lasting effects are most likely to be answered in terms of attachment theory. The quality of early attachments, it is proposed, gives rise to internal "working models" that shape our expectations of later relationships, inclining us to be hesitant or confident, trusting or doubtful, or able to recover from hurt or retreating at the first sign of difficulty.

The occurrence of lasting effects is still a matter for debate. Needed, I suggest, is not simply the accumulation of more data but also an integration of the underlying models.

To date, for example, there have been few attempts to bring together accounts from attachment theory and accounts that emphasize interpretive processing steps (Grusec, Hastings, and Mammone, 1994, is an exception). More broadly, there has been little integration of two models of influence to be found in the social science literature. In one of these, effects from experience are assumed to be long lasting unless moderated. In the other, effects are seen as needing to be sustained, to be given a constant boost in order to counteract a constant trend toward evanescence, transformation, or reconstruction. The former model tends to predominate in developmental psychology, the latter to be more common within analyses in anthropology and sociology that focus on the construction and maintenance of meanings. We would now benefit from asking not which model has the greater truth value but when each model applies: when family influences are likely to be long lasting, when they require constant maintenance, and what the differences might be between the two kinds of situations.

☐ Combining Contributions From Within and Outside the Family

Families are clearly not the only influence on the way our lives unfold. There are other social worlds: worlds populated by peers, teachers, neighbors, and figures encountered in books or on screen. How are these several worlds related to one another?

In some accounts, the issue is brushed aside. The family has been seen, for example, as simply a microcosm or a reflection of the larger society. This type of proposal, however, does not fit well with occasions during which family members feel at odds with the world around them.

In other accounts, two opposed worlds have been proposed. The family, for example, is regarded as "a haven in a heartless world." Or, the family is described as "private," the rest of the world as "public." These "opposition" proposals also do not fit well with the facts. Families are often the site of stress, violence, or oppression, making "the heartless world" seem easy by comparison. Families are also far from being "private" areas. The concept of families as "private" may slow down the giving of advice or the occurrence of intervention. (The "private" view has been noted, for instance, as one factor slowing down reports of abuse within families and the taking of action with regard to abuse.) Advice, gossip, and intervention nonetheless occur.

The more reasonable proposals cover a variety of links that go beyond simple opposition. These links may be of many kinds, and I shall break them into two sets.

Additive and Interactive Effects

One way to deal with a variety of contributing sources is to simply add up a variety of experiences. Suppose you start life, for example, with low birth weight or a juvenile illness. You then experience unresponsive parents, rigid or oppressive schools, a violent neighborhood or frequent changes in residence, peers who are in trouble with the law, or time in a residential institution of some kind. The sheer number of these experiences may be what matters rather than any single specific factor. What may matter also is timing, with the worst impact stemming from a second disaster arriving before recovery from the previous one is complete.

The alternative possibility is that some particular experiences or some particular combinations of experiences may have particular significance. One good relationship along the way, with a parent, a sibling, a teacher, or a neighbor, may act as a "buffer," offsetting the impact of several negatives. One negative (low birth weight, for example) may matter only if it occurs in combination with some specific other events, such as poor health services or the inability of parents to provide the care that would offset a disadvantageous start.

At the moment, both additive and interactive possibilities are under consideration (cf. Rutter, Champion, Quinton, Maughan, & Pickles, 1995). What we need especially to determine at this point are the situations where one or the other type of model best fits the data.

The Family as Preparation for Life Outside It

For many sociologists, the preparation is for entry into the world of paid work. The father's work experience, for example, is regarded as leading him to encourage his children to develop the values of conformity or autonomy that he sees as needed for them to succeed or survive in their later paid work.

For psychologists, the relevant nonfamily world tends to be more immediate and more social. Parents, for example, may work at preparing their children for a world that they perceive as full of dangers or bad examples. They may present the family as the only set of people you can trust or they may give children practice in how to deal with anticipated encounters with discrimination. Parents may also seek to act as guides, mentors, or gatekeepers. In so far as they are able, parents select schools, choose neighborhoods, foster some friendships rather than others, and interpret in preferred ways the events that children experience in school or see on television (see Maccoby & Martin, 1983; Parke & Buriel, 1997).

These forms of management of children's experiences may seem far less direct than the immediate management of, say, a display of temper, sibling rivalry, or a reluctance to go along with family routines. They provide, however, important and explorable ways of looking up from life within the family and of bringing that life into connection with events that occur outside the home.

☐ A Final Comment

I shall end this chapter by noting that to some extent family researchers have invited skepticism about the significance of families to the development of their members. The more that psychologists mistake the part for the whole, for example, the easier it becomes to point out that the case is being overstated and the more tempting it becomes to suggest that perhaps all of the proposals for the significance of families are unsound. To the extent, for instance, that families are narrowed down to parents, and parents are narrowed down to exerting influence only by virtue of their control styles or their responsiveness in the first years of life, the easier it becomes to argue that families are only a small part of outcomes such as school achievement, children's well-being, adolescents' social skills, or the course of adult life. The real challenge is always one of asking what part families play, in combination with other experiences and in relation to the circumstances that family members face.

Are there then no particular reasons for paying attention to family events? For three reasons, I would argue, families occupy a special place among influences on development. One is that families are for children often a first world of experience, creating the possibility that these first impressions, similar to many other first impressions, shape the way later events are interpreted and experienced. A second is that families are places of intense relationships, relationships loaded with affect and meaning. Throughout life, what we experience in relation to other family members is difficult to ignore, simply because it is so emotionally charged. It is not simply that family experiences are often first experiences but also that these experiences are affect laden and the emotions reverberate. Finally, family events and circumstances warrant a special place by virtue of the relationships being lifelong and being expected to remain so. Friendships may come and go, but family relationships, in principle and usually in practice, persist regardless of whether they are pleasant or aversive. Unraveling the links between family features and the paths we take over the life course is a task full of challenges. It is, however, a task worth undertaking.

☐ References

Beach, S. R. H., Tesser, A., Fincham, F. D., Jones, D. J., Johnson, D., & Whitaker, D. J. (1998). Pleasure and pain in doing well together: An investigation of performance-related affect in close relationships. *Journal of Personality and Social Psychology,* 923–938.

Berk, S. F. (1985). *The gender factory: The apportionment of work in American households.* New York: Plenum Press.

Collins, W. A., Gleason, T., & Sesma, A. (1997). Internalization, autonomy, and relationships: Development during adolescence. In J. E. Grusec & L. Kuczynski (Eds.), *Parenting and children's internalization of values* (pp. 78–102). New York: Wiley.

Collins, W. A. , & Luebker, C. (1994). Parent and adolescent expectancies: Individual and relational significance. In J. G. Smetana (Ed.), *Beliefs about parenting* (pp. 65–80). San Francisco: Jossey-Bass.

Dunn, J. (1988). *The beginnings of social understanding.* Cambridge, MA: Harvard University Press.

Fiese, D. (1992). Dimensions of family rituals across two generations: Relation to adolescent identity. *Family Process, 31,* 151–162.

Garborino, J., Dubrow, N., Kostelny, K., & Pardo, C. (1992). *Children in danger: Coping with the consequences of community violence*. San Francisco: Jossey-Bass.

Goodnow, J. J. (1994). Acceptable disagreement across generations. In J. G. Smetana (Ed.), *Beliefs about parenting* (pp. 51–64). San Francisco: Jossey-Bass.

Goodnow, J. J. (1996a). Acceptable ignorance, negotiable disagreement: Alternative views of learning. In D. R. Olson & N. Torrance (Eds.), *Handbook of education and human development* (pp. 345–368). Oxford: Blackwell.

Goodnow, J. J. (1996b). From household practices to parents' ideas about work and interpersonal relationships. In S. Harkness & C. Super (Eds.), *Parents' cultural belief systems* (pp. 313–344). New York: Guilford.

Goodnow, J. J., Miller, P. J., & Kessel, F. (1995). *Cultural practices as contexts for development*. San Francisco: Jossey-Bass.

Grusec, J. E., & Goodnow, J. J. (1994). The impact of parental discipline methods on the child's internalization of values: A reconceptualization of current points of view. *Developmental Psychology, 30*, 4–19.

Grusec, J. E., Hastings, P., & Mammone, N. (1994). Parenting cognitions and relationship schemas. In J. G. Smetana (Ed.), *Beliefs about parenting* (pp. 5–20). San Francisco: Jossey-Bass.

Kuczynski, L., & Hildebrandt, N. (1997). Models of conformity and resistance in socialization theory. In J. E. Grusec & L. Kuczynski (Eds.), *Parenting and children's internalization of values* (pp. 227–258). New York: Wiley.

Maccoby, E. E., & Martin, J. A. (1983). Socialization in the context of the family: Parent-child interaction. In M. E. Hetherington (Ed.), *Handbook of child psychology* (Vol. 4, pp. 1–101). New York: Wiley.

Parke, R. A., & Buriel, R. (1997). Socialization in the family: Ethnic and ecological perspectives. In N. Eisenberg (Ed.), *Handbook of child psychology* (Vol. 4, pp. 463–522). New York: Wiley.

Reiss, D. (1989). Families and their paradigms: An ecological approach to understanding the family in its social world. In C. M. Ramsey (Ed.), *Family systems in medicine* (pp. 119–134). New York: Guilford Press.

Ruble, D. (1983). The development of social comparison processes and their role in achievement-related self-socialization. In E. T. Higgins, D. N. Ruble, & W. W. Hartup (Eds.), *Social cognition and social development* (pp. 134–157). New York: Cambridge University Press.

Rutter, M., Champion, L., Quinton, D., Maughan, B., & Pickles, A. (1995). Understanding individual differences in environmental-risk exposure. In P. A. Moen, G. H. Elder Jr., & Luscher, K. (Eds.), *Examining lives in context* (pp. 61–96). Washington, DC: American Psychological Association.

Shweder, R. A., Arnett Jensen, L., & Goldstein, W. (1995). Who sleeps by whom revisited: A method for extracting the moral goods implicit in practice. In J. J. Goodnow, P. J. Miller, & F. Kessel (Eds.), *Cultural practices as contexts for learning* (pp. 21–40). San Francisco: Jossey-Bass.

Steinberg, L., Darling, N. E., & Fletcher, A. C. (1995). Authoritative parenting and adolescent adjustment: An ecological journey. In P. A. Moen, G. H. Elder Jr., & Luscher, K. (Eds.), *Examining lives in context* (pp. 423–466). Washington, DC: American Psychological Association.

Werner, E. E., & Smith, R. S. (1982). *Vulnerable but invincible: A longitudinal study of resilient children and youth*. New York: McGraw-Hill.

6

Paul L. Harris

Acquiring the Art of Conversation: Children's Developing Conception of Their Conversation Partner

☐ An Insular Backward Glance

Over the past quarter century, there have been two waves of innovative research on the early development of social cognition. Both were especially vigorous in Britain, and I describe their impact from that admittedly insular perspective. First, in the 1970s, several studies undermined the classical notion of the egocentric infant, disengaged from sharing and mutuality. Meltzoff observed the newborn's imitative sensitivity to a partner's facial and manual gestures (Meltzoff, 1976; Meltzoff & Moore, 1977). Trevarthen elaborated the concept of early intersubjectivity (Trevarthen & Hubley, 1978). Scaife and Bruner (1975) discovered that infants younger than 12 months can engage in joint attention by following an adult's gaze, and Butterworth went on to plot the origins and extension of that capacity (Butterworth & Cochran, 1980).

With that socially disposed infant in mind, and struggling against the prevailing emphasis on the child's syntactic wizardry, Bruner (1973) approached early language acquisition by emphasizing the communicative function, or the so-called pragmatics, of early utterances with the help of speech–act theory. A distinctive feature of Bruner's approach was its acknowledgment that acts of communication, including the syntactic structure of the utterance, are embedded in joint action and joint attention and are guided by the child's engagement with, and conception of, their interlocutor. By implication, the development of the child's communication is intertwined with the development of social cognition.

Since that period, the study of joint attention has turned into a sustained research program (Moore & Dunham, 1995) in which investigators are alert to its potentially foundational role for later psychological understanding (Baron-Cohen, 1995) and for early language (Baldwin, 1995; Carpenter, Nagell, & Tomasello, 1998). At the same time, research on the pragmatic aspect of early conversation continues to be overshadowed by the analysis of semantic and syntactic development, despite Bruner's pioneering efforts.

In the 1980s, a new wave of research focused on the social cognition, or "theory of mind" as it came to be known, of preschool children rather than of infants. From one perspective, the experimental results were yet another demonstration of an early lack of egocentricity; by the age of 4 years at any rate, children distinguish nicely between what they know to be the case and what someone else might wrongly believe to be the case. Moreover, they realize that beliefs, true or false, constrain actions (Wimmer & Perner, 1983). However, these findings were not inspired by the notion that human infants have a gift for sharing or communication. Their intellectual progenitor was Sarah, a chimpanzee invited to watch and calculate the next move of a human agent by Premack and Woodruff (1978) as they sought to assess the existence of a theory of mind among nonhuman primates.

On the theoretical front, Wimmer and Perner's (1983) findings, along with several ingenious variants, set fire to a debate about the extent to which young children can represent mental states and how they come to do so (Astington & Gopnik, 1988; Perner, 1988; Leslie, 1988). This attempt to penetrate into the child's mental machinery meant that the social context in which that machinery might operate and, more specifically, the potential links between the development of social cognition and of communication took a back seat. Admittedly, there were cogent reminders of that social context (Dunn, 1988) and there were provocative theoretical analyses that underlined the links between communicative and social–cognitive deficits among children with autism (Frith, 1989, Chapter 8). Still, the most contentious theoretical issue was inside the mind of the child: does he or she grasp the notion of metarepresentation?

In this essay, I explore a neglected recess, tucked in between the two age periods and the two preoccupations discussed above: the period beyond infancy but ahead of what we conventionally regard as the preschool phase. I argue that an analysis of children's conversation during that period, from approximately 18 to 36 months: (i) allows us to re-examine the connections between communication and social cognition; and (ii) raises the possibility that the child's emerging grasp of the mental states of knowing and thinking is initially embedded in the context of communication. If this essay succeeds at all, it will demonstrate that the apparently distinct theoretical motifs and experimental preoccupations of the 1970s as compared with the 1980s have a deeper continuity provided we look in the right place. Before laying out this argument, I first need to describe a pattern of findings that has emerged from research on the child's theory of mind and my own flawed attempt to explain it.

☐ Desires and Beliefs

A relatively well established claim is that young children initially elaborate a desire- or goal-based conception of other people and subsequently come to attribute beliefs. Eventually, by the age of approximately 4 years, these two main pillars for an understanding of human behavior are each in place. By implication, however, there is an early period in which children do not take beliefs into account and instead construe other people in terms of their goals or desires. Support for this claim has emerged from a variety of sources. First, experimental work has indicated that normal children take account of variation between people in their desires before taking account of variation in their beliefs both in explaining their actions (Bartsch & Wellman, 1989) and in predicting their emotions (Harris, Johnson, Hutton, Andrews, & Cooke, 1989).

A gap between the understanding of beliefs and of desires has also emerged in research on children with autism. Although there is a great deal of evidence indicating their difficulties in understanding beliefs (Yirmiya, Erel, Shaked, & Solomonica-Levi, 1998) there is no convincing evidence of an equivalent impairment in their understanding of desires (Tan & Harris, 1991; Baron-Cohen, 1991).

Evidence for the lag has also been gathered from children's spontaneous utterances. Normal children talk informatively about desires throughout much of the third year (Bartsch & Wellman, 1995), whereas talk about thoughts and beliefs only starts to take off around the third birthday. In addition, children with autism rarely talk about thoughts and beliefs, but they do talk about desires (Tager-Flusberg, 1992, 1993).

In an earlier discussion of this developmental sequence, I suggested that the notion of belief might be interlinked with the child's developing facility at conversation (Harris, 1996). My idea was that children initially think of other people as *agents*, or creatures who pursue various goals and get things done. Then, as a result of their involvement in conversation, which provides a constant tutorial in the ways that interlocutors may differ in the information that they have at their disposal, children come to think of other people as *epistemic subjects*, or creatures who can take in, store, and exchange information. This emphasis on the tutorial role of conversation led to various predictions (Harris, 1996). Two are particularly straightforward and important.

First, early references to *know* and *think* will be couched in terms of their conversational function rather than in terms of mental states in the strict sense. Thus, a term like *know* will be frequently used to mark the speaker's ignorance in response to a question ("I don't know"), to seek information or action or both from an interlocutor ("Do you know what that is?") or to introduce information ("Know what?"). Three studies of children's use of cognitive verbs provide evidence that this is indeed the pattern in the third year (Bartsch & Wellman, 1995; Furrow, Moore, Davidge, & Chiasson, 1992; Shatz, Wellman, & Silber, 1983). At first, references to mentation outside the domain of conversation are rare, whereas conversational references (e.g., "Know what?") that direct the flow of the conversation are more frequent. At around 3 years, references to more autonomous states of knowing and thinking increase in frequency and eventually occur as often as references to desires.

The second prediction was that performance on theory of mind tasks should be linked to children's sensitivity to the pragmatic aspects of language: their ability to respond in a relevant and informative fashion to a conversation partner. Support for this prediction has emerged from a variety of studies of children with varying language profiles. On the one hand, those children who have difficulties with the syntax of language rather than with its pragmatic aspect, for example, children with specific language impairment, respond well on theory of mind tasks (Leslie & Frith, 1988; Ziatas, Durkin, & Pratt, 1998). Similarly, children with Williams syndrome, who display considerable skill in conversation despite severe visual–spatial deficits, also perform well on theory of mind tasks (Tager-Flusberg, Sullivan, & Zaitchik, 1994). On the other hand, the well-known difficulties that many children with autism have with theory of mind tasks are associated with pragmatic impairments in language: those children with autism who fail the false belief task perform worse on standardized assessments of communication skills than those who pass (Eisenmajer & Prior, 1991; Frith, Happé, & Siddons, 1994).

Especially indicative of an important role for conversation is the finding that deaf children perform poorly on standard false belief tasks (Peterson & Siegal, 1995). This can be plausibly attributed to the fact that many deaf children are born to hearing parents and therefore have limited opportunities for conversation. In line with this interpretation, a high proportion of deaf adolescents, who are presumably more able to converse in sign (Russell et al., 1998) and also those deaf children who are born to deaf parents and become native signers (Peterson & Siegal, 1997), show no difficulty on false belief tasks. Finally, it is worth noting that children with older siblings, who tend to be advanced in their conversational skills (but not their syntax) when compared with firstborns (Hoff-Ginsberg, 1994), also perform better on false belief tasks (Ruffman, Perner, Naito, Parkin, & Clements, 1998).

In short, the claim that conversation is a key context in which children construct an understanding of knowing, thinking, and believing seems plausible. However, one important component of my proposal was vague. If it is seriously maintained that children only come to construe other people as epistemic subjects as a result of acquiring the art of conversation, and if it is also claimed that young children at first think of other people primarily as planful, go-getting agents in pursuit of their goals, the obvious implication is that young children will initially engage in communication simply to orchestrate joint goal-directed action. They will not conduct a conversation with a view to exchanging information because that would presuppose some conception of their partner as an epistemic subject. It appears that such an instrumental approach to communication is taken by chimpanzees who have been trained to use a sign language or keyboard. For example, the pygmy chimpanzee Kanzi, possibly the most advanced signer to date among nonhuman primates, is not an engaging raconteur; many of his utterances are directed at getting his human caretakers to fetch, carry, and tickle (Greenfield & Savage-Rumbaugh, 1990). Children, by contrast, clearly do eventually adopt a different conception of conversation at some point because they do not remorselessly put it to purely instrumental use, like Kanzi. Still, my account left open the possibility that, for some considerable period, say, from the onset of language until around 3 years of age, there is not much difference between the way that children talk and the way that a chimpanzee, such as Kanzi, uses signs. That possibility does not seem very likely.

An alternative and more plausible hypothesis is that children increasingly think of their interlocutor as an epistemic subject not just in the fourth year as a result of their proficiency at conversation, but increasingly during the second and third year. On this view, the initially dominant function of communication might well be the regulation of action and attention, especially in the context of ongoing activity. However, between 18 and 36 months conversation would be used more and more for the purpose of exchanging information and comparing attitudes, independent of any ongoing activity. On this view, the human child and Kanzi would part company very early in their use of a communication system. Indeed, they might never be on the same track.

To decide between these alternatives, I consider several different aspects of early language: the pragmatics of early conversation; the emergence of displaced reference; the correction of an interlocutor who shows signs of misunderstanding; and the verbal updating of an uninformed partner.

☐ The Pragmatics of Early Conversation

Hitherto, a developmental description of the pragmatics of conversation in the second and third year has not been available. Investigators interested in pragmatics have concentrated on the one-word period and have rarely carried out a more sustained, longitudinal assessment. However, a recent report by Catherine Snow and her colleagues provides a longitudinal analysis of a large number of children at 14, 20, and 32 months (Snow, Pan, Imbens-Bailey, & Herman, 1996). One caveat is in order. The study was based on a structured exchange in the laboratory between the child and a parent during which children played with toys from four different boxes. Had the study taken place in the children's homes, or with other children present, a wider assortment of activities and conversational exchanges might have been observed. Nevertheless, the study provides an intriguing and plausible description of early pragmatic development at two levels: the more encompassing level of *verbal interchange* and the more restricted level of particular *utterances*. The two levels differ in that a verbal interchange can comprise one or more rounds of talk, so long as they all serve a single function. In reviewing the findings, I leave aside the findings from the 14-month-olds (who said very little) and focus on the changes that were found between 20 and 32 months.

At 20 months, almost all the children used verbal interchanges to negotiate the start, continuation, and ending of various activities, including their hearer's attention to entities in the environment. Children also went on to discuss such entities once a joint focus of attention had been established. One might reasonably conclude from these findings that conversation by 20-month-olds rests primarily on a notion of the interlocutor as an active and potentially cooperative agent in various common activities rather than as an epistemic subject.

Alongside this primary orientation, however, there are intimations of a different conception of the interlocutor. About half of the children aged 20 months engaged in two types of interchange that were almost certainly information oriented, rather than activity oriented. First, they mentioned some attribute or event that was related to an entity present in the environment but was not itself observable. For example, one child playing with a ball was reminded of a football game she had recently seen on television. Second, children tried to regulate comprehension: they discussed the clarification of a verbal message or confirmed that it had been understood. In each of these two types of interchange, children are not simply commenting on, or negotiating, some ongoing, nonverbal activity. However, if we look at the proportion of utterances that 20-month-olds devote to these two types of interchange it is very small relative to activity-oriented discussion.

Among the 32-month-olds, communication in the context of ongoing activity remains widespread and continues to take up a sizeable proportion of children's interchanges, just as it does at 20 months. However, more children now engage in information-oriented interchanges. Moreover, such remarks are less obviously tied to current activity in that approximately half the children talk about absent entities or recent events, having no obvious link to the here and now.

Turning to the microlevel of particular speech acts, a similar age change emerged. At both 20 and 32 months, the majority of children produced speech acts connected to their ongoing activity, such as a statement of intent, a suggestion for action, or an agreement to another's request. At the same time, there were clear signs that this age period marked an increasing sensitivity to the interlocutor's epistemic status. Less than a quarter of 20-month-olds posed a question even though the majority of children at this age answered questions. At 32 months, by contrast, the majority not only answered questions, they also asked them.

In summary, whether we examine interchanges of several turns or particular utterances, we find that children aged 20 and 32 months frequently converse in the context of an ongoing activity that they seek to regulate in various ways. Such remarks suggest that the interlocutor is construed primarily as a potential agent in various common enterprises. Nonetheless, alongside this dominant function, another mode of conversational exchange is becoming increasingly evident between 20 and 32 months. During such exchanges, there appears to be a cessation or lull in ongoing activity, and the conversational world takes on an autonomous existence. At such moments, children show an increasing propensity to do three things: (i) to comment on entities that are not found in the immediate environment; (ii) to offer clarification of what has been said; and (iii) to view conversation as a way to gain information from an interlocutor by way of posing questions. In the next sections, I take a closer look at each of these emerging functions.

The Emergence of Displaced Reference

When children talk about displaced topics, they are likely to be engaging in a type of interchange that has no obvious instrumental purpose. By implication, children realize that language may be used not just to orchestrate some ongoing activity but to exchange information with their interlocutor. This is the conclusion I have implied in the preceding section. However, an alternative interpretation is that children enjoy no such understanding. Instead, adults simply induct children into answering questions about displaced topics, especially about shared events in the recent past. The adult's questions might then provide a scaffold by means of which children end up supplying information, but that might not be what the children themselves initially intend. Certainly, several theorists have argued that this latter interpretation is a valid model of the child's recall of past events (Nelson, 1993). However, recent evidence suggests that this Vygotskyan model may not be an adequate account of the full range of children's utterances about the not here and the not now. This intriguing evidence will be reviewed, and we will then reconsider the wider question of whether children seek to exchange information via such conversations.

Morford and Goldin-Meadow (1997) studied the emergence of displaced reference to noncurrent topics among normal hearing children ranging in age from 14 to 43 months. They also compared their findings with the pattern observed among four profoundly deaf children studied longitudinally over a 2-year period starting in their third year or fourth year. The deaf children had not been exposed to any conventional sign system, and their spoken utterances were confined to single words. Nevertheless, they had developed their own well-structured but idiosyncratic gesture system.

Among the hearing children the proportion of topics that included at least one displaced reference (to some information that was not perceptible in the environment) climbed from almost zero at 16 months to more than a quarter in the middle of the third year and to well over a third around the third birthday. Morford and Goldin-Meadow distinguish among three different types of displaced reference. The simplest type was to a nonperceptible object, attribute, or affordance: this could include features belonging to a visible object (e.g., the possibility of kicking a ball illustrated in a picture book), but the named feature had to be nonperceptible. Note that such references are closely equivalent to those identified by Snow et al. (1996) as interchanges concerning objects or features related to current objects and events. Such simple displaced references were already apparent at 16 months.

By 21 months, a second form of displaced reference had also emerged: references to so-called distal events occurring before or after the utterance in question but still during the recorded session (which lasted for 1–2 hours). Such references differed from the earlier-appearing simple displaced references in that they embraced a whole event or transformation and not just a particular object or object feature. For example, having just flipped over on the couch, a child might say, "See, I flipped over."

By 31 months, children started to produce the third type of displaced communication: references to events outside of the observational session, which may include events that had happened in the more distant past, events that would or could happen in the future, and fantasy events. These references differed from the second type in terms of their degree of displacement from the present and could also differ in terms of their reality status—children now talked about possible or fantasy events as well as those that had just happened or were imminent.

This three-phase sequence was apparent for the deaf children using Homesign as well as for the hearing children, albeit with a lag of over a year and with proportionately less use of references to proximal and distal events as compared with the simplest kind of displaced reference, namely, to displaced objects and attributes.

With these descriptive data in mind, we may now reconsider the question asked above: is this expansion of the universe of discourse primarily attributable to the adult interlocutor's prompting and elicitation of such displaced information? Alternatively, does it reflect a reorganization of the way that the child conceives of conversation? To put it simply, is the child taking the initiative in starting to use conversation not for the regulation of current activity but in order to share information about these displaced topics? Morford and Goldin-Meadow tackled this question by looking at the extent to which displaced topics were initiated either by the adult caregiver or by the child. For the hearing children, the adult caretaker initiated approximately one quarter of the discussions concerning displaced topics. Thus, it was the children who took the initiative most of the time. This pattern was even more marked for the Homesign children. Their caretakers initiated only one tenth of the displaced discussions with the remainder being initiated by the children.

In sum, the data gathered by Morford and Goldin-Meadow (1997) offer a persuasive complement to those reported by Snow et al. (1996). In the course of the second and third year, normal hearing children increasingly refer to topics that lie outside the current zone of activity. In that respect, they use conversation more and more as a tool for exchanging information and not just as a tool for the regulation of ongoing plans. That developmental trend is undoubtedly expedited by the availability of a conventional language system. Recall that the appearance of displaced references was delayed by well over a year among the Homesign children and such references increased at a slower rate. Nonetheless, it would be wrong to conclude that children are simply being pressed into sharing information about displaced topics by their caretakers. Among hearing and deaf children alike, such topics were mostly initiated by the children themselves and not by their caretakers.

Correction of Misunderstanding

The longitudinal study of Snow et al. (1996) suggested that 2-year-olds seek to clarify ambiguous messages. My interpretation is that children are starting to conceive of conversation as an exchange of information that may go wrong. Still, it could be objected that clarifications simply have an instrumental purpose. If young children engage in conversation primarily in the context of ongoing activities, then their clarifications might be intended not to ensure that their interlocutor has understood but simply to promote success in whatever activity is being undertaken. Indeed, the trigger for clarification might not be children's appreciation that their interlocutor has not understood given what he or she says in response, but rather their realization that their request has not been met or their plan of action has been stymied. It is difficult to tease apart these two interpretations in the context of naturalistic conversation, as indicated by an inconclusive debate between Golinkoff (1986, 1993) and Shatz and O'Reilly (1990). It is feasible, however, to assess the two interpretations in a more structured, experimental setting.

Shwe and Markman (1997) created such a setting. Two-year-olds (aged 30 months) were presented with two objects, one that was quite dull (e.g., a sock) and one that was interesting and desirable (e.g., a toy pig that talked when its stomach was pushed). Children were prompted to ask for one of the two objects from the experimenter. They almost invariably opted for the desirable object and made their request by pointing, reaching, or naming. The experimenter then responded either by granting the request, by placing the undesirable object in a bucket and leaving the desirable one in front of the child, or alternatively by denying it, by placing the desirable object in a bucket and leaving the undesirable one in front of the child. A statement accompanied each of these two actions from the experimenter, implying either that she had or had not understood the request. For example, in granting the request, the experimenter might convey her accurate comprehension by saying, "You asked for the pig. I think you want the pig. I'm going to give you the pig. Here's the pig." Alternatively, again in granting the request, the experimenter might imply misunderstanding by saying, "You asked for the sock. I think you want the sock. I'm going to give you the pig. Here's the pig." The same message variation was introduced in denying the request: the experimenter either conveyed comprehension or incomprehension of what the child had wanted.

This design made it possible to assess whether children provided clarification only when they did not get what they wanted or, alternatively, when they were misunderstood. In fact, children tended to repeat their request more if the experimenter implied misunderstanding as opposed to comprehension and this difference emerged not just when children's request was denied but also when it was granted. Thus, children sought to clarify their request even though that clarification had no instrumental purpose, because they had already been granted the object that they wanted. Looking back, then, at the naturalistic data gathered by Snow et al. (1996), it is plausible to conclude that children's growing propensity in the course of the second and third year to clarify their utterances likely reflects some growing sensitivity to whether or not their interlocutor has understood them.

Updating an Uninformed Partner

So far, I have argued that 2-year-olds increasingly see their interlocutor not just as an agent but as someone with whom information may be exchanged independent of any ongoing activity. To the extent that children see their interlocutor as someone who can take in information, we might expect children to provide more or less information, depending on the information already available to that person. Specifically, in a partial reprise of the standard false belief task, we may ask whether children alter their message depending on whether an interlocutor has or has not observed a particular event. To explore this possibility, O'Neill (1996) created a situation in which 2-year-olds needed help from their parent to retrieve a toy in one of two containers. The experimental question was whether the children would provide more or less information to their parent depending on whether the earlier placement of the toy had occurred when the parent could see it or not.

O'Neill found that 30-month-olds named and pointed at the container holding the toy more often if the parent had not seen its placement. Moreover, in a follow-up study, still younger 2-year-olds (with a mean age of 27 months) also pointed more often at a container if their parent was uninformed about its contents. These two studies imply that when they are engaged in communication children assess their interlocutor's knowledge a good deal earlier than orthodox research on the child's theory of mind might lead us to expect.

Granted this discrepancy, we need to look closely at these findings and consider just what type of monitoring of the interlocutor they imply. In attempting to steer a course between attributing too much and too little understanding, O'Neill (1996) proposes that 2-year-olds make use of a fairly global monitoring heuristic. Without understanding exactly how perceptual input gives rise to knowledge, they may nonetheless keep track of a partner's engagement or disengagement from events that they themselves are processing. Following a period of such disengagement, children might have a generalized strategy of updating an interlocutor with respect to significant changes that have occurred during the period of disengagement.

This proposal has several plausible features. First, it is consistent with the long tradition of research in attachment theory showing that infants and toddlers are indeed sensitive to variations in their partner's responsiveness and especially likely to register sustained periods of disengagement or absence. Second, as O'Neill (1996) points out, it is consistent with a wider conversational strategy of updating conversation partners about significant events that they have not witnessed. This strategy has a wide utility in that it can serve the child's immediate pragmatic purpose (e.g., of retrieving a toy) as well as emotional goals and conversational goals, such as the elicitation of sympathy or the sharing of information.

Phrasing this proposal in slightly different terms, we might say that even before they start to use language for communication children are sensitive to whether or not a partner is attentive to the same object or topic as themselves. That sensitivity is carried over to conversation proper and is manifest even when the topic is not an ongoing, visible event but a displaced event, something that happened recently, as in O'Neill's experiment, or a desirable state of affairs, as in Shwe and Markman's experiment. In short, both preverbally and during the rise of conversation, children monitor their partner, assessing whether he or she is on or off topic and taking appropriate steps to reestablish a joint focus when it is needed.

☐ Conclusions and Implications

The above review has uncovered several characteristics of children's conversations that are increasingly evident in the course of the second and third year. Children are more likely to provide information about an event if their interlocutor had no opportunity to observe the event; they are more likely to reiterate information for an interlocutor who expresses misunderstanding as compared with one who expresses understanding, even when such reiterations serve no extralinguistic instrumental goal; and they engage in displaced reference not just with respect to the past (a topic that adult partners may well prompt) but also with respect to future or fantasy events.

When we take each of these findings separately, it is certainly possible to doubt that children below the age of 3 conceive of their conversation partners as epistemic subjects. When the evidence is considered as a whole, however, it is difficult to resist that conclusion. Moreover, there is a good deal of consistency between the findings based on naturalistic observation (the studies of children's speech acts and displaced reference) and those that are based on experimental analysis (the studies of children's corrections of misunderstanding and updating of an uninformed partner). Combining these more recent findings concerning the emerging art of conversation with the two waves of research on social cognition described in the introduction, we may sketch three developmental phases.

First, as the research from the 1970s demonstrated, in the course of the first 18 months, the nonegocentric infant becomes capable of drawing the attention, or following the attention, of a partner to an object or event of potentially mutual interest. Limited commentary, including expressions of interest and emotion or comments on its name or its attributes, is possible with regard to this object or event. The main restriction, and I take it to be a restriction both of the child's system of communication as well as the child's social cognition, is that the topic of communication whether for self or other is typically an external object or event with which the child is occupied. During this period, therefore, conversation is primarily an instrumental and expressive supplement to action and attention in the here and now.

From 18 to 36 months, as I have tried to document in this chapter, the child's conception of, and capacity for, communication undergoes a gradual revolution. The child increasingly comes to recognize that communication can involve information about a topic that is not part of any current activity or event but about a topic that is known to one of the conversing partners and can be shared with the other. To enter into that form of displaced communication, children must increasingly acknowledge that people are not just agents who act on, or attend to, current events, they are also knowers who can attend to, take in, and exchange information about noncurrent or displaced events. Exactly what drives this displacement is not yet clear. However, we may speculate that early communication itself will help children to discover that their interlocutor is capable of attending not just to objects of mutual interest but also to the message that the child wants to convey. Effectively, the child is given countless opportunities to learn that a verbal comment, and not just the external object or event to which the comment refers, can serve as an interlocutor's focus of attention. Accordingly, during this period, conversation can become less and less tied to ongoing activity and joint attention; instead, it can gradually become an activity, or art, in its own right. At this point, language itself is used to introduce a topic and direct the focus of attention.

As research during the 1980s amply demonstrated, children's social–cognitive understanding takes another step forward in the course of the fourth year. They begin to think of people, whether as interlocutors or as agents, as knowers who can take in and retain information that is partial or misleading. In my view, that development is one that builds on the child's earlier emerging skill in the art of conversation. As discussed in the introduction, conversation, especially conversation in which there is an exchange of information, provides a constant tutorial in the ways that interlocutors may differ in what they think and know. Every time children are posed a question, asked for clarification, or meet a counterassertion, they are confronted by an interlocutor whose knowledge base departs from, and even contradicts, their own (Tomasello, in press).

This three-phase history implies that normal development can be seen as a succession of pragmatic forms; an earlier form of communication provides the tutorial context in which children make the discoveries that permit them to move on to a later form. Accordingly, the problems of children with autism are best seen not simply as the absence of a theory of mind, nor indeed as the absence of prerequisites for a theory of mind such as joint attention, but rather as a cascade of successive and interdependent failures. Difficulties in the establishment of joint attention set the stage for disturbances in the child's engagement in conversation; and in the wake of those communication problems, the child's developing appreciation of other people as epistemic subjects is disrupted.

As I pointed out in the introduction, the preoccupations of research on social cognition were, on one reading at least, quite different during the 1970s as compared with the 1980s. The altercentric infant of the 1970s was busy engaging with a partner. The mind-minded 4- and 5-year-old, by contrast, was a spectator, or theorist of human behavior rather than a communicating member of a dyad. If my argument is correct, however, there is a way to create a bridge between those two forms of social cognition. After all, the infant who follows or draws the attention of a partner turns into the conversationalist who can exchange information; and the conversationalist, in turn, becomes someone who understands that people may differ in what they know and believe. The child's early history is reasonably seen as a connected whole, even if our own intellectual past is not always so coherent.

☐ References

Astington, J. W., & Gopnik, A. (1988). Knowing you've changed your mind: Children's understanding of representational change. In J. W. Astington, P. L. Harris, & D. R. Olson (Eds.), *Developing theories of mind*. New York: Cambridge University Press.

Baldwin, D. (1995). Understanding the link between joint attention and language. In C. Moore & P. J. Dunham (Eds.), *Joint attention. Its origins and role in development*. Hillsdale, NJ: Erlbaum.

Baron-Cohen, S. (1991). Do people with autism understand what causes emotion? *Child Development, 62*, 385–395.

Baron-Cohen, S. (1995). *Mindblindness*. Cambridge, MA: Bradford, MIT Press.

Bartsch, K., & Wellman, H. (1989). Young children's attribution of action to beliefs and desires. *Child Development, 60*, 946–964.

Bartsch, K., & Wellman, H. M. (1995). *Children talk about the mind*. New York: Oxford University Press.

Bruner, J. S. (1973). The ontogenesis of speech acts. *Journal of Child Language, 2*, 1–19.

Butterworth, G. E., & Cochran, E. (1980). Towards a mechanism of joint visual attention in human infancy. *International Journal of Behavioral Development, 3*, 253–272.

Carpenter, M., Nagell, K., & Tomasello, M. (1998). Social cognition, joint attention, and communicative competence from 9 to 15 months of age. *Monographs of the Society for Research in Child Development, 63*, Serial No. 255.

Dunn, J. (1988). *The beginnings of social understanding*. Oxford, UK: Blackwell.

Eisenmajer, R., & Prior, M. (1991). Cognitive linguistic correlates of "theory of mind" ability in autistic children. *British Journal of Developmental Psychology, 9*, 351–364.

Frith, U. (1989). Autism: Explaining the enigma. Oxford, UK: Blackwell.

Frith, U., Happé, F., & Siddons, F. (1994). Autism and theory of mind in everyday life. *Social Development, 3*, 108–123.

Furrow, D., Moore, C., Davidge, J., & Chiasson, L. (1992). Mental terms in mothers' and children's speech: Similarities and relationships. *Journal of Child Language, 19*, 617–631.

Golinkoff, R. M. (1986). "I beg your pardon?" The preverbal negotiation of failed messages. *Journal of Child Language, 13*, 455–476.

Golinkoff, R. M. (1993). When is communication a "meeting of minds"? *Journal of Child Language, 20*, 199–207.

Greenfield, P. M., & Savage-Rumbaugh, S. (1990). Grammatical combination in *Pan paniscus*: Processes of learning and invention in the evolution and development of language. In S. T. Parker & K. R. Gibson (Eds.), *"Language" and intelligence in monkeys and apes: Comparative developmental perspectives*, pp. 540–578. Cambridge, UK: Cambridge University Press.

Harris, P. L. (1996). Desires, beliefs and language. In P. Carruthers & P. K. Smith (Eds.), *Theories of theories of mind* (pp. 200–220). Cambridge, UK: Cambridge University Press.

Harris, P. L., Johnson, C. N., Hutton, D., Andrews, G., & Cooke, T. (1989). Young children's theory of mind and emotion. *Cognition and Emotion, 3*, 379–400.

Hoff-Ginsberg, E. (1994). Influences of mother and child on maternal talkativeness. *Discourse Processes, 18*, 105–117.

Leslie, A. M. (1988). Some implications of pretense for mechanisms underlying the child's theory of mind. In J. W. Astington, P. L. Harris, & D. R. Olson (Eds.), *Developing theories of mind* (pp. 19–46). New York: Cambridge University Press.

Leslie, A. M., & Frith, U. (1988). Autistic children's understanding of seeing, knowing and believing. *British Journal of Developmental Psychology, 6,* 315–324.

Meltzoff, A. N. (1976). Imitation in early infancy. Unpublished doctoral thesis. Department of Experimental Psychology, University of Oxford.

Meltzoff, A. N., & Moore, M. K. (1977). Imitation of facial and manual gestures by human neonates. *Science, 198,* 75–78.

Moore, C., & Dunham, P. J. (Eds.). (1995). *Joint attention. Its origins and role in development.* Hillsdale, NJ: Erlbaum.

Morford, J. P., & Goldin-Meadow, S. (1997). From here and now to there and then: The development of displaced reference in Homesign and English. *Child Development, 68,* 420–435.

Nelson, K. (1993). The psychological and social origins of autobiographical memory. *Psychological Science, 4,* 7–14.

O'Neill, D. K. (1996). Two-year-old children's sensitivity to a parent's knowledge state when making requests. *Child Development, 67,* 659–677.

Perner, J. (1988). Developing semantics for theories of mind: Connecting mental spaces. In J. W. Astington, P. L. Harris, & D. R. Olson (Eds.), *Developing theories of mind.* New York: Cambridge University Press.

Peterson, C. C., & Siegal, M. (1995). Deafness, conversation and theory of mind. *Journal of Child Psychology and Psychiatry, 36,* 459–474.

Peterson, C. C., & Siegal, M. (1997). Domain specificity and everyday biological, physical and psychological thinking in normal, autistic and deaf children. In H. M. Wellman & K. Inagaki (Eds.), The emergence of core domains of thought: Children's reasoning about physical, psychological, and biological phenomena. *New Directions in Child Development, Number 75.* San Francisco: Jossey-Bass.

Premack, D., & Woodruff, G. (1978). Does the chimpanzee have a theory of mind? *Behavioral and Brain Sciences, 1,* 515–526.

Ruffman, T., Perner, J., Naito, M., Parkin, L., & Clements, W. A. (1998). Older (but not younger) siblings facilitate false belief understanding. *Developmental Psychology, 34,* 161–174.

Russell, P. A., Hosie, J. A., Gray, C. D., Scott, C., Hunter, N., Banks, J. S., & Macaulay, M. C. (1998). The development of theory of mind in deaf children. *Journal of Child Psychology and Child Psychiatry, 39,* 903–910.

Scaife, M., & Bruner, J. S. (1975). The capacity for joint attention. *Nature, 253,* 265–266.

Shatz, M., & O'Reilly, A. (1990). Conversation or communicative skill? A reassessment of two-year-olds' behavior in miscommunication episodes. *Journal of Child Language, 17,* 131–146.

Shatz, M., Wellman, H. M., & Silber, S. (1983). The acquisition of mental terms: A systematic investigation of the first reference to mental state. *Cognition, 14,* 301–321.

Shwe, H. I., & Markman, E. M. (1997). Young children's appreciation of the mental impact of their communicative signals. *Developmental Psychology, 33,* 630–636.

Snow, C. E., Pan, B. A., Imbens-Bailey, A., & Herman, J. (1996). Learning how to say what one means: A longitudinal study of children's speech act use. *Social Development, 5,* 56–84.

Tager-Flusberg, H. (1992). Autistic children's talk about psychological states: Deficits in the early acquisition of a theory of mind. *Child Development, 63,* 161–172.

Tager-Flusberg, H. (1993). What language reveals about the understanding of minds in children and autism. In S. Baron-Cohen, H. Tager-Flusberg, & D. J. Cohen (Eds.),

Understanding other minds: Perspectives from autism (pp. 138–157). Oxford, UK: Oxford University Press.

Tager-Flusberg, H., Sullivan, K., & Zaitchik, D. (1994, July 27). Social-cognitive abilities in Williams syndrome. Paper presented at the Conference of the Williams Syndrome Association, San Diego, CA.

Tan, J., & Harris, P. L. (1991). Autistic children understand seeing and wanting. *Development and Psychopathology, 3,* 163–174.

Tomasello, M. (in press). *The cultural origins of human cognition.* Cambridge, MA: Harvard University Press.

Trevarthen, C., & Hubley, P. (1978). Secondary intersubjectivity: Confidence, confiding and acts of meaning in the first year. In A. Lock (Ed.), *Action, gesture, and symbol* (pp. 183–229). London: Academic Press.

Yirmiya, N., Erel, O., Shaked, M., & Solomonica-Levi, D. (1998). Meta-analyses comparing theory of mind abilities of individuals with autism, individuals with mental retardation and normally developing individuals. *Psychological Bulletin, 124,* 283–307.

Wimmer, H., & Perner, J. (1983). Beliefs about beliefs: Representations and constraining function of wrong beliefs in young children's understanding of deception. *Cognition, 13,* 103–128.

Ziatas, K., Durkin, K., & Pratt, C. (1998). Belief term development in children with autism, Asperger syndrome, specific language impairment and normal development: Links to theory of mind development. *Journal of Child Psychology and Child Psychiatry, 39,* 755–763.

CHAPTER 7

Willard W. Hartup

Peer Experience and Its Developmental Significance

☐ Normative Studies and Research Beginnings

Children's relations with other children have been studied for more than a century. In early investigations, Tripplett (1897) found that children wound fishing reels faster when working with other children than when working alone; Monroe (1898) conducted survey studies showing that children tend to idealize their friends with respect to attitudes and values. Considerable interest in these issues remains. Contemporary investigators continue, for example, to be interested in the social conditions that affect task performance in children. We now know that performance outcomes vary according to reward structures: Winner-take-all situations elicit better performance than shared-reward conditions on simple tasks that do not require coordinated interaction. Shared rewards, on the other hand, elicit better performance on tasks requiring social coordination, especially when rewards are distributed in proportion to each individual's contribution (French, Brownell, Graziano, & Hartup, 1977).

Although research on child–child relations thus has a substantial history, empirical studies were nevertheless rare during the first three decades of this century. One early investigator, Charlotte Bühler, became interested in the social relations and competencies of infants and toddlers as revealed in observations of babies from poor families at a milk station (Bühler, 1930). Clever methods such as the "baby party" were invented, and observations showed that considerable interest in other children is evident by 6 months of age and that 6-month-old babies incorporate simple coordinations into their social exchanges. Although these studies tell us much about the origins of social competence, further efforts to describe the social abilities of infants and toddlers were delayed for more than 30 years (see below).

Meanwhile, beginning in the late 1920s, investigators concentrated on the peer interactions of preschool- and school-aged children, partly because children of these ages were now available for study in laboratory schools in the United States and elsewhere (Renshaw, 1981). Children were found to show increased capacities during early childhood for engaging in coordinated interaction of many different kinds: Associative and cooperative activities were found to increase during the preschool years (Parten, 1932–1933); solitary play was thought to decline.[1] Rates of physical aggression were shown to increase and then decline (Goodenough, 1931); verbal aggression was shown to increase and then stabilize (Jersild & Markey, 1935). Conflict instigation and management were found to be moderated by children's relationships with one another, that is, whether or not they are friends (Green, 1933). Kindnesses were observed to increase in child–child interaction especially when social conditions favor them (Murphy, 1937).

Social collectives (gangs, groups, crowds) began to be studied both in vivo and in situ. Best known are the field experiments in which democratic group atmospheres were found to foster more felicitous social outcomes than authoritarian or laissez-faire ones (Lewin, Lippitt, & White, 1938). Somewhat earlier, Frederic Thrasher (1927) described the formation, location, membership, and behavior of adolescent gangs through the use of "participant observation," a methodology that has been widely used to study intergroup relations (Sherif, Harvey, White, Hood, & Sherif, 1961) and other aspects of child–child interaction.

No single theory drove the empirical studies published during the first three or four decades of the century. Most early investigators espoused structural/maturational views: nascent social competencies were assumed to be among the child's endowments, and the work of the scientist was to chart their unfolding. Most psychologists were not interested in socialization, that is, the processes through which the child is assimilated into society, a topic that was more appealing to sociologists (e.g., Cooley, 1909) and personality theorists (Freud, 1933). The sociologists who became known as the "symbolic interactionists" (e.g., Mead, 1934) were es-

---

[1]Solitary play is now known to change qualitatively (in task involvement and cognitive maturity) to a greater extent than quantitatively through early childhood (Rubin, Watson, & Jambor, 1978).

pecially interested in the manner in which "experts" foster child growth and development. Psychoanalytic writers were also concerned with parent–child relations as antecedents of self-control and social conformity in the child. Among psychologists, Watson (1913) formulated a theory that would explain socialization in terms of rewards and punishments, but it took the combined efforts of an interdisciplinary group of scholars at the Institute of Human Relations at Yale University to create the synthesis needed to transform learning theory into a theory of socialization.

The new synthesis was called social learning theory (Dollard & Miller, 1950). Consistent with psychoanalytic thinking, this theory took dependency and aggression as central substantive themes in child development. Processwise, the child was believed to undergo a "social molding" through which mature behaviors are instantiated and immature ones extinguished according to reinforcement theory (Zigler, 1970). The child was viewed as relatively passive in these transactions and the adult as active. It is not difficult to see, then, why the study of socialization became mainly the study of parenting and why the study of personality development became mainly the search for dispositional outcomes of parent–child relations (Maccoby, 1992). Virtually no interest was evident in peer relations during this time because children were regarded de facto as lacking the expertise to be effective socializers.

☐ New Views

Between 1960 and 1970, developmental psychologists began to change their views of the child. The revival of structuralism through the rediscovery of Piaget's works (Flavell, 1963) fostered views of the child as an active agent in commerce with the social world. In one work, *The Moral Judgment of the Child*, Piaget (1932) suggested that peer interaction is actually necessary to engendering the intrapsychic conflict among cognitive schemas that provokes higher levels of reasoning and thinking by the child. By the close of the 1960s, children were seen throughout developmental psychology as "socializing," not merely "social" (Bell, 1968; Rheingold, 1969), and "active" rather than "passive" in their interactions with the world.

Accordingly, child–child interaction took on a significance that it did not have during the years when social mold models dominated thinking about social and cognitive development. First, the interaction between two "inexpert" children could now be seen as affording a clear view of each child's social competence. Child–child interaction reflects what children can and cannot do; adult–child interaction, on the other hand, frequently masks the child's capabilities since adults "drive" the interaction and compensate for the child's immaturities (Heckhausen, 1987). Second, interaction between two children may contribute in its own right to socialization, especially to learning how to regulate one's behavior with social equals. These Zeitgeist changes, I believe, are directly responsible for the thousands of studies dealing with peer relations and their developmental significance that have appeared in the years since 1970 (Hartup, 1983; Rubin, Bukowski, & Parker, 1997).

Among the questions that have driven these newer investigations, one stands out: *What contributions are made by interactions and relationships between children to the growth and development of children as individuals, to their capacities to relate to others, regulate their actions, and work out effective adaptations?* My own first studies were designed to show that children are effective reinforcers of one another's actions both in laboratory settings and in the nursery school (Hartup, 1964; Charlesworth & Hartup, 1967). The social mold models of socialization clearly guided those efforts, because one child was regarded as "shaper" and the other as "shaped" in this work. At the same time, we were asking whether 4-year-olds were competent as socializing agents, which is a "new look" issue. And, a bit later, the question became not whether children *can* socialize one another but whether they socialize one another differently from the manner in which adults socialize them.

☐ The Importance of Peer Experience

Demonstrating the Egalitarian Prototype

Most investigators believe that the unique benefits of peer experience stem from the developmental equivalence of the participants and the egalitarian nature of their interaction. Extensive documentation now shows that peer interaction is structured differently from adult–child interaction, especially in what children spend time doing; what is expected in terms of affection, intimacy, personal support, and conflict; and the compliance strategies used with one's associates (Furman & Buhrmester, 1985; Newcomb & Bagwell, 1995). Children understand quite early, for example, that strong compliance strategies are more appropriate and more likely to work with other children than with adults. Conversely, weak strategies are understood to work better with adults (Cowan, Drinkard, & MacGavin, 1984). Children also learn to control the expression of emotions, especially aggression, sadness, and pain, to a greater extent with other children than with adults (Zeman & Garber, 1996). Children's relations with other children are thus structured differently from relations with adults both cognitively and behaviorally.

Deprivation and Satiation Experiments

The strongest methods for showing enduring effects of peer experience, which are deprivation and satiation experiments, are impossible to carry out with children. One or two "experiments of nature," including the famous case studies conducted by Anna Freud and Sophie Dann (1951) immediately after World War II, seem to show that children can provide one another with security and self-enhancement that, when adults are absent, support ego development. Owing to the many confounds involved, however, this evidence is weak.

Harry and Margaret Harlow (together with Steve Suomi) remain the investigators who, with deprivation and satiation experiments, most clearly demonstrated the unique developmental significance of peer interaction and relationships. These investigators (see Harlow, 1969) raised Rhesus monkeys under several conditions: (a) with mothers but without contact with other infants, and (b) with other juveniles but without mothers. Subsequent adaptation among neither of these groups of monkeys was as adequate as among individuals who had contact with *both* mothers and peers during early rearing. Maternal rearing without peer contact produced animals showing both immediate disturbances in play behavior and long-term disturbances in social and emotional development. Peer rearing without maternal contact provided a basis for social development, albeit a shaky one. Still other work (Suomi & Harlow, 1972) revealed that the social adaptation of young animals who were socially isolated in infancy improves as a result of contact with other juveniles who are somewhat younger than the isolates themselves.[2] On balance, then, peer experience appears to contribute uniquely to socialization among members of this species (the Rhesus), although just how much experience is needed, how regularly, and under what conditions is still not known.

Comparing Children Who Are Socially Accepted With Those Who Are Socially Rejected

Among strategies employed in research with children that reflect on peer relations and their developmental significance is comparing children whose peer relations are *poor* with children whose peer relations

---

[2]Later, we demonstrated similar therapeutic effects of contact between socially shy nursery school children and children somewhat younger than they were (Furman, Rahe, & Hartup, 1979).

are *good*. Consequently, researchers have spent considerable time study-ing the differences between children who are liked by other children and those who are disliked. Sociometric methods emerged, in part, to make these studies possible. Developed by J. L. Moreno (1934) in the course of his work with adults (prison inmates and psychiatric patients), these methods were quickly adapted to the study of social organization and in-terpersonal relations among children.

An enormous literature has accumulated showing that children who are disliked are at risk in social development as compared with those who are well-liked (Hartup, 1983; Parker & Asher, 1987; Rubin et al., 1997). Early studies revealed that being liked and being disliked are ac-tually two dimensions in social relations: (a) being disliked is only moderately correlated with being liked, and (b) being disliked and being liked have different correlates. Aggressiveness, for example, is positively correlated with being disliked but uncorrelated with being liked; friend-liness is positively correlated with being liked but uncorrelated with being disliked (Hartup, Glazer, & Charlesworth, 1967). The weight of the evidence that has accumulated over the years shows that being disliked is frequently associated with unsuccessful outcomes in social de-velopment, while being liked is associated with successful ones. Consis-tent as they are, however, these results constitute relatively weak support for the hypothesis that peer relations contribute uniquely to growth and development. Concurrent correlational studies tell one little about this question because they do not provide a basis for making causal inferences.

Merrill Roff (cf. Roff, 1961) as well as Emery Cowen and his col-leagues (1973) provided the earliest longitudinal studies that suggested that being disliked by one's associates in childhood constitutes devel-opmental risk. These studies established that mental health status in early adulthood was better predicted by sociometric status during mid-dle childhood than any other cognitive or social variable. Looking back on them, though, this work is still not completely convincing, because the studies were not as carefully cross-lagged as they need to be and certain other deficiencies are evident (Parker, Rubin, Price, & DeRozier, 1995). More recent studies with improved designs and sturdier analytic methods nevertheless confirm the earlier conclusions: Being disliked during early and middle childhood leads to more intensive rejection by other children as time goes on, relationships (by default) with chil-dren who themselves are antisocial and not well-socialized, and de-velopmental outcomes that are not good (Coie, Dodge, & Kupersmidt, 1990; Dishion, Patterson, & Griesler, 1994; Rubin, LeMare, & Lollis, 1990).

Although these studies are convincing, it remains difficult to assert that good peer relations are developmental necessities: First, being popular and being rejected are multifaceted constructs (Peery, 1979) and most scoring methods do not yield homogeneous groups: For example, one-half to two-thirds of children who are peer rejected (i.e., disliked) in the first grade will not be rejected in the second grade, and their first-grade behavior forecasts these different trajectories. Being disliked from one year to the next is twice as likely when first-grade children's antipathies are based on aggression and antisocial behavior, a behavioral disposition that is itself unusually stable throughout childhood and adolescence (Cillessen, Van Ijzendoorn, Van Lieshout, & Hartup, 1992).

Second, growth curve analysis, survival analysis, and other sophisticated methods for identifying developmental pathways are now regarded as necessary because peer experience seems to account for significant variance in developmental outcomes among some individuals but not others. Using such analyses, for example, Coie, Terry, Lenox, Lochman, and Hyman (1995) studied changes in antisocial behavior between sixth and tenth grade as a function, separately, of aggression and rejection in third grade. Only boys who were *both* rejected and aggressive in third grade showed increasing antisocial behavior across the transition to adolescence. Being aggressive *or* rejected (or neither) was associated with decreasing antisocial behavior during this period. Growth functions among girls depended on the data source: Early aggression predicted increases during adolescence according to self-reports, whereas peer rejection predicted increasing antisocial behavior according to parents' reports.

These results, too, must be interpreted cautiously. Coie and Dodge (1997) state it this way:

> The characteristics that distinguish rejected and non-rejected aggressive boys cannot be argued to have developed solely or even predominantly as a consequence of peer rejection because the immature and incompetent aspects of social functioning that characterize the rejected subgroup are, no doubt, the same factors that contributed to their rejection in the first place. In this sense, then, peer rejection may serve as both a marker variable for these other risk factors and as a catalyst for the escalation of antisocial behavior. (p. 831)

Other recent studies (cf. Loeber et al., 1993; Moffitt, 1993) also indicate that considerable differentiation exists among the developmental pathways that lead to antisocial orientations among adults. More than likely, then, the ultimate answer to our basic question of whether peer relations are necessities in growth and development is not straightforward. Rather, it is likely to be for some children and not others.

☐ The Importance of Friendship

One other strategy has been used to establish the significance of peer relations in growth and development, namely, assessing the behavioral outcomes that can be traced to children's friendships: having friends, who one's friends are, and the quality of these relationships (Hartup, 1996). Studies have established that, from early childhood through old age, the "social capital" contained in these relationships consists of social support on the one hand, and intimacy between equals on the other. This friendship "deep structure" is developmentally stable and seems to be mainly responsible for the value of friendships to psychological well-being and mental health (Hartup & Stevens, 1997). As we shall see, however, friendships carry risks with them along with the social capital they contain.

Having Friends

Most early studies were descriptive: We learned that friendships ordinarily become evident in the second or third year (about 75% of preschool-aged children have good friends and about 90% of adolescents). Friendship networks are relatively small among young children (about 1.8) but expand among adolescents (to about 5). Time spent with friends is greatest in middle childhood and adolescence, accounting then for about 30% of time spent awake. Although there is some instability among children's friendships, the majority last more than a year and those children who have friends at one age are likely to have friends later on (see Hartup & Stevens, 1997). Friendships are understood differently as children grow older: Among younger children, the social quid pro quo is concrete ("He gives me food and I give him some back"); children expect to play with their friends. Among older children, the quid pro quo is attitudinal and generalized; children regard these relationships as rooted in loyalty, trust, and intimacy (Bigelow, 1977).

Cross-sectional studies show, first, children who have friends are more socially competent than those who do not; second, children being clinically referred with psychosocial problems are more likely to be friendless than better-adjusted children; and, third, children and adolescents who have friends report a greater sense of well-being than those who do not (see Hartup & Stevens, 1997). Although consistent, these results are difficult to interpret. First, having friends in these studies is usually confounded with having *good* friends. The significance of this confound is clearly demonstrated by the discovery that *not* having problematic friendships is more closely related to well-being among adults than having supportive ones (Rook, 1984). Second, causal direction is impossible to specify: having friends may contribute to self-esteem and well-being, but the reverse may also be true.

Longitudinal studies are beginning to show that friendships represent valuable social capital and that access to these relationships are advantages in child development. School attitudes, for example, are better among kindergarten children (5-year-olds) whose friends enter school at the same time and who maintain these relationships than among children who do not (Ladd, 1990). In addition, access to friends predicts increases in self-esteem among preadolescents and decreases the frequency of psychosocial disturbances when children make changes from lower school to middle school and on to high school (Simmons, Burgeson, & Reef, 1988).

The social capital contained in friendships seems especially important to preadolescents and adolescents. Consider the children of divorce: Longitudinal studies show that the risk of being above the clinical cutoff for both internalizing and externalizing symptoms during childhood and early adolescence is about three times greater among children from divorced or remarried families or both than among nondivorced families (Hetherington, 1999). Consider, next, that *within divorced and remarried families*, discrimination between resilient and nonresilient offspring assessed as children depends mainly on the adequacy of the child's relationships with the custodial parent (usually the mother), amount of conflict between the custodial and noncustodial parents, and access to the noncustodial parent—*not* to relationships with siblings or friends. The social maturity of the child's parents and the supportiveness of their relationship with the child are both correlated with the child's resilience, showing the significance of family relationships in coping with divorce and remarriage during childhood. Among adolescents, family relationships remain important as social capital in these families, but having siblings who are mature and sensible as well as having friends also contribute to resilience. Among young adults (24-year-olds), friendships remain important as social capital for individuals from divorced and remarried families in addition to which dating, cohabiting, and spousal relationships provide similar benefits. At the same time, family relationships diminish greatly in the extent to which they furnish social capital to these adult offspring of divorce. Few studies show as dramatically as this one that the benefits of having friends depends on developmental status. Although having friends may be important to one's sense of well-being at all ages, these relationships may be most significant in coping with stress during adolescence and early adulthood.

Friendships may not contribute equally to every aspect of social adaptation. In one important study (Bagwell, Newcomb, & Bukowski, 1998), the investigators separately examined *popularity* and *having friends* during childhood as predictors of adaptation in early adulthood (12 years after the initial testing). Results show that: (a) childhood sociometric status (popular versus rejected) but not friendship status (having versus not having friends) significantly predicted school performance, job success, educational aspirations, and sociability in adulthood; (b) having childhood friends, on the other hand, predicted good attitudes toward family members among the young adults and, most important, general feelings of self-worth and the absence of depressive symptoms: Peer rejection did not predict these specific outcomes. Correlations between having friends in childhood and self-attitudes in adulthood remained significant even when the participants' perceptions of their social competence as children were factored out.

These results suggest, first, that sociometric status (being liked or being disliked by one's classmates as a whole) and having friends are two different dimensions in social relations during childhood. And, indeed, although it is hard to imagine that a child can be popular without having friends, it is *not* hard to imagine that children who are disliked may, at the same time, have steady companions and that these children call themselves friends. Accordingly, recent studies (George & Hartmann, 1996) show that more than 75% of rejected children have friends.

Second, across the transition from childhood to adulthood, peer rejection seems to be a more important predictor of social skill than having friends. Friendship experience, however, contributes to developmental outcome in two other domains, exactly the outcomes that one might expect: better family relationships, more positive attitudes toward family relationships, and self-esteem (as well as freedom from depression, a disorder frequently accompanied by low self-esteem). The connection in these data between childhood friendship and self-esteem in early adulthood is especially important because it supports one of the most basic propositions in Sullivan's (1953) theory of interpersonal relations, namely, that preadolescent friendships "provide opportunities for validation of self-worth and a unique context for exploration and development of personal strengths" (Bagwell et al., 1998, p. 150).

Still other studies suggest that friendships in childhood may be precursors of romantic relationships in adolescence. For example, having same-gender friends during middle childhood forecasts having romantic relationships during adolescence; subsequently, having same-gender friends during adolescence forecasts romantic relationships in early adulthood (Neemann, Hubbard, & Masten, 1995). Longitudinal studies following children from the first year of life through adolescence also show that having friends during middle childhood enhances success in early romantic relationships, even when quality of the parent–child relationship is factored out (Sroufe, Egeland, & Carlson, 1999). Since same-gender friendships forecast romantic relationships, but not vice versa, results are consistent with another of Sullivan's (1953) notions, namely, that same-gender friendships during the "juvenile era" support the formation and functioning of heterosexual relationships, mainly by the establishment of the need for intimacy.

Taken together, then, the weight of the evidence suggests that: (a) Childhood friendships are more than correlates of successful coping with the developmental demands of childhood; having friends supports successful coping later on. (b) The social capital encompassed by these relationships seems to be utilized according to developmental status, especially during preadolescence, adolescence, and early adulthood.

Who the Child's Friends Are

Since children make friends on the basis of common ground, friends ought to be similar to one another in interests, abilities, and outlook. Behavioral data, extending from early childhood through adolescence, accord with these expectations. More than 60 years ago, cooperativeness was found to be more concordant among preschool-aged friends than nonfriends (Challman, 1932). One recent investigation with school-aged children shows that friends, as compared with nonfriends, are more similar to one another across a wide behavioral range in prosocial behavior, antisocial behavior (in many different aspects), shyness and dependency, and being disliked by one's classmates (Haselager, Hartup, Van Lieshout, & Riksen-Walraven, 1998). Childhood friends are certainly not carbon copies of one another; effect sizes are small. Nevertheless, the commonalities are sufficiently great that they cannot be ignored in predicting developmental outcome.

Some of these similarities between friends undoubtedly derive from mutual selection through which children "shop" for friends who are similar to themselves and with whom they can reach shared goals. Children are not believed to choose friends on a rational basis, however, so much as on an experiential one—because it "feels right" (Dishion et al., 1994). Once two similar friends choose one another, though, the stage is set for becoming even more alike (Kandel, 1978).

Among relatively well-adjusted children, the mutual socialization occurring between friends is usually evinced in socially acceptable attributes. Since friends are more sociable, more task-oriented, more effective in managing conflicts, more mutually oriented, and more affirmative in their interactions with one another than nonfriends (Newcomb & Bagwell, 1995; Hartup, 1996), friendships constitute social capital that enhances social competence in most circumstances. Three kinds of data support the notion that competent children provide their friends with social resources of this kind: (a) School-aged friends with conventional social orientations and good social skills move further over time in the direction of normative behavior than in the direction of antisocial behavior (Ball, 1981; Kandel & Andrews, 1987). (b) When children are under stress (e.g., in the aftermath of divorce or remarriage), having socially skilled friends who have relatively few behavior problems promotes resilience, whereas having immature friends who have many behavior problems does not (Hetherington, 1999). (c) "Desisting" delinquency is forecast among children at risk for antisocial behavior more strongly by turning away from antisocial friends to more socially skilled friends than by any other variable (Mulvey & Aber, 1988). In other words, social capital for children does not reside merely in having friends but in having *socially competent* friends.

On the other side of the coin, antisocial behavior increases as a consequence of association with antisocial friends (Ball, 1981; Dishion, 1990). One reason is that antisocial friends often have poor social skills, but other reasons have to do with the nature of relationships between antisocial children. New studies show that friendships between aggressive children and between nonaggressive children differ markedly with these differences depending on the type of aggression that characterizes the children.

First, "overtly aggressive" friends (mostly boys) report more aggressiveness toward others than toward each other (Grotpeter & Crick, 1996), although their interactions with one another are more contentious and conflict ridden than matched controls (Dishion, Andrews, & Crosby, 1995). Both self-report and observational data also show that overtly aggressive children and adolescents are not notably intimate with one another and are not as exclusive in their relationship attitudes as matched controls (Grotpeter & Crick, 1996; Dishion et al., 1995). Friendships between overtly aggressive children, then, appear to rest on companionship and gaining status in a peer dominance hierarchy, rather than needs for warm, intimate intercourse. These relationships contain much developmental risk in addition to whatever social benefits they provide the participants, mostly through the encouragement and modeling of aggressive behavior toward others that occurs within them (Hartup, 1996).

Second, friendships between "relationally aggressive" children also differ from matched controls. These children (mostly girls) inflict harm by manipulating their relationships with others (e.g., by using the "silent treatment" or shunning, maliciously spreading lies and rumors so as to damage a child's status with other children, exclusion, and the like). Although relational aggression is more common among girls than boys, children of both sexes who show high levels of this activity exhibit significant concurrent and future adjustment difficulties (Crick, 1996). Friendships existing between relationally aggressive children are distinctive: they are extremely intimate and exclusive, and frequent displays of relational aggression occur between the children themselves (Grotpeter & Crick, 1996). This admixture of intimacy and relationship-oriented aggression characterizes certain other dysfunctional relationships (e.g., bad marriages) and also constitutes a developmental risk for the participants.

Overall, then, when antisocial children become friends, these relationships do not provide them with the same kind of social capital that friendships do among nonaggressive children. Rather than being protective factors or contributors to successful adaptation and adjustment, these relationships contain considerable "risk." Thus, friendships among aggressive children (whether the aggression is overt or relational) are mixed blessings: On the one hand, aggressive friends support ego development through the social support and increased sense of well-being they provide the children. On the other hand, aggressive friends are risk factors, since the children are poorly socialized and dispose themselves to increased aggressive behavior either toward others (in the case of overtly aggressive children) or toward relationship partners (in the case of relationally aggressive children).

Whether shy children (who sometimes have shy friends) mutually socialize one another toward increased shyness (thereby constituting developmental risk) remains to be seen. Social interaction between shy children and their friends may not be as maladaptive as interaction between aggressive children and their companions. Actually, adjustment may be achieved through the social interaction that these friends have with one another even though the children themselves are socially reticent or sad. Shy friends may not alleviate one another's shyness so much as the loneliness that accompanies and exacerbates the risk associated with it (Asher, Parkhurst, Hymel, & Williams, 1990). Once again, developmental diagnosis demands that we know who a child's friends are, not just whether he or she has friends.

Friendship Quality

Qualitative assessment of child and adolescent friendships involves two main strategies: (a) *dimensional analysis* through which one determines whether certain elements are present or absent in the social interaction between friends (e.g., intimacy, conflict), and (b) *typological analysis* through which one identifies patterns in social interaction believed to be critical to social development and adaptation.

Dimensional assessment of child and adolescent friendships is relatively new and no standard instrument exists for measuring relationship qualities, although several have been widely tested. In most instances, the new instrumentation encompasses both positive and negative friendship attributes showing factorial structures that include, for example, reciprocity of relations, self-disclosure, overt hostility, and covert hostility (Windle, 1994). Sometimes, factor analysis reveals very simple structures consisting of "positive" and "negative" dimensions, that is, intimacy and supportiveness, on the one hand, and criticism and poor conflict management on the other.

Categorical analysis has not yet produced a list of "friendship styles" or "friendship types" that can be used in either research or clinical practice. Shulman (1993) constructed a typological model based on the balance between closeness and individuation, using concepts drawn from family therapy. *Independent* friendships have been identified in which cooperation and independence are balanced; *disengaged* ones in which friends are disconnected in spite of efforts to remain in proximity; and *consensus-sensitive* or *enmeshed* friendships in which agreement and cohesion are maximized. Generally, though, we are unable to differentiate among friendships in terms of social capital or their developmental implications. Nevertheless, friendships are not all alike, and this truism needs to be taken into account in assessing social adjustment.

Supportiveness between friends (high versus low) is positively correlated with school involvement and achievement (Berndt & Hawkins, 1991) and negatively correlated with school-based problems (Kurdek & Sinclair, 1988) in both cross-sectional and longitudinal studies. Conversely, negativity between friends (including conflict and contentiousness) is negatively correlated across time with school attitudes, involvement, and achievement among children and adolescents. Using cross-lagged designs, investigators have discovered that neither the number of the child's friends nor the stability of these friendships forecasts school behavior although friendship quality does. And school behavior seems to be one outcome domain that shows pervasive effects of friendship quality.

A second domain linked to friendship quality is self-esteem: Supportiveness is negatively correlated with identity problems and positively correlated with self-esteem across the transition from adolescence to adulthood (Bagwell et al., 1998). Not surprisingly, then, negative correlations occur between friends' supportiveness and depression, among girls especially. But developmental pathways are complicated: Among boys, supportive friends *encourage* substance abuse and depression when life conditions are stressful and friends are troublemakers (Dubow, Tisak, Causey, Hryshko, & Reid, 1991). The evidence thus suggests that interaction effects are evident between friendship quality and who one's friends are. Other complications exist: Evidence shows that individual characteristics (e.g., delinquency and depression) forecast both overt and covert hostility between friends rather than vice versa (Windle, 1994). Causal direction, then, needs to be more clearly established. One can say, however, that the weight of the evidence suggests that good outcomes are most likely when one has friends, one's friends are well-socialized, and when one's relationships with these individuals are supportive. Otherwise, friendships are mixed blessings.

Much remains to be learned about the manner in which friendship attributes combine to determine developmental outcome. Among some individuals, having friends may account for more outcome variance than who one's friends are; this may not be true for others. Friendship quality (i.e., having supportive friends) may be the most important social capital that one can possess when facing certain challenges (e.g., school transitions), but the identity of one's friends may be most important in determining whether an adolescent will move into an adult criminal career. Comprehensive studies are needed, therefore, in which friendship is studied along with other predictors, including temperament and personality, rather than studied separately. Indeed, multiple developmental pathways undoubtedly exist in which friendship experience may account for significant variance in outcome for some children but not others. Sufficient evidence exists, however, to confirm the hypothesis that friendship experience should rarely be excluded from either research models in developmental psychopathology or developmental diagnoses. And, finally, the evidence shows that multidimensional assessment of these relationships is essential.

☐ Conclusion

The developmental significance of peer relations was recognized during the early years of the twentieth century. Empirical studies appeared infrequently, however, lagging behind studies of parent–child relations. This situation changed during the 1960s, coincidentally with changes occurring among scientists in their views of the child. Prior to this time, the child was regarded as a passive participant in the socialization process, one who is largely incapable of socializing others—adults or children. Since that time, children have been regarded as active, socializing creatures from birth onward, which is a view that supports a strong interest in child–child interaction.

Considerable effort has been made over the years to describe normative changes in modes of child–child interaction and to show, especially, the increasingly complex and differentiated social coordinations that children achieve in prosocial and antisocial behavior, conflict resolution, and group relations. One question that has preoccupied many investigators is the extent to which peer relations (including friendship experience) are developmental necessities. Deprivation and satiation experiments conducted with nonhuman primates suggest that, indeed, adult adaptation depends on childhood opportunities to interact with other youngsters. Studies of our own species are consistent with these animal models but, in themselves, cannot demonstrate that peer experience is necessary to becoming human. Friendship experience, too, appears to be a developmental advantage for children, but outcomes vary according to whether one has friends, who one's friends are, and friendship quality.

Researchers have come a long way toward demonstrating that children's relations with other children cannot be ignored in developmental science. Children's successes and failures in getting along with one another can no longer be regarded merely as interesting sidelights in the life course but as experiences through which earlier adaptations are linked to later ones in adolescence, adulthood, and old age. Children's lives, however, vary enormously in the circumstances under which peer experience occurs; many different pathways lead from infancy to adaptational success (or failure) in later life. Temperamental vicissitudes, parent–child relationships, sibling relationships, and peer relations are believed to combine in many different ways to affect adult lifestyles. Major "types" among these pathways have not yet been identified, but they need to be. Better understanding of relationship dynamics needs to be achieved, including adversarial relationships (bully–victim relationships and enemies) as well as friendships. Cultural and subcultural variations are virtually uncharted. Considering the relative sophistication of current research methods, however, the end-of-the-century agenda is as feasible as it is formidable.

☐ References

Asher, S. R., Parkhurst, J. T., Hymel, S., & Williams, G. A. (1990). Peer rejection and loneliness in childhood. In S. R. Asher & J. D. Coie (Eds.), *Peer rejection in childhood* (pp. 253–273). Cambridge, UK: Cambridge University Press.

Bagwell, C. L., Newcomb, A. F., & Bukowski, W. M. (1998). Preadolescent friendship and peer rejection as predictors of adult adjustment. *Child Development, 69,* 140–153.

Ball, S. J. (1981). *Beachside comprehensive.* Cambridge, UK: Cambridge University Press.

Bell, R. Q. (1968). A reinterpretation of the direction of effects in studies of socialization. *Psychological Review, 75*, 81–95.

Berndt, T. J., & Hawkins, J. A. (1991). *Effects of friendship on adolescents' adjustment to junior high school.* Unpublished manuscript, Purdue University, Department of Psychological Sciences, West Lafayette, IN.

Bigelow, B. J. (1977). Children's friendship expectations: A cognitive developmental study. *Child Development, 48*, 246–253.

Bühler, C. (1930). *The first year of life.* New York: John Day.

Challman, R. C. (1932). Factors influencing friendships among preschool children. *Child Development, 3*, 146–158.

Charlesworth, R., & Hartup, W. W. (1967). Positive reinforcement in the nursery school peer group. *Child Development, 38*, 993–1002.

Cillessen, A. H. N., Van Ijzendoorn, H. W., Van Lieshout, C. F. M., & Hartup, W. W. (1992). Heterogeneity among peer-rejected boys: Subtypes and stabilities. *Child Development, 63*, 893–905.

Coie, J. D., & Dodge, K. A. (1997). *Aggression and antisocial behavior.* In W. Damon (Series Ed.) & N. Eisenberg (Vol. Ed.), *Handbook of child psychology, Vol. 3, Social, emotional, and personality development* (pp. 779–862). New York: Wiley.

Coie, J. D., Dodge, K. A., & Kupersmidt, J. (1990). Peer group behavior and social status. In S. R. Asher & J. D. Coie (Eds.), *Peer rejection in childhood* (pp. 17–59). Cambridge, UK: Cambridge University Press.

Coie, J. D., Terry, R., Lenox, K. Lochman, J. E., & Hyman, C. (1995). Childhood peer rejection and aggression as predictors of stable patterns of adolescent disorder. *Development and Psychopathology, 7*, 697–713.

Cooley, C. H. (1909). *Social organization.* New York: Scribner.

Cowan, G., Drinkard, J., & MacGavin, L. (1984). The effect of target, age, and gender on use of power strategies. *Journal of Personality and Social Psychology, 47*, 1391–1398.

Cowen, E. L., Pederson, A., Babijian, H., Izzo, L. D. & Trost, M. (1973). Long-term follow-up of early detected vulnerable children. *Journal of Consulting an Clinical Psychology, 41*, 438–446.

Crick, N. R. (1996). The role of overt aggression, relational aggression, and prosocial behavior in the prediction of children's future social adjustment. *Child Development, 67*, 2317–2327.

Dishion, T. J. (1990). The peer context of troublesome child and adolescent behavior. In P. Leone (Ed.), *Understanding troubled and troublesome youth* (pp. 128–153). Newbury Park, CA: Sage.

Dishion, T. J., Andrews, D. W., & Crosby, L. (1995). Anti-social boys and their friends in early adolescence: Relationship characteristics, quality, and interactional process. *Child Development, 66*, 139–151.

Dishion, T. J., Patterson, G. R., & Griesler, P. C. (1994). Peer adaptations in the development of antisocial behavior: A confluence model. In L. R. Huesmann (Ed.), *Current perspectives on aggressive behavior* (pp. 61–95). New York: Plenum.

Dollard, J., & Miller, N. E. (1950). *Personality and psychotherapy.* New York: McGraw-Hill.

Dubow, E. F., Tisak, J., Causey, D., Hryshko, A., & Reid, G. (1991). A two-year longitudinal study of stressful life events, social support, and social problem-solving skills: Contributions to children's behavioral and academic adjustment. *Child Development, 62*, 583–599.

Flavell, J. H. (1963). *The developmental psychology of Jean Piaget.* Princeton, NJ: Van Nostrand.

French, D. C., Brownell, C. A., Graziano, W. G., & Hartup, W. W.(1977). Effects of cooperative, competitive, and individualistic sets on performance in children's groups. *Journal of Experimental Child Psychology, 24*, 1–10.

Freud, A., & Dann, S. (1951). An experiment in group upbringing. In R. Eissler, A. Freud, H. Hartman, & E. Kris (Eds.), *The psychoanalytic study of the child* (Vol. 6, pp. 127–163). New York: International Universities Press.

Freud, S. (1933). *New introductory lectures in psychoanalysis.* New York: Norton.

Furman, W., & Buhrmester, D. (1985). Children's perceptions of the personal relationships in their social networks. *Developmental Psychology, 21,* 1016–1024.

Furman, W., Rahe, D. F., & Hartup, W. W. (1979). Rehabilitation of socially-withdrawn preschool children through mixed-age and same-age socialization. *Child Development, 50,* 915–922.

George, T. P., & Hartmann, D. P. (1996). Friendship networks of unpopular, average, and popular children. *Child Development, 67,* 2301–2316.

Goodenough, F. L. (1931). *Anger in young children.* Minneapolis: University of Minnesota Press.

Green, E. H. (1933). Friendships and quarrels among preschool children. *Child Development, 4,* 237–252.

Grotpeter, J. E., & Crick, N. R. (1996). Relational aggression, overt aggression, and friendship. *Child Development, 67,* 2328–2338.

Harlow, H. F. (1969). Age-mate or peer affectional system. In D. S. Lehrman, R. A. Hinde, & E. Shaw (Eds.), *Advances in the study of behavior* (Vol. 2, pp. 333–383). New York: Academic Press.

Hartup, W. W. (1964). Friendship status and the effectiveness of peers as reinforcing agents. *Journal of Experimental Child Psychology, 1,* 154–162.

Hartup, W. W. (1983). Peer relations. In P. H. Mussen (Series Ed.) & E. M. Hetherington (Vol. Ed.), *Handbook of child psychology: Vol. 4. Socialization, personality, and social development* (pp. 103–196). New York: Wiley.

Hartup, W. W. (1996). The company they keep: Friendships and their developmental significance. *Child Development, 67,* 1–13.

Hartup, W. W., Glazer, J., & Charlesworth, R. (1967). Peer reinforcement and sociometric status. *Child Development, 38,* 1017–1024.

Hartup, W. W., & Stevens, N. (1997). Friendships and adaptation in the life course. *Psychological Bulletin, 119,* 355–370.

Haselager, G. J. T., Hartup, W. W., Van Lieshout, C. F. M., & Riksen-Walraven, M. (1998). Similarities between friends and nonfriends in middle childhood. *Child Development, 69,* 1198–1208.

Heckhausen, J. (1987). Balancing for weaknesses and challenging developmental potential: A longitudinal study of mother-infant dyads in apprenticeship interactions. *Developmental Psychology, 23,* 762–770.

Hetherington, E. M. (1999). Social capital and the development of youth from nondivorced, divorced, and remarried families. In W. A. Collins & B. Laursen (Eds.), *Relationships as developmental contexts: Minnesota Symposia on Child Psychology* (Vol. 30, pp. 177–209). Mahwah, NJ: Erlbaum.

Jersild, A. T., & Markey, F. U. (1935). Conflicts between preschool children. *Child Development Monographs No. 21.* New York: Columbia University Press.

Kandel, D. B. (1978). Similarity in real-life adolescent friendship pairs. *Journal of Personality and Social Psychology, 36,* 306–312.

Kandel, D. B., & Andrews, K. (1987). Processes of adolescent socialization by parents and peers. *International Journal of the Addictions, 22,* 319–342.

Kurdek, L. A., & Sinclair, R. J. (1988). Adjustment of young adolescents in two-parent nuclear, stepfather, and mother-custody families. *Journal of Consulting and Clinical Psychology, 56,* 91–96.

Ladd, G. W. (1990). Having friends, keeping friends, making friends, and being liked by peers in the classroom: Predictors of children's early school adjustment? *Child Development, 61*, 1081–1100.

Lewin, K., Lippitt, R., & White, R. K. (1938). Patterns of aggressive behavior in experimentally created "social climates." *Journal of Social Psychology, 10*, 271–299.

Loeber, R., Wung, P., Keenan, K., Giroux, B., Stouthamer-Loeber, M., Van Kammen, W., B., & Maughan, B. (1993). Developmental pathways in disruptive child behavior. *Development and Psychopathology, 5*, 103–133.

Maccoby, E. E. (1992). The role of parents in the socialization of children: An historical overview. *Developmental Psychology, 28*, 1006–1017.

Mead, G. H. (1934). *Mind and society*. Chicago: University of Chicago Press.

Moffitt, T. E. (1993). Adolescence-limited and life-course-persistent antisocial behavior: A developmental taxonomy. *Psychological Review, 100*, 674–701.

Monroe, W. S. (1898). Social consciousness in children. *Psychological Review, 5*, 68–70.

Moreno, J. L. (1934). *Who shall survive?* Washington, DC: Nervous and Mental Disease Publishing Company.

Mulvey, E. P., & Aber, M. S. (1988). Growing out of delinquency: Development and desistance. In R. Jenkins & W. Brown (Eds.), *The abandonment of delinquent behavior: Promoting the turn-around*. New York: Prager.

Murphy, L. B. (1937). *Social behavior and child personality*. New York: Columbia University Press.

Neemann, J., Hubbard, J., & Masten, A. (1995). The changing importance of romantic relationship involvement to competence from late childhood to late adolescence. *Development and Psychopathology, 7*, 727–750.

Newcomb, A. F., & Bagwell, C. (1995). Children's friendship relations: A meta-analytic review. *Psychological Bulletin, 117*, 306–347.

Parker, J. G., & Asher, S. R. (1987). Peer relations and later personal adjustment: Are low-accepted children at risk? *Psychological Bulletin, 102*, 357–389.

Parker, J. G., Rubin, K. H., Price, J., & DeRozier, M. E. (1995). Peer relationships, child development, and adjustment: A developmental psychopathology perspective. In D. Cicchetti & D. Cohen (Eds.), *Developmental psychopathology, Vol. 2, Risk, disorder, and adaptation* (pp. 96–161). New York: Wiley.

Parten, M. B. (1932–1933). Social participation among preschool children. *Journal of Abnormal and Social Psychology, 27*, 243–269.

Peery, J. C. (1979). Popular, amiable, isolated, rejected: A reconceptualization of sociometric status in preschool children. *Child Development, 50*, 1231–1234.

Piaget, J. (1932). *The moral judgment of the child*. Glencoe, IL: Free Press.

Renshaw, P. D. (1981). The roots of peer interaction research: A historical analysis of the 1930s. In S. R. Asher & J. M. Gottman (Eds.), *The development of children's friendships* (pp. 1–25). Cambridge: Cambridge University Press.

Rheingold, H. L. (1969). The social and socializing infant. In D. A. Goslin (Ed.), *Handbook of socialization theory and research* (pp. 779–790). Chicago: Rand McNally.

Roff, M. (1961). Child social interactions and adult bad conduct. *Journal of Abnormal and Social Psychology, 63*, 333–337.

Rook, K. S. (1984). The negative side of social interaction: Impact on psychological well-being. *Journal of Personality and Social Psychology, 46*, 1097–1108.

Rubin, K. H., Bukowski, W. M., & Parker, J. G. (1997). Peer interactions, relationships, and groups. In W. Damon (Series Ed.) & N. Eisenberg (Vol. Ed.), *Handbook of child psychology, Vol. 3, Social, emotional, and personality development* (pp. 619–700). New York: Wiley.

Rubin, K. H., LeMare, L. J., & Lollis, S. (1990). Social withdrawal in childhood: Developmental pathways to peer rejection. In S. R. Asher & J. D. Coie (Eds.), *Peer rejection in childhood* (pp. 217–249).Cambridge, UK: Cambridge University Press.

Rubin, K. H., Watson, K., & Jambor, T. (1978). Free play behaviors in preschool and kindergarten children. *Child Development, 49,* 534–536.

Sherif, M., Harvey, O. J., White, B. J., Hood, W. R., & Sherif, C. W. (1961). *Intergroup conflict and cooperation: The Robbers Cave experiment.* Norman, OK: The University Book Exchange.

Shulman, S. (1993). Close friendships in early and middle adolescence: Typology and friendship reasoning. In B. Laursen (Ed.), *Close friendships in adolescence* (pp. 55–72). San Francisco: Jossey-Bass.

Simmons, R. G., Burgeson, R., & Reef, M. J. (1988). Cumulative change at entry to adolescence. In M. Gunnar & W. A. Collins (Eds.), *Development during the transition to adolescence: Minnesota Symposia on Child Psychology* (Vol. 21, pp. 123–150). Hillsdale, NJ: Erlbaum.

Sroufe, L. A., & Egeland, B., & Carlson, E. (1999). One social world: The integrated development of parent-child and peer relationships. In W. A. Collins & B. Laursen (Eds.), *Relationships as developmental contexts: Minnesota Symposia on Child Psychology* (Vol. 30, pp. 241–261). Mahwah, NJ: Erlbaum.

Sullivan, H. S. (1953). *The interpersonal theory of psychiatry.* New York: Norton.

Suomi, S. J., & Harlow, H. F. (1972). Social rehabilitation of isolate-reared monkeys. *Developmental Psychology, 6,* 487–496.

Thrasher, F. M. (1927). *The gang.* Chicago: University of Chicago Press.

Tripplett, N. (1897). The dynamogenic factors in pacemaking and competition. *American Journal of Psychology, 9,* 507–533.

Watson, J. B. (1913). Psychology as the behaviorist views it. *Psychological Review, 20,* 158–177.

Windle, M. (1994). A study of friendship characteristics and problem behaviors among middle adolescents. *Child Development, 65,* 1764–1777.

Zeman, J., & Garber, J. (1996). Display rules for anger, sadness, and pain: It depends on who's watching. *Child Development, 67,* 957–973.

Zigler, E. (1970). Review of research on social class and the socialization process. *Review of Educational Research, 40,* 87–110.

R. Peter Hobson

Developmental Psychopathology: Revolution and Reformation

☐ Introduction

...what was believed in as the most reliable—
And therefore the fittest for renunciation.

T. S. Eliot, *Four Quartets*

If developmental psychology is the most challenging of humanistic disciplines, then developmental psychopathology may yet prove to be the most revolutionary. In this brief essay, I shall try to say why.

Perhaps it has always been the case that those who have reflected on the nature and growth of the human mind have speculated on whether to address or ignore abnormal conditions or less-than-rational states of mind such as dreams. When we take a specifically developmental orientation to psychological functioning, the challenge is to see whether we can locate the sources of "abnormal conditions" in unusual factors that distort the typical pathways of human development. Although this may seem rather obvious, it is only recently that clinicians working in the field of mental disorder have become accustomed to adopting a developmental perspective on the conditions they identify and treat.

One source of insight into human psychopathology, then, has been to measure abnormal developmental trajectories against the yardstick of what we observe in the "normal" case. From a complementary perspective, and it is here that developmental psychopathology has revolutionary potential, one may come to view typical development in a quite different way when one seeks to encompass phenomena from the atypical and normal case within a single theoretical framework. The fact is that we can overlook pivotal features of normal development simply because they are so familiar to us. In the abnormal case, these features may stand out and demand attention. When this happens, we have either to modify our account of typical development in order to accommodate the newly recognized phenomena, or we have to specify how these phenomena arise as deviations from the normal case and then give an account of the developmental repercussions that ensue.

If I were to try to cover the field of developmental psychopathology, and take up how we are redefining the place of genetics or neuropsychology or systems theory or culture in our developmental theory, then I would need to assemble a veritable catalogue of facts and references. Such material may be sought in invaluable overviews that are available elsewhere (e.g., Cicchetti & Cohen, 1995; Lewis & Miller, 1990; and in the pages of the journal *Development and Psychopathology*, edited by Cichetti and Nurcombe). I shall select just a few issues and studies to illustrate both the achievements and future potential of this approach to the study of psychology.

☐ Development and Psychopathology

As far as I recall, my training as a psychiatrist at the Maudsley Hospital included little emphasis on the developmental approach to understanding mental disorder. There were two exceptions to this: one was in the area of child psychiatry, naturally enough (especially because the training in child psychiatry was shaped by a champion of developmental psychopathology, Michael Rutter), and the other was in the field of psychodynamic psychotherapy. In fact it was rather curious that in general adult psychiatry we were taught to conduct systematic interviews that included questions about a patient's early life, but when it came to presenting a psychiatric formulation, there seemed to be little scope to integrate what was gleaned from such questions with the really important matter in hand, mostly, a detailed analysis of the patient's phenomenology. I think it is one of the achievements of developmental psychopathology that this situation is changing. Increasingly, the developmental perspective is becoming integral to our understanding not just of child psychiatric disorders but also of all mental illness.

What difference does this make? To consider schizophrenia as a neurodevelopmental disorder, or personality disorders as "relational disorders" for which early experiences are amongst critical predisposing factors, or depression as the outcome of multiple interacting biological and experiential factors such as early and recent losses, is to set the current psychopathological picture in the context of the lifetime of the person and his or her nervous system. Not only do we gain a fresh view of the pathogenesis of these conditions, but also we are in a position to identify risk and protective factors that become targets for intervention. As Rutter (1996) has argued eloquently, it is no longer tenable for psychiatrists to employ outdated disease concepts that have assumed single causes operating in a direct, one-step fashion. By tracing the origins of disorders with an overt onset in adult life, and by determining the adult outcome of child psychopathology, one comes not only to appreciate the vital importance of adopting a life-span perspective, but also to discover where there is underlying coherence in psychological continuity despite variation in presenting features, for example, where neurodevelopmental impairments and social malfunction in childhood lead to the psychotic manifestations of schizophrenia in adult life.

Perhaps it is worth adding that one cannot *presume* that a developmental perspective is important for understanding a given psychopathological disorder. What is exciting is the attempt to establish whether or not it is and, if it is, in what way.

So, too, one cannot presume whether cases of psychopathology such as eating disorders or depression or conduct disorder represent extremes of the normal continuum, or something qualitatively different: one has to find out. Developmental psychopathology has been a major source of ideas about how to do so. For example, Rende and Plomin (1990) discuss how quantitative genetic research can elucidate etiological factors in psychopathology and breaks between the normal and abnormal. If quantitative dimensional data are obtained on individuals with psychological abnormality, their relatives, and the population, it is possible to assess the extent to which the genetic and environmental causes of abnormality differ from those of variation in the normal population. For example, siblings of mildly retarded individuals are below average in IQ, and the familial resemblance is much the same as in the normal population; but the siblings of severely retarded individuals have IQ scores in the normal range, so the condition appears to be etiologically distinct. As in longitudinal approaches to developmental and behavioral continuities and discontinuites, the search for underlying mechanisms of disorder can change our very definitions of diagnostic categories.

Although it is extremely valuable to apply the principles of developmental psychopathology to psychiatric conditions considered one by one (e.g., Rutter & Garmezy, 1983), I shall be taking a complementary approach by emphasizing another direction of influence: the impact of the study of psychopathology on our theories in developmental psychology. I recall Neil O'Connor, a pioneer in the field, describing to me how in the early days of his collaborative work with Beate Hermelin, psychology conference audiences would evaporate when they realized that the subject matter of a presentation was something so peripheral to their interests as mental retardation or autism. Now the situation is very different, not least because of the influence of these two researchers and their erstwhile students. Why the change?

There are many reasons. We have become aware of the ways that genetic factors influence developmental change and continuity and the shaping and selection of environments, as well as individual differences in susceptibility to environmental risks. We find from longitudinal research just how far individuals may change over time—not least, how they can move between pathological and nonpathological forms of functioning (Cicchetti, 1993)—and how we need to explain stability as well as change. Studies in developmental psychopathology have highlighted dimensional risk factors that bear upon individual differences in the normal as well as abnormal range of variation. Just as disordered patterns of behavior are illuminated by considering usual patterns of adaptation in relation to the developmental issues of a given period (Sroufe & Rutter, 1984; so that for example childhood affective disturbances predict adult depression only in the context of other indices of adaptational failure such as poor peer relations and conduct disturbances) so too developmental pathways are only fully defined by considering *both* the normal and abnormal outcomes. As Sroufe (1990) has argued, one cannot demonstrate the critical importance of any developmental issue without examining its consequences, nor delimit the range of normal adaptive patterns without demarcation of the pathological.

I shall leave it to the reader to remember that I have indicated the enormous potential of "biological" research in developmental psychopathology (for which see, for example, Lenzenweger & Haugaard, 1996), as I now focus on four issues.

The first is the potential for developmental psychopathology to broaden the scope of our theories, and in so doing, transform how we think about development. *If* one decides that psychopathological phenomena of one sort or another are not beyond the pale of normal developmental psychology, then in order to encompass such phenomena in our theories, we may find that some of our most cherished beliefs are indeed the fittest for renunciation. Not surprisingly, the threat of this generates much controversy. By way of illustration, in what follows I shall consider psychoanalytic approaches to development.

My second point will be that when methodologies from mainstream developmental psychology are applied to abnormal conditions, the effect may be to draw the latter into a "normal" developmental framework, and at the same time, to enrich our interpretation of what those methodologies yield for understanding development. Here I shall consider the case of attachment research.

The third point will be that the study of psychopathological conditions enables us to pursue empirical investigations in areas that are otherwise largely inaccessible. In particular, one can see how particular psychological abilities and disabilities that usually develop in tandem may become dissociated from one another in the abnormal case. This affords an invaluable perspective on the structuring of the mind, both at a given point in time and as development unfolds. We find out which abilities seem to depend on which other developmental achievements. It is almost like finding psychological nature carved at its joints. My example here will be that of early childhood autism.

The final point is related to and arises out of the other three. Studies in developmental psychopathology may bear upon our choice among theories in developmental psychology, especially what one might call higher-level theories that represent alternative approaches to understanding the processes that underpin development (constructivism, contextualism, etc.). I shall illustrate what I mean in a concluding section on the reformation of developmental psychology.

Revolutionary Potential

I am going to begin with perhaps the most controversial examples of all. These are taken from what I see as a (but not *the*) once and future core component of developmental psychopathology, that of psychoanalysis. Part of my justification for this choice is that Freud's work is a dazzling exemplification of the principles of developmental psychopathology. Despite this, there is a well-entrenched tendency to acknowledge Freud's inspiration but then to sideline the contribution of psychoanalysis as unscientific and therefore unworthy of serious consideration. This is not a stance that passes unchallenged, however, and there is a growing body of work that attempts to achieve a synthesis or accommodation between certain psychoanalytic concepts and those of academic developmental psychology (e.g., Bretherton, 1998; Carlson & Sroufe, 1995; Fonagy, 1995; Hobson, 1997; Main, 1995; Stern, 1985; Steele & Steele, 1998). In the present context, I shall take two examples of psychoanalytic thinking to illustrate how these could revolutionize not only what we consider to be normal and abnormal, but also how we think development proceeds.

Consider two of Freud's proposals about sexuality. First, he discerned in patients' clinical presentation that sexuality involves much more than sex. Not only can sexual excitement arise from and be associated with other bodily zones and activities than those involving the genitals, an observation that is startling for its obviousness and one that assumes significance only in a developmental perspective, but also the seemingly bizarre psychopathological phenomena of perversions such as fetishism may be comprehensible in terms of *normal* elements of early sexual life being channeled along abnormal developmental pathways. What results is a view of infants as polymorphously perverse, not in the sense of their having perversions, but in the sense of the fluidity and potential malleability of aspects of psychological functioning that will shape their later sexual conduct. According to this view, the foundations of both normality and abnormality are to be found in the starting state of human sexual life, or, if one prefers, in those components of early experience that will in due course make a telling contribution to adult sexual life. What matters is the developmental trajectory that these components follow.

My second example comes from Kleinian psychoanalytic theory (e.g., Klein, 1946). This posits that early in life, before a "realistic" understanding of the nature of other people has been acquired, infants experience others in a way that is suffused with their own impulses. In particular, the paranoid-schizoid position (which is not truly a stage in development, rather a quality of relatedness to others) is one in which the infant faces a nightmarish, fairytale, black-and-white world in which persecutors are experienced as split from idealized figures. If and only if the infant receives good-enough parenting in which her anxieties are responded to and contained, then a different kind of relating becomes established in which the infant's basic anxieties are of losing or harming a valued and depended-on figure who is recognized as having a mental life of her own. Once again, the idea is that the elements of abnormal experiences—or, strictly, what will become abnormal experiences later in life—are present in normal infancy, and the appropriate account of development is as much about the integration and transformation of potentially psychopathological states of mind as about the fostering and augmentation of what we consider as normal. The implications for developmental theory are considerable. Not only does one start with a much more elaborated view of the innate building blocks of infant social experience, but also one is led to consider the role of an infant's caregivers in "containing" relatively fragmented mental states and thereby enabling the infant to achieve more integrated functioning.

My purpose is not to argue for the accuracy of either of these accounts, which is anyway an especially complex task for the reason that one is using language in a special way in order to capture what infantile experiences might be like. Rather, I am trying to indicate the radical nature of developmental psychopathology.

Suppose for a moment that the accounts are valid to some degree. Suddenly we find that aspects of human psychology that had largely escaped our theoretical net no longer elude us: all those elements of "normal" adult sexuality that seem both related to and yet different from perverse activities (for example, what lovers do with their mouths) find a place within a single theoretical account, and certain "normal" yet disturbed experiences such as feelings of persecution (think of your dreams) become recognizable as the vestigial aftermath of the turmoils of infancy. At the same time, psychopathological conditions such as perversions and severe personality disorders become comprehensible as developmental disorders. In each case, the depth and breadth of human psychological life encompassed by our developmental theories is greatly extended.

No wonder such theoretical approaches are controversial. And, of course, they may be wrong. Eminent figures as contrasting as Rutter and Stern have expressed dismay that one should wish to build accounts of normal development on the basis of abnormal mental phenomena. The point I am making is that what counts as normal or abnormal depends on your perspective, and that perspective may be altered by the study of developmental psychopathology. The battles still rage over whether Freud hoodwinked us into believing absurd things or whether, as Auden (1966) put it,

> so many long-forgotten objects
> revealed by his undiscouraged shining
> are returned to us and made precious again

Whatever the final verdict, such accounts arise through attention to psychopathological phenomena that are most visible in the abnormal case but are also discernible in normal people, and a belief that through a developmental perspective we can understand their place in human mental life.

I now turn to my second theme, the far-reaching effects of applying methods from development psychology to cases of psychopathology.

Attachments

The study of the development of relationships from an attachment perspective reveals what one needs for a success story in any scientific field: a good theory and some effective ways to measure what the theory addresses. In their introduction to the first book on the *Clinical Implications of Attachment,* Belsky and Nezworski (1988) observed:

> Only a decade ago, students of human development were routinely taught that individual differences in infant functioning in the first year

of life were not predictive of later development. . . A virtual revolution has taken place in our understanding of early human development. (pp. 3–4)

The central idea in attachment theory is that an individual's relationships are underpinned by an attachment motivational system that finds expression in various but related types of behavior that can be organized in different ways. Through the Strange Situation procedure of Ainsworth, Blehar, Waters, and Wall (1978), with its emphasis on the infant's behavior when it reunites with its caregiver after a brief separation, infant–caregiver dyads are classified into the categories of secure, insecure–avoidant, insecure–resistant, or disorganized.

Psychopathological conditions need not have stimulated the thinking that lay behind attachment theory, but it is no coincidence that this was in fact the case. Bowlby conducted his early (1944) study of 44 juvenile thieves because he was interested in seemingly affectionless characters, and ever since the Strange Situation took center stage in the study of attachments, mental health workers have had the explanation of different patterns of child and adult relationships firmly in their sights. Yet it was only after the work of Erickson, Egeland, and Sroufe (1985) and Lewis, Feiring, McGuffog, and Jaskir (1984) pointed to an increased risk for behavior problems in children who as infants had been insecurely attached to their mothers, that researchers came to investigate how early attachments predict not only a range of "normal" social abilities and levels of self-esteem in children, but also conditions that extend beyond the normal range into psychopathology (e.g., contributions to Atkinson & Zucker, 1997).

Over the last decade, research in this area has been propelled forward by the introduction of the Adult Attachment Interview (AAI) of George, Kaplan, and Main (1985). These investigators invited parents who had been tested with their infants on the Strange Situation five years earlier to reflect on aspects of their own childhood relationships with caregivers. What they found was that in correspondence with the attachment classification of the mother–infant dyads, mothers could be distinguished by the formal qualities of their discourse.

Transcripts are classified into three major categories: free to evaluate attachments, where individuals talk coherently and objectively about their early relationships; dismissing of attachments; and preoccupied (or enmeshed) in attitudes toward attachment, where the influence of parents or attachment-related experiences can neither be coherently described nor dismissed, and where such relationships seem to preoccupy attention. In addition, individuals may be "unresolved/disorganized/

disoriented" with respect to loss and trauma if they show lapses in reasoning, unfounded fear or guilt, or irrational thought process when the individual is talking about these issues.

Why is this interview so important? First, it is a measure of "mental representation" that appears to reflect or shape, or both, interpersonal relations. Recall that AAI categories were originally derived from a study of mothers whose attachment classifications with their own infants were the independent measure. There is now evidence that evaluations of AAI transcripts of mothers *antenatally* can predict mother–infant Strange Situation attachment classifications at the end of the first year of the infant's life (Fonagy, Steele, & Steele, 1991). It seems reasonable to suppose that the index of mental representation was related to the mother's behavior with her infant, which in turn determined the separation–reunion reactions.

What, then, might the AAI reveal about psychopathology? Consider individuals with borderline personality disorder, who amongst other things show marked instability in their interpersonal relations with initial clinging followed by devaluation, as well as abrupt swings in mood. I and my colleagues (Patrick, Hobson, Castle, Howard, & Maughm, 1994) identified one group of women with the diagnosis of borderline personality disorder and another with chronic depression. The two groups were similar in age, intellectual history, socioeconomic status, and current mood state. When administered the AAI, it turned out that all 12 of the borderline patients, but only 4 out of 12 depressed patients, were classified as preoccupied. Of the borderline patients, 10 out of 12 fell into one particular preoccupied category, appearing "confused, fearful and overwhelmed" in relation to past experiences with attachment figures. Not one depressed patient was classified in this way. There were also significantly more borderline individuals classified as "unresolved" in relation to trauma and loss. All 9 out of the 9 borderline patients who reported trauma or loss had failed to assimilate these difficult experiences, whereas only 2 of the 10 depressed patients who had reported similar events were classed as unresolved.

So specific patterns of disturbed relationships were found to correspond with specific difficulties in *thinking about* early relationships. According to psychoanalytic thinking, failures in emotional containment or emotional sensitivity in early infancy may lead to these kinds of disruption in the capacity to think about the contents of one's own mind (see also Fonagy et al., 1995). It is especially noteworthy that "unresolved" status in mothers is associated with the very kind of disorganized (D) behavior in their infants that is being linked with subsequent psychopathology (e.g., Lyons-Ruth, Alpern, & Repacholi, 1993). What is now accessible is a truly life-span and transgenerational developmental picture relating maternal psychopathology to syles of mental representation *and* patterns of mother–infant relatedness, which in turn can be studied with reference to the infant's own ways of coping with interpersonal stress and eventually to possible psychopathology and mental representation in the infant–grown-up.

Moreover, this area of study returns us full circle to the issue of how much our theories of development may need to encompass. The reason is that borderline conditions are *also* characterized by the person's proneness to psychoticlike experiences such as states of intense and unfounded persecution or ideas of reference, and it is not unusual for them to receive a diagnosis of schizophreniform illness. Moreover, they often include perverse sexual inclinations. So, how abnormal is abnormal? Perhaps even some psychoticlike and perverse states are the developmental outcome of failures of the kinds of interpersonal provision that in the normal case contains and integrates such experiences.

My next topic is how the study of an abnormal condition—in this case, early childhood autism—enables us to study the structure of the developing mind in ways that are otherwise impossible.

Autism

Childhood autism is a cause celebre of developmental psychopathology.

Autism is a syndrome. It is not a "condition" such as, say, tuberculosis, with a defined medical cause and underlying physical pathology. A syndrome is a constellation of clinical features that tend to occur together. It was first described by the American child psychiatrist Kanner in 1943, who gave a detailed clinical account of 11 cases of children with a characteristic set of abnormalities that include profound impairment in interpersonal relations, restrictions in imaginative play, delays and oddities of language, and a variety of additional features such as rituals and stereotypies. Why do these particular abnormalities cluster together?

Associations Among Impairments

It *could* be that this syndrome has relatively circumscribed interest for the developmental psychologist. For example, suppose it were discovered that almost all of the clinical features of the disorder were the behavioral expression of physical damage to or dysfunction of a particularly vital part of the brain that normally subserves nonverbal communication, imagination, language, and flexible thinking, but also a part of the brain that is *not* needed for those aspects of psychological functioning such as jigsaw-type skills that are relatively spared in autism. If this were the case, then we should have learned a lot about neuropsychology, but not very much from a specifically developmental point of view, beyond some insights into children's ways of adjusting to these severe handicaps.

In fact, however, no such part of the brain appears to exist. True, there is much jostling among neuropsychologically inclined investigators to identify the part or parts of the brain that are not working properly in individuals with autism, and although it is striking and probably telling that there is very little agreement in this respect, the endeavor is all to the good. What is being sought is a dysfunction that through cascading psychological-cum-neurological effects *over the course of early development* eventuates in the familiar features of the syndrome. In other words, largely because of the failure of alternative approaches, we have arrived at the view that *only* by identifying either one or several abnormalities that are "basic" to autism and accounting for the other features of the disorder with reference to the developmental sequelae of those abnormalities shall we arrive at a satisfactory theory of autism. This approach requires that we draw on, or if necessary evolve, an adequate account of normal early development.

So now the challenge is to delineate what is basic to what in autism and then to explain the developmental links in the story. Is the basic abnormality some essentially linguistic ability that leads to disruption in the other areas of psychological function? This view was once prevalent, but it no longer seems adequate except in a partial and modified form (e.g., Goodman, 1989). Is the basic abnormality a cognitive deficit, such as one in the computation of particular forms of mental representation (e.g., Leslie, 1987)? If so, then whatever cognitive ability is lacking may be of great significance for our understanding of the developmental bases of normal interpersonal relations and imaginative thought. Should we instead focus upon the executive function deficits in autism, the ways in which affected individuals seem limited in their ability to inhibit prepotent responses to a situation, and relatively poor at thinking and acting flexibly in relation to changing contexts (e.g., the contributions to Russell, 1997)? Or might we even return to Kanner's original formulation of autism as a biologically based impairment in the children's affective contact with other people, and explain much else about the syndrome as the developmental outcome of a disorder in the intersubjective patterning of social relations (Hobson, 1993)?

Obviously I do not have space to deal with each of these possibilities. I shall try to illustrate how they represent fundamentally different ways of conceptualizing normal as well as abnormal development, by dwelling on what is probably the most renowned topic in contemporary developmental psychology—the origins and early development of theory of mind. The reason for considering the issue at this point is that theory of mind abilities may provide a fulcrum for understanding the constellation of abnormalities in autism.

A groundbreaking study was conducted by Baron-Cohen, Leslie, and Frith (1985) titled: "Does the autistic child have a 'theory of mind'?" These investigators employed a task originally devised by Wimmer and Perner (1983). There was a basket in front of a doll called Sally and a box in front of a doll called Anne. Sally first placed a marble into her basket. Then she left the scene, and while she was away Anne transferred the marble from Sally's basket into her own box, where it was hidden from view. When Sally returned, the experimenter asked the critical "belief question": "Where will Sally look for her marble?" Only 4 out of 20 autistic children, but the majority of the children with Down's syndrome and normal children who were generally lower in mental age than the autistic group, demonstrated their understanding that their own knowledge of where the marble really was differed from the "incorrect" belief held by the doll.

Since this study there has been an industry in administering theory of mind tasks to people with autism (see contributions to Baron-Cohen, Tager-Flusberg, & Cohen, 1993). It appears that in a number of related abilities such as understanding the distinction between appearance and reality, or recognizing the "mental" functions of the brain, children with autism show relatively specific deficits.

Now suppose that for whatever reason children with autism fail to acquire a sophisticated understanding of the mind. The possibility arises that the associations among the *ab*normalities in autism point to something about a very important association among developing *abilities* in normal young children and, in particular, between early understanding of minds and the emergence of creative symbolic play and context-sensitive language around the middle of the second year of life. This is exactly what Leslie (1987) suggested. He proposed that toward the end of infancy, through the operation of an innately determined *decoupling mechanism*, children acquire the ability to represent not only the world, but also these representations themselves: it is as if children are quoting someone else, lifting out the representation, without committing themselves to the truth of whatever the person said or thought. The block of wood "is" a car, the doll "can" speak, and so on. In this way, they acquire the ability to engage in pretend symbolic play. Leslie complemented this account with the hypothesis that autistic children have an absence or malfunction of the decoupling mechanism and are thereby impaired in forming metarepresentations and show deficits in symbolic play and in theory of mind abilities.

It is here that we see how a fundamentally different kind of theory can be applied to the same set of phenomena. Perhaps the "decoupling mechanism" is what we should explain, not merely describe. Let me make an attempt. When toward the end of the first year of life infants begin to identify with the attitudes of *someone else* as these are directed toward a shared world, they are lifted out of an immediate, egocentric, unreflective, "concrete" apprehension of the environment. They are now in a position to recognize that the same things can be the objects of different attitudes, and that therefore things are different from thoughts, and with this realization they become able to "represent" attitudes. As a result, the child can knowingly confer novel attitudes (thoughts) onto familiar things in symbolic play and can appreciate how she herself as well as others can capture and intentionally convey attitudes and thoughts in language.

If developmental psychopathology has motivated these theories of normal as well as atypical development, then can it also provide evidence to help decide between them?

One principle of developmental psychopathology is that it is worthwhile to explore whether several conditions might illuminate one other. So, for example, congenitally blind children cannot see how other people's attitudes are *directed* at a world that is also the world experienced by the child herself. This, too, might handicap a child in relating to someone else's relation to the world and in coming to represent attitudes. On the other hand, there is no reason to think a supposedly innate decoupling mechanism would be inoperative in blind children.

Colleagues and I have now conducted systematic observations on 24 congenitally blind children between the ages of 3 and 9 years of age and have found that no fewer than 10 of the children satisfied the standard diagnostic criteria for autism (Brown, Hobson, Lee, & Stevenson, 1997). In addition, the upper-ability children who were mostly not autistic differed from matched sighted children in their relations to people, verbal and nonverbal communication, interactive play, and immediate echolalia. Now why should blind children without coincident neurological disorder be echolalic, if not because, like sighted children with autism, they adopt phrases wholesale rather than adjusting the form of language in relation to the speech roles of speaker and listener? Moreover in a separate study with nonautistic able blind children over the age of 4 years (Minter, Hobson, & Bishop, 1998), we found that over half the blind children but very few of the sighted children failed in at least one part of a modified theory of mind task involving a teapot unexpectedly found to contain sand. This evidence tips the balance toward a social–developmental account of "decoupling."

If associations among features of psychopathology provide one route to new developmental theory, then dissociations open up another.

Dissociations Among Abilities and Impairments

What I want to illustrate is how, when we consider dissociations among impairments in autism, one set of observations leads to another, until we arrive at a quite different view of our starting point and at a new vision of the cascading effects of abnormalities over the course of early development.

Let us begin with cognitive development, narrowly conceived. When the effects of general mental retardation are taken into account, even quite young autistic children are relatively unimpaired in such abilities as visuo-spatial pattern recognition, the understanding of means–ends relations, and the awareness of the permanence of objects. On the other hand, in clinical descriptions such as the classic case history of the idiot savant "L" described by Scheerer, Rothmann, and Goldstein (1945), as well as in profiles of performance in IQ tests, one may observe that even the verbally fluent autistic individual may have difficulties in defining objects, in locating absurdities, in understanding metaphor, and in wresting himself from a fixed and rigid point of view.

Now the focus shifts to language itself. Some children with autism are surprisingly adept at aspects of syntax, semantics, and grammar, even though they may show more restricted uses of the grammatical structures they have available (Tager-Flusberg, 1989). It seems that it is especially in the adjustment of speech to the social context of language, that is, in the pragmatics of language use, that people with autism are abnormal (e.g., "What did you have for dinner?" "Meat and cabbage and potatoes and gravy and salt and jam tart and custard and orange juice and cup of tea"; Ricks & Wing, 1975).

Thus we move on to the broader topic of communication. What dissociations occur here? In a seminal study, Wetherby and Prutting (1984) reported how autistic children used a high proportion of communicative acts that led to an environmental consequence that satisfied a physical want or need such as requesting objects, requesting actions, and protesting. On the other hand, there were few communications that fully acknowledged the other person and drew attention to the children themselves, few that involved requests for information and permission, and few that commented on objects for the adult through pointing, describing, and so on. Subsequent systematic research (summarized in Mundy, Sigman, & Kasari, 1993) has confirmed that there appears to be a dissociation between the ability both to use and to recognize gestures of requesting from those involved in achieving "joint attention" such as pointing and showing, and the development of language and play may be associated with the development of the latter abilities (e.g., Mundy, Sigman, & Kasari, 1990).

This carries us further to consider the forms of interpersonal relatedness that are present or absent (or limited) in people with autism. There may be *specific* forms of interpersonal engagement that are relatively lacking, and these may prove to be the developmental source of at least some of the abnormalities in communication, language, and thought already outlined.

Consider the following study of how individuals with autism perceive (and therefore stand in relation to) other people. Moore, Hobson, and Lee (1997) presented autistic children with brief videotaped sequences of a moving person visible only as points of light emanating from reflective patches attached to the person's limbs and body. For example the point-light person enacted emotional gestures, as when a "sad" person walked forward slowly, sighed, sat down on a chair limply, lifted his hands slowly, and put his head in his hands. Subjects were asked to say what was happening. Ten out of 13 autistic subjects, but only 1 out of 13 nonautistic individuals, *failed* to refer to emotional states (whether correctly or incorrectly) on all 5 presentations of basic emotions. Typical responses for autistic participants were "walking and sitting down on a chair" for sad, and "standing up and moving backward" for scared. Unlike control subjects, they remarked on the actions, but not the attitudes, of the point-light person. In a further task, there was *not* a significant difference between autistic and nonautistic subjects on naming actions when specifically asked to do so, but the autistic subjects achieved significantly lower scores on a task involving judgments of emotion-related states.

The findings are relevant for accounts of autistic individuals' impairments in understanding as well as perceiving "persons" as beings with their own subjective psychological orientations (e.g., Hobson, 1993). Autistic children's relative failure to attend to and identify with such attitudes is likely to have far-reaching consequences for their capacity to adopt the attitudes of other people, and thereby to distance themselves from their own "egocentric" attitudes to the world, which takes us right back to the beginning of this section and the nature of the cognitive and linguistic abilities that are abnormal or spared in autism. Many of the abilities that are spared do not require such distancing. It seems that there are dissociable *pathways* to different aspects of cognitive and language functioning. The study of autism is mapping these pathways.

☐ The Reformation of Developmental Psychology

If developmental psychopathology is so revolutionary for perspectives on the human mind, what will our reformed developmental psychology look like? Here I shall not try to be even-handed in approach, keeping the possibilities abstract and all the options open. I shall simply say what I think is going to happen.

First, we shall see more clearly how and why early interpersonal relations are central to the development of thought and are frequently important in explaining individual differences in thinking. We shall also continue to clarify how interpersonal relations are formative for one's relations with oneself, including one's self-reflective awareness, self-control, and self-punitiveness. Of course, the debate about the relative contributions of individual and social influences in early psychological development is long-running, and encompasses disagreements about the very processes of change. Was Vygotsky correct in suggesting that the higher cognitive functions emerge from the interiorization of interpersonal processes, or do we need an account more like that of Piaget or some computationalists who want to account for development in more individualistic terms? Were Werner and Kaplan (1984) correct in supposing that symbolic function was the outcome of "distancing" among symbolizer, symbols, and their referents, but, as they remarked (italics mine), "There is little direct information about the stages, *in the normally developing child,* of this emergence of objects and symbols from the interpersonal matrix" (p. 71).

I think that developmental psychopathology is yielding answers to these questions. Individual differences in interpersonal relations, personality, and thinking in certain psychopathological conditions allow for examination of the nature of those differences, so that the separable processes that go into the development of thinking or personality can be delineated. In addition, one can observe just what is or is not "interiorized" and how this takes place. At the same time, we see the strengths but also the limitations of computational approaches to mental functioning, the strengths having much to do with the explanation of subpersonal cognitive operations and the limitations being that the approaches leave out the critical contribution of the social. Just as psychiatrically defined conditions, such as conduct disorder or psychopathy, will yield to explanation only when interpersonal/psychodynamic factors are accorded greater significance, so investigations of such disorders will provide the impetus for corresponding shifts in theoretical emphasis in general developmental psychology.

The issues go deeper than this, however.

First, there is the matter of how we are to characterize the nature of social relations and their representation in the mind. For example, how far do we need to posit innately configured "dialogic structures" in the mind, whether in psychoanalytic fashion or in terms more familiar to academic psychology (e.g., Fernyhough, 1996; Stern, 1985)? The study of abnormal (e.g., persecuted) states of mind, of psychopathology in relationships, and of autism (perhaps the exception that proves the rule?) is bound to influence the answer to this question. Through applying a creative combination of methods (including those of child psychiatry, experimental child psychology, psychoanalysis, la methode clinique, ethology, genetics, and so on) to normal and abnormal conditions in tandem, we shall arrive at a fresh and deeper view of the origins and development of interpersonal relations.

Second, how are we to theorize about early cognitive development? Does it really make sense to follow the hallowed tradition of separating cognition, conation, and affect, and then to study their interrelationships from early infancy onward? Many people who have thought about infancy have said no, these aspects of mental life are intertwined, but that is not good enough unless one can put some other conceptual distinctions in place of the ones being jettisoned. Once again, the issue pertains to contemporary controversies in cognitive science, and in particular about the nature of "representations" and how these manage to be "about" something and why computers fail to interpret their own symbols and so fail to model human functioning.

What we shall find is that we need to derive a scheme that distinguishes among modes of relatedness between the infant and its social and nonsocial world. The concept of "modes of relatedness" is an organizational construct, just like attachment, and, like the concept of attachment, it cannot be applied to computers! Our developmental account will explain how, out of infant-level modes of relatedness, cognitive abilities emerge in such a way as to become relatively independent of particular occasions of their use. Piaget had an approach such as this, but he focused on actions to the relative neglect of attitudes. Attitudes, which have phenomenology as well as behavioral expressions, are what constitute the psychological linkage between the infant and its world, and the biologically based coordination of attitudes between and across individual people is what lifts the infant out of a kind of embeddedness in its own ways of relating to the world and eventually yields symbolic thought. This is not to say that all forms of thought depend on the social, and autism illustrates how much as well as how little can develop with minimal truly interpersonal exchange (although we still need to define those important aspects of social connectedness that children with autism do experience).

A great deal else follows for our reformed developmental psychology. We shall find that a host of concepts need to be transformed to accommodate the new point of view, to the discomfort of reductionists who are ill at ease with what they see as "vague" notions such as relatedness rather than affect or cognition, or attitudes rather than "behaviors" or feelings. In the social–developmental sphere, we shall think in terms of infants apprehending persons rather than perceiving bodies or representing minds, interiorizing aspects of social and nonsocial experience, and identifying with rather than merely imitating other people. Issues to do with the origins and nature of the self and its development, now set within the broader context of abnormalities of self-experience in abnormal conditions, will lead to a deepening of our view of what it is to be an individual who experiences herself to have a mind of her own.

It is here that we can see how psychology will be impelled to return to its philosophical roots by the thrust of considerations from developmental psychopathology. We shall find that the gaps and weaknesses in our conceptual framework will provide impetus not merely to find out more facts, but also to reconsider the terms in which theory should be framed to make sense of those facts. Such a turn of events is already amounting to a minor revolution in its own right!

Meanwhile, there are all those things I have neglected that need to be brought back into the picture. Surely the future is full of promise that we shall make progress in understanding how different levels of functioning, from the biochemical to the societal, relate one to the other. Happily, we need not be bullied into thinking that "biology" drives "psychology"; as Rutter (1996) asserts, the causal arrows run in both directions. Happily, too, thanks largely to developmental psychopathology, we are being given theoretical license and methodological tools to claim back for scientific study the different paths that *individuals* follow in their lives. On an even more personal but still scientific level, we can reevaluate how far elements of "psychopathology" constitute an inevitable and perhaps even enriching dimension to a "normal" individual's mental life.

In conclusion, these are exciting times for developmental psychology, and this is partly because of the arrival of a new family member who, like many a toddler just finding his feet, threatens to overturn some of the furniture and challenge the status quo. Making room for this newcomer is not going to be easy, and few have realized the revolution and reformation it may entail. What many do accept is that the developmental study of "abnormalities" in psychological functioning is now a mainstream research venture.

☐ **References**

Ainsworth, M. D., Blehar, M., Waters, E., & Wall, S. (1978). *Patterns of attachment.* Hillsdale, NJ: Erlbaum.

Atkinson, L., & Zucker, K. J. (1997). *Attachment and psychopathology.* New York: Guilford.

Auden, W. H. (1966). In memory of Sigmund Freud. In *Collected shorter poems, 1927–1957* (pp. 166–170). London: Faber.

Baron-Cohen, S., Leslie, A. M., & Frith, U. (1985). Does the autistic child have a "theory of mind"? *Cognition, 21,* 37–46.

Baron-Cohen, S., Tager-Flusberg, H., & Cohen, D. J. (1993). *Understanding other minds: Perspectives from autism.* Oxford, UK: Oxford University Press.

Belsky, J., & Nezworski, T. (1988). Clinical implications of attachment. In J. Belsky & T. Nezworski (Eds.), *Clinical implications of attachment* (pp. 3–17). Hillsdale, NJ: Erlbaum.

Bowlby, J. (1944). Forty-four juvenile thieves: Their characters and home-life. *International Journal of Psycho-Analysis, 25,* 19–53.

Bretherton, I. (1998). Attachment and psychoanalysis: A reunion in progress. *Social Development, 7,* 132–136.

Brown, R., Hobson, R. P., Lee, A., & Stevenson, J. (1997). Are there "autistic-like" features in congenitally blind children? *Journal of Child Psychology and Psychiatry, 38,* 693–703.

Carlson, E. A., & Sroufe, L. A. (1995). Contribution of attachment theory to developmental psychopathology. In D. Ciccheti & D. J. Cohen (Eds.), *Developmental psychopathology. Theory and methods* (pp. 581–617). New York: Wiley.

Cicchetti, D. (1993). Developmental psychopathology: Reactions, reflections, projections. *Developmental Review, 13,* 471–502.

Cicchetti, D., & Cohen, D. J. (1995). *Developmental psychopathology.* New York: Wiley.

Erickson, M., Egeland, B., & Sroufe, L. A. (1985). The relationship between quality of attachment and behavior problems in preschool in high risk sample. In I. Bretherton & E. Waters (Eds.), *Growing points in attachment theory and research* (pp. 147–186). *Monographs of the Society for Research in Child Development, 50* (1–2, Serial No. 209).

Fernyhough, C. (1996). The dialogic mind: A dialogic approach to the higher mental functions. *New Ideas in Psychology, 14,* 47–62.

Fonagy, P. (1995). Psychoanalytic and empirical approaches to developmental psychopathology: An object-relations perspective. In T. Shapiro & R. N. Emde (Eds.), *Research in psychoanalysis: Process, development, outcome* (pp. 245–260). Madison, CT: International Universities Press.

Fonagy, P., Steele, H., & Steele, M. (1991). Maternal representations of attachment during pregnancy predict the organisation of infant-mother attachment at one year of age. *Child Development, 62,* 891–905.

Fonagy, P., Steele, M., Steele, H., Leigh, T., Kennedy, R., Mattoon, G., & Target, M. (1995). Attachment, the reflective self, and borderline states. The predictive specificity of the Adult Attachment Interview and pathological emotional development. In S. Goldberg, R. Muir, & J. Keer (Eds.), *Attachment theory. Social, developmental, and clinical perspectives* (pp. 233–278). Hillsdale, NJ: Atlantic Press.

George, C., Kaplan, N., & Main, M. (1985). *The attachment interview for adults.* Unpublished manuscript. University of California, Berkeley.

Goodman, R. (1989). Infantile autism: A syndrome of multiple primary deficits? *Journal of Autism and Developmental Disorders, 19,* 409–424.

Hobson, R. P. (1993). *Autism and the development of mind.* Hove, UK: Erlbaum.

Hobson, R. P. (1997). Psychoanalysis and infancy. In G. Bremner, A. Slater, & G. Butterworth (Eds.), *Infant development: Recent advances* (pp. 275–290). Hove, UK: Psychology Press.

Kanner, L. (1943). Autistic disturbances of affective contact. *Nervous Child, 2,* 217–250.

Klein, M. (1946). Notes on some schizoid mechanisms. *International Journal of Psycho-Analysis, 27,* 99–110.

Lenzenweger, M. F., & Haugaard, J. J. (1996). *Frontiers of developmental psychopathology.* Oxford, UK: Oxford University Press.

Leslie, A. M. (1987). Pretense and representation: The origins of "theory of mind". *Psychological Review, 94,* 412–426.

Lewis, M., Feiring, C., McGuffog, C., & Jaskir, J. (1984). Predicting psychopathology in six-year-olds from early social relations. *Child Development, 55,* 123–136.

Lewis, M., & Miller, S. M. (1990). *Handbook of developmental psychopathology.* New York: Plenum.

Lyons-Ruth, K., Alpern, L., & Repacholi, B. (1993). Disorganized infant attachment classification and maternal psychosocial problems and predictors of hostile-aggressive behavior in the preschool classroom. *Child Development, 64,* 572–585.

Main, M. (1995). Discourse, prediction, and recent studies in attachment: Implications for psychoanalysis. In T. Shapiro & R. N. Emde (Eds.), *Research in psychoanalysis: Process, development, outcome* (pp. 209–244). Madison, CT: International Universities Press.

Minter, M. E., Hobson, R. P., & Bishop, M. (1998). Congenital visual impairment and "theory of mind". *British Journal of Developmental Psychology, 16,* 183–196.

Moore, D. G., Hobson, R. P., & Lee, A. (1997). Components of person-perception: An investigation with autistic, non-autistic retarded and typically developing children and adolescents. *British Journal of Developmental Psychology, 15,* 401–423.

Mundy, P., Sigman, M., & Kasari, C. (1990). A longitudinal study of joint attention and language development in autistic children. *Journal of Autism and Developmental Disorders, 20,* 115–128.

Mundy, P., Sigman, M., & Kasari, C. (1993). The theory of mind and joint-attention deficits in autism. In S. Baron-Cohen, H. Tager-Flusberg, & D. Cohen (Eds.), *Understanding other minds: Perspectives from autism* (pp. 181–203). Oxford, UK: Oxford University Press.

Patrick, M., Hobson, R. P., Castle, D., Howard, R., & Maughan, B. (1994). Personality disorder and the mental representation of early social experience. *Development and Psychopathology, 6,* 375–388.

Rende, R. D., & Plomin, R. (1990). Quantitative genetics and developmental psychopathology: Contributions to understanding normal development. *Development and Psychopathology, 2,* 393–408.

Ricks, D. M., & Wing, L. (1975). Language, communication and the use of symbols in normal and autistic children. *Journal of Autism and Childhood Schizophrenia, 5,* 191–221.

Russell, J. (1997). (Ed). *Autism as an executive disorder.* Oxford, UK: Oxford University Press.

Rutter, M. (1996). Developmental psychopathology: Concepts and prospects. In M. F. Lenzenweger & J. J. Haugaard (Eds.), *Frontiers of developmental psychopathology* (pp. 209–237). Oxford, UK: Oxford University Press.

Rutter, M., & Garmezy, N. (1983). Developmental psychopathology. In P. H. Mussen (Ed.), *Handbook of Child Psychology* (pp. 775–911). Chichester, UK: Wiley.

Scheerer, M., Rothmann, E., & Goldstein, K. (1945). A case of "idiot savant": An experimental study of personality organisation. *Psychological Monographs, 58 (whole no. 269),* 1–63.

Sroufe, L. A. (1990). Considering normal and abnormal together: The essence of developmental psychopathology. *Developmental Psychopathology, 2,* 335–347.

Sroufe, L. A., & Rutter, M. (1984). The domain of developmental psychopathology. *Child Development, 55,* 17–29.

Steele, H., & Steele, M. (1998). Attachment and psychoanalysis: Time for a reunion. *Social Development, 7,* 92–119.

Stern, D. N. (1985). *The interpersonal world of the infant.* New York: Basic Books.

Tager-Flusberg, H. (1989). A psycholinguistic perspective on language development in the autistic child. In G. Dawson (Ed.), *Autism: Nature, diagnosis and treatment* (pp. 92–115). New York: Guilford.

Werner, H., & Kaplan, B. (1984). *Symbol formation.* Hillsdale, NJ: Erlbaum.

Wetherby, A. M., & Prutting, C. A. (1984). Profiles of communicative and cognitive-social abilities in autistic children. *Journal of Speech and Hearing Research, 27,* 364–377.

Wimmer, H., & Perner, J. (1983). Beliefs about beliefs: Representation and constraining function of wrong beliefs in young children's understanding of deception. *Cognition, 13,* 103–128.

CHAPTER   Mark H. Johnson

Developmental Cognitive Neuroscience

☐ Introduction

More than any other area of psychology, developmental psychology can trace its roots to the study of biology. In this chapter I argue that the most promising future avenue for developmental psychology lies in a closer association with developmental biology, but in a more circumspect import of ideas from evolutionary biology. The dissociation of cognitive development from developmental biology over the past few decades has, in my view, been counterproductive due to the investment of time and resources into the exploration of hypotheses and models that while perhaps philosophically attractive were biologically implausible. The close association between developmental psychology and biology is not only important for the continuing success of the former. I suggest that the newly emerging interdisciplinary field of developmental cognitive neuroscience will also be critical for our general understanding of the brain basis of adult cognitive, social, and emotional function.

☐ The Biological Roots of Developmental Psychology

While most branches of psychology can trace their earliest roots to experimental studies of philosophy of mind, developmental psychology largely arose from the hands of biologists. For example, one of the first scientific observational studies of child development was Charles Darwin's *The expression of emotion in man and animals* (1965, originally published in 1872). Like Darwin, Jean Piaget viewed human behavioral development through the perspective of evolution (e.g., Piaget, 1954). Piaget, who was originally trained as a biologist, also imported current theories of embryological development, mainly due to C. H. Waddington, to generate his accounts of human cognitive development (Waddington, 1975). Some of Waddington's notions have recently been resurrected by those interested in nonlinear dynamic systems approaches to cognitive development (Thelen & Smith, 1994; Elman et al., 1996). A curious aspect of Piaget's biological approach to human cognitive development was his relative neglect of the importance of brain development. Segalowitz (1994) suggests that this neglect was due to a lack of information about brain development and function resulting in Piaget being unable to articulate an integrative theory of brain and cognitive development. Two of the founders of American developmental psychology, McGraw and Gesell, both focused primarily on motor development, but they extended their conclusions to mental and social development (e.g., Gesell, 1929; McGraw, 1943). These scientists and their colleagues described a large number of stages in the development of motor abilities, from prone positions to walking and stair climbing. McGraw proposed that the transition between these stages could be explained in terms of the maturation of motor cortex and its inhibition of subcortical pathways and thus adopted a biological approach in which brain development was considered to be a critical element of the explanation for behavioral change in infants and children.

Why has developmental psychology been so closely related to evolutionary and developmental biology? One of the important factors is that underlying both disciplines there is the fundamental question of how complex organic structures, such as the human brain and the mind it supports, can arise from apparently much simpler stuff. In both disciplines there have been several approaches to answering this underlying question. I will argue in what follows that a return to some of the assumptions adopted by the founding fathers of developmental psychology, but subsequently discarded, would be productive. However, as I will discuss later, this does not mean that developmental psychology should be essentially reducible to evolutionary psychology in the way that some so-called evolutionary psychologists would have us believe.

Pre-Darwinian theories of evolution were largely based on preformationism: the idea that a creator, or creative force, "designed" the final forms of species (see Gottlieb, 1992; Oyama, 1985). In contrast, Darwin outlined a specific mechanism through which complex species evolve gradually from simpler, more primitive varieties. The evolution of species was viewed as the product of an interaction between genetic variation and random mutation on the one hand, and the demands of a particular environment on the other. The process was not directed, but like a "blind watchmaker" (Dawkins, 1987). An important point to note is that as a species evolved, its effective environment changed. For example, as sense organs improve, the detail of information that can be extracted from the environment increases; or as wings evolve, the effective environment of insects dramatically increases.

There have been theories of cognitive and behavioral development that share the common assumption that the emergence of more complex functions can, and should, be attributed to some preexisting source of information. The extreme manifestation of these pre-Darwinian views of ontogeny are nativism, in which it is believed that information in the genes "codes for" aspects of brain and mental structure (that are merely triggered by aspects of the environment),[1] and empiricism, in which it is believed that simple but powerful learning mechanisms absorb information about the structure of the environment. While nativism and empiricism are commonly viewed as two extreme ends of a continuum of theories about development, in fact they both share the underlying assumption that the information necessary for the final state of the organism precedes it, somewhat like an architect's plans for a building (see Oyama, 1985). Both approaches also attempt to minimize the extent of the transition from simple starting stuff to complex final state. For nativists, the original stuff is more complex than it seems: genes contain complex codes with all the necessary information for building neural circuits dedicated to language or arithmetical computation, and infants are viewed as being born with prespecified dedicated modules for various functions, which merely require to be triggered by appropriate environmental input. For empiricists, the end stuff is actually simpler than it seems; the brain may be viewed as composed of relatively simple but powerful learning devices. In both cases much of the mystery of development is thankfully eliminated by reference to simple explanatory concepts.

Nativism comes in several varieties, but they all share the common assumption that genes, either directly or indirectly, build brain structures, often argued to be domain specific, which underlie specific types of com-

---

[1] See later for discussion of some more sophisticated versions of nativism.

putation in the brain. Changes in behavior during infancy or childhood are thus often attributed to "brain maturation." Gottlieb (1992) has characterized this type of viewpoint as "causal epigenesis." Causal epigenesis implies a one-way causal relation from gene to brain to behavior. This basic assumption about development has several consequences. The first of these consequences is that a behavioral change, or the presence of an ability, not easily attributable to learning is considered not to be the concern of the cognitive scientist. The role of the nativist cognitive "developmentalist" in this case is merely to describe the steady state of the cognitive system of the infant or child before and after the transition. There is no need to give a cognitive explanation of the actual change between these states, nor the initial presence of a state since this is the domain of the neuroscientist (brain maturation) and the molecular biologist (gene expression). Thus, the range of phenomena in ontogeny that require explanation for the nativist are relatively restricted, and a duality between brain and cognitive development is maintained. Further, by this view much of ontogeny (i.e., individual development) can be explained by reference to phylogeny (i.e., species adaptation), since it represents an unfolding pattern of gene expression selected for in previous generations. This brand of nativism has resulted in the recent emergence of so-called evolutionary psychology in which aspects of human cognition are attributed to specific species adaptations (Cosmides & Tooby, 1994; Baron-Cohen, 1994).

In summary, for nativists of all varieties many (but not all) of the problems of change during ontogeny are essentially reducible to phylogeny. However, this has the paradoxical consequence that developmental biology can be maintained as a separate discipline from psychological development, less germane to the questions of interest than, for example, the cognitive psychology of adults. These tendencies were undoubtedly reinforced by the popular view among cognitive scientists in the 1970s and 1980s that the "software" of the mind was best studied without reference to the "hardware" of the brain.

Empiricist accounts of cognitive and behavioral development lost popularity in the past few decades when it became apparent that in several domains infants and children are capable of going beyond the (environmental) information given to them (e.g., Bruner, 1963) and that the cognitive capacities of young infants had been grossly underestimated. However, rejection of empiricist views is not grounds for rejection of an alternative way of thinking about development, which is constructivism. Further, most empiricist models involve a static environment that imposes itself on the child's brain. As with evolution, we should be aware that the effective environment for the organism is likely to change as it develops.

☐ Constructivism and Development

Whereas both nativism and empiricism share the assumption of preexisting information (be it in the genes or in the environment), constructivist theories of ontogeny, like Darwinist accounts of phylogeny, do not. Constructivism is an orthogonal dimension of developmental theory to the nature/nurture debate and is primarily focused on the mechanisms of change and emergence of new structure through interactive processes. It views development as a constructive process through which genes interact with their environments at various different levels, including the environment external to the organism, resulting in organic structures that are more specified or differentiated than those that preceded them. Thus, it puts an emphasis on the activity-dependent nature of development. As we will see, this activity-dependent nature is appropriate at a number of different levels including the cellular and organismal.

Piaget was one of the first to adopt a constructivist approach to psychological development, although the approach has a much longer history in biological development (e.g., Waddington, 1975; see Gottlieb, 1992). Indeed, as is well known, Piaget based his theories of cognitive change partly on accounts of embryological development. Although Piaget's general approach to psychological development may have been sound, the particular theory he advanced clearly looks dated today. Among a number of weaknesses were the rather vague and underspecified mechanisms of change such as "assimilation" and "accommodation," the neglect of the importance of brain development, and his gross underestimation of the abilities of young infants. The latter was no doubt due to the relative lack of procedures for studying infant abilities during the 1950s and early 1960s. (It took another biologist, Robert Fantz, to adapt methods from animal behavior experiments to develop the first infant preference testing procedures.) However, although much of Piaget's theory has been correctly rejected by empirical evidence, this does not mean we should reject his general approach and throw out the baby with the bathwater. As earlier mentioned, there has been a tendency by those of a nativist inclination to conflate constructivism with empiricism and to use the same arguments against both types of theories. For example, arguments from the poverty of the stimulus in language acquisition are commonly used to support a nativist position, when in fact they only refute an empiricist stance (Johnson, 1998). It is in no way inconsistent with a contructivist approach in which developmental change results in structures that go beyond the information immediately available in either the environment or intrinsic factors.

☐ What Can We Learn From the Brain?

Philosophical debates regarding ways of thinking about development are all very well, but which of these positions has the most plausibility when we consider the organ in question, the human brain? It is outside the scope of this chapter to review all that is known about primate brain development (see Johnson, 1993, 1997, for reviews). However, what follows are a number of important summary statements drawn from my own and others' reviews of this literature.

- In a recent review of pre- and postnatal brain development, Nelson and Bloom (1997) summarize: "An unfortunate misconception of developmental neurobiology is that most aspects of brain development during the pre- and immediate postnatal periods reflect rigidly deterministic, genetic programs that are implemented at different points in time. . . This view is inappropriate for even the very earliest stages of brain development" (p. 979).
- During both pre- and postnatal life, neural circuits, especially those within the cerebral cortex, are remodeled in interaction with their input. Recent evidence indicates that during prenatal life much of this input comes from internally generated spontaneous activity (see Katz & Shatz, 1996, for review). With maturation of sense organs and input from the environment in postnatal life there is a gradual shift to effects of input from the external environment.
- Human brains do not contain any new structures or parts not found in other primates. Rather, our brain development is characterized by (i) greater volume, particularly in the cerebral cortex, and (ii) greatly slowed development and in particular an extended period of postnatal plasticity (see Johnson, 1997, for review). This relatively delayed sequence of brain development makes our species more open to influence by interactions with the postnatal environment.

Thus, recent reviews of pre- and postnatal brain development have come to the conclusion that brain development is not merely a process of unfolding of a genetic plan, or a passive response to environmental input, but is an activity-dependent process at molecular, cellular, and organismal levels involving probablistic epigenesis (bidirectional relations between genes, brain, and behavior). In humans this process extends further into postnatal life than in other primates. What we need now are some concrete examples of how this general view of brain development can be applied to the area of interest to the developmental psychologist: postnatal behavioral change. In the next section I review a domain in which to consider the merits of the neuroconstructivist approach, the development of face processing.

☐ Contemporary Constructivist Approaches to Cognitive Development: The Case of Face Processing

One of the topics in which there has been considerable debate between nativist and empiricist perspectives concerns face recognition abilities in young infants. On the empiricist side of the debate, many studies supported the view that it takes the infant about two or three months to learn about the arrangement of features that compose a face (for reviews see Maurer, 1985; Nelson & Ludemann, 1989). From this it was assumed that face processing was an acquired skill developed through prolonged exposure to faces.

On the nativist side, two lines of evidence are commonly invoked to support the idea of an "innate cortical module" for face processing. The first is that several studies have shown evidence that newborn human infants preferentially respond to facelike patterns. For example, Goren, Sarty, and Wu (1975) showed that newborns around 10 minutes old would track, by means of head and eye movements, facelike patterns further than various "scrambled" face patterns, a study which was replicated by Johnson, Dziurawiec, Ellis, & Morton, (1991) with some improvements to the methodology. The second source of evidence comes from recent functional neuroimaging studies, which show that particular regions of the cortex, such as the "fusiform gyrus face area," are specifically activated following the presentation of faces (Kanwisher, Tong, & Nakayama, 1998). The assumption is that such specificity within the cortex results from genetic and molecular-level interaction, and not visual experience. As discussed in detail by Elman et al. (1996), such assumptions can be erroneous.

By considering evidence from biology, Morton and Johnson (1991) presented an alternative, constructivist account of the development of face processing in which they argued that there are at least two interacting brain systems in operation. One of these systems, termed Conspec, is present from birth and underlies the tendency for newborn infants to orient toward faces, while the other system was hypothesized to acquire information about faces through exposure to them. Importantly, the first system was argued to bias the input (preferentially toward faces) to the second system, thus ensuring that it specialized for learning about faces.

In developing their theory, Johnson and Morton (1991) used two sources of evidence from biology: evidence from the differential development of brain systems, and evidence from conspecific recognition in another species, the domestic chick. The primary source of evidence from other species (ethology) that we used to interpret the human infancy results concerned filial imprinting in the domestic chick, a process by which young precocial birds, such as chicks or ducklings, recognize and develop an attachment for the first conspicuous object that they see after hatching (Bolhuis, 1991; Bolhuis & Honey, 1998). The results of a series of experiments on the brain basis of imprinting led to the proposal that there are two independent neural systems that underlie filial preference in the chick (Horn, 1985; Johnson, Bolhuis, & Horn, 1985). The first of these is a specific predisposition for the chick to orient toward objects resembling others of its own species. This system appears to be specifically tuned to the correct spatial arrangement of elements of the head and neck region (Johnson & Horn, 1986) and is sufficient to pick out the mother hen from other objects the chick is likely to be exposed to in the first few days after hatching. The neural basis for this predisposition is currently unknown, but the *optic tectum,* the homologue of the mammalian superior colliculus, is a likely candidate.

The second brain system acquires information about the objects to which the young chick attends and involves a particular part of the chick forebrain called the IMHV (the IMHV is within a part of the chick brain similar to the mammalian cortex). A variety of neurophysiological and behavioral manipulations, such as damage to the IMHV, have been shown to dissociate the two systems (see Horn, 1998; Bolhuis & Honey, 1998, for recent reviews of this work). In the natural environment, we argued that the first system ensures that the second system acquires information about the particular individual mother hen close by. In other words, the effective environment of the chick is changed such that it is biased more toward conspecifics than it would be otherwise.

The other source of biological data that we used to generate an account of human infant face recognition came from the postnatal development of the human cerebral neocortex. Both neuroanatomical and neurophysiological data indicate that visually guided behavior in the newborn infant is largely mediated by subcortical structures such as the superior colliculus and pulvinar, and that it is not until 2 or 3 months of age that cortical circuitry comes to dominate subcortical circuits (see Johnson 1990, 1995). Consistent with these arguments is the hypothesis that visually guided behavior in human infants, like that in domestic chicks, is based on activity in at least two distinct brain systems. Since these systems have distinct developmental time courses, they may differentially influence behavior in infants of different ages.

Figure 9.1. A 6-month-old infant wearing a geodesic sensor net. This system is able to record electrical changes at the scalp surface when groups of neurons fire within the cerebral cortex.

These two sources of biological evidence led Johnson and Morton (1991; Morton & Johnson, 1991) to propose the two-process theory outlined above. The first process involves a system accessed via the subcortical visual pathway (but possibly also involving some cortical structures) and which underlies the preferential orienting to faces observed in newborns. However, the influence of this system over behavior declines (possibly due to inhibition) during the second month of life. This is reflected in the fact that infants no longer preferentially track faces by 2 months (Johnson et al., 1991). The second process depends upon cortical maturity, and exposure to faces over the first month or so, and begins to influence infants' behavior and responses to faces in a graded manner from 2 to 4 months of age.

However, it remains possible that the "cortical module" for face processing is "prewired" by genetic interactions and that it is only activated by visual input or by neurochemical changes at 2 months of age. In order to differentiate between this notion and that of gradual specialization, my colleagues and I conducted some experiments in which we examined the extent of cortical specialization for face processing in 6-month-old infants through the use of a noninvasive functional brain imaging system (see Figure 9.1). The results of this study showed that although some degree of functional specialization for face processing has taken place by 6 months of age, it still has not reached the adult level of localization or specialization. For example, the infants were less localized in their face processing than adults (e.g., they did not clearly show the right hemisphere localization seen in adults) and less specialized (e.g., unlike adults they showed the same response to upright monkey faces that they did to upright human faces; de Haan, Oliver, & Johnson, 1998). This evidence that there are dynamic changes in the cortical processing of faces during the first year of life is more consistent with a process of gradual specialization/localization than the activation of a preexisiting dedicated circuit.

Thus, in this example of human development at least three factors contribute to the brain specialization that emerges: first, the primitive tendency of newborns to orient toward facelike patterns, second, the presence of many faces in the normal environment of the young infant, and, third, the architecture of cerebral cortical circuits activated when faces are within the visual field. These three factors acting in concert ensure the inevitable outcome of a brain specialized for processing the biologically important stimulus of faces. This specialization is not "coded for" by genes, or is not just the result of passive exposure to faces, but it is the result of an active process in which the infant's own behavior selects the appropriate input for its still-developing brain.

☐ Future Prospects

In this section I would like to suggest some directions for research for the future. The first of these concerns the use of neural network modeling, and other new technologies, for understanding the course of normal brain and cognitive development, while the second focuses on the implications of the new approach for work on developmental disorders.

Taking a constructivist approach to neurocognitive development is all very well, but it is still open to the criticism that the underlying mechanisms remain somewhat vague, and, as discussed earlier, this is one reason why Piaget's mechanisms of change are given less credibility these days. Fortunately, this is why closer contact with brain development and, in particular, models of neural networks and their cognitive cousins, connectionist nets, can be of value. To illustrate this, I will consider a neural network model of one of the processes mentioned in the last section, visual imprinting in the chick.

As mentioned earlier, a particular region of the chick forebrain (cortex) has been identified as being critically involved in imprinting. The wiring patterns of connections between neurons found in this part of the

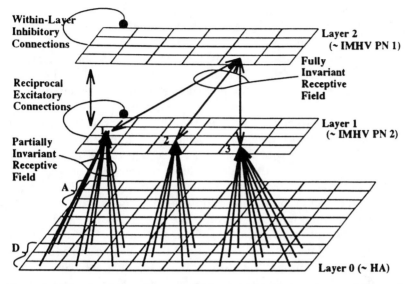

Figure 9.2. The detailed architecture of the model is designed around the anatomical connectivity of IMHV and its primary input area, the hyperstriatum accessorium (HA). The model is based on a set of layers, each of which have lateral inhibition within them. The "input" layer of the network, layer 0, represents HA. HA then projects to one subpopulation of IMHV PN cells (Type 1 PNs). This is layer 1 of the IMHV component of the model. Note that the laminar distinction in the model between these two component cells of IMHV is not intended to suggest that the cells are arranged as such in the IMHV itself, but rather serves to reflect the functional distinction between the two types of PN. The axons from the Type 1 neurons project to the Type 2 projection neurons, as well as onto the local inhibitory neurons. This composes the second layer of the models "IMHV" component. The Type 2 PNs then send a bifurcating axon both back to the Type 1 PNs and the inhibitory cells (layer 2), and to other areas, which are not modeled. Within each layer of the model, strong lateral inhibition exists in the form of relatively large negative weights between all units in the layer. This reflects the presence of a large number of GABAergic inhibitory interneurons in IMHV and its relatively low levels of spontaneous activity. The strong inhibition in this layer of the model resulted in only one unit in each layer becoming active at any time.

brain have been studied and used to construct a neural network model by O'Reilly and Johnson (1994). This model implemented four cell types and their pattern interconnectivity in a way that resembled those seen in the real animal. A particular feature of this circuitry was the existence of positive (excitatory) feedback loops between some of the principal neurons and extensive inhibitory circuitry mediated by local circuit neurons. The detailed architecture of the model is shown in Figure 9.2.

The model was trained in a similar way to chicks during imprinting in that it was presented with "objects" that moved across the visual fields. The strength of links (synapses) in the model were adjusted during training according to a biologically plausible associative (Hebbian) learning rule in which coactive nodes have their links strengthened, while nodes that do not have correlated activation have their links weakened. Some of the units in the network learn to become responsive to a particular object, in much the same way as they do in the chick brain as the animal imprints onto the first conspicuous object that it sees after hatching. Importantly, these nodes are able to learn to recognize the object regardless of where it appears in the visual field. A combination of factors, including the excitatory feedback loop, are responsible for this location-invariant object recognition. To get an intuitive sense of how the model works, imagine moving a pen laterally across your visual field. As the pen moves it is still clearly recognizable as a pen. The neural network model learns to "bind" together the features of an object such as a pen by detecting that the same features (the nib, the top, and the barrel of the pen) move together as one in time. Nodes that are able to integrate information over several points in time are able to detect that a particular set of features cooccur and therefore respond to it anywhere in the visual field.

Using this model O'Reilly and Johnson (1994) were able to successfully simulate a range of phenomena associated with imprinting in the chicks. Perhaps the major characteristic of visual imprinting of interest to the developmental psychologist is the notion of a sensitive or critical period within which the learning must occur to be effective. This was examined in the model by first training it on one object for a period, and then training it on a different one. The data from the model closely paralleled that from chicks, with reversibility of preferences only being possible after shorter periods of initial training on the first object. It is important to point out that the sensitive period, and other aspects of imprinting behavior, were not "built in" to the model by O'Reilly and Johnson (1994). Rather, these properties emerged from the neural architecture and learning rule used in the model. The purpose of such models is not just to simulate nature, however, but to understand it better. This was done by analyzing the reasons why the network shows the performance it does (an interaction between the neural architecture and the learning rule) and by making novel predictions that can be tested on the real organism. One of the predictions made on the basis of the model by O'Reilly and Johnson (1994) concerned the effects of training on rapidly alternating objects. From the model it was predicted that such circumstances would generate a "blended" representation of the two objects. This would have the subsequent effect of making it harder for a chick to differentiate the two objects than if they had received no prior training, or if they had been trained on the objects separately in time. Evidence from chicks supported these predictions.

Although such neural network models can be developed for well-studied neural circuits in animals, at present we have insufficient knowledge of the circuitry underlying similar neural computations in human infants. However, we can construct "neurally inspired" network (connectionist) models that provide a concrete instantiation of some of the principles underlying a constructivist approach to development. One of these assumptions is that development is a graded process, in which functioning within a domain can be partial. One example of the use of connectionist modeling to investigate the graded development of partial representations concerns object permanence (Piaget, 1954). Recent experiments on the ability of infants to maintain in mind objects that are occluded (disappear) have provided conflicting evidence depending on whether the measure (response) is looking at the location of the hidden object or reaching for it. It appears that although infants of 6 months will look at the location of an object that is occluded, at least for a short period after its disappearance, they will not reach toward it. Only toward the end of the first year will infants reach for occluded objects. Munakata and colleagues (Munakata, McClelland, Johnson, & Siegler, 1997) constructed connectionist nets that were trained on stimulus presentations in which "objects" moved behind occluders. After some training the network's internal representation of the object (a particular pattern of activations across a particular set of nodes) tends to persist for some time after the occlusion of the object. With a small amount of training, the weak representation of an occluded object may be sufficient to drive a low threshold output such as looking. With further training the representation of an occluded object gets stronger, allowing it to guide more complex forms of output such as reaching.

Perhaps more so than other areas of developmental psychology, progress in developmental cognitive neuroscience will depend on technological developments. One set of tools relate to brain imaging: the generation of "functional" maps of brain activity based on either changes in cerebral metabolism, blood flow, or electrical activity produced as groups of neurons fire within the brain. Some of these imaging methods, such as positron emission tomography (PET), are of limited utility for studying transitions in behavioral development in normal infants and children due to their invasive nature (requiring the intravenous injection of radioactively labeled substances) and their relatively coarse temporal resolution. Two brain imaging techniques are currently being applied to development in normal children: event-related potentials (ERPs) and functional magnetic resonance imaging (fMRI). ERPs involve measuring the electrical activity of the brain generated as groups of neurons fire synchronously by means of sensitive electrodes that rest on the scalp surface. These recordings can either be of the spontaneous natural rhythms of the brain (EEG), or the electrical activity induced by the presentation of a stimulus (ERP). Normally the ERP from many trials is averaged, resulting in the spontaneous natural rhythms of the brain that are unrelated to the stimulus presentation averaging to zero. With a high density of electrodes on the scalp, algorithms can be employed that infer the position and orientation of the brain sources of electrical activity (dipoles) for the particular pattern of scalp surface electrical activity (see Figure 9.1). Functional MRI allows the noninvasive measurement of cerebral blood flow (Kwong et al., 1992), with the prospect of millimeter spatial resolution and temporal resolution on the order of seconds. Although this technique has been applied to children (Casey et al., 1997), the distracting noise and vibration, and the unknown possible effects of high magnetic fields on the developing brain, make its usefulness for children under 4 or 5 years of age unclear.

Developmental psychobiological research on animals has contributed greatly to our understanding of the relation between developing brain and behavior, and recent techniques in molecular genetics open up new possibilities. For example, it is now possible for us to "knock out" specific genes from the genome of an animal and study effects on subsequent development. An example of this approach was the deletion of the alpha-calcium calmodulin kinase II gene, which results in rats being unable to perform certain learning tasks when adults (Silva, Paylor, Wehner, & Tonegawa, 1992; Silva, Stevens, Tonegawa, & Wang, 1992). The method may open new vistas in the analysis of genetic contributions to cognitive and perceptual change in animals. However, it should be noted that lesioning a single gene is likely to have a cascade of effects caused by the abnormal, or absent, interactions with other genes and thus may be complex to interpret.

Finally, another useful approach for linking brain development to behavior is the "marker task." This method involves the use of specific behavioral tasks that have been linked to a brain region or pathway in adult primates and humans by neurophysiological, neuropsychological, or brain imaging studies. By testing infants or children with versions of such a task at different ages, the researcher can use the success or otherwise of individuals as indicating the functional development of the relevant regions of the brain.

The view that the later stages of human brain specialization are to some extent constructed through interaction between the child and his or her environment offers a new perspective on wide-ranging aspects of development psychology including the study of development disorders.

Karmiloff-Smith (1998) and Oliver, Johnson, Karmiloff-Smith and Pennington (in press), among others, have argued that it is an error to approach developmental disorders in the same way as adults with acquired brain damage. It became popular in the past decade to use the methods of adult neuropsychology (such as the search for "double dissociations") to analyze developmental disorders such as autism, dyslexia, and Williams syndrome. The focus was very much on searching for specific cognitive deficits (usually in school-age children or even adults) and then attempting to identify the cortical regions and genetic precursors of these deficits (see Frith & Happé (1998) for a defense of the specific cognitive deficits approach to developmental disorders). In contrast to this approach, the constructivist approach assumes that (i) most developmental disorders will involve widespread neural and cognitive deficits, (ii) patterns of association between disorders can be as informative as dissociation, and (iii) cognitive disorders are likely to lie on a continuum, rather than being discrete and specific. These changed assumptions alter the way that developmental disorders are approached in that the focus is on longitudinal studies from early infancy, on similarities as well as differences between disorders, and on an interdisciplinary approach in which cause is not seen as necessarily unidirectional (see Box 6 of Karmiloff-Smith (1998) for details). Of course, there is no doubt that the constructivist approach to developmental disorders is a harder type of science to do, requiring as it does interdisciplinary and longitudinal studies. Fortunately, however, some of the new methods that have become available to development cognitive neuroscience will make it feasible.

☐ Goals for the Next Millenium

As should be evident from the preceding text, I believe that we are on the verge of an exponential increase in our knowledge of the developing mind and brain. I argued that we need to increase the exchange of hypotheses between developmental biology and psychological development to facilitate this progress. In particular, we need to focus on working out detailed examples of how preexisting brain/mental structure selects aspects of the environment to contribute to the further tuning of neural circuits. In other words, we need theories of the child as an active contributor to his or her own subsequent brain specialization and theories of how the effective environment changes with age. With regard to evolutionary biology we need to be more careful of how we proceed. I proposed that reducing ontogeny to phylogeny ("evolutionary psychology") is not a helpful step, but importing mechanistic notions, such as dynamic changes in the environment resulting from earlier development, may be more fruitful. Finally, another goal for the next millennium will be to understand and characterize developmental disorders in terms of types of deviation from the normal developmental pathway, rather than simply as static end states, and to develop a framework within which different developmental trajectories can be analyzed and compared together, rather than viewed in isolation.

☐ References

Baron-Cohen, S. (1994). How to build a baby that can read minds: Cognitive mechanisms in mindreading. *Currrent Psychology of Cognition, 13,* 513–552.

Bolhuis, J. J. (1991). Mechanisms of avian imprinting: A review. *Biological Reviews, 66,* 303–345.

Bolhuis, J. J. & Honey, R. C. (1998). Imprinting, leaning and development: From behaviour to brain and back. *Trends in Neurosciences, 21,* 306–311.

Bruner, J. S. (1963). *Beyond the information given: Studies in the psychology of knowing.* New York: Norton.

Casey, B. J., Trainor, R. J., Orendi, J. L., Schubert, A. B., Nystrom, L. E., Giedd, J. N., & Xavier Castellanos, J. L. (1997). A developmental functional MRI study of prefrontal activation during performance of a go-no-go task. *Journal of Cognitive Neuroscience, 9*(6), 835–847.

Cosmides, L., & Tooby, J. (1994). Origins of domain specificity: The evolution of functional organization. In L. A. Hirschfield & S. A. Gelman (Eds.). *Mapping the mind.* New York: Cambridge.

Darwin, C. R. (1965). *The expression of emotions in man and animals.* Chicago: University of Chicago Press. (Original work published in 1872)

Dawkins, R. (1987). *The blind watchmaker.* New York: Norton.

de Haan, M., Oliver, A., & Johnson, M. H. (1998). Electrophysiological correlates of face processing by adults and 6-month-old infants. *Journal of Cognitive Neuroscience Annual Meeting Supplement, 36.*

Elman, J., Bates, E., Johnson, M. H., Karmiloff-Smith, A., Parisi, D., & Plunkett, K. (1996). *Rethinking innateness: A connectionist perspective on development.* Cambridge, MA: MIT Press.

Frith, U., & Happé, F. (1998). Why specific developmental disorders are not specific: On-line and developmental effects in autism and dyslexia. *Developmental Science, 1*(2), 267–272.

Gesell, A. (1929). *Infancy and human growth.* New York: Macmillan.

Goren, C. C., Sarty, M., & Wu, P. Y. K. (1975). Visual following and pattern discrimination of face-like stimuli by newborn infants. *Pediatrics, 56,* 544–549.

Gottlieb, G. (1992). *Individual development and evolution.* New York: Oxford University Press.

Horn, G. (1985). *Memory, imprinting and the brain: An inquiry into mechanisms.* Oxford, UK: Clarendon Press.

Horn, G. (1998). Visual imprinting and the neural mechanisms of recognition memory. *Trends in Neuroscience, 21,* 300–305.

Johnson, M. H. (1990). Cortical maturation and the development of visual attention in early infancy. *Journal of Cognitive Neuroscience, 2*(2), 81–95.

Johnson, M. H. (1993). *Brain development and cognition and cognition: A reader.* Oxford, UK: Blackwell.

Johnson, M. H. (1995). The development of visual attention: A cognitive neuroscience perspective. In M. S. Gazzinga (Ed.), *The cognitive neurosciences* (pp. 735–747). Cambridge, MA: MIT Press.

Johnson, M. H. (1997). *Developmental cognitive neuroscience: An introduction.* Oxford, UK: Blackwell.

Johnson, M.H. (1998). Developmental cognitive neuroscience: Looking ahead. *Early Development and Parenting, 7,* 163–169.

Johnson, M. H., & Horn, G. (1986). An analysis of a predisposition in the chick. *Behavioral Brain Research, 20,* 108–109.

Johnson, M. H., & Morton, J. (1991). *Biology and cognitive development: The case of face recognition.* Oxford, UK: Blackwell.

Johnson, M. H., Bolhuis, J. J., & Horn, G. (1985). Interaction between acquired preferences and developing predispositions during imprinting. *Animal Behaviour, 33,* 1000–1006.

Johnson, M. H., Dziurawiec, S., Ellis, H. D., & Morton, J. (1991). Newborns' preferential tracking of face-like stimuli and its subsequent decline. *Cognition, 40,* 1–19.

Kanwisher, N., Tong, F., & Nakayama, K. (1998) The effect of inversion on the human fusiform face area. *Cognition, 68,* B1–B11.

Karmiloff-Smith, A. (1998). Development itself is the key to understanding developmental disorders. *Trends in Cognitive Sciences, 2*(10), 389.

Katz, L. C., & Shatz, C. J. (1996). Synaptic activity and the construction of cortical circuits. *Science, 274,* 1133.

Kwong, K. E., Belliveau, J. W., Chesler, D. A., Goldberg, I. E., Weisskoff, R. M., Poncelet, B. P., Kennedy, D. N., Hoppel, B. E., Cohen, M. S., Turner, R., Cheng, H. M., Brady, T. J., & Rosen, B. R. (1992). Dynamic magnetic resonance imaging of human brain activity during primary sensory stimulation. *Proceedings of the National Academy of Sciences, 89,* 5675–5679.

Maurer, D. (1985). Infants perception of facedness. In T. N. Field & N. Fox (Eds.), *Social Perception in Infants.* New York: Ablex.

McGraw, M. B. (1943). *The neuromuscular maturation of the human infant.* New York: Columbia University Press.

Morton, J., & Johnson, M. H. (1991). CONSPEC and CONLERN: A two-process theory of infant face recognition. *Psychological Review, 98*(2), 164–181.

Munakata, Y., McClelland, J. L., Johnson, M. H., & Siegler, R. S. (1997). Rethinking infant knowledge: Toward an adaptive process account of successes and failures in object permanence tasks. *Psychological Review, 104*(4), 686–713.

Nelson, C. A., & Bloom, F. E. (1997). Child development and neuroscience. *Child Development, 68*(5), 970–987.

Nelson, C. A., & Ludemann, P. M. (1989). Past, current and future trends in infant face perception research. *Canadian Journal of Psychology, 43,* 183–198.

Oliver, A., Johnson, M. H., Karmiloff-Smith, A., & Pennington, B. (In press). Deviations in the emergence of representations: A neuroconstructionist framework for analyzing developmental disorders. *Developmental Science.*

O'Reilly, R., & Johnson, M. H. (1994). Object recognition and sensitive periods: A computational analysis of visual imprinting. *Neural Computation, 6,* 357–390.

Oyama, S. (1985). *The ontogeny of information.* Cambridge, UK: Cambridge University Press.

Piaget, J. (1954). *The construction of reality in the child* (Cook, M., Trans.). New York: Basic Books.

Segalowitz, S. J. (1994). Developmental psychology and brain development: A historical perspective. In G. Dawson & K. W. Fischer (Eds.), *Human behavior and the developing brain* (pp. 67–92). New York: Guilford Press.

Silva, A. J., Paylor, R., Wehner, J. M., & Tonegawa, S. (1992). Impaired spatial learning in alpha-calcium-calmodulin kinase II mutant mice. *Science, 257,* 206–211.

Silva, A. J., Stevens, C. F., Tonegawa, S., & Wang, Y. (1992). Deficient hippocampal long-term potentiation in a-calcium-calmodulin kinase II mutant mice. *Science, 257,* 201–206.

Thelen, E., & Smith, L.B. (1994). *A dynamic systems approach to the development of cognition and action.* Cambridge, MA: MIT Press.

Waddington, C. H. (1975). *The evolution of an evolutionist.* Edinburgh, UK: Edinburgh University Press.

CHAPTER

Frank C. Keil

Cognition, Content, and Development

☐ Introduction

The child's developing mind is looking rather different to researchers today than it did even as few as 20 years ago. A wave of new discoveries has occurred usually in close correspondence with new theories. Moreover, the links between the study of cognitive development and the rest of cognitive science are vastly stronger and more mutually beneficial than many would have even imagined when cognitive science was first held up as a new way of studying the mind. There are threads connecting many of these recent advances to developmental research and theory spanning back to the beginning of this century; but these recent advances have been far more than incremental steps forward. They are changing our views of children's minds and suggest that developmental research in the next century may have a radically different character than it did for most of this century. In this essay, I summarize four dimensions of contrast that have been highlighted by this research and which are likely to be major parts of any research program for the next several decades.

We seem to be reconceptualizing cognitive development because of the following ways of framing problems: domain specificity versus generality, hybrid versus homogeneous learning architectures, implicit versus explicit forms of knowledge, and abstract versus concrete forms of thought. In some cases the contrast itself is much more salient than it used to be, while in others there is now much more emphasis on a different end of the dimension or on a different way of viewing the contrast itself. All of these contrasts also highlight the need to take a realist stance to the world around us. In essence, cognitive development can no more study the acquisition of knowledge by merely looking at the machinery inside the head than visual neurophysiology can study the retina by merely looking at retinal anatomy and not considering the nature of light. This common theme will emerge as each of the contrasts is discussed in turn.

☐ Domain Specificity Versus Generality

Although the notion of different developmental patterns in different realms of cognition has been with us for many years (e.g., Galton, 1883), in the last two decades it has become a central idea in much of cognition and cognitive development (e.g., Keil, 1981; Chi, 1989; Gigerenzer & Hug, 1992; Cosmides & Tooby, 1994; Hirschfeld & Gelman, 1994; Wellman & Gelman, 1998). It has offered an alternative to accounts of cognitive development where change occurred in roughly the same way across all kinds of knowledge and at roughly the same time. These domain general accounts were common to many of the best-known developmental theorists of this century. Although they may have disagreed dramatically on many things, Piaget, Bruner, Vygotsky, and Werner all proposed patterns of developmental change that swept across all domains of knowledge.

It now seems, however, that our routes to mature knowledge and thought might be quite different in character depending on the kind of knowledge involved. Increasing proficiencies in using mental maps to guide our way around in the world may look very different from increasing proficiencies in language or arithmetic. Even in those cases where the pattern of change seems similar across two domains, the time when it happens may vary dramatically, such as when novice-to-expert shifts occur in toddlers and in graduate students (e.g., Chi, Feltovich, & Glaser, 1981; Chi & Koeske, 1983).

We are only beginning to realize the implications and limitations of thinking about development in terms of domain specificity. One problem concerns different senses of the word "domain." If we see a domain as simply a bounded area of knowledge, there are hundreds of thousands of local areas of expertise that could be called domains. A child could be an expert in the "domain" of cartoon heroes on a certain television channel on Saturday mornings, a stock consultant might be an expert on the profit margins of hard disk drives in laptop computers. The list of such local domains is nearly endless and is updated daily as new technologies and television shows are produced. Contrast those local cases with domains that virtually every person masters and has done so for thousands of years: numbers, physical object mechanics, biology, and folk psychology. These seem to be very different senses of domain with correspondingly different patterns of development; yet they often are conflated.

How does one distinguish between these two kinds of domains other than simply on the basis of their size? Universality across individuals and cultures seems to be one strong difference. But those criteria alone are not enough. Virtually all cultures encounter clouds, yet knowing the cloud "domain" seems far different from knowing biology. There is a sense of depth and interconnectedness in domains such as biology and folk psychology that does not seem as apparent for more local cases. It is tempting to equate this depth with the idea of an intuitive theory; but a clear sense of "theory" is equally problematic. With domains such as language and spatial knowledge most adults are not considered to have theories of either their own languages or of their cognitive maps, at least in the sense of being able to understand or explain properties of their grammar or of their spatial representations.

One might want to draw the distinction on the basis of innate domain-specific constraints, assuming that they only apply to the acquisition and use of very broad areas of knowledge. Thus, our understandings of mechanics, biology, and other minds might be sharply limited to only a very small class of possible alternatives, making only certain kinds of knowledge in those areas conceptually natural. Humans, however, are well known to be "prepared" to have fears about quite specific kinds of things such as snakes and spiders (Tomarken, Mineka, & Cook, 1989; McNally, 1987); yet these phobias hardly cover large-scale domains of knowledge. It has also been argued that broad domains, such as knowledge of physical objects, can emerge from learning architectures not subject to domain-specific constraints (Munakata, McClelland, & Siegler, 1997). Even if the end-state knowledge has distinctive and unique characteristics, it might not have to start out that way.

Similarly, until recently it seemed that these different senses of domains could be distinguished on the extent to which there were distinct neural structures for encoding them, structures that could be damaged selectively and that might contain built-in architectural specializations for distinct kinds of information. It is now clear, however, that a distinct region of the brain could come to be specialized for processing a certain kind of information and yet not be innately predetermined. In essence, different patterns of information could be sequestered in different brain regions not because of any a priori constraints for that kind of information, but because some very simple perceptual cues shunted information to a specific brain region where that information was further processed by completely general mechanisms. For example, Johnson and Morton (1991) have argued that neural specializations for processing human faces may have developed from a simple sensitivity to two vertically symmetrical dots in an oval. That sensitivity then resulted in sending face-related information to a particular region of neural tissue that, over time, came to be a specialized face-processing area even though nothing about that area contained face-related information at the start. (See Johnson, this volume.)

Perhaps the differences between small local pockets of expertise and sweeping universal ones are not important, and the lessons we learn from studying the development of knowledge of cartoon superheroes or clouds will apply equally well to learning language or a folk psychology. My strong preference is to reject such a move and to maintain that the different senses of domain are psychologically important. Indeed, a key challenge in the next several years is to develop much clearer ways of contrasting broad domains from local areas of expertise.

At present there is only the intuition of an important difference between "true" domains of knowledge and what we might call areas of expertise, which tend to be much smaller in scope. One way of making the distinction may rest more in characterizing how patterns in the world cluster according to lawful regularities, with the broad domains being characterized by much more distinctive and interconnected principles. Clouds would differ from biology, because there are few principles unique to clouds. Rather, more general principles concerning gases are at work. By contrast, a large set of interrelated principles make living kinds a distinct domain (e.g., Atran, 1996). In short, analyses of real-world structures may be critical to understanding different senses of domains.

Putting the issue of the scope of a domain aside, it is becoming more apparent that the study of cognitive development can no longer proceed in a solipsistic fashion where one talks about only internal mental machinery. Almost 50 years ago James and Eleanor Gibson started on programs of research showing that, for perception, one needed to characterize the structure of what is perceived and how those informational patterns might be detected and used in an organism's ecology (J. Gibson, 1966; E. Gibson, 1970). It is now evident that similar analyses must be undertaken not just for what is perceived, but also for what is thought about. We need to describe the distinctive informational properties of a domain and then to consider how a mind might apprehend those properties. A domain-specificity approach suggests that different kinds of cognitive structures optimally resonate with different kinds of real-world relations. The mental structures that help us remember where we are in a three-dimensional space are different from those that tell us how physical objects interact just because the informational patterns associated with three-dimensional layout and object interactions are different.

It is hardly remarkable to claim that humans might have different structures tailored for different kinds of informational patterns that exist in the world. The anatomies of the eyes, ears, and nose are optimized in very different ways to pick up patterns of light, high frequency pressure variations, and airborne chemicals. That we should also have mental structures specialized for different kinds of informational patterns does not seem such a large leap. Moreover, in the realms of artificial systems, it is common to have different kinds of processors dedicated to processing only certain kinds of information, such as video arrays, mathematical computations, or chess configurations. Current efforts in the philosophy of science to ask whether the nature of thought and the structure of knowledge is different across the sciences (e.g., Boyd, 1991; Salmon, 1989) also provide a useful guide in considering possible domains for which we might have different cognitive specializations. Paying attention to the informational patterns that exist in the world does not mean that world comes with dotted lines, saying, "Carve me up this way." There are often several different ways of usefully organizing a group of things. A group of animals can be seen as pets and nonpets, as edible and inedible, as predators and prey, and so on. My claim here is not that there is one right way to pick out informational patterns. Rather, the claim is that the patterns are not merely arbitrary, especially in those cases where causal interactions cause certain property clusters to be stable.

In the next few decades, we are likely to have clearer sets of principled ways of distinguishing broad foundational domains from local ones of expertise. We may discover that more than two senses of domain are needed. Thus, there may be large domains that are laden with intuitive but accessible theories and explanations. These might include folk psychology. There may also be domains that are broad and governed by domain-specific constraints but are much more resistant to conscious reflection or awareness. These might include natural language grammars. Finally, there might be the highly local domains either explicitly known, such as cartoon superheroes, or implicitly so, as in principles governing learned taste aversions. Any developmental psychology of the future will have to deal with these senses of domains and their implications for models of development. I am suggesting that one key to doing so successfully will be to link any accounts of kinds of knowledge to descriptions of how the world is structured, especially in causal terms.

☐ Hybrid Versus Homogeneous Architectures

All too often debates in psychology swirl around absolute dichotomies. Is a representation analog or propositional? Is a memory explicit or implicit? Is development stagelike or continuous? Such oppositions may help promote debates, but they can obscure the possibilities of more mixed models. With the development of knowledge, it often seems that models usually propose qualitatively distinct kinds of representations at different points of development. A young child is considered association-ist, or concrete, or exemplar-based in her representations, while an older child is considered rule-governed, abstract, or principle-based in her representations. There are major developmental differences to be sure, but they may not rest on such dichotomies. In particular we can ask if a hybrid architecture might not be more reasonable in many cases. Such hybrids are rarely offered in some ecumenical spirit of weak eclecticism; rather they reflect the ways in which the acquisition of knowledge in a domain might require several kinds of learning architectures working in tandem. To return to the biology analogy again, many bodily organs work through simultaneous functioning of several distinct components that mutually reinforce each other, whether they are the components of the immune system or the kidneys. For example, the kidneys have several complementary mechanisms for optimally filtering waste products out of the blood. No one mechanism is adequate on its own and does not dominate at some point in an organism's development.

The study of concepts in adults has repeatedly come across a need for two kinds of architectures, sometimes called similarity versus rules (e.g., Sloman & Rips, 1998), but more generally considered as associationist versus symbolic representations. We no longer envision many concepts as being composed of simple sets of singly necessary and jointly sufficient properties, embodied as a set of simple analytic rules (Medin, 1989). The abandonment of that "classical" view, however, has led to two themes: concepts as mirrors of probabilistic patterns in the world and concepts as mirrors of causal, logical, and mathematical patterns (the "concepts as theories" view). While both themes can point to supporting phenomena, neither seems sufficient on its own for handling how we use most adult concepts.

Whether it be in computer science (Jordan & Russell, in press), linguistics (Pinker, 1993), or psychology (Murphy, in press), there is a recurrent need for a system that not only tabulates the frequencies of properties and their intercorrelations but also represents rules, principles, and mechanisms. When a person taxonomizes animals, or vehicles, or tools, that person uses a mixture of principled reasons for sorting categories as well as brute force comparisons of some feature sets. We can never explain away all aspects of members of a category or devise rules to model those properties exhaustively. I may sort mammals from reptiles on grounds that are principled and motivated by explanatory concepts in biology, but some features of each may be simply remembered because they are more commonly associated with each. Moreover, when much more local contrasts are considered, such as a Labrador retriever versus a Chesapeake Bay retriever, one may have no rules, explanatory schemas, or mechanisms that explain their differing features. At some point theory-laden aspects of knowledge may only serve to identify the sorts of features to tabulate in a more associative manner. Thus, theory will suggest that a dog's coat color, size, and ear shape should be tabulated into a probabilistic matrix but not the most common color of its collar, the number of syllables in its name, or the social class of its owner, even though some of these might well be correlated with some breeds (e.g., certain breeds are favored by the very affluent).

Each component feeds on and nourishes the other. Theory-laden parts help constrain enormously what sorts of features and feature interrelations are likely to be important, while associative processes make order out of patterns where theories can no longer suggest distinctions.

This acknowledgment of the need for hybrid structures in adult concepts has raised the obvious question of how such a hybrid might emerge in development. This question then feeds back onto the adult model by suggesting which aspects of a concept might be more primitive and unchangeable. It has often been proposed that younger children might be largely associative thinkers and that only later do they consider rules and principles (e.g., Werner & Kaplan, 1963). This view, in turn, has led to the claim that adult concepts are mostly associative as well and that the theory-laden parts are seen only when people engage in careful reflection.

In many ways the developmental conjecture is appealing. Young children certainly are different in how they talk about the world around them, and it would seem that those differences might in turn reflect differences in how they represent reality. If children seem to focus on the most typical features in their descriptions of things and if they rarely offer reasons as to why certain features are associated with a category, it would seem that they are basing their concepts on typicality structure.

There are many studies that could be cited to support such a claim. One example comes from my own laboratory, where a "characteristic to defining shift" in word meaning is described (Keil & Batterman, 1984). Younger children are more likely to judge category membership on the basis of an example having the most typical features associated with a category even if it lacks critical defining ones. Thus, they judge a penin-

sula with palm trees, buried treasures, and a warm climate to be an island, while rejecting a cold forbidding spot surrounded by water on all
sides (Keil & Batterman, 1984; Keil, 1989). Similarly, with natural kinds
such as a skunk versus a raccoon, younger children seemed to base category membership decisions on salient surface features rather than on
deeper more theory-laden ones (Keil, 1986; 1989).

A closer look at those studies, however, as well as at many others, suggests a far different interpretation. Young children are not at all at the
exclusive mercy of typicality information. In the absence of theory they
might fall back on typicality patterns sooner, assuming that such patterns
were linked to deeper processes; but where they did have more principled beliefs, such beliefs would often trump purely associative information. Moreover, the features that were probabilistically tabulated were
almost always still selected in the context of a broader set of principled
and explanatory schema. The child who declares a peninsula an island
because of its palm trees, climate, and beaches might well have mistakenly inferred that islands were characterized by their functional roles
rather than by geography. But that same child would not rely on other
features that may have been typically associated with islands but were
not associated with their roles. For example, a child might have encountered a set of islands that ended in vowels (Hawaii, Bermuda, Jamaica,
and Tahiti), but she is unlikely to weight those properties much even
if she noticed them. Similarly, children who falsely labeled kind, gift-
giving male friends of a child's parents as uncles would pick up on various social roles fulfilled by uncles and not the biological relation; but
they would not consider properties unrelated to those roles, such as
whether the uncles wore glasses or were left handed (Keil, 1989).

Many aspects of cognition may be hybrid architectures at all points in
development, whether they be for concepts, the past tense forms for
verbs (Pinker, 1993), or arithmetic calculations (Miller, 1995). At the
same time, more subtle aspects of the hybrid structure may change with
development. Here I have described two. A younger child may have
fewer encompassing theories that explain less of the information. That
child would then fill in the larger number of explanatory gaps with more
associative tabulations of information, but still constraining on theoretical grounds which features to tabulate. A younger child may also have a
different theory that focuses on a different set of relations such that associative information for an older child might be theory-laden information
for the younger child, and vice versa.

Finally, a third developmental difference in hybrid structure concerns
how closely the child links typical features to core relations. Younger
children seem to think that highly typical features are more likely to be
linked to deeper more essential or theory-laden features; that is, they

more strongly reject the idea of mere correlations. For example, if one describes a vehicle that puts out fires, young children might readily agree that it is a firetruck; yet if that truck is also said to be bright blue, younger children may reject that possibility, saying that fire trucks must be red. This kind of effect can be found in a wide array of tasks such as categorization, explanation choice, and induction. Younger children are less likely to think that any features of a kind could be arbitrary or accidental. They may well realize the centrality of some theory-laden features, but they may also see highly typical features as central even if they have no account as to why. As children get older they are more able to discount highly typical features if they are not compatible with any relevant theory. Using the highly typical to look for deeper explanatory insight is a good strategy, since most highly correlated and distinctive features are associated with a category for a reason. Even adult college students have to frequently be cautioned about the difference between causation and correlation.

Major questions remain concerning the nature of hybrid cognitive structures in development. Is there just one dichotomy, such as associations versus propositions, or are there several related dichotomies? Perhaps there are trichotomies such as associations, formal rules, and causal beliefs. How does associative information interact with the more propositional form? Could one of these forms be illusory? Perhaps layers of correlations and contingencies can look like mentally represented causal laws where they are nothing more than stored associations facilitated by temporal and spatial contiguities (Glymour, 1998). I strongly doubt that the distinctions will turn out to be ephemeral, especially given almost a century of intuitions about the duality of thought (Sloman, 1996; Neisser, 1963); but even if the distinctions are ephemeral, at the least we need to explain how a single system gives rise to the subjective experience of two.

☐ Implicit Versus Explicit Forms of Knowledge

There has been a flurry of interest in recent years in implicit and explicit cognition, especially with respect to memory (Tulving, Squire, & Schacter, 1987) but also with respect to stereotypes (Greenwald & Banaji, 1995) and learning of artificial categories (Brooks, 1978). It has proven vastly more difficult however to come up with principled ways of characterizing the differences between implicit and explicit knowledge. There is a tendency to characterize implicit knowledge as simpler, more perceptually grounded, and perhaps more associationistic in nature; but a closer look at the contrasts in the literature does not show a systematic pattern of differences. Yet that tendency to see implicit nonverbalized knowledge as simpler and more primitive also pervades views of cognitive development. In particular it often seems that the ability to encode or express thoughts in language represents a major change in the nature of cognition. This view, with roots going at least as far back as Vygotsky (1934/1986), can result in the assumption that, if children cannot verbally express a belief, then they could not have such a belief. Children's inabilities to talk about a wide range of phenomena, ranging from aspects of biology to numbers, have been taken as evidence for lack of any knowledge or understanding in those areas. This inference may be mistaken, however, and the last decade of research has intensified the debate over the nature of implicit knowledge and how it helps us understand the nature of cognitive development. The rise of connectionism in particular has enabled some to declare that not only are there no belieflike states in implicit cognition, such states might be illusory in explicit cognition as well (Churchland, 1981).

Taken together, however, the studies of the last decade seem to suggest just the opposite. Not only do older children and adults live mental lives dominated by well-elaborated belief systems, there is good reason to suspect the existence of such systems in younger children and even infants. In addition, the study of language acquisition has revealed a model of learning and developmental change in which highly elaborated belieflike mental structures function at a level that almost always functions outside of awareness. Consider first work on infant cognition. There has been a recent reaction warning against tendencies to impute adultlike mental states to infants (e.g., Haith & Benson, 1998). No doubt there are profound differences in thoughts entertained by 6-month-olds and 6-year-olds, but those differences may have little to do with the kinds of thoughts involved as much as with their contents.

It is not clear that preverbal or nonverbalizable behavior is always implicit. Thus, one might have a vivid awareness of how a machine works but have great difficulty putting that understanding into words. Indeed, some of Piaget's classic studies on language and thought documented cases where young children seemed to understand how a device worked, but they were grossly incompetent in passing on that understanding to another person (Piaget, 1926). The possibility of such kinds of knowledge highlights two alternatives for infant cognition: truly implicit knowledge that guides behavior while being outside of awareness or knowledge that is very much in the infant's awareness but cannot be expressed to others. Such a distinction may be difficult or impossible to distinguish in a preverbal infant, but it is important to models of how their knowledge might develop into more mature forms.

We now know that infants seem to understand a great deal about their physical world and aspects of their social worlds. While investigators may disagree on the details of their understandings of physical objects (e.g., Spelke, 1994; Baillargeon, Kotovsky, & Needham, 1995), they see physical objects as solid impenetrable entities that honor principles of spatio-temporal continuity and the principle of no action at a distance. Infants dishabituate when objects appear to pass through each other or seem to go out of existence and then reappear while on a trajectory (Baillargeon et al., 1995).

There is a degree of compartmentalization to some of these behaviors that might be taken as showing that the underlying mental states are not fully belieflike. An infant whose dishabituation patterns suggest that they do not understand how principles of inertia constrain object trajectories may seem to show such an understanding when perceptual motor behavior is studied. For example, infants do not dishabituate when objects change their path of motion without external forces being applied (Spelke, Kestenbaum, Simons, & Wein, 1995); yet in their attempts to manually catch moving objects, their hand movements seem to be powerfully guided by the expectations that free objects travel on straight-line trajectories (Von Hofsten, Vishton, Spelke, Feng, & Rosander, 1998). At first glance, this apparent dissociation of knowledge about physical objects across two different tasks would seem to be evidence for a form of knowledge that is highly implicit and developmentally primitive. A closer look at adult knowledge, however, reveals that closely related dissociations occur in all of us on a daily basis. There are now many compelling lines of evidence for different visual processing streams, one that supports visual pattern recognition of the sort that would occur in any passive observer of a scene and one that supports perceptual motor interactions with objects. Thus, individuals with particular patterns of brain damage to these visual processing streams can be selectively impaired such that they have almost total inability to recognize objects, yet they will approach them in perceptually guided ways that reveal considerable processing of the object's properties (Milner & Goodale, 1995). These sorts of results make comparable differences in performance among groups of infants far less indicative of a developmentally primitive mode of thought.

There are two related themes here. Some aspects of cognition may be more encapsulated than others, and the encapsulated forms tend to be more implicit (Fodor, 1983). Explicit knowledge is thought to lead to more of a meaning holism where everything is interconnected in a "web of belief" (Fodor, 1983; Quine & Ulian, 1973). But such patterns exist in adults as well as children and infants and do not necessarily mean there is a profound developmental difference. For almost 25 years it has been speculated that younger children and infants do have more encapsulated forms of knowledge and that development consists of increasing access to and flexibility with those forms (Rozin, 1976). This proposal may still be correct, but we need to consider the strength of the evidence. In particular, we should not confuse the ability to verbally express one's knowledge with it being explicit. It is a sufficient condition to be sure, but it does not seem to be a necessary one. Yet, repeatedly, preverbal children are said to be "procedural" in how they represent their knowledge. They then are said to shift to declarative knowledge when language skills become evident.

It seems just as likely that infants have a language of thought full of belief structures long before they can express those beliefs in a public language (Fodor, 1975). All of us from time to time have beliefs that we have great difficulty putting into words. Why should infants be so different and bereft of beliefs? To deny infants beliefs is to raise the difficult issue of how they make a transition from a prebelief state to having beliefs. To grant language the power of generating beliefs in children where there were none before gives language a causal power that seems to go far beyond the real nature of language alone.

The implications of this analysis extend to older children who seem to not do well on tasks requiring explicit articulation of reasons for their responses. If a child judges that only certain biological properties are inherited and not psychological ones (e.g., Hirschfeld, 1996) but is unable to explicitly justify her responses, she may not be credited with any biological knowledge. If a child cannot explain the mechanisms that are responsible for how cars work, she may well be said to have no understanding of cars. These sorts of conclusions are rampant throughout the literature and for obvious reasons; yet they are almost surely wrong in many cases. In some quarters the mismatch between explicit understandings and implicit ones are well-documented. For example, in studies of gesture, there are impressive demonstrations that children will show with gestures a newly emerged insight long before they do so explicitly with their language (Goldin-Meadow, Wein, & Chang, 1992).

The failure to consistently acknowledge the potentially rich and belieflike nature of implicit knowledge is intimately related to an assumption that development must proceed from the associative to the concrete and mechanistic to the abstract. Werner was perhaps the most straightforward in his descriptions of a concrete to abstract shift, but the same theme can be seen in Vygotsky, Bruner, and Piaget. But such a progression is not necessary and certainly does not follow some sort of logical progression. Moreover, once one allows abstract insights to precede concrete ones, it becomes much easier to see how children might have some degree of explanatory understanding that is implicit and precedes that of mechanism. Consider knowledge of "causal potency." This level corresponds to knowing that some kinds of properties are more likely to be central to mechanistic explanations in some domains as opposed others, even if one does not know those mechanisms. Moreover, that knowledge is more than simply associating kinds of properties with things, because some highly associated properties might still be seen as not being causally potent in a domain. In a series of recent studies we have been able to show that children often have a sense of a unique pattern of causal potencies for a domain long before they have much insight into specific mechanisms (Keil, Smith, Simons, & Levin, 1998). A 5-year-old might be able to articulate many systematic differences between the general categories of artifacts and living things yet might consistently see very different sorts of properties as being causally central. Artifacts, for example, tend to have a fairly narrow range of sizes and reference to human intentions as explanatorily central, whereas color and surface markings are usually seen as irrelevant. By contrast, biological kinds tend to have color and surface markings as more causally potent, but allow more size variation and make little use of human intentions (Keil et al., 1998). Few children, even those much older than 5, can articulate such differences, but they display such knowledge when they are asked to make judgments about whether something is still of the same kind if it fails to have a specific property. Similarly, they will judge causally potent properties in a domain as being more inductively projectible. These understandings are not merely associative. Some artifacts (e.g., tires, videocassettes, and personal computers) tend to have specific colors associated with most instances, whereas some living kinds (e.g., dogs, flowers) can have huge variations in colors and surface markings. The children nonetheless see color as more central to the living kinds.

In a sense, these patterns have been known for a long time in a domain of cognition that often seems to be artificially separated from the rest of cognition, namely, natural language. Much of linguistic knowledge is acquired in an implicit manner and appears to be subject to a rich array of abstract constraints (Chomsky, 1986). Moreover, recent attempts to explain even the earliest stages of language learning in infancy in purely associative terms (e.g., Saffran, Aslin, & Newport, 1996) are now being challenged on the grounds that infants will abstract away rules that are quite distant from patterns based on individual tokens (Marcus, Vijayan, Rao, & Vishton, 1998). It has therefore been a respectable view for many years that natural languages are acquired by a child who starts out with abstract constraints on possible rules and only gradually makes those rules more concrete and language specific. There is no obvious reason why such a view that seems so plausible for language would seem implausible for other domains of knowledge.

☐ Abstract Versus Concrete Modes of Thought

The implicit and explicit knowledge contrast is related to a classic theme in cognitive development: children start off representing the world in concrete terms and only later shift to more abstract representations. Despite a certain intuitive appeal to such a view, difficulties have always existed in trying to be more precise about what such a shift would really mean, and research in the last few decades makes such difficulties especially clear. It could not mean that children initially think in terms of what they can perceive and only later think in terms of concepts removed from the here and now. We now know that even very young children acquire word meanings for things that they cannot see, such as "idea," "story," or "dream" (Bloom, in press). We know that infants can think about objects while they are out of view (e.g., Baillargeon, 1991). Even levels of categorization such as "vehicle" might appear earlier than the seemingly more concrete basic level (Mandler & McDonough, 1993). Finally, as mentioned earlier, the acquisition of a natural language often seems to start at the most abstract level.

If it is so difficult to characterize thought as progressing from concrete to abstract, why does the idea seem so compelling at first glance? Part of the reason may have do to with implicit and explicit forms of knowledge. Ask children who seem to have learned the concept of a dream about the properties of dreams and many of them will ascribe to the dream's physical properties, which makes it appear that they can only think about dreams in physical terms. Talking about dreams as mental events or as kinds of informational content is much more difficult for them. But such difficulties hold for adults as well. Ask someone to talk about what gravity is and they might well try to describe it in terms of physical objects or events rather than as a force. I write this paragraph on a laptop computer while watching a group of 8- and 9-year-olds rehearse in a youth choir. The choir director is trying to explain a subtle theme in the music where the children in the youth choir are meant to represent a spirit that links together all the older members of the choir. She repeatedly says, "It's very hard to explain, but I know exactly what it means." The point is simple. We should not leap from an inability to easily talk about some abstract things to the conclusion that one cannot easily think about such things.

In many cases it seems that development might best proceed in the opposite direction, namely, from the abstract to the concrete. Such cases seem especially vivid when we think about explanatory knowledge. Most of the things we know, we only know in the sketchiest terms. The sky is blue because something happens to light when it passes through the atmosphere. Viruses are difficult to treat because there are no antibiotics for them. Ice can be destructive because it expands when it freezes. For each of these "explanations" most people can hardly go any further and provide anything like a concrete mechanistic account of what occurs. What is it about the atmosphere that makes the light turn blue? Why can't we make antibiotics for viruses? Why does water expand when it freezes unlike most other liquids? Science may indeed try to uncover general laws and principles, but it often does so by uncovering ever-more-detailed mechanisms. If infants do indeed have an intuitive folk physics and psychology, the forms of those theories must surely be in abstract terms, waiting for experience to fill in the details. Indeed, nativist proposals tend to gain the most credibility when the developmental account they describe is from abstract to concrete. They are most implausible when full-fledged concrete ideas or mechanistic beliefs spring from the minds of the newborn. Sadly, that is how many modern-day empiricists tend to caricature nativist points of view (e.g., Elman et al., 1996). In recent years there have been several attempts to characterize early, or even innate, knowledge in terms that allow it to be abstract. Dennet talks about stances, mental perspectives taken toward types of phenomena, such as the intentional, physical, and teleological stances. Others talk about early frameworks or skeletal representations (e.g., Gelman, 1990). Following a theme in linguistic theory, I have talked about abstract constraints on knowledge (Keil, 1981) and more recently about modes of construal (Keil, 1994). Finally, in the realm of biological thought, there are now many cases where preschoolers will have a very general sense of how disease is spread, how properties are inherited, or how the heart works without having any sense of the details (see Keil et al., 1998, for more on this).

In short, the more complex the knowledge and the earlier it emerges in development, the more likely the developmental pattern will be from abstract forms to those that include more concrete components. There are several nativist accounts that adopt such a model, but one of the most interesting new trends is a surge of empiricist attempts to also model abstract-to-concrete shifts. At first blush, such shifts would seem to be incompatible with an account that has an infant slowly building up expectations about the world based on frequencies and correlations among perceptual primitives. But such learning systems can yield structures and show patterns of developmental change much closer to a case where superordinate general insights precede more local ones linked to specific instances. For example, multilayered connectionist systems might develop a set of network weights that represented high-level generalizations about a domain while forgetting most low-level details. This sort of process has been compared with the process of factor analysis, where complex patterns of variation yield a few high-level factors (Hinton & Ghahramani, 1997). Similarly, a recent "latent semantic analysis" model looks at second-order correlations among word cooccurrences and abstracts away a level of analysis with a few hundred dimensions rather than relying on patterns among the hundreds of thousands words at lower levels (Landauer & Dumais, 1997). Thus, what appear to be quite abstract and general categories can emerge in a network structure and play a dominant role in guiding the further operations of much lower units.

Whether such network accounts can really model the acquisition of complex natural domains of knowledge without having a much richer set of a priori constraints remains a hotly debated topic (e.g., Marcus, in press). The point here is simply to note that some of the more recent and promising attempts to do so might well be modeling abstract-to-concrete shifts in cognition. At the least, we need to be vastly more cautious in making claims about developmental trends involving "abstract" and "concrete" aspects of thought. Whatever criteria we adopt to define these terms, there is no obvious primacy of concrete thought early, on except perhaps what children find it easiest to talk about.

☐ Conclusions

These themes all seem quite different, yet they all arise from a more attentive stance toward the world in which cognition develops. This stance is not the same as the situated cognition movement, where cognition itself is distributed not only across minds, but even across cultural artifacts (e.g., Kirshner & Whitson, 1997). While some effects along those lines certainly do occur, the emphasis here is on the simple idea that one cannot remain completely agnostic with respect to the structure of the world and hope to have an adequate account of cognitive development. There is indeed an infinite number of ways to carve up reality, to form categories, and probably even to hiearchically embed them (although there I am not so sure the number is infinite). And there are an indefinitely large number of potential correlations to notice in the environment, dooming any truly purely associative learner to a life of failed inductions (e.g., Peirce, 1960–1966). Those truths compel us to acknowledge some sorts of constraints on learners, constraints that help us pick out meaningful and important relations over senseless ones. But those constraints in turn are impossible to understand without some sense of the organism, the environment, and their ecology. Domain specificity means that there is a special adaptive resonance between one realm of cognition and one aspect of the environment. This sense is different from the simple compartmentalizations of knowledge that might occur for informationally equivalent bodies of information. There are many cases where two bodies of expertise are formally isomorphic, but experts in one have little or no insight into the other (e.g., Simon, 1975). If expert knowledge is both structurally the same in nature and only the tokens differ, such differences are not what is meant here by domain specificity.

No one, neither child nor adult, can know much of the world in any sort of detail. We rely greatly on a division of cognitive labor that allows us to access areas of expertise in others when we need it (Wilson & Keil, 1998). We get along with much sketchier understandings that somehow do enough work to be useful to us. Knowing that adult cognition usually works this way should help us see much more continuity between us and children.

☐ References

Atran, S. (1996). From folk biology to scientific biology. In D. R. Olson & N. Torrance (Eds.), *Handbook of education and human development: New models of learning, teaching, and schooling*, . Cambridge, UK: Blackwell.

Baldwin, J. M. (1897). *Mental development in the child and the race*. New York: Macmillan.

Baillargeon, R. (1991). Reasoning about the height and location of a hidden object in 4.5- and 6.5-month-old infants. *Cognition, 38*(1), 13–42.

Baillargeon, R., Kotovsky, L., & Needham, A. (1995). The acquisition of physical knowledge in infancy. In D. Sperber (Ed.), *Causal cognition: A multidisciplinary debate. Symposia of the Fyssen Foundation* (pp. 79–116). New York: Clarendon Press/Oxford University Press.

Bloom, P. (in press). Theories of word learning: Rationalist alternatives to associationism. In T. K. Bhatia & W. C. Ritchie (Eds.), *Handbook of language acquisition*, New York: Academic Press.

Boyd, R. (1991). On the current status of scientific realism. In R. Boyd, P. Gaspar, & J. D. Trout (Eds.), *The philosophy of science* (pp. 195–222) Cambridge, MA: MIT Press.

Brooks, L. (1978). Nonanalytic concept formation and memory for instances. In E. Rosch & B. B. Lloyd (Eds.), *Cognition and categorization*. Hillsdale, NJ: Earlbaum.

Chi, M. T. H. (1989). How inferences about novel domain-related concepts can be constrained by structural knowledge. *Merrill-Palmer Quarterly, 36*, 27–62.

Chi, M., Feltovich, P. J., & Glaser, R. (1981). Categorization and representation of physics problems by experts and novices. *Cognitive Science, 5*, 121–152.

Chi, M. T. H., & Koeske, R. D. (1983). Network representations of a child's dinosaur knowledge. *Developmental Psychololgy, 19*, 29–39.

Chomsky, N. (1986). *Knowledge of language*. New York: Fontana.

Churchland, P. M. (1981). Eliminative materialism and the propositional attitudes. *Journal of Philosophy, 78*, 67–90. Reprinted in A Neurocomputational Perspective (MIT Press, 1989)

Cosmides, L., & Tooby, J. (1994). The evolution of Domain specificity: The evolution of functional organization. In L. A. Hirschfeld & S. A. Gelman (Eds.), *Mapping the mind: Domain specificity in cognition and culture*. Cambridge, UK: Cambridge University Press.

Elman, J. L., Bates, E. A., Johnson, M. H., Karmiloff-Smith, A., Parisi, D., & Plunkett, K. (1996). Rethinking innateness. Cambridge, MA: MIT Press.

Fodor, J. A. (1975). *The language of thought*. New York: Thomas Y. Crowell.

Fodor, J. A. (1983). *Modularity of mind*. Cambridge, MA, MIT Press.

Galton, R. (1883). *Inquiries into human faculty and its development*. London: Macmillan.

Gelman, R. (1990). First principles organize attention to and learning about relevant data: Number and animate-inanimate distinction as examples. *Cognitive Science, 14*, 79–106.

Gibson, J. J. (1966). *The senses considered as perceptual systems*. Boston: Houghton Mifflin.

Gibson, E. J. (1970). The development of perception as an adaptive process. *American Scientist, 58*, 98–107.

Gigerenzer, G., & Hug, K. (1992). Domain-specific reasoning: Social contracts, cheating, and perspective change. *Cognition, 43*, 127–171.

Glymour, C. (1998). Learning causes: Psychological explanations of causal explanation. *Minds and Machines, 8*, 39–60.

Goldin-Meadow, S., Wein, D., & Chang, C. (1992). Assessing knowledge through gesture: Using children's hands to read their minds. *Cognition and Instruction, 9*, 201–219.

Greenwald, A. G., & Banaji, M. R. (1995). Implicit social cognition: Attitudes, self-esteem, and stereotypes. *Psychological Review, 102*, 1–27.

Haith, M. M., & Benson, J. B. (1998). Infant cognition, In D. Kuhn & R. Siegler (Eds.), *Cognition, perception and language Vol 2. of Handbook of Child Psychology (5th ed.)*. New York: Wiley.

Hinton, G. E., & Ghahramani, Z. (1997). Generative models for discovering sparse distributed representations. *Philosophical Transactions Royal Society B, 352*, 1177–1190.

Hirschfeld, L. (1996). *Race in the making: Cognition, culture, and the child's construction of human kinds*. Cambridge, MA: MIT Press.

Hirschfeld, L. A., & Gelman, S. A. (Eds.). (1994). *Mapping the mind: Domain specificity in cognition and culture*. Cambridge, UK: Cambridge University Press.

Johnson, M. H., & Morton, J. (1991). *Biology and cognitive development: The case of face recognition*. Cambridge, MA: Blackwell.

Jordan, M., & Russell, S. Computational intelligence. In R. Wilson & F. Keil (Eds.), *The MIT encyclopedia of cognitive sciences*, Cambridge, MA: MIT Press

Keil, F. C. (1981). Constraints on knowledge and cognitive development. *Psychological Review, 88*, 197–227.

Keil, F. C. (1986). The acquisition of natural kind and artifact terms. In W. Demopoulos & A. Marras (Eds.), *Language learning and concept acquisition* (pp. 133–153). Norwood, NJ: Ablex.

Keil, F. C. (1989). *Concepts, kinds and cognitive development*. Chester, NJ: Bradford Books.

Keil, F. C. (1994). The birth and nuturance of concepts by domains: The origins of concepts of living things. In L. A. Hirschfeld & S. A. Gelman (Eds.), *Mapping the mind: Domain specificity in cognition and culture* (pp. 234–254). Cambridge, UK: Cambridge University Press.

Keil, F. C., & Batterman, N. (1984). A characteristic-to-defining shift in the development of word meaning. *Journal of Verbal Learning and Verbal Behavior, 23*, 221–236.

Keil, F. C., Smith, C. S., Simons, D., & Levin, D. (1998). Two dogmas of conceptual empiricism, *Cognition, 65*, 103–135.

Kirshner, D., & Whitson, J. A. (1997). *Situated cognition: Social, semiotic, and psychological perspectives*. Mahwah, NJ: Erlbaum.

Landauer, T. K., & Dumais, S. T. (1997). A solution to Plato's problem: The Latent Semantic Analysis theory of the acquisition, induction, and representation of knowledge. *Psychological Review, 104*, 211–240.

Mandler, J. M., & McDonough, L. (1993). Concept formation in infancy. *Cognitive Development, 8*(3), 291–318.

Marcus, G. F. (in press). *The algebraic mind: Reflections on connectionism and cognitive science*. Cambridge, MA: MIT Press.

Marcus, G., Vijayan, S., Rao, S., & Vishton, P. M. (1998). 7-month-old infants can learn rules. *Science*,

McNally, R. J. (1987). Preparedness and phobias: A review. *Psychological Bulletin, 101*, 283–303.

Medin, D. (1989). Concepts and conceptual structure. *American Psychologist, 44*, 1469–1481.

Miller, K. F. (1995). Origins of quantitative reasoning. In R. Gelman & T. Au (Eds.), *Handbook of perception and cognition, Vol. 13: Perceptual and cognitive development*. Orlando, FL: Academic Press.

Milner, A. D., & Goodale, M. A. (1995). *The visual brain in action*. Oxford, UK: Oxford University Press.

Murphy, G. (in press). In F. C. Keil & R. A. Wilson (Eds.), *Cognition and explanation*. Cambridge, MA: MIT Press.

Munakata, Y., McClelland, J. L., & Siegler, R. (1997). Rethinking infant knowledge: Toward an adaptive process account of successes and failures in object permanence tasks. *Psychological Review, 104*, 686–713.

Neisser, U. (1963). The multiplicity of thought. *British Journal of Psychology, 54*, 1–14.

Peirce, C. S. (1960–1966). *Collected papers*. Cambridge, MA: Belknap Press of Harvard University Press.

Piaget, J. (1926). *The language and thought of the child*. New York: Harcourt, Brace & World.

Pinker, S. (1993). Rules of language. In P. Bloom (Ed.), *Language acquisition: Core readings*. New York, London: Harvester Wheatsheaf.

Pinker, S. (1994). *The language instinct*. New York, Harper.

Quine, W. V. O., & Ulian, J. S. (1973). *The web of belief*. New York: Random House.

Rozin, P. (1976). The evolution of intelligence and access to the cognitive unconscious. In J. M. Sprague & A. A. Epstein (Eds.), *Progress in psychobiology and physiological psychology*. New York: Academic Press.

Saffran, J. R., Aslin, R. N., & Newport, E. L. (1996). Statistical learning by 8-month-old infants. *Science, 274*, 1926–1928.

Salmon, W. C. (1989). *Four decades of scientific explanation*. Minneapolis: University of Minnesota Press.

Schacter, D. L. (1987). Implicit memory: History and current status. *Journal of experimental psychology: Learning, memory, and cognition, 13*, 501–518.

Schacter, D. L., Chiu, C.-Y. P., (1993). Implicit memory: A selective review. *Annual Review of Neuroscience, 16*, 159–182.

Simon, H. A. (1975). The functional equivalence of problem solving skills. *Cognitive Psychology, 7*, 268–288.

Sloman, S. A. (1996). The empirical case for two systems of reasoning. *Psychological Bulletin, 119*(1), 3–22.

Sloman, S. A., & Rips, L. J. (Eds.). (1998). *Similarity and symbols in human thinking (Cognition Special Issues)*, Cambridge, MA: MIT Press.

Spelke, E. (1994). Initial knowledge: Six suggestions. *Cognition, 50*, 431–445.

Spelke, E. S., Kestenbaum, R., Simons, D. J., & Wein, D. (1995). Spatiotemporal continuity, smoothness of motion and object identity in infancy. *British Journal of Developmental Psychology, 13,* 113–142.

Tomarken, A. J., Mineka, S., & Cook, M. (1989). Fear-relevant selective associations and covariation bias. *Journal of Abnormal Psychology, 98,* 381–394.

Tulving, E., & Schacter, D. L. (1990). Priming and human memory systems, *Science, 247,* 301–306.

Von Hofsten, C., Vishton, P. M., Spelke, E. S., Feng, Q., & Rosander, K. (1998). Predictive action in infancy: Tracking and reaching for moving objects. *Cognition, 67,* 255–285.

Vygotsky, L. S. (1934/1986). *Thought and language.* Cambridge, MA: MIT Press.

Wellman, H. M., & Gelman, S. A. (1998). Knowledge acquisition in foundational domains. In D. Kuhn & R. Siegler (Eds.), *Cognition, perception and language (Vol 2, 5th ed.).* New York: Wiley.

Werner, H., & Kaplan, B. (1963). *Symbol formation: An organismic-developmental approach to language and the expression of thought.* New York: Wiley.

Wilson, R. A., & Keil, F. C. (1998). The shadows and shallows of explanation, *Minds and Machines, 8,* 137–159.

CHAPTER   Katherine Nelson

The Developmental Psychology of Language and Thought

☐ Introduction

Language has been a major focus of the human sciences, humanities, and philosophy over the past century. In the beginning the focus was on the logical foundations of language (Russell, 1956; Wittgenstein, 1961) and on language structure (Saussure, 1959). But of equal interest have been the questions: "How does language determine our lives, our thoughts, our selves, our societies, and our intellectual endeavors?" Within psychology generally and developmental psychology in particular, however, language has sometimes played a minor role, has sometimes been treated as an alien topic, and has sometimes seemed to disappear entirely. As Wierzbicka (1994, p. 431) put it, "Mainstream modern psychology . . . at times seems to behave as though language is irrelevant to the study of the mind."

Yet the theories of Sapir and Whorf, of Wittgenstein, and of Chomsky and Fodor are all of major relevance to developmental psychology, particularly to issues of cognitive development. Equally relevant are the related discussions of the evolution of language, literacy, discourse, social constructionism, and narrative that are abundant at century's end. It is obviously impossible to consider in any detail the many important ideas about the relation between language and thought that have been considered over the past century within an essay of this length. In this chapter these theories serve as the background for how the relation of language and thought is treated in developmental psychology. The two dominant cognitive developmental theorists of the century, Piaget and Vygotsky, viewed this relation very differently, and their influence can be traced in the major strands of research at the century's end. In addition, the most prominent linguist of the last half century, Noam Chomsky, has influenced the thinking of developmentalists in a different direction. We can view these three major theorists as taking three divergent paths that lead to quite different launching points for the next round of developmental research and theory.

☐ The Nativist Perspective

Although not the first to come to prominence in developmental psychology, nativist approaches to cognition and language are quite prevalent at this century's end. In part this has come about through a renewed emphasis on biology and evolution, suggesting in the common parlance, "It's all in the genes," or "in the head." The anticipated success of the human genome project in decoding the genetic basis of human life, in conjunction with the claims of sociobiologists and evolutionary psychologists for the ultimate explanation of all human behavior, seem to provide the basis for believing that the development of human cognition, including human language, is simply a matter of an unfolding of a set of prepared brain "modules."

Modular theorizing began with Chomsky in the 1960s and 1970s, in claims that human language is determined by a specialized "language organ" or module situated in the brain with specialized learning mechanisms based in Universal Grammar (UG) (Chomsky, 1965). UG is claimed to represent language structures that are the basis for all human languages, present at birth in every child, ready to be realized in the particular natural language of the community into which the child is born. The details of this theory (which have changed many times over the past 40 years) are irrelevant to its influence. Among the influences on developmental thinking is the claim for the specialness of language, which has had the result of blocking language off from influence by other systems, social or cognitive, and, reciprocally, the perhaps unintended result of blocking it off from influencing these other systems in turn. Rather, as Fodor (1983) discussed, the language module (actually a set of modules, including phonology, syntax, and lexicon) is believed to be analogous to perceptual systems such as vision, which are autonomous and encapsulated; that is, they cannot be influenced by other processes and are essentially unchanged in developmental time. Two other major influences from nativist theorizing include innately available structure and content of cognitive systems, for example, knowledge of the physical world and of number, and the idea of deep theories, inaccessible to conscious reflection, that structure the surface manifestations of thought.

However, oddly, Chomsky himself eschews the idea that Darwinian evolution was responsible for the emergence of the language module. Rather he attributes it to some kind of massive genetic change, as yet unexplained (Pinker & Bloom, 1992). Nevertheless, most nativist thinking has drawn heavily from neo-Darwinism and sociobiology (Barkow, Cosmides, & Tooby, 1992). The position has also been reinforced by revolutionary research into the capacities of infant cognition, including such previously undiscovered capacities as number recognition, phonetic categorization, long-term memory, and object categorization. These capacities appear to support the idea of an organism prepared to know the world in specific ways or according to basic principles (Gelman, 1991) that will support further knowledge. The extent of nativist claims varies depending upon the specificity of principles, but the ubiquity of nativist thinking in cognitive developmental theory at the end of the century is certainly notable, from Gopnik's (1993) claim that children are born with theories of mind (which change as they encounter data that require further work) to P. Bloom's (1996) claims about the basis for lexical acquisition or Wynn's (1992) claims about arithmetic understanding in infants.

The question as usually posed by nativists is, "what is 'built in' to the 'hardware'?" Or "What does the child begin with in terms of categories, theories, grammars, or whatever?" Piaget's great effort was to assume that the infant began with nothing but reflexes and built up cognitive categories and logics from there. It is interesting that for Piaget the structure of language was no problem, whereas the structure of logical categories was. The same could be said of Vygotsky. Chomsky, however, claimed that the theory of language (basically a Saussurian theory) that both were basing their assumptions on was in error. The true theory according to Chomsky involves underlying abstract categories that cannot be learned, induced, or constructed on the basis of experience and must therefore be innately specified in the mind itself. But the assumption of innate content or innate structure that involves abstract concepts (such as noun, verb, noun phrase, etc.) poses its own unsolvable problems. How did this content get there originally if it is not acquirable from the experiential environment? We need a different theory of language than that offered by Chomsky to solve this problem. In particular we need a theory that posits language based on human cognition, rather than a theory in which human cognition is based on language.

How does nativist theorizing work out in relation to language and thought? First, it should be noted that it has little backing from the philosophers and social scientists of the earlier period, such as Whorf

(1956) or the later Wittgenstein (1953). As suggested previously, a major fallout is the blocking off of cognition from language as well as the reverse, on the grounds that cognitive domains, including language, develop in domain-specific ways according to domain-specific learning principles This has resulted in the major neglect of language as in any way relevant to issues in cognitive development, however important language might be seen to be in its own right as a subject of study or as a means of communication. Whole areas of research, such as the currently popular study of children's theory of mind, have been carried on for decades with no interest whatsoever in the relation of language, discourse, or narrative in children's understanding of mental life. (However, see Harris, this volume.)

Despite the alleged importance of understanding evolution from a Darwinian standpoint, thus seeking the origins of human social behavior in evolutionary adaptations in prehistory, there seems to be little interest among nativists in seeking to understand the extraordinary emergence in evolution of language as a species-specific characteristic in relation to its influence on human cognition. This is rather a topic of interest to those with a bent toward social constructionism rather than toward neonativism or neo-Darwinism. This outcome is ironic: language is surely one of the most dramatic species-specific characteristics of humans. The questions of what functions language serves in human life and thought and how these functions develop seem critical from a nativist as well as a nonnativist perspective.

The question "What role does the biological (innate brain structure, genetic input, evolutionary basis, modularity) play in the development of language and thought?" is at base misguided in that individual development is both a product of biological evolution, necessary to the continuation of the species, and in the human case a product of cultural institutions, especially the family, necessary to the nurturance and growth to adulthood of initially helpless individuals. There is no either/or here, no nature/nurture choice; both are not only necessary but indivisible. It is possible to break the system apart, to examine brain function, for example, but then the system is no longer functioning as a system (i.e., it is no longer active in its environment). Our analytic categories in this enterprise are by their nature artificial.

Yet if language emerged originally from human cognition, the latter cannot be cognition as we know it in present-day adults who already speak a language. Nor can it be the cognition of present-day children who do not speak the language that they will learn because the child mind is not shaped nor does it have the capacity of the adult mind. Thus we are sent back into human evolutionary history to ask what kind of mind might have constructed language in the first place. (See Deacon,

1997; Donald, 1991, for some proposals. Unfortunately, space does not permit pursuing this topic here.)

☐ Cognitive Constructivism

Piaget was without doubt the most influential theorist in the field of cognitive development during the twentieth century, although he characterized his work as a theory of genetic epistemology, and his primary concern was with constructing a theory of the origins of logical scientific thought. His developmental theory borrowed from earlier theorists, particularly James Mark Baldwin (1902), thus continuing a line of thinking throughout the century. Piaget published important theoretical papers for over 60 years, but his greatest period of influence on Anglo-American developmental psychology covered a much shorter period, roughly from the early 1960s to the early 1980s, a period during which most of his major works were translated and published in English. This period coincided with the establishment of developmental psychology as a major academic specialty in psychology departments that had previously been dominated by behavioral experimental psychology, and it also coincided with the establishment of cognitive psychology as a dominant specialty replacing the previously dominant behaviorism. Thus Piaget's influence on the emergence of cognitive development as a subspecialty is hardly surprising, and his enduring influence reflects in part the rejection of his major theoretical claims by some of the most central figures in the field. The influence endures in the setting of the major questions, problems, and themes to be addressed in cognitive development.

Because of his dominant and continuing influence on the field, Piaget must bear some of the responsibility for the neglect of language in the study of cognitive development. He viewed language as a component of the representational function, but not as an important contributor to cognition per se. Language acquisition was viewed as depending upon the completion of the sensori-motor period in terms of the establishment of the concept of permanent objects and means–ends operations, and the emergence of representational thought. Prior to this point (e.g., early in the second year) language forms (early words) might have appeared but they reflected the child's individual symbolism, not conventional signs as true language must.[1]

---

[1]Piaget uses symbols in a way similar to Freud (Piaget, 1962) rather than Peirce; thus symbols are considered meaning laden and idiosyncratic, rather than abstract and social, while signs are logical and conventional, whereas for Peirce the term "sign" incorporates multiple levels of semiotic relations of which the symbol is the most abstract.

Probably best known of Piaget's writings on the subject of language and thought was his first book published in English in 1926 under the title *The Language and Thought of the Child*, a work still in print and still enjoying considerable popularity. In this book he outlined his theory of egocentric speech. Basically he claimed that very young children used speech as reflections of their own activity. While they might seem to be addressing their peers as they engaged in related activities (playing with clay or drawing, for example) actually they were simply expressing themselves. Consequently, peers did not address each other directly and did not expect others to respond but engaged in what Piaget referred to as collective monologue.

Piaget's ultimate concern, however, was with the development of logical thought, a product of logicomathematical constructions based in action. Under his influence the Geneva school viewed language as a reflection of thought, not as contributing to the development of thought. An argument can be made that Piaget did not neglect the role of social interaction in developing cognition (Piaget, 1970), but the reciprocal role of language per se on cognitive constructions was not considered. To my mind this is a major failing of his theory. Is it a necessary failing of all theories of cognitive construction? Evidently not. Several theories of what one might call "representational constructionism" have emerged in which language usually plays a constructive, not a merely reflective, role (Bickhard, 1987; Karmiloff-Smith, 1992; Nelson, 1986; see also Donald, 1991, for an evolutionary counterpart). These theories view language as an individual tool of constructing new levels of cognition, without necessarily invoking a social agent. For example, Piaget's notion of reflective cognition is reconceptualized in Karmiloff-Smith's theory as representational redescription, or explicitation. In Donald's theory representation in language offers for the human an articulation and reification of abstract objects that makes a new level of cognition possible. This possibility was foreshadowed by Bruner, Over, and Greenfield (1966) and postulated again by Nelson (1996). Most current theories of cognitive construction, however, incorporate Piaget's basic teleology with the end point being a level of logical or scientific thought, rather than an open-ended evolution of cognition (as in Donald, 1991), and they treat cognition independently of language and its development.

☐ Social Constructivism

Beginning in the 1960s but initially overshadowed by the "debate" between Piaget and Chomsky (an event that actually took place in 1977 in Paris; see Piattelli-Palmarini, 1980), a third major theorist of the mid-twentieth century began to influence Anglo-American developmental psychology, namely, Lev Vygotsky. Vygotsky, like Piaget, had been known in international circles in the 1930s, but his work had been obscured and lost during the years after his death in Soviet Russia in 1934. Fortunately, his contributions had been kept alive by his former colleagues, particularly Luria, who became internationally renowned as a physiological psychologist, and Vygotsky's ideas were resurrected for the English-speaking academic community with the renewed interest in Soviet psychology in the 1960s. Vygotsky's last major work, *Thought and Language,* was first published in English in 1962 with an introduction by Jerome Bruner (later republished in a longer version as *Thinking and Speech,* 1987). As the title suggests, but unlike Piaget's work with a similar title (see previous section), Vygotsky alone, of the theorists thus far discussed, was centrally concerned with the relation between thinking and language. In this he was in tune with many others at the time in Europe and America in attempting to understand how language might come to both reflect and influence thought and how different languages might affect thought in different ways. Vygotsky introduced the term "semiotic mediation" to express the idea that for humans thought was mediated by the language used by the community. Vygotsky's ideas were formulated in accord with the cultural–historical social theory of Marxist–Leninism, and within that theory the relation of language and thought is highly complex.

Nonetheless, Vygotsky's theory was explicitly psychological, designed to explain how the individual could incorporate the social thinking of the community by linguistic means. Thus the influence of language on thought was through its social uses. This sets him in contrast to a writer such as Whorf (1956), who actually came later in time within American anthropology and who viewed the influence of language as a system incorporating hidden culturally determined categories that structure thought, invisible to the individual who uses them in habitual thinking. For Vygotsky the influence of language on thought is more open and explicit. Vygotsky's approach seems more in tune with Wittgenstein's (1953) later philosophy in which concepts are displayed through language as it is used by the community of speakers.

The contrast with Piaget can be seen best in their contrasting views of egocentric speech. In *Thought and Language* Vygotsky specifically addressed Piaget's theory, published almost a decade earlier. The Russian theorist viewed children's nonsocial talk as "private speech," a development on the way from social speech toward "inner speech" or verbal thinking, an advanced form of thought that made higher forms of cognition, including logical thinking, possible. In this view language begins as a social communicative function, its evolution toward a private cognitive function reflecting the advance toward higher cognitive levels accessible to humans and opening the possibility of cultural influence through educational means. Piaget responded to Vygotsky's account in a post-mortem epilogue to the 1962 version of *Thought and Language,* primarily reinterpreting Vygotsky's empirical work and seeming to foreclose empirical distinctions between the two theories. Nonetheless, the two approaches on this pivotal development in early childhood nicely contrast their divergent views on the relation of language and thought, one seeing social influence through language leading to individual development, the other seeing individual development reflected first in private, then in social language.

Contemporary developmental psychologists who have embraced aspects of Vygotsky's theories have not always emphasized the influence of language on thought to the same extent that Vygotsky himself did. Among present-day theorists in this "school" James Wertsch stands out as the primary exponent of the language view, and he has supplemented Vygotsky's theory with that of Bakhtin (a Russian literary theorist who was a contemporary of Vygotsky's but who continued to work into the 1970s). What Bakhtin's theory adds is the social–psychological dynamic of "voices in the mind." Whereas Vygotsky implied an individual private inner voice that emerged in response to the social functions of language, Bakhtin's conception is of "multivoicedness" or the reenvoicing of others' talk. Thus parental talk may "infect" the mind in ways that the individual may or may not recognize. This is a more personalized version of the language and thought relation, one that is more compatible with versions of psychodynamic theorizing, but that may also hold a key to the mystery of how language may become interiorized (Wertsch, 1991).

Other present-day theorists influenced by Vygotsky tend to a version of cultural psychology (e.g., Cole, 1996) that focuses more on activity theory (the idea that cognitive work is carried out in the context of specific activities and development of cognitive skill is thus functionally specific) and on educational applications, based on the idea of apprenticeship (Lave & Wenger, 1991; Rogoff, 1990) and scaffolding in "the zone of proximal development." In these versions the specific influence of language on cognition is no more apparent than in other versions of cognitive development; language is necessary to the scaffolding process and to the activity task but is incidental to the work that proceeds. Cultural psychology emphasizes in different degrees the social, cultural, and historical contexts and specific environments that affect cognitive functioning and knowledge acquisition. Although language is obviously crucial to these contexts, it is not the focus of analysis. In these works language remains a social, not an important cognitive tool.

A specific application of the *Thought and Language* theory in current developmental work can be found in the socialization theory of autobiographical memory development. In this theory (Fivush, 1994; Nelson, 1993; Nelson & Fivush, in press) the episodic memories of early childhood, which are initially unaccessible to long-term verbal recall (i.e., the phenomenon of childhood amnesia), are shaped through a dialectic process in which adults elicit and scaffold memories of shared past experiences with their children. In this way the young child learns to value the memory-sharing process and acquires the narrative forms that structure recalled experiences into stories that may be retained as part of one's self-history. This process in turn enables the child to recall for self and to shape her own memories for future recall and personal significance. Whereas this theory incorporates the scaffolding process that is seen as crucial to the apprenticeship version of Vygotskyan theory, it in addition emphasizes the linguistic source and structure of the memory formation. Verbal narratives, whether individual or group (e.g., group histories or myths), are postulated as specifically critical to the formation of long-enduring autobiographical memories and the offset of childhood amnesia.

☐ Interdependence

Vygotsky's theory postulated that language and thought originated independently, with language evolving from communicative forms such as those used by other primates and thought evolving from sources of animal intelligence. In human development the two were assumed to grow independently according to different "streams," coming together in the later preschool years in the form of inner speech, which becomes verbal thought with the potential for logical thinking. It was this coming together that provided the power of human intelligence in Vygotsky's view. In his (1986, p. 256) closing words, "The word is a direct expression of the historical nature of human consciousness."

An alternative to the convergence theory is the proposition that in human development thought and language emerge together from the beginning in a process of interdependence in which they mutually influence each other as development continues. Vygotsky's theory incorporated this view as well: "Verbal thought appear[s] as a complex, dynamic entity, and the relation of thought and word within it as a movement through a series of planes. . . . The development may stop at any point in its complicated course: an infinite variety of movements to and fro, of ways still unknown to us, is possible" (1986, pp. 253–254).

In one version of this theory (e.g., Nelson, 1996) human cognition and communication are seen as a singly interdependent process of representation for oneself (individual cognition) and for others (social communication). Communication need not involve conventional language, but may be conveyed by nonverbal expressions, gestures, and so on. Similarly, cognition need not involve symbols, whether natural language or other, but may be unconscious and nonsymbolic, iconic, or action based. Layers and levels of representational forms may yield different cognitive and communicative processes and products. When conventional language forms are acquired, usually beginning in the second year of life, they may reshape previously formed cognitive elements into the categories of the language being learned so as to make social communicative exchange through the common language possible. This early beginning in turn makes available to the child a means of expressing and learning through the common language, and using language forms to articulate thoughts previously left implicit (see Karmiloff-Smith, 1992, for related ideas).

As language becomes established as a complex system of symbolic representation the possibilities of using language in thought become more varied. Language is not simply a mediator of cultural ideas but a tool for analyzing and restructuring existing ideas and for forming new emergent concepts. The categories of the cultural system of language become established through use (Wittgenstein, 1953) in personal ideations along the lines of Whorf (1956), although not recognized by the individual as categories that shape thought. Thus thought becomes socialized and language becomes personal. But unlike the "voices in the mind" of Bakhtin and Wertsch, individual minds in this theory reconstruct and transform the communicative messages of others, even significant others, so that the cognitive environment of any individual is a unique product of individual constructions based on direct active experience and internalized linguistically based communications of the social–cultural world, together reconstructed through a kind of reflective cognitive process such as envisioned by Piaget or Karmiloff-Smith (1992). In this theory the developing person is never the autonomous individual theorized by Piaget and cognitive science generally nor the cultural product theorized by social constructionists. Interdependent growth of language and thought in a social–cultural environment implies a co-construction of the emerging person, in terms of cognition, personality, and self.

This interdependent growth or collaborative construction theory (Nelson, 1996) rebalances the equation to provide for the uniqueness and integrity of the self-organizing individual while recognizing the significance and essential support of the social. What about the biological basis? As stated earlier, and as Vygotsky and Piaget, together with many earlier theorists such as James Mark Baldwin, explicitly recognized, individual human development is both a biological product of evolution and a product of social and cultural institutions and interactions. In this sense the social and cultural are as natural as the biological. Language and thought each depend upon both sources as they develop interdependently. It is the developmental process that is of significance, not the apportionment to one "influence" or "input" or another.

☐ Language and Thought in Current Research

How people in general and children in particular form categories at different levels of abstraction, and how they acquire words that reference those categories are topics that have been central to psychology throughout the present century, and a central issue in contemporary developmental research is how words and categories are learned. Early in the century the topic was considered from the perspective of infant development, and much of the literature was derived from parent diaries (e.g., Stern & Stern, 1928; see Clark, 1973, for a summary of much of this early literature). Three findings of significant interest emerged from this work.

(1) First words tended to be "overextended" from the point of view of adult categories. For example, "dog" might be used for all four-legged animals, and even to name moving carriages or designs on a rug. Much discussion of this phenomenon and its meaning has appeared in the literature over the past 30 years (see review by Griffiths, 1986). The effect has not disappeared, but its meaning has diminished in importance, as the related phenomenon of "underextension" has been recognized, and pragmatic explanations have been proposed, such as the child's effort to communicate, or recognition of similarities. Different theories place emphasis on different aspects of these suggestions and ignore others or neglect the finding altogether.

(2) Although first words tend to appear at the beginning of the second year, a distinct change in acquisition patterns is usually observed midway into that year (about 18 to 20 months) when vocabulary growth accelerates in a vocabulary "spurt" resulting in the rapid accumulation of 100 to 200 words over the course of a few months (Bloom, 1993; McCarthy, 1954; Nelson, 1973). Again this phenomenon has been subject to a variety of interpretations from the Sterns' (1928) claim that it indicated that the child has a sudden insight that "everything has a name" to the current claim by Bates and Carnevale (1993) that the spurt is a mathematical artifact of the exponential function of the cumulation of items. Again, though, psy-

chologically speaking, this shift in the shape of the curve must have some implication for the child's understanding of the language. The timing is such that it is accompanied very closely by the onset of word combinations, the beginnings of grammar. This suggests that there is a cognitive–linguistic shift toward the end of the second year that supports the further acquisition of language in the third and fourth year. That this shift may be related to a better understanding of categories of both verbal and nonverbal types is suggested from work by Gopnik and Meltzoff (1986), as well as by the diminishing of the tendency to over- and underextend new words.

(3) The use of early words to express whole phrases, sentences, or speech acts, the "holophrastic hypothesis," was an accepted part of the description of early language in the first half of the century, but it has vanished from view in recent years. To DeLaguna (1927) it indicated that language was first used socially for communicative purposes (see Bruner, 1983). To some others inclined toward UG accounts of grammar it indicated that the child was equipped at the outset with the concept "sentence" but did not have the requisite vocabulary or memory to construct one (McNeill, 1970). The former view appears to have interesting implications for the relation of language and thought and would fit a Vygotskian approach very well. It is less consonant with cognitive views that suggest that the child is expressing his or her ideas about the world (Bloom, 1993), unless those ideas are held to be themselves holistic, that is, undifferentiated into parts (Nelson & Lucariello, 1985).

Thus far the puzzles posed by these early observations remain unresolved either through theoretical argument or empirical study. There remain multiple explanations for each phenomenon, and to a large extent the phenomena themselves have tended to be ignored in recent work. Children's early category structures and children's word learning have continued as major interests of developmental researchers over the past 10 or 15 years, but those concerned primarily with the acquisition of grammar or with language per se, rather than with development or with the language–thought relation, have tended in recent years to neglect the phenomena identified in the earlier work as of little interest to the main issues at stake today.

A very brief characterization of one major contemporary approach to these issues (e.g., Markman, 1987, 1991) can be outlined as follows: (1) Very young children tend to organize their knowledge of the world thematically, and when asked to group items together, they tend to form thematic groups (e.g., a dog and his bone) rather than "taxonomic" groups (e.g., a dog, cow, and giraffe). This characterization of preschool-age children is based on studies by Piaget and Vygotsky, as well as long-standing Anglo-American research. (2) Language categories, including nouns applying to "basic level" categories (such as dog, car, apple), superordinates (such as animal, vehicle, fruit), or subordinates (such as poodle, Toyota Camry, Granny Smith), apply taxonomically, that is, to all things defined in terms of relevant characteristics of similarity and not to thematic groupings (what similarity aspects are relevant is another issue). Thus if a child is to learn what words refer to, he or she must have a rule that specifies that words refer taxonomically. (3) It follows that in order to learn the language, to acquire words in the first place, children must be equipped to begin with principles such as "words apply to whole objects" and "words apply to taxonomic sets." (The actual principles suggested are not necessary to the argument, and some have been suggested to be learned as the language is being acquired; see Golinkoff, Mervis, & Hirsh-Pasek, 1994.)

Much research effort has been spent in recent years in documenting the use of such principles. Early research focused on children in the preschool years, where the tendency to group by thematic principles was shown to be overcome when a word was used to name the target superordinate group (Markman & Hutchinson, 1984; Waxman & Gelman, 1986). Current efforts are aimed at documenting the effect of words on object categorization in preverbal infants (Waxman & Markow, 1995).

The rationale advanced for the principles approach is based on an argument from analytic philosophy (Quine, 1960) stating essentially that the referent of a word cannot be reliably induced from its use in context. Rather, according to Quine, language is a wholistic structure and the reference and meaning of words is defined in terms of the whole theory within which the language is defined. This argument applies ideally to the language of science; its extension to natural language, and especially to the language-learning child, is refuted by Wittgenstein's (1953) arguments that language is a functional system and that meaning is derived from use by the community. One essential part of that argument that applies forcefully to the language-naive child comes from Wittgenstein's use of the "language game" metaphor, where the aim of the game is to learn how words are used within a particular context. To learn a language, according to Wittgenstein, is to learn a form of life. The aim is not to learn the correct rule, but to learn when to apply one term rather than another. In the child's game there are no scores kept and no penalties for wrong guesses.

Note that the logic of the principles argument, applied to the early stages of development, runs against the observations of under- and overextension, of holophrastic usage, and of a shift in the vocabulary acquisition function leading to accelerated growth of nouns. The claims for principles such as "words name whole objects" at the beginning of language acquisition also conflict with descriptions of the content of early vocabularies, which show that on average fewer than 40% of the words learned in the first half of the second year are object labels. The rest fall into a variety of categories that are not easily covered by any principles thus far promulgated (Bloom, 1993; Nelson, 1973, 1996). There is a widespread assumption that object label nouns are universally the first words learned by children, but this assumption is contradicted by the findings of distinct individual and language differences among children, many of whom acquire very few words for objects. There is evidence from languages such as Korean and Chinese that children learning those languages begin by learning primarily verbs rather than nouns (Choi & Gopnik, 1995; Tardif, 1996). In addition there is no explanation of where the alleged principles come from or how they develop, save in terms of innate specifications. The most troublesome problem for the principles approach is that it is limited in scope to concrete vocabulary (object nouns and simple actions and attributes), whereas word learning is a project that is lifelong and involves terms for abstract entities and relations that are not definable in terms of the kind of rules that principles theorists propose (Kripke, 1982; Wittgenstein, 1953). In summary, it appears that we need a more complex theory of the relation of infant cognition and language development than the "principles" account provides.

Two alternative accounts have been put forward in recent years. One, related to Piagetian assumptions, is that children begin learning words in the effort to communicate their ideas, as these ideas become more complex in relation to their actions (Bloom, 1993). This "individual expression" theory is based on extensive observation and analysis of toddlers' emerging language expressions, emotional expressions, and actions in regard to objects in play. The theory can account well for all of the observations noted previously of holophrastic expressions, under- and overextensions, and the vocabulary spurt, as well as individual differences.

A second theory focuses on children's social–communicative competence, and particularly their intersubjective interpretations of others' intentions during the period leading up to and into the early language learning period. This theory, espoused by Tomasello (1992; Tomasello & Kruger, 1992; see also Bruner, 1986), focuses on the question of how the child can understand others' intentions in a language-using situation, and thus how they infer the meanings of as-yet-unknown words. This is a subtly different version of the problem addressed by the "principles" theory, which views the issue as that of inducing the reference of a word independent of contextual guidance, whether from speakers or the general communicative situation. In the real world of adult and child, as many observations and experiments have demonstrated, there are numerous social and situational clues to the referential intentions of speakers, and toddlers are highly sensitive to these clues. Of course, children are not always successful in decoding intentions; again, the game is not one of winning or losing, or being right or wrong, but of achieving communication between speaker and listener.

An integration of the "expressive" theory and the "intentional" theory of how children come to understand and use the language beginning in the second year is not only possible, but it also solves many questions that each leaves unaddressed. In particular, the expressive theory does not really address the issue of how children interpret the language of others, which the intentional theory is specifically addressed to. The latter, in turn, pays little attention to the interests and cognitive efforts of the child, and does not address issues of individual differences, or other indications of variation among children and parents as a function of temperament, cognitive style, culture, or language. What the child is interested in expressing and attending to modulates the effects of the general conditions of the learning situation, which is emphasized by the intentional theory, and is needed to account for the wide variation in both rate and pattern of learning in the first few years of language acquisition.

A general theory of word learning must also account for the rapid acquisition of vocabulary, not only in the second year but throughout the preschool and subsequent school years. For this a theory that accounts for the learning of words for abstract concepts and relations is more important than that addressed to whole objects and taxonomic categories, which constitute a minority of the words learned, in the early as well as the later years (Nelson, 1995; Nelson, Hampson, & Kessler Shaw, 1993). How children learn verbs has been relatively neglected, but has been addressed by a number of researchers in the last 10 years (Tomasello & Merriman, 1995). As many have pointed out, the referents of verbs are less easy to recognize than object nouns, because, unlike objects, actions and states do not have easily identified boundaries and shapes; verbs encode a rich variety of aspects of action, including direction, manner, and causality. With the exception of object labels, most nouns also have less obvious reference to the world of things and require more induction on the part of the learner (Nelson et al., 1993), as do relational terms for cause and time, for example (Bloom, Lahey, Hood, Lifter, & Fiess, 1980; Nelson, 1996). The word-learning child is faced with a formidable task in building a vocabulary that includes these abstract types of words, but children are remarkably successful at it. What social and cognitive capacities do they draw on for this task?

In addressing the issue of how children learn abstract words and their meanings, Levy and I proposed (Nelson, 1996; Levy & Nelson, 1994) that children learn to use words in context, as Wittgenstein implied, and that they engage in "use without meaning" for many words prior to acquiring the aspects of meaning implied by adult uses. This approach has been demonstrated for temporal terms, causal terms, and in recent work for mental state terms (Kessler Shaw, 1999). There is broad agreement that older children and adults learn the meanings of words not from direct instruction, but from use in context, from oral discourse or written texts (Sternberg & Powell, 1983). This conclusion takes us beyond the narrow focus of much of the recent work on children's lexical acquisition to situate word learning within the larger framework of how language is used in discourse, and how children make sense with language and through other means. In so doing it moves the study of words and meanings from the rule-driven static code toward a dynamic creative process. It emphasizes the dialectical nature of the word–concept relation in development. To focus on an unknown word is to recognize the absence of a meaning structure or concept in one's mental repertoire, while at the same time recognizing an empty slot in an otherwise familiar context. Knowing the nonverbal context set up by the verbal utterance provides the beginnings of the meaning that can be attributed to the word. Attending to the word in additional contexts and using it in similar ways progresses to the construction of a new concept through linguistic means.

Understanding of the semantics of words is now revealed to be as complex a process as the understanding of larger segments of discourse. In particular, word forms are polysemous (standing for many meanings), and the meaning of a word can thus only be understood in the context of its use. But by the same token, the possible meanings of a word can only be inferred from experiencing the word in many different contexts. Even simple, nonpolysemous words (by standard analyses) may be taken as implying one aspect rather than another in different discourse contexts, as Wittgenstein's (1953) unpacking of the meaning of the word "game" indicated. Out of context we can only understand the meaning of this word in terms of a "family resemblance" structure. In context we can only understand its meaning in terms of the kinds of game in focus, whether chess, basketball, tag, Monopoly, or politics. Future investigations of the developmental beginnings of integrating language and thought through the learning of words based on these more complex understandings of contexted meanings in discourse promise to reveal more of the deep relation between using words to think and to express one's thoughts to others. In this way word meaning and use can shed light on important current issues involved in children's understanding of time, of self, and of other minds, all topics of current interest to those who see language as critical to cognitive development and knowledge acquisition.

The word–concept dialectic displays in a microcosm the larger language and thought problems raised at the outset of this discussion. Discourse and its development, literacy and written texts, metaphor comprehension and interpretation, narrative and stories, all active areas of current inquiry, inevitably encounter similar problems of the interplay between language and cognition, although often the problems lie more deeply embedded in methodological and theoretical assumptions than in the area of early word learning where they are more explicit. These larger linguistic constructions also lay open the unavoidable social and cultural nature of linguistic thought. The word–concept relation can be (ill-)conceived as an individual matter, as "in the head," but these larger discourse forms are socially produced and socially owned. Deriving word meanings from use in discourse thus inevitably infects the child's mind with social and cultural concepts.

In particular, the ubiquity of narrative in human thinking, in individual stories and societal myths, has been newly recognized as a hallmark of human thought and linguistic product (Bruner, 1986, 1990; Donald, 1991). As Donald put it, "narrative is the natural product of language." Theorists of narrative understanding, whether in written texts, oral tales, or television dramas, emphasize the psychological process of piecemeal construction of plot, calling on real-world knowledge, causal relations, interpretations of mental dispositions, as well as the contexted meanings of individual words and syntactic constructions (Bruner, 1990; van den Broek, Bauer, & Bourg, 1997). To understand and produce narrative, even the skeletal personal narratives about "what happened" by the 3-year-old, it is necessary to combine understanding of action, causality, conventional event structures, intentions, motivations, goals, emotions, ideas and other mental constructions, and the relations between people, including sex and age differences, among many other constructs.

Recognizing narrative as the natural product of language is to recognize the central role of language in the interpretation of human experience. Of course narrative is not the only interpretive genre that we educated, literate folk can call on (exposition and argumentation come to mind), but it is often the most "ready to hand" and the earliest acquired in childhood. As Carrithers (1991) argued, narrative rests on and incorporates all of the larger concerns of human experience; thus language enters and shapes "our lives, our thoughts, our selves, our societies, and our intellectual endeavors."

☐ References

Baldwin, J. M. (1902). *Development and evolution.* New York: Macmillan.

Barkow, J. H., Cosmides, L., & Tooby, J. (Eds.). (1992). *The adapted mind: Evolutionary psychology and the generation of culture.* New York: Oxford University Press.

Bates, E., & Carnevale, G. F. (1993). New directions in research on language development. *Developmental Review, 13,* 436–470.

Bickhard, M. H. (1987). The social nature of the functional nature of language. In M. Hackmann (Ed.), *Social and functional approaches to language and thought.* New York: Academic Press.

Bloom, L. (1993). *The transitions from infancy to language: Acquiring the power of expression.* New York: Cambridge University Press.

Bloom, L., Lahey, M., Hood, L., Lifter, K., & Fiess, K. (1980). Complex sentences: Acquisition of syntactic connectives and the semantic relations they encode. *Journal of Child Language, 7,* 235–261.

Bloom, P. (1996). Controversies in language acquisition: Word learning and the part of speech. In R. Gelman & T. Au (Eds.), *Handbook of perceptual and cognitive development.* New York: Academic Press.

Brumm, J. S. (1983). *Child's talk: Learning to use language.* New York: Norton.

Bruner, J. S. (1986). *Actual minds, possible worlds.* Cambridge, MA: Harvard University Press.

Bruner, J. S. (1990). *Acts of meaning.* Cambridge, MA: Harvard University Press.

Bruner, J. S., Over, R. R., & Greenfield, P. M. (1966). *Studies in cognitive growth.* New York: Wiley.

Carrithers, M. (1991). Narrativity: Mindreading and making societies. In A. Whiten (Ed.), *Natural theories of mind: Evolution, development and simulation of everyday mindreading* (pp. 305–318). Oxford, UK: Blackwell.

Choi, S., & Gopnik, A. (1995). Early acquisition of verbs in Korean: A cross-linguistic study. *Journal of Child Language, 22,* 497–529.

Chomsky, N. (1965). *Aspects of a theory of syntax.* Cambridge, MA: MIT Press.

Clark, E. V. (1973). What's in a word? On the child's acquisition of semantics in his first language. In T. E. Moore (Ed.), *Cognitive development and the acquisition of language.* New York: Academic Press.

Cole, M. (1996). *Cultural psychology: A once and future discipline.* Cambridge, MA: Harvard University Press.

Deacon, T. W. (1997). *The symbolic species: The co-evolution of language and the brain.* New York: Norton.

DeLaguna, G. (1927). *Speech: Its function and development.* New Haven, CT: Yale University Press.

Donald, M. (1991). *Origins of the modern mind.* Cambridge, MA: Harvard University Press.

Fivush, R. (1994). Constructing narrative, emotion, and self in parent-child conversations about the past. In U. Neisser, (Ed.), *The remembering self: Construction and accuracy in the self-narrative* (pp. 136–157). New York: Cambridge University Press.

Fodor, J. (1983). *Modularity of mind.* Cambridge, MA: MIT Press.

Gelman, R. (1991). Epigenetic foundations of knowledge structures: Initial and transcendent constructions. In S. Carey & R. Gelman (Eds.), *The epigenesis of mind: Essays on biology and cognition* (pp. 293–322). Hillsdale, NJ: Erlbaum.

Golinkoff, R., Mervis, C. B., & Hirsh-Pasek, K. (1994). Early object labels: The case for a developmental lexical principles framework. *Journal of Child Language, 21,* 125–156.

Gopnik, A. (1993). How we know our minds: The illusion of first-person knowledge of intentionality. *Behavioral and Brain Sciences, 16,* 1–14.

Gopnik, A., & Meltzoff, A. (1986). Words, plans, and things: Interactions between semantic and cognitive development in the one-word stage. In S. Kuczaj & M. Barrett (Eds.), *The development of word meaning* (pp. 199–223). New York: Springer-Verlag.

Griffiths, P. (1986). Early vocabulary. In P. Fletcher & M. Garman (Eds.), *Language acquisition: Studies in first language development* (2nd ed., pp. 279–306). London: Cambridge University Press.

Karmiloff-Smith, A. (1992). *Beyond modularity.* Cambridge, MA: MIT Press.

Kessler Shaw, L. (1999). *Acquiring the meaning of know and think.* Unpublished doctoral dissertation, City University of New York Graduate Center.

Kripke, S. A. (1982). *Wittgenstein on rules and private language.* Cambridge, MA: Harvard University Press.

Lave, J., & Wenger, E. (1991). *Situated learning: Legitimate peripheral participation.* New York: Cambridge University Press.

Levy, E., & Nelson, K. (1994). Words in discourse: A dialectical approach to the acquisition of meaning and use. *Journal of Child Language, 21,* 367–390.

Markman, E. M. (1987). How children constrain the possible meanings of words. In U. Neisser (Ed.), *Concepts and conceptual development: Ecological and intellectual factors in categorization* (pp. 255–287). New York: Cambridge University Press.

Markman, E. M. (1991). The whole-object, taxonomic, and mutual exclusivity assumptions as initial constraints on word meanings. In S. A. Gelman & J. P. Byrnes (Eds.), *Perspectives on language and thought: Interrelations in development.* New York: Cambridge University Press.

Markman, E. M., & Hutchinson, J. E. (1984). Children's sensitivity to constraints on word meaning: Taxonomic vs. thematic relations. *Cognitive Psychology, 16,* 1–27.

McCarthy, D. (1954). Language development in children. In L. Carmichael (Ed.), *Manual of child psychology* (2nd ed.). New York: Wiley.

McNeill, D. (1970). *The acquisition of language: The study of developmental psycholinguistics.* New York: Harper & Row.

Nelson, K. (1973). Structure and strategy in learning to talk. *Monographs of the Society for Research in Child Development, 38* (1–2, Serial No. 149).

Nelson, K. (1986). *Event knowledge: Structure and function in development.* Hillsdale, NJ: Erlbaum.

Nelson, K. (1988). Where do taxonomic categories come from? *Human Development, 31,* 3–10.

Nelson, K. (1993). The psychological and social origins of autobiographical memory. *Psychological Science, 4,* 1–8.

Nelson, K. (1995). The dual category problem in lexical acquisition. In W. Merriman & M. Tomasello (Eds.), *Beyond names for things.* Hillsdale, NJ: Erlbaum.

Nelson, K. (1996). *Language in cognitive development: The emergence of the mediated mind.* New York: Cambridge University Press.

Nelson, K., & Fivush, R. (in press). Socialization of memory. In E. Tulving & F. Craik (Eds.), *Handbook of memory.* New York: Oxford University Press.

Nelson, K., Hampson, J., & Kessler Shaw, L. (1993). Nouns in early lexicons: Evidence, explanations, and implications. *Journal of Child Language, 20,* 61–84.

Nelson, K., & Lucariello, J. (1985). The development of meaning in first words. In M. D. Barrett (Ed.), *Children's single word speech.* Chichester, UK: Wiley.

Piaget, J. (1926). *The language and thought of the child.* New York: Harcourt, Brace.

Piaget, J. (1962). *Play, dreams, and imitation in childhood.* New York: Norton.

Piaget, J. (1970). Piaget's theory. In P. H. Mussen (Ed.), *Carmichaels' handbook of child development* (3rd ed., Vol. I, pp. 703–732). New York: Wiley.

Piattelli-Palmarini, M. (Ed.). (1980). *Language and learning: The debate between Jean Piaget and Noam Chomsky.*

Pinker, S., & Bloom, P. (1992). Natural language and natural selection. In J. H. Barkow, L. Cosmides, & J. Tooby (Eds.), *The adapted mind: Evolutionary psychology and the generation of culture* (pp. 451–494). New York: Oxford University Press.

Quine, W. V. O. (1960). *Word and object.* Cambridge, MA: MIT Press.

Rogoff, B. (1990). *Apprenticeship in thinking: Cognitive development in social context.* New York: Oxford University Press.

Russell, B. (1956). *Logic and knowledge.* London: Allen and Unwin.

Saussure, F. D. (1959). *Course in general linguistics.* New York: The Philosophical Library, Inc. (Original work published in 1915)

Stern, C., & Stern, W. (1928). *Die kindersprache: Eine psychologische und sprachtheoretische unterserchung* (4th ed.). Leipzig: Barth.

Sternberg, R. J., & Powell, J. S. (1983). Comprehending verbal comprehension. *American Psychologist, 39,* 878–891.

Tardif, T. (1996). Nouns are not always learned before verbs: Evidence from Mandarin speakers' early vocabularies. *Developmental Psychology, 32,* 492–504.

Tomasello, M. (1992). The social bases of language acquisition. *Social Development, 1,* 67–87.

Tomasello, M., & Kruger, A. C. (1992). Joint attention on actions: Acquiring words in ostensive and non-ostensive contexts. *Journal of Child Language, 19,* 313–333.

Tomasello, M., & Merriman, W. E. (Eds.). (1995). *Beyond names for things: Young children's acquisition of verbs.* Hillsdale, NJ: Erlbaum.

van den Broek, P., Bauer, P., & Bourg, T. (Eds.). (1997). *Developmental spans in event comprehension and representation: Bridging fictional and actual events.* Hillsdale, NJ: Erlbaum.

Vygotsky, L. (1962). *Thought and language* (E. Hanfmann & G. Vakar, Trans.). Cambridge, MA: MIT Press.

Vygotsky, L. (1986). *Thought and language.* Cambridge, MA: MIT Press.

Vygotsky, L. S. (1987). *Problems of general psychology (including the volume Thinking and Speech)* (Vol. I). (N. Minick, Trans.). New York: Plenum Press.

Waxman, S., & Gelman, R. (1986). Preschoolers' use of superordinate relations in classification and language. *Cognitive Development, 1,* 139–156.

Waxman, S. R., & Markow, D. B. (1995). Words as invitations to form categories: Evidence from 12- to 13-month-old infants. *Cognitive Psychology, 29,* 257–302.

Wertsch, J. (1991). *Voices in the mind.* Cambridge, MA: Harvard University Press.

Whorf, B. L. (1956). *Language, thought and reality: Selected writings of Benjamin Lee Whorf.* Cambridge, MA: MIT Press.

Wierzbicka, A. (1994). Cognitive domains and the structure of the lexicon: The case of the emotions. In L. A. Hirschfeld & S. A. Gelman (Eds.), *Mapping the mind* (pp. 431–452). New York: Cambridge University Press.

Wittgenstein, L. (1953). *Philosophical investigations.* New York: Macmillan.

Wittgenstein, L. (1961). *Tractatus logico philosophicus.* London: Routledge.(Original work published in 1921)

Wynn, K. (1992). Addition and subtraction by human infants. *Nature, 358,* 749–750.

CHAPTER

Josef Perner

Theory of Mind

☐ Introduction

Theory of mind has become the name of the research area that investigates our *folk psychological* concepts for imputing mental states to others and ourselves: what we *know, think, want, feel,* etc. My first encounter with the expression "theory of mind" was in quite distinct fields. In philosophy, Fodor (1978) spoke of the "representational theory of mind" as a proposal of how cognitive science should deal with our folk psychology. In animal psychology Premack and Woodruff (1978) asked the provocative question, "Does the chimpanzee have a theory of mind?" These authors argued that imputing mental states requires a theory because (1) mental states are not directly observable but need to be inferred like theoretical terms in science, and because (2) one can predict behavior on the basis of these inferred mental states much better than one could without them. Many people object to "theory" as being too intellectual a term for chimpanzees and young children; readers who feel that way can safely substitute "coherent body of knowledge" for theory. Soon the term appeared in developmental psychology (Bretherton, McNew & Beeghley-Smith, 1981) where it became the agreed label for the field, with two symposia in 1986 (contributions to both published in Astington, Harris, & Olson, 1988).

Although my concern is with the development of a theory of mind in humans, it is worth mentioning these other fields because it is a characteristic of theory of mind research that there is a lively exchange among different fields (e.g., Carruthers & Smith, 1996). Notably philosophers of mind and cognitive science (e.g., Fodor, 1987; Churchland, 1984) debate the question whether our folk psychology is a good starting point for a scientific psychology or not. Evolution theorists and primatologists ask at which step in evolution a theory of mind emerged and for what reason (perhaps a Macchiavellian advantage in the social power struggle; Byrne & Whiten, 1988), and whether it may have been the motor behind the large size of human brains (Dunbar, 1998).

☐ Predecessor Traditions in Developmental Psychology

Before the field had been given its new identity as "theory of mind," similar issues were investigated within different intellectual traditions. The most important tradition is that on visual perspective-taking that started with Piaget and Inhelder's (1956) three-mountain problem, in which children had to indicate the picture showing the view from another person's perspective of three toy mountains. This culminated in Flavell, Everett, Croft, and Flavell (1981) showing that very young children, even 1-year-olds (Lempers, Flavell, & Flavell, 1977), understand what people can and cannot see, but have problems until 4 years or later understanding that people can see different things in the same drawing (Chandler & Boyes, 1982). This work was also extended into emotional perspective-taking (Flavell, Botkin, Fry, Wright, & Jarvis, 1968; Borke, 1971; Chandler & Greenspan, 1972) and cognitive perspective-taking, or what people know or do not know (Marvin, Greenberg, & Mossler, 1976).

A psycholinguistically inspired tradition (Macnamara, Baker, & Olson, 1976: pretend, forget, and know; Johnson & Maratsos, 1977: think and know; Wellman & Johnson, 1979: remember and forget) investigated when children understand certain prerequisites for the use of mental verbs, for instance, that one has to have known something before one can forget it. Within this tradition investigators also looked at the frequency of use of mental verbs in very young children (Shatz, Wellman, & Silver, 1983).

Another relevant tradition is that of children's story understanding (Stein & Trabasso, 1981). It is now clear that any decent story centers around protagonists' motives, emotions, and deceptions. Analyses in artificial intelligence (Schank & Abelson, 1977; Bruce & Newman, 1978; Hendrix, 1979) have given interesting cognitive analyses of these stories and made them amenable to theoretically interesting manipulation. And philosophers' comments on Premack and Woodruff's (1978) paper indicated how to construct decisive tests for understanding the mind. Out of this came our (Wimmer & Perner, 1983) false belief test that played a crucial role in assessing children's appreciation of mental perspective.

The False Belief Test

Three- to 5-year-old children are told a story that is enacted with toy figurines on a small stage: "Maxi puts his chocolate into the cupboard. He goes out to play. While he is outside he can't see that his mother comes and transfers the chocolate from the cupboard into the table drawer. She then leaves to visit a friend. When Maxi comes home to get his chocolate, where will he look for it?" Most studies report that practically all children below the age of 3 years give the wrong answer and say that Maxi will look in the drawer where the chocolate actually is. And they do so even though many of them can remember where Maxi put it in the beginning and that he could not see it being transferred. By 3 years a few children start getting it right by saying that he will look in the cupboard where the chocolate used to be. After 4 years most children give this answer, although in some studies even some 5- and 6-year-olds are not perfect (e.g., Ruffman, Perner, Naito, Parkin, & Clements, 1998, Experiment 2).

In the last 10 years a massive onslaught of clever experimenting has been aimed at showing that much younger children can be shown to understand false belief. Although several of the experimental manipulations had some success in producing correct performance several months earlier, the basic developmental trend was not affected. This was recently shown in a massive metanalysis by Wellman, Cross, and Watson (1999) of 177 false belief experiments.

Why has this paradigm become so popular and why is it carried out under the label of theory of mind rather than in the Piagetian tradition of "cognitive perspective-taking"? I like to think that this popularity is due to the conceptual analysis that makes theory of mind research distinctive.

☐ What Makes Theory of Mind Research Distinctive? Conceptual Analysis

It is in conceptual analysis where the affinity with philosophy of mind is most apparent. This is so because philosophers of mind (within the tradition of analytical philosophy) make their living by analyzing the deep structure of how we adults talk about the mind (naive folk psychology).

Since developmental psychologists study how children acquire the adults' theory, philosophers' insights are of particular value.

The philosophical analyses make one thing very clear: there is an important difference between our naive folk physics (our everyday knowledge of how physical objects behave) and our naive folk psychology. Our knowledge about the physical world consists of representations of how the world is, whereas our knowledge of the mind goes a step higher. It consists of knowledge of how these representations of the world are used by sentient beings. This is brought out very clearly in the so-called representational theory of mind (Fodor, 1978; Field, 1978) that tries to make our folk psychology amenable to cognitive science. Let me explain with a modified version of our false belief story. Maxi got a beginner's set of an electric train: just one line connecting the train shed with the station. Maxi can flip the control switch left and the train goes from the station back into the shed, or he can flip it to the right and the train goes from the shed into the station.

Aristotle in his Practical Syllogism noted that if I know what someone wants and what he thinks (believes) about how he can achieve it, then I have the basis for a behavioral prediction. So, if Maxi wants the train to be in the station and he thinks (knows) that it is in the shed, then we can predict that he will flip the switch to the right. In our folk psychology we express Maxi's mental life with the familiar terms "want" and "think." Philosophers have characterized these terms as *propositional attitudes,* because they relate an organism (Maxi) to a proposition:

Organism ——————— (attitude) ————→ proposition
Maxi ——————— (thinks) ————→ the train is in the shed

The interesting point is that with the *proposition* we express how Maxi *represents* the world. The *attitude* describes how Maxi *uses* this representation. In philosophy this functional use of representations is identified with functional boxes that contain these representations like a *belief box* (B-box) and a *desire box* (D-box), and cognitive scientists speak similarly of a data base and a goal box. So, in our example Maxi's mind would consist of two boxes:

B-box: "The train is in the shed."
D-box: "The train is in the station."

What defines the boxes are the different roles they play in determining Maxi's behavior. That is, the B-box has the function to show the world *as it is,* the D-box how Maxi *wants* the world to be, and they fulfill their function in that they make Maxi flip the switch so that the train will go from the shed to the station, and not the other way around.

An important point here is that propositional attitudes do not describe higher-order representations. That is, when we say "Maxi wants the train to be in the station," then we do not mean that Maxi has such a representation in his data base (B-box). If he has such a representation in his B-box, then that would mean that *he believes that he wants the train to be in the station,* but believing that one wants something does not mean one actually wants it, that is, that one is actually poised to do something in order to attain it.

Conversely, actually wanting the train to be in the station requires that one has the representation "train in station" in one's D-box, but that does not mean that one knows what one wants. To have that knowledge the higher-order representation "I want the train to be in the station" has to be in the B-box. In other words, one can have desires without knowing about (loosely speaking, being conscious of) them. But to know about it one needs a concept of desire (want), that is, the relevant part of a theory of mind.

The clear distinction between the contents of our mental states (the representations in a box) and the function that they serve (the kind of box the content is in) helps us see the nature of various long-standing problems, to which we now turn.

The Problem of Introspection

What we know and believe is that which is represented in our B-box. However, the functional use of our representations (that we know, that we want something, etc.) is not represented in our B-box. So how do we know that? The common intuition is that we simply know. René Descartes referred to this saying that our mind can freely introspect so that it is transparent to itself. This Cartesian idea of mental transparency is used in *simulation theory* (Goldman, 1993; Harris, 1992), which assumes that children know their own minds directly by introspection. The real developmental problem is to understand what goes on in other minds. This is gradually mastered by taking the other person's perspective and simulating with one's own mind the experiences in such a situation.

The opposing position is the so-called theory theory (NB: "*theory* of mind" is sometimes used in the more specific way to denote this theoretical position), where the mental terms are considered theoretical terms of a theory that get their meaning from how they relate to other terms in the theory and in particular to the observable. One weakness of this position is that nobody has yet managed to specify a coherent body of theoretical laws (but then nobody has yet managed to give a satisfactory specification of the grammatical rules of English). However, they might be something like this in relation to our Maxi problem: "If someone doesn't *see* an object moved (or has other kinds of information about it), then he *thinks* that the object remains where it is. A person *looking* for an object goes to where she or he *thinks* the object is." The terms "see," "look," "think," etc., get their meaning from the role they play in laws like this.

One distinguishing implication of these positions is that the introspectionist simulation theory predicts that children should have problems mostly with understanding other minds, not their own. However, theory theory predicts that understanding one's own mind and understanding other people's mind should follow a similar developmental course. The available evidence favors the latter (Gopnik, 1993; Gopnik & Wellman, 1992). For instance they can predict Maxi's false belief at about the same time as they can remember their own false belief (Gopnik & Astington, 1988). However, theory theory remains intuitively unsatisfactory since it denies the primacy of knowledge of our own mind. For instance take the case of knowing where the train is after having seen it inside the station. Theory theory claims that we know of our own knowledge just in the same way as we know that Maxi knows. There are two main ways of checking whether Maxi knows. We can see him look inside or we can check whether he can give the right answer. If he can give the right answer but we made sure that he could not have looked inside, then we conclude that he does not know and just made a lucky guess. In our own case it is quite different. We may have forgotten that we had looked inside and yet we still know whether we know or not.

A nonintrospectionist version of simulation theory developed by Gordon (1995) may do justice to this intuition. Gordon realized that in our own case everything that is a fact (for us) is something that we know. So if we have "the train is in the station" in our B-box as a fact, then we can safely add (Gordon calls this an "ascent routine") the higher-level description, "I know that the train is in the station," to our B-box, without any introspection of the functional use of the basic level representation.

The issue of whether we understand the mind by theory or by simulation is still far from settled, largely because there are many interesting ideas and claims but no good empirical methods for assessing the issue. We (Perner, Gschaider, Schrofner, & Kühberger, 1999) have test run one method on adults, but we have not yet used it on the developmental issues.

The Problem of Pretense and Reasoning

Another interesting problem is whether all we need is a B- and a D-box, or whether we need many more functional boxes, for instance, one for pretend play. Leslie (1987) suggested that the difference between what is believed and what is pretended is made by means of metarepresentation. For example, the child represents (presumably in the B-box) that she is pretending that the banana is a telephone:

B-box: "I pretend this (banana) is a telephone."

This has the advantage that when the child is pretending she also knows that she is pretending. It has the disadvantage that it does not explain how believing that one is pretending should result in pretend action (just as believing that one wants something does not serve the function of wanting something). For this reason Nichols and Stich (1999) and Currie and Ravenscroft (in press) suggested that pretense must have a different function, that is, they posit a possible-world box (PW-box) in addition to B-box and D-box. One unsatisfactory feature of this proposal is that it entails that children can indulge in pretend play without knowing that they do so (since there need be no representation of their pretence in their B-box). My proposal (Perner, 1991, pp. 33–35 and Chapter 3) was that pretend representations are in the B-box but are differentiated from straight beliefs by metarepresentational comments (or markers) that serve a dual function. They give the marked representations a different function and they represent that the so-marked content is not real. In other words, the metarepresentational markers amount to a PW-box within the B-box. Of course, Leslie's proposal can be easily amended in this way by stipulating that the "I pretend" part induces a different function, which makes our proposals very similar.

Leslie's proposal: B-box: "I pretend this (banana) is a telephone."
My proposal: B-box: "PW-box: This (banana) is a telephone."

in contrast to

Nichols and Stich: PW-box: "This (banana) is a telephone."

Despite their similarity there is an important difference between my proposal and that of Leslie. The difference is that in my proposal a pretending child only needs to represent the difference between reality and a possible world. In contrast, in Leslie's proposal the child represents the mental (functional) state of pretending. That implies that the child needs to understand the difference between pretending and believing. My theory (e.g., Perner, Baker, & Hutton, 1994) entails that the 3-year-old child who fails the false belief test does not understand this. These children can understand that people act according to the real world or according to a possible world (pretend scenario), but they do not understand that someone with a false belief, intent to act according to the real world, ends up acting according to a possible (counterfactual) world because the person mistakes that possible world for the real world (or we could say, because the person takes a false proposition as true; Perner, Leekam, & Wimmer, 1987). The mastery of the false belief task shows that children understand this.

This developmental transition can also be characterized in the following way. Younger children understand that people act for a reason (Davidson, 1963). In the normal case, the world gives reason to act a particular way in order to reach one's goal. If Maxi is after his chocolate, then he has good reason to go to the drawer where his chocolate is. If he pretends that his chocolate is in the empty cupboard, then within his pretend world he has good reason to go there. Three-year-olds understand this, as noted by Henry Wellman (1990), who spoke of a "desire psychology." The critical point is that these children understand that people have reasons to act in those ways that bring them closer to their goals. Mistaken action is difficult to explain. Maxi has no good reason to look for his chocolate in the empty cupboard when he wants to really get it. To understand how this can happen the child needs to understand that action is based on a mistaken belief that gives no good reason for going to the wrong place, which is at best an excuse. It provides an excuse once one understands that beliefs cause action; that is, even though Maxi does not further his goal by going to the empty cupboard, the belief makes him go there because it is not the world directly that governs Maxi's action but his belief about the world. I spoke of understanding beliefs (and other mental states) as causally effective mental representations and characterized the child who passes the false belief test as a "representation theorist" (Perner, 1988, 1991).

In sum, there are principally two reasons for why the study of children's understanding of false belief has enjoyed such great popularity. It is partly due to the fact that (besides desire) belief is the central concept in our theory of mind. The other reason is that there are interesting analyses of deeper intellectual changes in the child that help link false belief development to other, often seemingly unrelated, changes at this age. This, however, holds the greatest promise for the future. So let me first take stock of the established developmental findings.

☐ Achievements and Gaps: General Development

Early Infancy

The investigation of theory of mind in infancy has just started. Investigations center on early awareness that people's actions are governed by intentions to reach a goal. Gergely, Nadasdy, Csibra, and Biro (1995) used habituation–dishabituation to displays of animated, moving objects, such as a small ball moving to a large ball. Children around 9 and 12 months appear to be "teleologists" who expect spontaneously moving objects to approach a goal on the most direct physically possible path. Spelke, Phillips, and Woodward (1995) reported for a similar age that children expect a person who is looking at one of two objects to then manipulate that one rather than the other object. Woodward (in press) reports that even at 5 months infants who were habituated to a person grasping a particular object dishabituated more strongly to a change in goal object than to a change in the grasping movement. At this point, however, it is not clear how much these young infants understand about intentions. It could be that the other person's action aimed at a goal object is apt to focus the child's attention on that object, so that a shift in goal object requires a shift in the infant's attention, which then registers as prolonged dishabituation. The infant need not have a concept of intention and goals beyond this attentional sensitivity.

At 18 Months

Fairly sharply around 18 months, some drastic changes have been documented in children's understanding of goals and desire. Meltzoff (1995) found that children observing a failed action, for example, trying to pull one of the balls off a small dumbbell, then imitate the intended successful action, not the actually observed action. Thus, they must have inferred the intended goal.

Repacholi and Gopnik (1997) gave 18-month-olds the choice between a tasty cracker and a (for most children) repulsive piece of broccoli. The infants observed one of the experimenters express the opposite preference supported by clear vocal and facial expressions (e.g., "Ugh, this cracker is yucky! Hmm, this broccoli is yummy"). Children were then requested by that person to hand her something to eat. Most of the younger half of 18-month-olds handed her the crackers, whereas most of the older half handed her the broccoli. It seems that sharply at 18 months children start to understand that food preferences are subjective.

At 18 months other theory-of-mind-related abilities emerge. Early reports of pretend play fall into this period (Piaget, 1945), and children show clear signs of empathic behavior when observing another person in distress (an ability that emerges with self-recognition in the mirror; Bischof-Köhler, 1988).

From 1 and One-Half to 3 Years

Children's pretense becomes demonstrably sophisticated in terms of tracking the counterfactual consequences of pretense (Leslie, 1994; Harris & Kavanaugh, 1993). For instance, when naughty Teddy is pretending to have tea in his cup and tilts the cup over a piece of chocolate, children are able to state that the piece of chocolate is now wet (within the pretense when, of course, it remained perfectly dry). However, Lillard (1993) has cautioned that there are still severe limitations on these children's understanding of pretense. When told that a troll has never seen a kangaroo and he does not know what one is, when he hops (like a kangaroo) children before the age of 4 or 5 years nevertheless say that the troll is pretending to be a kangaroo. Lillard concluded that young children conceive of pretense in a nonmental way, simply as acting alike. There is controversy on this point. Custer (1996; also Bruell & Woolley, 1998; Gerow, Taylor, & Moses, 1998; Rosen, Schwebel, & Singer, 1997) found that if a story character who had a boot on his fishing line was pretending that he had caught a fish, then children tended to agree (they pointed to the relevant think bubble) that he was thinking of a fish rather than thinking of a boot. Lillard's finding might not have picked up so much on a specific problem about pretense but on a very important different problem about understanding mental states, namely, that someone who has a mental state about something (e.g., pretending to be or wanting a kangaroo) has to have a concept of it (kangaroo), i.e., know what it is. This connection may not be understood until 4 or 5 years.

Children are also becoming increasingly sophisticated about understanding people's desires and their emotional consequences. For instance Nicola Yuill (1984; Wellman & Banerjee, 1991) found that by 3 years children understand that a person will feel happier when he achieves what he wants (e.g., throws a ball to a particular person) than when he fails to do so (e.g., another person catches the ball).

Children's growing understanding of pretense and desire is also reflected in the increasingly frequent use of words such as "pretend," "want," "feel" in this period (Bartsch & Wellman, 1995). The word "think," however, is not much used before the age of 3 years.

From 3 to 5 Years

A major change that takes place in this period is the understanding that things can be conceived of as being different than they really are. This enables children to come to grips (as outlined above) with false belief (Wimmer & Perner, 1983) and related concepts such as the distinction between appearance and reality (Flavell, Flavell, & Green, 1983). The earliest onset of this ability emerges around 3 years as a particular kind of understanding that we (Clements & Perner, 1994) have called "implicit understanding." This can be demonstrated in the original false belief paradigm, except that the story protagonist (instead of Maxi we used Sam the Mouse) disappears from the child's view to *reappear* either at location A (where he thinks the desired object is) or at location B (where the object really is). With this change one can check where children are looking in anticipation of Sam's return when Sam's desire for his piece of cheese is mentioned. There is a sharp onset around 3 years (2 years and 10 months and 3 years and 2 months) where a majority of children look to location A, almost all of whom answer the explicit question about where Sam will reappear with location B. Importantly, in a knowledge control condition in which Sam saw the cheese being moved to B, children did not look to A where the cheese had originally been.

We also found (Clements & Perner, 1997) that when children had to *act,* for example, quickly move a welcoming mat into place, many moved that mat to location A provided they acted spontaneously and quickly. Those children who hesitated tended to move it to B. This provided one more reason to call this early knowledge implicit, because it seems to dissociate from conscious, explicit knowledge in a similar way as implicit from explicit knowledge when visual illusions are involved (e.g., illusory motions of a dot, Bridgeman, Kirch, & Sperling, 1981; Bridgeman, Peery, & Anand, 1997; Milner & Goodale, 1995; Wong & Mack, 1981; see Perner & Clements, in press, for analogy to our finding).

A similar finding that implicit knowledge (expressed in manual gestures) precedes explicit knowledge (expressed in answers to questions) has been reported by Church and Goldin-Meadow (1986) for Piagetian conservation tasks and for math problems (Perry, Church, & Goldin-Meadow, 1988). This group of researchers, Goldin-Meadow, Alibali, and Church (1993), also made the interesting suggestion that the appearance of implicit knowledge marks the zone of proximal development (Vygotsky, 1978) within which instructions and helpful scaffolding (Wood, Bruner, & Ross, 1976) become effective. This may explain some of the claims (e.g., Judy Dunn, this volume) that in natural interactions children show earlier competence than in the experimental test situations.

Take the case of deception. Deception in stories seems to be understood as, or slightly after, children master the false belief test (Wimmer & Perner, 1983; Sodian, 1991). Active deception (Sodian, Taylor, Harris, & Perner, 1991) even when emotionally extremely involved (Peskin,

1992), is not reliably and flexibly employed in novel situations until that age (mothers and nursery teachers think so, too; Stouthamer-Loeber, 1986; see Perner, 1991, Figure 8.7). It is true that in standard situations children do behave deceptively by the age of 3. For instance when accused of some wrongdoing they seemingly deny having done it with a firm, "No" (Lewis, Stanger, & Sullivan, 1989). However, this kind of evidence is multiply ambiguous. As Stern and Stern (1909) observed a long time ago, we do not know whether these "No's" are genuine acts of deception or pleas for not being accused. If successful, they may work deceptively (the adult is genuinely made to believe that the child did not do it) but without the child realizing that that is how the trick works, i.e., by inducing a false belief in the accusing adult. From the child's point of view, saying "no" simply had beneficial effects in the past.

This ambiguity of interpretation of real-life acts of deception, by the way, is a source of festering controversy in the animal literature about primates being or not being able to understand false belief. Primatologists observing apes in the wild or the zoo (e.g., De Waal, 1982; Byrne, 1995) present ample anecdotes of seemingly convincing acts of deception. These acts look convincing as uses of a theory of mind because *if we* engaged in these acts *we would* understand the mental effects on the victim. However, experimental attempts to demonstrate flexible acts of deception that indicate an understanding of false belief (or even knowledge) consistently meet with failure (Woodruff & Premack, 1979; Povinelli & Eddy, 1996) as do direct attempts at testing false belief in chimps (Call & Tomasello, in press).

From 4 to 6

Children's understanding of false belief comes with an understanding that perceptual access (e.g., seeing what is in a box) is important for knowing. However, for them the importance of perceptual access seems to override other sources of knowledge such as inference (Sodian & Wimmer, 1987). As a consequence, they fail to see the point in memory cues (e.g., put a police car outside the house where the policeman is visiting in order to remember where he is; Sodian & Schneider, 1990) because such cues enable retrieval of knowledge without direct perception. At this age children also do not appreciate that different properties are gained through different sense modalities, for example, that you need your eyes to learn what color an object is, but your hands (to lift the object) in order to learn how heavy it is (O'Neill, Astington, & Flavell,

1992). This understanding develops between 4 and 6 years and might be the basis for genuine episodic memories, as I will argue below.

After 6

It is not that theory-of-mind development stops at age 6, but less research effort has been devoted to exploring the many important developments in later childhood. Children's ability to introspect (for us almost self-evident) aspects of their own thoughts develops surprisingly late (Flavell, Green, & Flavell, 1995). For instance (Flavell, Green, & Flavell, 1998), a group of 5-and-one-half and 8-and-one-half-year-olds were to sit in the special "Don't Think" chair, and they were instructed to not think for a while. After about 20 seconds they were allowed to move over to the normal chair and were asked: "While you were sitting over there in that Don't Think chair, you tried not to have any thoughts. What happened? Did you have no thoughts at all or did you have some thoughts anyway?" Very few 5-year-olds (15%) but most 8-year-olds (75%) and adults (100%) admitted to having had some thoughts.

Higher-order false beliefs (e.g., what John mistakenly thinks that Mary thinks where the ice cream van is; Perner & Wimmer, 1985) are understood at around 6 or 8 years. However, the complexity of the story narrative has a much greater influence at this stage than for the acquisition of understanding first-order beliefs (Núñez, 1993; Sullivan, Zaitchik, & Tager-Flusberg, 1994). A relevant implication is that children cannot really distinguish more complicated speech acts, such as irony from lies. Lies as well as irony (and jokes) are false statements, and they are *intended* to be false by the speaker. The difference emerges at the second-order level: the speaker does *intend* the listener to *believe* the lie, whereas a joke or irony is not *intended* to be *believed* (Leekam, 1991; Winner & Leekam, 1991).

Children this age also have problems with promises (Astington, 1990). Fortunately they do understand what is important, namely, that promises need to be kept. Rather, their problem is that they see too much commitment as being associated with a promise. For instance, Mant and Perner (1988) told stories such as the following: A boy tells his friend that he will go swimming and she regrets not to be able to join because she has to help mother. He later decides to stay home. She finds out that mother does not need her and goes to the pool, where she is lonely and disappointed. Up to the age of about 9 years children judged the boy as naughty for not having gone to the pool. It is as if stating what one wants to do constitutes a commitment to doing it. The difficulty is in seeing that there are exceptions. There is an interesting age parallel to understanding exceptions to the reprehensibility of lying: white lies are not bad and even socially desirable (Walper & Valtin, 1992). Children's problems understanding the function of lies, promises, and social commitment are also of interest in connection with children's competency as witnesses in court (Perner, 1997).

And there is much else left to be discovered about the mind for the older children. As Chandler (1988) points out, all the rapidly increasing evidence of understanding the mind in early childhood does not show that children conceive of the mind as truly constructive, and that they fully realize the relativity of human knowledge. Much of this awareness develops later and contributes to the self-doubt and *Existenzangst* during puberty and young adulthood.

Summary

Although we know little about early infancy, we have a good picture of how theory of mind develops in early childhood, and we have some idea of how that links to important social skills at this age (e.g., deception) and how later development influences the more subtle social abilities of irony and white lies and the ability to introspect.

☐ Achievements and Gaps: Individual Differences

Normal Development: Siblings and Parental Interaction

Although the acquisition of a theory of mind follows some fairly clear progression, there are also individual differences in the normal population, largely investigated with children's mastery of the false belief task. There is some circumstantial evidence, which has not yet been extensively investigated, that children from lower socioeconomic families are delayed (Holmes, Black, & Miller, 1996; Ruffman et al., 1998, Experiment 2). Furthermore, we know that early interactions between child and siblings and parents have an influence (Dunn, this volume; Ruffman, Perner, & Parkin, in press). We also know that the number of siblings is beneficial (Perner, Ruffman, & Leekam, 1994) and older siblings in particular (Lewis, Freeman, Kyriakidou, Maridaki-Kassotaki, & Berridge, 1996; Ruffman et al., 1998). This finding speaks strongly against the view that theory of mind development is due to purely endogenous maturation, since it is unlikely that speed of acquisition is genetically linked to the number of older siblings a child has. However, there are also genetic factors that have severe effects on the acquisition of a theory of mind.

Autism

Autism has a clear genetic component (Frith, 1989). Baron-Cohen, Leslie, and Frith (1985) found that children with autism, despite a mental age (verbal and nonverbal intelligence) of well over 4 years, have a severe deficit on our Maxi task (which has become the "Sally-Ann test" in the autism literature). In contrast, children with Down's syndrome matched on IQ had no comparable deficit. Moreover, the few children with autism who master false belief, even the very intelligent and highly verbal ones (Asperger syndrome), still have problems with higher-order theory of mind problems such as second-order beliefs and indirect speech acts, like irony (Happé, 1994; see "After 6" above). It seems fairly clear that autism brings a theory-of-mind deficit with it. However, it is less clear that the theory-of-mind deficit is defining of autism since other groups show a similar deficit. For instance, a recent metanalysis by Yirmiya, Erel, Shaked, & Solomonica-Levi (1998) shows that children with mental retardation of unknown etiology (in particular not caused by Down's syndrome) are also impaired in their theory of mind performance, in particular, on the false belief test, and are more similar to autistic children than children with Down's syndrome.

Deafness

Gale, de Villiers, de Villiers, & Pyers (1996) report that orally taught deaf children (who have a good education but because they are not taught sign language are delayed in their language development) trail in their mastery of tasks such as the false belief task by about 3 years. Jill and Peter de Villiers (in press) argue that language competence reflects the development of certain grammatical mechanisms that also govern our language of thought required for thinking about someone's false belief and related mental states. Although this is an intriguing proposal, the available evidence still leaves more mundane possibilities viable. In particular, there is the plausible possibility that language is a very or even *the* most important database for working out a theory of mind. Our best and most precise source of information about other people's mind is what they themselves say about it. Building a theory of mind from just observing people's behavior would be a tough order.

Summary

Environmental factors clearly influence the acquisition of a theory of mind, but the search for the relevant factors has just started. Impairments of linguistic communication (deafness) is certainly one of the most important. Genetic factors are equally important, and the case of autism is one very striking example.

☐   Prospects: Implications for Own Mind

My brief review of achievements has also shown obvious gaps. There are many exciting prospects for theory of mind research filling these gaps. However, I would like to concentrate here on a particular aspect: the application of theory of mind to one's own mind and how one's mind is related to the world it represents. With this issue we touch on the highly popular phenomenon of consciousness of whose development we know little. Theory of mind research should be able to help.

Consciousness

The *higher-order thought theory* of consciousness (Armstrong, 1980; Carruthers, 1996; Rosenthal, 1986) makes clear that consciousness requires some theory of mind. For instance, if I am consciously aware (as I am) that I am typing these lines, then I am not just seeing and knowing (first-order mental states) that I am doing this, but I am also aware (higher-order state) of the first-order state; that is, I am aware that I am *seeing* myself typing. There is controversy over whether this captures the nature of consciousness, but, surely, it must be a necessary condition. It seems inconceivable that I could genuinely claim that I am conscious of my typing and, yet, claim that I have no idea whether I *see* myself typing or *just dream* about it or *want* myself to type. Consequently, since being conscious of my typing implies awareness of seeing myself typing, consciousness requires mental concepts such as seeing, that is, some theory of mind.

We do not yet understand enough about consciousness to say what kinds of concepts are minimally required for those higher-order mental states implied by consciousness. Moreover, the theory of mind research in infancy, where the first mental concepts are acquired, is still in its beginning. Because of the importance of this topic, progress in investigating the earliest theory of mind development holds great promise.

We are not only conscious of what happens in the world. A higher form of consciousness concerns our awareness of how we are linked to our world, in particular, how the experience of events leads to (causes) our knowledge and memory of these events, and how our intentions to act are responsible for (cause) our actions. Searle (1983) referred to mental states such as memory and intentions as "causally self-referential," since, for example, my memory has to encode not only a past state ("I was typing the above lines") but also how it (the memory itself) came about (was caused by the remembered event: my typing via my experiencing it caused my knowledge and memory of my typing). There is now some evidence suggesting that the prerequisite theory-of-mind development for this kind of self-referential awareness enables episodic memory and self-control.

Episodic Memory

Tulving (1985) reintroduced the self-referential aspect into modern memory research. To capture this aspect he characterized *episodic memory* as "autonoetic (self-knowing)." Episodic memory is the remembering of personally experienced events that need, in Ebbinghaus' (1885) words, "to be recognised as something formerly experienced." When reading Tulving's paper I realized that there is relevant evidence from theory of mind development (Perner, 1990). Children between 4 and 6 years acquire the prerequisite for forming episodic memories in this specific sense because, as mentioned above, around this age children become able to represent how they know something (Wimmer, Hogrefe, & Perner, 1988).

And, indeed, we were able to show a connection (Perner & Ruffman, 1995). We used the difference between free recall and cued recall as a measure that is (according to Tulving, 1985) sensitive to the availability of episodic traces. We found that this difference depended significantly on children's ability to, for example, explain why they know what is in a box ("because you've shown me" or "because you told me") or understand that they need to look inside a tunnel to find out what color the object is but use their hand to find out how heavy it is (O'Neill et al., 1992).

We now also know that passing these theory of mind tests coincides with children becoming less suggestible (Leichtman, 1996; Welch-Ross, 1997), presumably because true episodic memories give a firmer grip on reality than mere knowledge about the past, with obvious implications for children's use as witnesses in court.

Executive Control

Theory of mind cannot only be applied to memory (input side) but also to actions (output side). Heinz Wimmer (1989) once suggested that the better one understands one's own mind the better one should be able to control one's actions that are governed by one's mind. There is now increasing evidence that children's mastery of the false belief task and related tasks around the age of 4 years also brings an increase in executive control (Carlson, 1997; Frye, Zelazo, & Palfai, 1995; Hughes, 1998a, 1998b; Perner, Lang, & Stummer, 1998; Russell, Mauthner, Sharpe, & Tidswell, 1991). In particular, children master tasks that I like to characterize as *executive inhibition* tasks.

In the normal case there is *automatic inhibition* (in the model of control by Norman and Shallice, 1986, this is the level of *contention scheduling*). Concentrating on performing an action activates the relevant action schema, which in turn inhibits incompatible schemata. The tasks that require executive inhibition (Norman and Shallice's supervisory attentional system, or for short SAS) have the particularly nasty feature that by concentrating on the intended action an old action tendency, too, gets activated and, thus, becomes likely to interfere with the intended action (Perner, Stummer, & Lang, 1999). Hence, the usual automatic control does not suffice; conscious inhibition from the SAS is required.

A typical example where this is required is a children's version of Luria's (Luria, Pribram, & Homskaya, 1964) hand game. The child (C) is first to imitate what the experimenter (E) does: flat hand → fist → flat hand → . . . Then the game changes so that the child has to do the opposite of what the experimenter does, i.e.,

E: flat hand → fist → flat hand → . . .
C: fist → flat hand → fist → . . .

The natural tendency is to imitate. Hence, that tendency is likely to interfere with what one is supposed to do. In order to inhibit this natural tendency it is not sufficient to just concentrate more on one's proper task because that task involves concentrating on what the experimenter does and that enhances the interfering natural tendency to imitate. That is, automatic inhibition is thwarted and executive inhibition is needed. Executive inhibition consists of representing the existence of the interfering action tendency in order to inhibit that tendency.

There is now a healthy controversy in the literature (5 competing theories; see Perner & Lang, in press) about how to explain why the false belief task and executive inhibition tasks are mastered at the same time. I will mention a couple of these theories that make specific predictions about why the false belief task in particular should be mastered at the same time as executive inhibition tasks. Russell et al. (1991; Hughes & Russell, 1993) suggested that the false belief task itself is an executive function task requiring the inhibition of a predominant response, namely, to answer with the object's real location. This, however, is unlikely, because the so-called explanation version of the false belief task shows the same correlation (Hughes, 1998a). In that task (Wellman & Bartsch, 1988) the child watches Maxi look in the wrong cupboard and is asked to explain why he did so. Children who do not understand false belief tend to say nothing, which means there is no prepotent answer strategy that needs to be inhibited.

Another explanation is based on my analysis of excecutive control (Perner, 1998). One way of explaining the basic idea is that children around 4, as outlined above, understand mental states as something that make people act (something with causal power) even if people have no good reasons to act like that. In the case of our false belief task, the false belief makes Maxi look for his chocolate in the empty cupboard, even though he does not really want to look in an empty cupboard. Similarly, the child can only start to understand the need for inhibiting an existing response tendency when it is understood that response tendencies can make one act in a way contrary to one's actual intentions. An evaluation of the different proposals in view of existing data can be found in Perner & Lang (in press).

Summary

I have emphasized the cases of episodic memory and executive control as illustrations of how the conceptual analysis of mental concepts (typical of theory-of-mind research) helps make cross connections to otherwise unrelated areas. Existing research holds great promise that these connections will be strengthened. And my hope is that new insights in the very early theory of mind development during infancy will help us understand the development of consciousness.

☐ Conclusion

The investigation of children's theory of mind has its ancestry in Piaget's work and other traditions of cognitive/linguistic/social development. It gets its particular flavor from its link with philosophy of mind, which focuses on the functional use of mental representations and less on the form of mental representations as in traditional cognitive psychology.

The last 20 years have given us an intensive picture on how theory of mind unfolds from 3 to 6 years, less on the preceding and following years, and hardly anything on early infancy. The particular analysis of mental states pursued by theory of mind research allows us to see cross connections to other intellectual achievements. I have mentioned episodic memory and self-control. They are particularly interesting since they pertain to aspects of consciousness. The greatest prospect for theory of mind research is that it will shed light on the development of consciousness.

☐ References

Armstrong, D. (1980). *The nature of mind and other essays.* Ithaca, NY: Cornell University Press.

Astington, J. W. (1990). Metapragmatics: Children's conception of promising. In G. Conti-Ramsden & C. Snow (Eds.), *Children's language* (pp. 223–244). Hillsdale, NJ: Erlbaum.

Astington, J. W., Harris, P. L., & Olson, D. R. (1988). *Developing theories of mind.* New York: Cambridge University Press.

Baron-Cohen, S., Leslie, A. M., & Frith, U. (1985). Does the autistic child have a "theory of mind"? *Cognition, 21,* 37–46.

Bartsch, K., & Wellman, H. M. (1995). *Children talk about the mind.* Oxford, UK: Oxford University Press.

Bischof-Köhler, D. (1988). Über den Zusammenhang von Empathie und der Fähigkeit, sich im Spiegel zu erkennen. *Schweizer Zeitschrift für Psychologie, 47,* 147–159.

Borke, H. (1971). Interpersonal perception of young children: Egocentrism or empathy? *Developmental Psychology, 5,* 263–269.

Bretherton, I., McNew, S., & Beeghley-Smith, M. (1981). Early person knowledge as expressed in gestural and verbal communication: When do infants acquire a "Theory of Mind"? In M. E. Lamb & L. R. Sherrod (Eds.), *Infant social cognition* (pp. 333–373). Hillsdale, NJ: Erlbaum.

Bridgeman, B., Kirch, M., & Sperling, A. (1981). Segregation of cognitive and motor aspects of visual function using induced motion. *Perception and Psychophysics, 29,* 336–342.

Bridgeman, B., Peery, S., & Anand, S. (1997). Interaction of cognitive and sensorimotor maps of visual space. *Perception & Psychophysics, 59* (3), 456–469.

Bruce, B., & Newman, D. (1978). Interacting plans. *Cognitive Science, 2,* 195–233.

Bruell, M. J., & Woolley, J. D. (1998). Young children's understanding of diversity in pretense. *Cognitive Development, 13,* 257–277.

Byrne, R. W. (1995). *The thinking ape: Evoluntionary origins of intelligence.* Oxford, UK: Oxford University Press.

Bryne, R. W., & Whiten, A. (1988). *Machiavellian intelligence: Social expertise and the evolution of intellect in monkeys, apes and humans.* Oxford, UK: Clarendon Press.

Call, J., & Tomasello, M. (in press). A nonverbal false belief task: the performance of children and great apes. *Child Development.*

Carlson, S. M. (1977, April). *Individual differences in inhibitory control and children's theory of mind.* Poster presented at the biennial meeting of the Society for Research in Child Development. Washington, DC.

Carruthers, P. (1996). *Language, thought and consciousness. An essay in philosophical psychology.* Cambridge, UK: Cambridge University Press.

Carruthers, P., & Smith, P. K. (1996). *Theories of theories of mind.* Cambridge, UK: Cambridge University Press.

Chandler, M. J. (1988). Doubt and developing theories of mind. In J. W.Astington, P. L Harris, & D. R.Olson (Eds.), *Developing theories of mind* (pp. 387–413). New York: Cambridge University Press.

Chandler, M. J., & Boyes, M. (1982). Social-cognitive development. In B. B. Wolman (Ed.), *Handbook of developmental psychology* (pp. 387–402). Engelwood Cliffs, NJ: Prentice-Hall.

Chandler, M. J., & Greenspan, S. (1972). Ersatz egocentrism: A reply to H. Borke. *Developmental Psychology, 7,* 104–106.

Church, R. B., & Goldin-Meadow, S. (1986). The mismatch between gesture and speech as an index of transitional knowledge. *Cognition, 23,* 43–71.

Churchland, P. M. (1984). *Matter and consciousness: A contemporary introduction to the philosophy of mind.* Cambridge, MA: MIT PressClements, W. A., & Perner, J. (1994). Implicit understanding of belief. *Cognitive Development, 9,* 377–397.

Clements, W. A., & Perner, J. (1994). Implicit understanding of belief. *Cognitive Development, 9,* 377–397.

Clements, W., & Perner, J. (1997). *When actions really do speak louder than words—but only implicity: Young children's understanding of false belief in action.* Unpublished manuscript.

Currie, G., & Ravenscroft, I. (in press). The development of pretence. In G. Currie & I. Ravenscroft (Eds.), *Meeting of minds: Thought, perception and imagination.* Oxford, UK: Oxford University Press.

Custer, W. L. (1996). A comparison of young children's understanding of contradictory representations in pretense, memory, and belief. *Child Development, 67,* 678–688.

Davidson, D. (1963). Actions, reasons, and causes. *Journal of Philosophy, 60,* 685–700.

de Villiers, J., & de Villiers, P. (in press). Linguistic determinism and the understanding of false beliefs. In P. Mitchell & K. J. Riggs (Eds.), *Children's reasoning and the mind.* Hove, East Sussex: Psychology Press.

De Waal, F. (1982). *Chimpanzee politics.* London: Unwin.

Dunbar, R. I. M. (1998). The social brain hypothesis. *Evolutionary Anthropology, 6,* 178–190.

Ebbinghaus, H. (1885). *Über das Gedächtnis.* Leipzig: Duncker und Humblot.

Field, H. (1978). Mental representation. *Erkenntnis, 13,* 9–61.

Flavell, J. H., Botkin, P., Fry, C., Wright, J., & Jarvis, D. (1968). *The development of role-taking and communication skills in children.* New York: Wiley.

Flavell, J. H., Everett, B. A., Croft, K., & Flavell, E. R. (1981). Young children's knowledge about visual perception: Further evidence for the Level 1–Level 2 distinction. *Developmental Psychology, 17,* 99–103.

Flavell, J. H., Flavell, E. R., & Green, F. L. (1983). Development of the appearance-reality distinction. *Cognitive Psychology, 15,* 95–120.

Flavell, J. H., Green, F. L., & Flavell, E. R. (1995). Young children's knowledge about thinking. *Monographs of the Society for Research in Child Development, 60* (1, Serial No. 243).

Flavell, J. H., Green, F. L., & Flavell, E. R. (1998). *Development of children's awareness of their own thoughts.* Unpublished manuscript, Stanford, CA: Stanford University.

Fodor, J. A. (1978). Propositional attitudes. *The Monist, 61,* 501–523.

Fodor, J. A. (1987). Modules, frames, fridgeons, sleeping dogs, and the music of the spheres. In J. L. Garfield (Ed.), *Modularity in knowledge representation and natural-language understanding* (pp. 25–36). Cambridge, MA: MIT Press.

Frith, U. (1989). *Autism: Explaining the enigma.* Oxford, UK: Basil Blackwell.

Frye, D., Zelazo, P. D., & Palfai, T. (1995). Theory of mind and rule-based reasoning. *Cognitive Development, 10,* 483–527.

Gale, E., de Villiers, P., de Villiers, J., & Pyers, J. (1996). Language and theory of mind in oral deaf children. In A. Stringfellow, D. Cahana-Amitay, E. Hughes, & A. Zukowski (Eds.), *Proceedings of the 20th annual Boston University Conference on Language Development. Volume 1.* Somerville, MA: Cascadilla Press.

Gergely, G., Nadasdy, Z., Csibra, G., & Biro, S. (1995). Taking the intentional stance at 12 months of age. *Cognition, 56,* 165–193.

Gerow, L. E., Taylor, M., & Moses, L. J. (1998). *Children's understanding that pretense is based on mental representation.* Unpublished manuscript, University of Oregon.

Goldin-Meadow, S., Alibali, M. W., & Church, R. B. (1993). Transitions in concept acquisition: Using the hand to read the mind. *Psychological Review, 100,* 279–297.

Goldman, A. I. (1993). The psychology of folk psychology. *Behavioral and Brain Sciences, 16,* 15–28.

Gopnik, A. (1993). How we know our minds: The illusion of first-person knowledge of intentionality. *Behavioral and Brain Sciences, 16* (1), 1–113.

Gopnik, A., & Astington, J. W. (1988). Children's understanding of representational change and its relation to the understanding of false belief and the appearance-reality distinction. *Child Development, 59,* 26–37.

Gopnik, A., & Wellman, H. M. (1992). Why the child's theory of mind really is a theory. *Mind & Language, 7,* 145–171.

Gordon, R. M. (1995). Simulation without introspection or inference from me to you. In M. Davies & T. Stone (Eds.), *Mental simulation: Evaluations and applications* (pp. 53–67). Oxford, UK: Blackwell.

Happé, F. (1994). *Autism: An introduction to psychological theory.* Cambridge, MA: Harvard University Press.

Harris, P. L. (1992). From simulation to folk psychology: The case for development. *Mind & Language, 7,* 120–144.

Harris, P. L., & Kavanaugh, R. D. (1993). Young children's understanding of pretence. *Society for Research in Child Development Monographs (Serial No. 237).*

Hendrix, G. C. (1979). *Encoding knowledge in partitioned networks.* New York: Academic Press.

Holmes, H. A., Black, C., & Miller, S. A. (1996). A cross-task comparison of false belief understanding in a head start population. *Journal of Experimental Child Psychology, 63,* 263–285.

Hughes, C. (1998a). Executive function in preschoolers: Links with theory of mind and verbal ability. *British Journal of Developmental Psychology, 16* (2), 233–253.

Hughes, C. (1998b). Finding your marbles: Does preschoolers' strategic behavior predict later understanding? *Developmental Psychology, 34* (6), 1326–1339.

Hughes, C., & Russell, J. (1993). Autistic children's difficulty with mental disengagement from an object: Its implication for theories of autism. *Developmental Psychology, 29,* 498–510.

Johnson, C. N., & Maratsos, M. P. (1977). Early comprehension of mental verbs: Think and know. *Child Development, 48,* 1743–1747.

Leekam, S. R. (1991). Jokes and lies: Children's understanding of intentional falsehood. In A. Whiten (Ed.), *Natural theories of mind: Evolution, development, and simulation of everyday mindreading* (pp. 159–174). Oxford, UK: Blackwell.

Leichtman, M. D. (1996). *What gets remembered? Patterns of memory and reminiscence in early life.* Paper presented at the International Conference on Memory, Padua, Italy, July 1996.

Lempers, J. D., Flavell, E. R., & Flavell, J. H. (1977). The development in very young children of tacit knowledge concerning visual perception. *Genetic Psychology Monographs, 95,* 3–53.

Leslie, A. M. (1987). Pretense and representation: The origins of "Theory of Mind". *Psychological Review, 94,* 412–426.

Leslie, A. M. (1994). Pretending and believing: Issues in the theory of ToMM. *Cognition, 50,* 211–238.

Lewis, C., Freeman, N. H., Kyriakidou, C., Maridaki-Kassotaki, K., & Berridge, D. M. (1996). Social influences on false belief access: Specific sibling influences or general apprenticeship? *Child Development, 67,* 2930–2947.

Lewis, M., Stanger, C., & Sullivan, M. W. (1989). Deception in 3-year-olds. *Developmental Psychology, 25,* 439–443.

Lillard, A. S. (1993). Young children's conceptualization of pretense: Action of mental representational state? *Child Development, 64,* 372–386.

Luria, A., Pribram, K. H., & Homskaya, E. D. (1964). An experimental analysis of the behavioural disturbance produced by a left frontal arachnoidal endothelioma (meningioma). *Neuropsychologia, 2,* 257–280.

Macnamara, J., Baker, E., & Olson, C. (1976). Four-year-olds' understanding of pretend, forget, and know: Evidence for propositional operations. *Child Development, 47,* 62–70.

Mant, C. M., & Perner, J. (1988). The child's understanding of commitment. *Developmental Psychology, 24,* 343–351.

Marvin, R. S., Greenberg, M. T., & Mossler, D. G. (1976). The early development of conceptual perspective taking: Distinguishing among multiple perspectives. *Child Development, 47,* 511–514.

Meltzoff, A. N. (1995). Understanding the intentions of others: Re-enactment of intended acts by 18-month-old children. *Developmental Psychology, 31,* 838–850.

Milner, D. A., & Goodale, M. A. (1995). *The visual brain in action.* Oxford, UK: Oxford University Press.

Nichols, S., & Stich, S. (1999). *A cognitive theory of pretense.* Unpublished manuscript, College of Charleston.

Norman, D. A., & Shallice, T. (1986). Attention to action. Willed and automatic control of behavior.Center for Human Information Processing Technical Report No. 99. Reprinted in revised form in. In R. J. Davidson, G. E. Schwartz, & D. Shapiro (Eds.), *Consciousness and self-regulation (Vol. 4)* (pp. 1–18). New York: Plenum.

Núñez, M. (1993). Teoría de la mente: Metarrepresentación, creencias falsas y engaño en el desarrollo de una psicología natural (Theory of mind: Metarepresentation, false beliefs and deception in the development of a natural psychology) (pp. 333–382). Unpublished doctoral thesis. Universidad AuÝónoma de Madrid, Spain.

O'Neill, D. K., Astington, J. W., & Flavell, J. H. (1992). Young children's understanding of the role that sensory experiences play in knowledge acquisition. *Child Development, 63,* 474–490.

Perner, J. (1988). Developing semantics for theories of mind: From propositional attitudes to mental representation. In J. W. Astington, P. L. Harris, & D. R. Olson (Eds.), *Developing theories of mind* (pp. 141–172). New York: Cambridge University Press.

Perner, J. (1990). Experiential awareness and children's episodic memory. In W. Schneider & F. E. Weinert (Eds.), *Interactions among aptitudes, strategies, and knowledge in cognitive performance* (pp. 3–11). New York, Berlin, Heidelberg, London, Paris, Tokyo, Hong Kong: Springer-Verlag.

Perner, J. (1991). *Understanding the representational mind.* Cambridge, MA: MIT Press.

Perner, J. (1997). Children's competency in understanding the role of a witness: Truth, lies, and moral ties. *Applied Cognitive Psychology, 11,* 21–35.

Perner, J. (1998). The meta-intentional nature of executive functions and theory of mind. In P. Carruthers & J. Boucher (Eds.), *Language and thought* (pp. 270–283). Cambridge, UK: Cambridge University Press.

Perner, J., Baker, S., & Hutton, D. (1994). Prelief: The conceptual origins of belief and pretence. In C. Lewis & P. Mitchell (Eds.), *Children's early understanding of mind: Origins and development.* Hove, UK: Erlbaum.

Perner, J., & Clements, W. A. (in press). From an implicit to an explicit theory of mind. In Y. Rossetti & A. Revonsuo (Eds.), *Interaction between dissociated implicit and explicit processing.* Amsterdam: John Benjamins.

Perner, J., Gschaider, A., Kühberger, A., & Schrofner, S. (1999). Predicting others through simulation or by theory? A method to decide. *Mind & Language, 14,* 57–79.

Perner, J., & Lang, B. (in press). Theory of mind and executive function: Is there a developmental relationship? In S. Baron-Cohen, H. Tager-Flusberg, & D. Cohen (Eds.), *Understanding other minds: Perspectives from autism and developmental cognitive neuroscience.* Oxford, UK: Oxford University Press.

Perner, J., Lang, B., & Stummer, S. (1998). *Theory of mind and executive function: Which depends on which.* Unpublished manuscript, University of Salzburg.

Perner, J., Leekam, S. R., & Wimmer, H. (1987). Three-year olds' difficulty with false belief: The case for a conceptual deficit. *British Journal of Developmental Psychology, 5,* 125–137.

Perner, J., & Ruffman, T. (1995). Episodic memory an autonoetic consciousness: Developmental evidence and a theory of childhood amnesia. Special Issue: Early memory. *Journal of Experimental Child Psychology, 59* (3), 516–548.

Perner, J., Ruffman, T., & Leekam, S. R. (1994). Theory of mind is contagious: You catch it from your sibs. *Child Development, 65,* 1228–1238.

Perner, J., Stummer, S., & Lang, B. (1999). Executive functions and theory of mind: Cognitive complexity or functional dependence? In P. D. Zelazo, J. W. Astington, & D. R. Olson (Eds.), *Developing theories of intention: Social understanding and self-contol* (pp. 133–152). Mahwah, NJ: Erlbaum.

Perner, J., & Wimmer, H. (1985). "John thinks that Mary thinks that . . .": Attribution of second-order beliefs by 5- to 10-year old children. *Journal of Experimental Child Psychology, 39,* 437–471.

Perry, M., Church, R. B., & Goldin-Meadow, S. (1988). Transitional knowledge in the acquisition of concepts. *Cognitive Development, 3,* 359–400.

Peskin, J. (1992). Ruse and representations: On children's ability to conceal information. *Developmental Psychology, 28,* 84–89.

Piaget, J. (1945). *Play, dreams, and imitation in childhood.* New York: W. W. Norton.

Piaget, J., & Inhelder, B. (1956). *The child's conception of space.* London: Routledge and Kegan Paul.

Povinelli, D. J., & Eddy, T. J. (1996). What young chimpanzees know about seeing. *Monographs of the Society for Research in Child Development, 61,* 1–152.

Premack, D., & Woodruff, G. (1978). Does the chimpanzee have a theory of mind? *The Behavioral and Brain Sciences, 1,* 516–526.

Repacholi, B. M., & Gopnik, A. (1997). Early reasoning about desires: Evidence from 14- and 18-month-olds. *Developmental Psychology, 33* (1), 12–21.

Rosen, C. S., Schwebel, D. C., & Singer, J. L. (1997). Preschoolers' attributions of mental states in pretense. *Child Development, 68* (6), 1133–1142.

Rosenthal, D. M. (1986). Two concepts of consciousness. *Philosophical Studies, 49,* 329–359.

Ruffman, T., Perner, J., Naito, M., Parkin, L., & Clements, W. A. (1998). Older (but not younger) siblings facilitate false belief understanding. *Developmental Psychology, 34* (1), 161–174.

Ruffman, T., Perner, J., & Parkin, L. (in press). Parental disciplinary intervention and the development of theory of mind. *Social Development.*

Russell, J., Mauthner, N., Sharpe, S., & Tidswell, T. (1991). The "windows task" as a measure of strategic deception in preschoolers and autistic subjects. *British Journal of Developmental Psychology, 9,* 331–349.

Schank, R. C., & Abelson, R. P. (1977). *Scripts, plans, goals and understanding.* Hillsdale, NJ: Erlbaum.

Searle, J. (1983). *Intentionality.* Cambridge, UK: Cambridge University Press.

Shatz, M., Wellman, H. M., & Silver, S. (1983). The acquisition of mental verbs: A systematic investigation of the first reference to mental state. *Cognition, 14,* 301–321.

Sodian, B. (1991). The development of deception in young children. *British Journal of Developmental Psychology, 9,* 173–188.

Sodian, B., & Schneider, W. (1990). Children's understanding of cognitive cuing: How to manipulate cues to fool a competitor. *Child Development, 61* (3), 697–704.

Sodian, B., Taylor, C. , Harris, P. L., & Perner, J. (1991). Early deception and the child's theory of mind: False trails and genuine markers. *Child Development, 62,* 468–483.

Sodian, B., & Wimmer, H. (1987). Children's understanding of inference as a source of knowledge. *Child Development, 58,* 424–433.

Spelke, E. S., Phillips, A., & Woodward, A. L. (1995). Infant's knowledge of object motion and human action. In D. Sperber, D. Premack, & A. J. Premack (Eds.), *Causal cognition. A multidisciplinary debate* (pp. 44–78). Oxford.

Stein, N. L., & Trabasso, T. (1981). What's in a story: Critical issues in comprehension and instruction. In R. Glaser (Ed.), *Advances in the psychology of instruction (Vol. 2).* Hillsdale, NJ: Erlbaum.

Stern, C., & Stern, W. (1909). *Monographien über die seelische Entwicklung des Kindes. 2. Band: Erinnerung, Aussage und Lüge in der ersten Kindheit.* Leipzig: Barth.

Stouthamer-Loeber, M. (1986). *Adults' perception of verbal misrepresentation of reality in four-year-olds.* Unpublished manuscript, Western Psychiatric Institute and Clinic, University of Pittsburgh.

Sullivan, K., Zaitchik, D., & Tager-Flusberg, H. (1994). Preschoolers can attribute second-order beliefs. *Developmental Psychology, 30* (3), 395–402.

Tulving, E. (1985). Memory and consciousness. *Canadian Psychology, 26,* 1–12.

Vygotsky, L. S. (1978). *Mind in society.* Cambridge, MA: Harvard University Press.

Walper, S., & Valtin, R. (1992). Children's understanding of white lies. In R. J. Watts, S. Ide, & K. Ehlich (Eds.), *Politeness in language* (pp. 231–251). Berlin, New York: Mouton de Gruyter.

Welch-Ross, M. K. (1997, April 3–6). *Children's understanding of the mind: Implications for suggestibility.* Poster presented at the Biennial Meeting of the Society for Research in Child Development, Washington, DC.

Wellman, H. M. (1990). *The child's theory of mind.* Cambridge, MA: MIT Press.

Wellman, H. M., & Banerjee, M. (1991). Mind and emotion: Children's understanding of the emotional consequences of beliefs and desires. *British Journal of Developmental Psychology, 9,* 191–124.

Wellman, H. M., & Bartsch, K. (1988). Young children's reasoning about beliefs. *Cognition, 30,* 239–277.

Wellman, H. M., Cross, D., and Watson, J. K. (1999). *A meta-analysis of theory of mind development: The truth about false-belief.* Paper presented at the Biennial Meeting of the Society for Research in Child Development. Albuquerque, New Mexico, April 15–18, 1999.

Wellman, H. M., & Johnson, C. (1979). Understanding of mental processes: A developmental study of "remember" and "forget". *Child Development, 50,* 79–88.

Wimmer, H. (1989). Common-sense mentalismus und emotion: Einige entwicklungspsychologische Implikationen. In Roth (Ed.), *Denken und Fühlen.* Berlin: Springer-Verlag.

Wimmer, H., Hogrefe, J., & Perner, J. (1988). Children's understanding of informational access as source of knowledge. *Child Development, 59,* 386–396.

Wimmer, H., & Perner, J. (1983). Beliefs about beliefs: Representation and constraining function of wrong beliefs in young children's understanding of deception. *Cognition, 13,* 103–128.

Winner, E., & Leekam, S. (1991). Distinguishing irony from deception: Understanding the speaker's second-order intention. *British Journal of Developmental Psychology, 9,* 257–270.

Wong, E., & Mack, A. (1981). Saccadic programming and perceived location. *Acta Psychologica, 48,* 123–131.

Wood, D., Bruner, J. S. , & Ross, G. (1976). The role of tutoring in problem solving. *Journal of Child Psychology and Psychiatry and Allied Disciplines, 17,* 89–100.

Woodruff, G., & Premack, D. (1979). Intentional communication in the chimpanzee: The development of deception. *Cognition, 7,* 333–362.

Woodward, A. L. (in press). Infants selectively encode the goal object of an actor's reach. *Cognition.*

Yirmiya, N., Erel, O., Shaked, M., & Solomonica-Levi, D. (1998). Meta-analyses comparing theory of mind abilities of individuals with autism, individuals with mental retardation, and normally developing individuals. *Psychological Bulletin, 124* (3), 283–307.

Yuill, N. (1984). Young children's coordination of motive and outcome in judgements of satisfaction and morality. *British Journal of Developmental Psychology, 2,* 73–81.

Behavioral Genetics

☐ Introduction

Imagine the following. You mail a small tube along with your hyperactivity questionnaire to the parents of children in your study. The tube contains some cotton swabs in a teaspoon of solution. Parents are asked to use the cotton swabs to rub the inside of their children's cheeks and put the cotton swabs back in the tube. They return the tube with the questionnaire in the mail. You bring the tubes to the lab and DNA is extracted in a couple of hours at a cost of about £2 ($3) per sample. You now have enough DNA to relate thousands of genes to the components of hyperactivity that interest you. Because DNA lasts forever, you can continue to use it as additional genes are found that might be relevant. However, there are several genes that you want to look at right away because they seem like good candidates in relation to hyperactivity in children. So you ask the lab to genotype your subjects for these genes. If you genotype each individual the old way, it would cost about £3 per marker for each subject. However, if you have groups of subjects, for example, if you select subjects high and low on some aspect of hyperactivity, the DNA from individuals in each group can be pooled so that you have one pool of DNA from the high group and another pool of DNA from the low group. This means that genotyping each gene costs only £6, because it is as if you only have two individuals to genotype. This allows you to screen many genes to see if they are related to your questionnaire. You can compare the results of the genotyping the next day to see if the high and low group differ in the expected direction for any of the genes. If the pooled DNA results indicate differences for certain genes, you could decide to genotype each individual for those genes so that you can investigate why these genes have effects for some individuals and not others, as discussed below. Although it is still very new, you might have access to the new "DNA chips." DNA chips, about the size of a credit card, can genotype thousands of genes in less than an hour. Although you have to use the genes that are on the chip, new chips are being created that give different selections of genes.

You are less interested in finding genes yourself than in using genes that have been found by others to help answer questions about the development of hyperactivity. One question you want to investigate is how early in development does the association between a particular gene and hyperactivity emerge? Although you cannot really measure hyperactivity itself in infancy, is the gene associated with related traits in infancy such as novelty preference or behavioral inhibition? What about later in development? Is the gene associated with different sorts of problems in adolescence and adulthood?

You can also ask questions that try to break down hyperactivity into its components (heterogeneity). For example, is the gene associated more strongly with a particular component of hyperactivity such as activity level, attention, or impulsivity? You can also ask whether genes for hyperactivity relate to other problems (comorbidity) such as learning disabilities or peer problems. You might be interested in studying the psychological mechanisms that lie between genes and behavior, for example, asking whether a particular gene affects cognitive processing or brain functioning. Another large category of questions involves the interplay with the environment. Does a particular form of the gene (allele) interact or correlate with environmental risk factors? That is, children with an allele associated with hyperactivity might be more likely to be exposed to environmental risk factors, for example, by selecting peers that exacerbate their impulsive behavior (gene–environment correlation). They might also be more susceptible to environmental risk factors such as chaotic households or unruly peers (gene–environment interaction). Treatment and prevention are especially important aspects of gene–environment interaction. If an allele could be shown to predict response to treatment, for example, which hyperactive children will respond especially well to Ritalin or to cognitive therapy, this could be helpful for planning individually tailored treatment programs. The most exciting potential of DNA is prevention. If you can predict genetic risk for hyperactivity, it might be possible to intervene to prevent hyperactivity before it creates a cascade of other cognitive and social problems at school.

☐ The Future

You probably read the opening paragraphs of this essay assuming that I had begun by predicting the future. However, amazing as it seems, this is the present! Everything described above can be, and is, being done at the moment (Plomin & Rutter, 1998). In addition, in the next few years, the Human Genome Project will complete the entire sequence of 3 billion nucleotide bases (steps in the spiral staircase of the double helix of DNA), which will greatly facilitate genetic research on complex traits. Differences between people in the DNA sequence of the genome will also be available. About 1 in 1,000 DNA bases varies significantly among people for a total of 3 million DNA differences. It is the differences in DNA that can account for differences in behavior such as why one child becomes hyperactive and another does not.

What the future holds is the likelihood that many of the specific genes responsible for the widespread influence of genes in psychology will be identified. Genes have already been reported for personality (Hamer & Copeland, 1998), reading disability (Cardon et al., 1994), and intelligence (Chorney et al., 1998), as well as several areas of psychopathology (McGuffin, Owen, O'Donovan, Thapar, & Gottesman, 1994). Although attention is focused now on finding genes, few psychologists are likely to join the hunt for genes because it is difficult and expensive. However, it is easy and inexpensive to use genes that have already been identified in order to ask questions about development at the psychological level of analysis. Knowledge of specific genes related to specific behaviors will greatly improve the ability of psychologists to ask more refined and powerful questions such as the questions mentioned above about development, heterogeneity and comorbidity, and gene–environment interplay. No longer will we be limited to the use of twin and adoption studies to address rudimentary questions about how much variation in behavior is genetically influenced. We will be able to make the transition from such "black box" inferences regarding genetic influences to the measurement of specific genes. This will open up new scientific horizons of immense potential that will transform psychological research.

Here is what the future might look like for clinical psychologists. DNA will be routinely collected. Genes will be used to aid in diagnosis and to plan treatment programs. As indicated above, the most powerful potential for DNA is to predict risk so that steps can be taken to prevent problems before they happen. Such primary prevention for complex psychological traits is not likely to take the form of high-tech genetic engineering, because many genes are involved. Even in the case of simple single-gene disorders, environmental interventions are more likely than genetic engineering. For example, phenylketonuria (PKU) is a type of severe mental retardation caused by a single gene on chromosome 12. This form of mental retardation has been largely prevented, not by high-tech solutions such as correcting the mutant DNA or by eugenic programs, but rather by a change in diet that prevents the mutant DNA from having its damaging effects on the developing brain. Once the damage has been done, there is no way to ameliorate the profound retardation it causes. For this reason, all newborns are screened for this genetic disorder in order to determine which of the 1 in 10,000 babies has the disorder so that their diet can be changed.

The importance of primary prevention may well lead to screening for genetic profiles of risk for common diseases as well as for behavioral problems. This is likely to involve DNA chips that can screen for thousands of genes and create genetic profiles even for complex traits like behavior that involve many genes. The problem is that we do not yet know how to intervene to prevent disorders even if we could identify all of the genes involved. This is less of a problem for some disorders than for others. For example, if genes for alcoholism were known, it might help people to know that they are at increased genetic risk for becoming dependent on alcohol because people cannot become alcoholic unless they drink a lot of alcohol. People who know that they are at genetic risk for alcoholism might watch more carefully for the signs of alcohol dependence. When we do not know how to intervene to prevent a genetic risk from becoming reality, the decision to screen is more difficult. For example, a gene on chromosome 19 (apolipoprotein-E) quadruples risk for Alzheimer's disease, a dementia that affects as many as 15% of individuals over 80 years of age. If you have this genetic risk factor for dementia, there is nothing at the moment that you can do to prevent dementia other than avoiding head injuries (especially boxing) and exposure to lead, which increase the risk of dementia for the genetically vulnerable. Because this gene is the only known risk factor for Alzheimer's disease, an intense research effort is aimed at preventing or at least delaying this common form of dementia later in life. If genetic profiles of risk are created for diseases and disorders, genetic strengths will inadvertently be profiled as well, because some genes that are "bad" for one thing might be "good" for another. This profiling of genetic strengths could be done more systematically so that schools, for example, are able to maximize students' strengths rather than only worrying about minimizing their weaknesses.

This picture of the future will confirm some people's worst fears about DNA. They fear that finding out about genetic risk when no prevention or cure is available will label people in ways that might lead to discrimination for insurance and employment. Knowing about genetic risk might also become a self-fulfilling prophecy, for example, if a child is labeled as at risk for learning disorders. Parents using in vitro fertilization might select embryos with fewer genetic risks and more genetic strengths. These are serious problems, but it should be noted that most advances in science create new problems as well as new potential for doing good. For example, when amniocentesis was developed two decades ago to screen for genetic problems prenatally, it led to a minefield of problems involving abortion, especially the specter that society might force this procedure on women at risk. However, mothers voted with their feet by choosing amniocentesis when they had specific genetic risks in their family or when they were older than 40, which increases the risk for chromosomal abnormalities such as the most common form of mental retardation, Down's syndrome (trisomy 21). There have been abuses of amniocentesis as well. In India, for example, where sons are considered more valuable than daughters, some parents have used amniocentesis to abort female fetuses. Clearly, society has some serious thinking to do to capitalize on the potential of the genetics revolution while circumventing the hazards. Despite the new problems created by advances in genetics, it would be a mistake, and futile as well, to try to cut off the flow of knowledge and its benefits in order to avoid having to confront new problems.

Some of the fears derive from misunderstandings about what genetics can and cannot do (Rutter & Plomin, 1997). The main misunderstanding is to think that genes determine outcomes in a hard-wired, there-is-nothing-we-can-do-about-it way. For thousands of rare single-gene disorders, such as the gene on chromosome 4 that causes Huntington's disease, it is the case that genes determine outcomes. If you inherit the Huntington's disease allele, you will die from the disease regardless of your other genes or your environment. However, behavioral disorders and dimensions are complex traits influenced by many genes as well as many environmental factors. For complex traits, genetic factors operate in a probabilistic fashion like risk factors rather than determining outcomes. Fears about cloning, for example, are fueled by the misguided notion of genetic determinism. We already have clones (identical twins are clones who even share the same embryo) and we know that they are by no means identical in behavioral traits. Indeed, genetic studies using twin and adoption designs provide the best available evidence for the importance of environmental influences, as discussed in the next section.

For these reasons, it is crucial that psychologists of the future not be afraid of genetics. Psychology departments must teach their students about genetics in order to prepare them for this future. Otherwise, this opportunity will slip away by default to geneticists, and genetics is much too important a topic to be left to geneticists!

☐ The Past

The fundamental accomplishment of genetic research in psychology to date has been to demonstrate the ubiquitous importance of genetics throughout psychology. This evidence consists of twin studies that compare the similarity of identical and nonidentical twins and adoption studies that consider, for example, the resemblance of adopted-away children to their biological parents. These methods and the theory that underlies them are called *quantitative genetics* in contrast to *molecular genetic* studies that attempt to identify specific genes. Behavioral genetics includes both quantitative and molecular genetic approaches to investigate genetic influences on individual differences in behavior. This latter phrase should be emphasized. Behavioral genetics focuses on questions of why individuals within a species differ in behavior (for example, why children differ in rates of language acquisition), whereas most research in developmental psychology asks questions about species-typical behavior (for example, when on average do children use two-word sentences). Descriptions and explanations of species-typical behavior bear no necessary relationship to descriptions and explanations of individual differences within a species. For example, evolution and genetics accounts for the fact that our species uses two-word sentences at the average age of 18 months, but this does not mean that genetics is the reason why some children do not use two-word sentences until much later in development. The controversy that swirled around behavioral genetics research in psychology during the 1970s has largely faded. During the 1980s and especially the 1990s, psychology became much more accepting of genetic influence, as can be seen in the increasing number of behavioral genetic articles in mainstream psychology journals and in research grants. One symbol of this change was the 1992 centennial conference of the American Psychological Association. In preparation for the conference, a committee selected two themes that best represented the past, present, and future of psychology. One of the two themes chosen was behavioral genetics (Plomin & McClearn, 1993). In my view, this is one of the most dramatic shifts in the modern history of psychology. Indeed, the wave of acceptance of genetic influence in psychology is growing into a tidal wave that threatens to engulf the second message coming from behavioral genetic research. The first message is that genes play a surprisingly important role throughout psychology. The second message is just as important: Individual differences in complex psychological traits are due at least as much to environmental influences as they are to genetic influences. In some areas of psychology, especially psychopathology, the pendulum representing the accepted view may be swinging too far from environmental determinism to genetic determinism.

Consider schizophrenia. Until the 1960s, schizophrenia was thought to be environmental in origin, with theories putting the blame on poor parenting to account for the fact that schizophrenia clearly runs in families. The idea that schizophrenia could run in families for genetic reasons was not seriously considered. Twin and adoption studies changed this view. Twin studies showed that identical twins are much more similar than nonidentical twins, which suggests genetic influence. If one member of an identical twin pair is schizophrenic, the chances are 45% that the other twin is also schizophrenic. For nonidentical twins, the chances are 17%. Adoption studies showed that the risk of schizophrenia is just as great when children are adopted away from their schizophrenic parents at birth as when children are reared by their schizophrenic parents, which provides dramatic evidence for genetic transmission. There are now intense efforts to identify some of the specific genes responsible for genetic influence on schizophrenia.

In the 1960s when schizophrenia was thought to be caused environmentally, it was important to emphasize the evidence for genetic influence such as the concordance of 45% for identical twins. Now that evidence for the importance of genetic influence throughout psychology has largely been accepted, it is important to make sure that the pendulum stays in the middle in between nature and nurture by emphasizing that identical twins are *only* 45% concordant for schizophrenia, which means that in half of the cases these pairs of genetically identical clones are discordant for schizophrenia. This discordance cannot be explained genetically; it must be due to environmental factors. It should be noted that the word *environment* in genetic research really means *nongenetic,* which is a much broader definition of environment than is usually encountered. That is, environment denotes all nonheritable factors, including possible biological events such as prenatal and postnatal illnesses, not just the usual psychosocial factors that are usually considered in psychology. The point is that genetics can often explain half of the variance of psychological traits, but this means that the other half of the variance is *not* due to genetic factors.

For nearly every area of psychology that has been studied, twin and adoption studies have shown genetic as well as environmental influence (Plomin, DeFries, McClearn, & Rutter, 1997). For example, genetic research has consistently shown genetic influence in many traditional areas of psychological research such as psychopathology, personality, cognitive disabilities and abilities, and drug use and abuse. Some areas showing strong genetic influence are more surprising such as school achievement (see below), self-esteem, interests, and attitudes. You might be surprised to learn that differences in weight are almost as heritable as height. Even though we can control how much we eat and are free to go on crash diets, differences among us in weight are more a matter of nature than nurture. Moreover, these are not merely statistically significant effects of genes. The influence of genetic factors is substantial, often as important as all other factors put together.

☐ The Present

Although there are areas of psychology still largely untouched by genetic research, including some of the oldest areas such as perception and learning, genetic research is moving beyond merely demonstrating the importance of genetic factors. In part this is because it is of little interest merely to show that genetic factors influence yet another area in psychology. More importantly, there are more interesting things that can be done with quantitative genetic designs. Five of these new areas of research are described in this section. Rather than summarizing all research on these topics, examples from my research are used in order to make these issues more concrete and personal. An overview of these topics and details concerning the methods used are included in a textbook on behavioral genetics (Plomin, DeFries et al., 1997).

Developmental Change

One way in which current genetic research is moving beyond simply demonstrating genetic influence is to ask questions about genetic change and continuity during development. As you might expect, genetic influences tend to be stable developmentally, but there are some interesting examples of genetic changes during development. One of the more striking findings of genetic change involves general cognitive ability, often called intelligence and assessed by IQ tests. The magnitude of genetic influence (indexed by a statistic called heritability) increases steadily from infancy to childhood to adolescence to adulthood (McGue, Bouchard, Iacono, & Lykken, 1993). This is surprising because most people would think that environmental factors become increasingly important as experiences accumulate during the life course. It is not known why heritability increases during development, but it may be due to what is called *genotype-environment correlation,* which refers to correlations between genetic propensities and exposure to experiences. That is, small genetic differences may snowball as we go through life creating environments that are correlated with our genetic propensities.

An example comes from an ongoing adoption study that I began with John DeFries in 1974 called the Colorado Adoption Project (CAP). CAP began with 245 children adopted away at birth from their biological mothers and adopted into adoptive families in the first few weeks of life. A similar number of nonadopted control children were studied in families matched to the adoptive families. This adoption design makes it possible to disentangle nature and nurture in development because it includes parents who are related genetically but not environmentally to their children (biological parents whose children are adopted away at birth), parents who are related environmentally but not genetically to their children (adoptive parents), and parents who are related both genetically and environmentally to their children (nonadoptive control parents). CAP also includes adoptive siblings (genetically unrelated children adopted into the same family) and nonadoptive siblings (genetically related control siblings).

The children have been studied yearly since infancy in order to investigate questions about nature and nurture in development. Results for the development of general cognitive ability from infancy through adolescence show genetic change, as illustrated in Figure 13.1 (Plomin, Fulker, Corley, & DeFries, 1997). Correlations between parents and children for nonadoptive control families increase from less than .20 in infancy to about .20 in middle childhood to about .30 in adolescence. The correlations between biological mothers and their adopted-away children follow a similar pattern, thus indicating that parent–offspring resemblance for general cognitive ability is due to genetic factors and that genetic influence increases from infancy through adolescence. Parent–offspring correlations for adoptive parents and their adopted children hover around zero. This finding indicates that environmental factors that contribute to cognitive development are not correlated with parents' cognitive ability, a topic to which we shall return later. Similar results were found in CAP for specific cognitive abilities such as verbal, spatial, memory, and speed of processing.

The trend toward increasing heritability continues into adulthood. As one gets older, the other end of the life course becomes more interesting. Because hardly any behavioral genetic research looked at the entire second half of the life span, I was interested in studying individual differences in behavioral functioning later in life. An opportunity arose when on a trip to Stockholm in 1979 I found that there were hundreds of pairs of elderly twins who had been reared apart from early in life who were included in the Swedish Twin Registry of 26,000 pairs of twins. An inter-

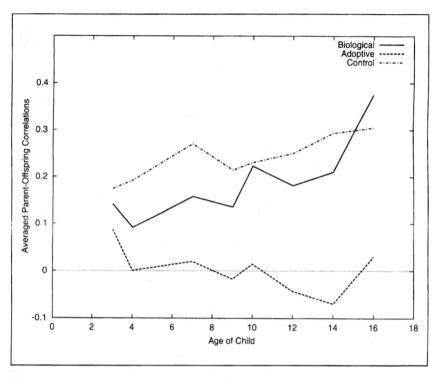

Figure 13.1. Parent–offspring correlations for general cognitive ability from infancy to adolescence in the Colorado Adoption Project (CAP) at 3, 4, 7, 9, 10, 12, 14, and 16 years. (Thanks go to Blackwell Publishers for permission to reprint this figure from "Nature, nurture and cognitive development from 1 to 16 years: A parent–off-spring adoption study" by Plomin, Fulker, Corley, & DeFries (1997), *Psychological Science, 8,* 442–447.)

national collaboration was formed to study twins reared apart who were over 50 years of age and matched pairs of twins who had been reared to-gether. The study was called the Swedish Adoption/Twin Study of Aging (SATSA). In the first report of older twins tested at the average age of 60 years, heritability of general cognitive ability was estimated as 80% in SATSA (Pedersen, Plomin, Nesselroade, & McClearn, 1992), a result that was replicated when the SATSA twins were retested three years later (Plomin, Chipuer, & Neiderhiser, 1994). This is one of the highest heri-tabilities reported for any behavioral dimension or disorder. We ex-tended this Swedish study to include 350 pairs of reared-together twins 80 years old or older. The first results from this study showed that high heritability of general cognitive ability persist into old age (McClearn et al., 1997).

In addition to changes in heritability during development, another important developmental advance is the application of behavioral genetic methods to longitudinal data in order to investigate genetic sources of age-to-age change as well as continuity. For the most part, genetic factors contribute to continuity, but there examples of change. Change in genetic effects does not necessarily mean that genes are turned on and off during development, although this does happen. Genetic change simply means that genetic effects at one age differ from genetic effects at another age. One example from CAP involves cognitive development: Longitudinal genetic analysis showed that genetic factors contribute to change in general cognitive ability from early childhood to middle childhood, which all theories of cognitive development recognize as a major important transition (Fulker, Cherny, & Cardon, 1993). This finding means that if we found genes associated with general cognitive ability, we would expect that some of these genes would be different in early childhood and in middle childhood. Despite this evidence for genetic change, it should be noted that most genetic influences on general cognitive ability in childhood continue to have their effect even in adulthood.

Multivariate Genetic Analysis

Another example of going beyond estimating heritability is multivariate genetic analysis. Rather than analyzing the variance of a single trait, multivariate genetic analysis focuses on the covariance (correlation) between traits. It asks whether genetic factors that affect one trait also affect another trait. For example, the twin partners of schizophrenic identical twins have a 45% chance of being schizophrenic, but they have no greater chance of being manic-depressive. This finding suggests that genetic factors that affect schizophrenia are different from those that affect manic-depression. In contrast, genetic factors that contribute to depression are the same genetic factors that affect anxiety. This means that if genes are found that contribute to depression, the same genes can be expected to contribute to anxiety.

CAP has helped to clarify the origins of differences and similarities among cognitive abilities. Current cognitive neuroscience assumes a modular model of intelligence, in which different cognitive processes are isolated anatomically in discrete modules in the brain. This modular model implies that specific cognitive abilities are also genetically distinct. That is, genetic effects on verbal ability, say, should not overlap substantially with genetic effects on spatial ability. However, it has long been known that most cognitive abilities intercorrelate moderately. That is, people who perform well on one type of test also tend to do well on other types. Correlations between verbal and spatial abilities, for example, are usually about 0.5.

Multivariate genetic analyses of CAP data indicate that genes are responsible for most of the overlap between cognitive abilities such as verbal and spatial ability (Cardon & Fulker, 1993). Indeed, hardly any genetic influence is unique to verbal ability or to spatial ability. In other words, if genes are found that are associated with verbal ability, they are also likely to be associated with spatial ability. This evidence supports a decidedly nonmodular view of intelligence as a pervasive or global quality of the mind. The Swedish twin studies also support the hypothesis of genetic nonmodularity later in life (Pedersen, Plomin, & McClearn, 1994; Petrill et al., 1998).

Moreover, this genetic nonmodularity even extends to school achievement. CAP and other studies show that genes have almost as much effect on school achievement as they do on cognitive abilities. These results are surprising in and of themselves because educators have long believed that achievement is more a product of effort than of ability. Even more interesting is the multivariate genetic finding that genetic factors that affect school achievement are the same genetic factors that influence cognitive abilities (Wadsworth, 1994).

Genetic Links Between the Normal and Abnormal

Another example of genetic research that goes beyond heritability involves attempts to ask about the genetic links between the normal and abnormal for which new quantitative genetic methods have been developed called DF extremes analysis (DeFries & Fulker, 1985, 1988). DF extremes analysis estimates genetic and environmental contributions to the average difference between an extreme group and the rest of the population using quantitative measures of a dimension rather than a qualitative diagnosis. The genetic estimate from DF extremes analysis is called *group heritability* to distinguish it from the traditional *individual heritability* that focuses on individual differences rather than average differences between groups.

This distinction is important because the relative influence of genetic and environmental factors on individual differences in the normal range could differ from the magnitude of genetic and environmental effects at the extreme of the distribution. In general, however, genetic effects at the extremes tend to be similar in magnitude to the rest of the distribution. For example, reading disability appears to represent the genetic extreme of a continuous distribution. That is, genetic effects on reading disability appear to be merely the genetic extreme of a continuum of genetic effects on reading ability. In other words, if genes are found for reading disability (and replicated linkages have been reported), we would predict that the same genes are responsible for normal variation in reading ability. If a disorder is merely the extreme of the same genetic and environmental factors that affect variation in the normal range, it implies that the disorder is not really a disorder but rather the low end of a continuous dimension.

Ideally, analyses of the links between the normal and abnormal would involve a normal sample of twins sufficiently large to include enough abnormal cases for analysis so that direct comparisons can be made between the normal and abnormal. When I moved to London in 1994, I decided to launch a large twin study that could tackle this issue. Because there has never been a twin study of language delay or mild mental retardation or the association between these cognitive delays and behavioral problems, I decided to focus on this triad of developmental problems. Given the evidence for genetic influence on cognitive abilities, one might suppose that cognitive disabilities must also show genetic influence. However, this does not necessarily follow. For example, severe mental retardation does not run in families. Severe retardation is caused by genetic and environmental factors (novel mutations, birth complications, and head injuries, to name a few) that do not come into play in the normal range of intelligence. Researchers need to assess, rather than assume, genetic links between the normal and the abnormal, between the traits that are part of a continuum and true disorders that are etiologically distinct from the continuum of normal variation.

The Twins Early Development Study (TEDS) focuses on the triad of language delays, nonverbal cognitive delays, and associated behavioral problems at 2, 3, and 4 years of age using a sampling frame of all twins born in England and Wales in 1994, 1995, and 1996. TEDS analyses have been conducted for more than 3,000 2-year-old twin pairs in the 1994 cohort. The most interesting result so far concerns delay in vocabulary at 2 years of age, defined as the lowest 5% of the distribution (Dale et al., 1998). Two years is a particularly appropriate age to study vocabulary development because it follows a period of rapid acceleration in the use of words at about 18 months and the beginning use of word combinations at about 20 months. Although a substantial proportion of language delays resolve themselves in the preschool or early school years, early language delay is important, because nearly all language impairments in school children are preceded by early language delay. In this first twin study of language delay, vocabulary delay was highly heritable, yielding a group differences heritability of 73%, which suggests that early vocabulary delay may be one of the most highly heritable aspects of early behavioral development. Moreover, heritability of vocabulary delay (73%) was significantly greater than individual heritability of normal variability in vocabulary (25%). This is the first time that a significant difference has been found between the heritabilities of the normal and the abnormal, and it supports the view of language delay as a genetically distinct disorder.

For nonverbal cognitive delay (lowest 5% of a battery of nonverbal tests), group heritability was more modest (37%), and not significantly greater than the heritability of individual differences in the normal range (20%). Mental handicap is usually assessed as a composite of both verbal and nonverbal disabilities. Despite the high heritability for vocabulary delay, a composite measure of vocabulary and nonverbal cognitive ability, used as an index of mild mental retardation, showed moderate heritability both for the lowest 5% of the distribution (37%) and for the entire distribution (21%). Given these results, it was surprising to find that the comorbid cases in which children were selected who were in the lowest 5% of *both* the verbal and nonverbal measures, heritability was extremely high (91%), although the sample size for this analysis was small because only 22% of the verbal delay and nonverbal delay children were in both the verbal delay and nonverbal delay groups. Together, these results suggest the hypothesis that verbal delays, nonverbal cognitive delays, and comorbid verbal-plus-nonverbal delay may be genetically distinct (Eley et al., 1998).

The Importance of Nonshared Environment

Genetic research is changing the way we think about the environment. Genetic research tells us that the way the environment works in development must be very different from the way it has been thought to work. Instead of making two children growing up in the same family similar to one another, which is what theories of socialization generally assume, genetic research shows that environmental influences that affect behavioral development operate to make children in the same family different (Plomin & Daniels, 1987). We know this, for example, because genetically unrelated children growing up in the same adoptive family scarcely resemble each other for personality, psychopathology, and cognitive abilities after adolescence. Other behavioral genetic results converge on this surprising conclusion that growing up in the same family does not make siblings similar for environmental reasons (Plomin, Chipuer, & Neiderhiser, 1994). Siblings are similar, of course, but for genetic rather than environmental reasons. The environment is important, but environmental influences operate to make children in the same family different, not similar. This topic is called nonshared environment, because these environmental influences are not shared by children growing up in the same family.

This finding does not mean that family environment is unimportant. Environmental influences in development have their effect on an individual-by-individual basis rather than on a family-by-family basis. The key question is why children growing up in the same family are so different. Nonshared environment is a crucible for environmental research. Unless an environmental variable can be shown to be experienced differently by siblings growing up in the same family, it cannot be an important environmental predictor of developmental outcomes. In developmental psychology, it has often been assumed that the key environmental influences on children's development are shared by siblings such as their parents' personalities and childhood experiences, the quality of their parents' marital relationships, their parents' educational background and socioeconomic status, the neighborhood in which they grow up, and their parents' attitudes about parenting. Yet to the extent that these influences are shared by children growing up in the same family, they cannot account for the differences we observe in their development. Consider divorce. Whether or not their parents have been divorced is the same for two children in the family. Assessed in this family-general way, divorce cannot be a source of differences in siblings' outcomes because it does not differ for two children in the same family. However, research on divorce has shown that divorce affects children in a family differently (Hetherington & Clingempeel, 1992). If divorce is assessed in a child-specific way (for example, by the children's different perceptions about the stress caused by the divorce), it could well be a source of differential sibling outcome.

Because psychologists had seldom studied more than one child per family, little was known until recently about different experiences of children in the same family. Research so far suggests that children in the same family experience quite different environments. For example, if you ask adolescent siblings about differences in their parents' treatment of them, you get an earful! Most importantly, if you observe children interacting with their parents, you find that parents do in fact act quite differently toward their two children. The discovery of the importance of nonshared environment has sparked research in psychology that studies more than one child per family and asks why they turn out so differently (Dunn & Plomin, 1990). As discussed later, it is important to embed such research in genetically sensitive designs, because one of the reasons why siblings differ is that siblings are 50% different genetically, which means that genetic differences between them might be responsible for differences in the way they are treated by their parents.

The largest study of nonshared environment, begun over a decade ago, is the Nonshared Environment and Adolescent Development (NEAD) project. NEAD was designed as a collaboration between environmentalists (David Reiss and E. Mavis Hetherington) and behavioral geneticists (Robert Plomin and Jenae Neiderhiser) in order to identify specific sources of nonshared environment relevant to adolescent adjustment in the context of a genetically sensitive design (Reiss, Neiderhiser, Hetherington, & Plomin, in press). NEAD includes more than 720 families with twins, full siblings, half siblings, and genetically unrelated siblings who were visited in their homes twice for two to three hours. All family members completed questionnaires about family interactions and are videotaped in various groupings discussing family issues.

The results from NEAD showed that differences in family experiences were strongly related to differences in adjustment outcomes in the adolescent siblings. Especially strong were relations between differences in negative parenting behavior such as hostility and conflict and differences in adolescents' negative outcomes such as antisocial behavior and depression. Differences in parents' positive behavior were less influential. Results such as these suggested that the source of nonshared environment for adolescent adjustment lies in differential family experiences. However, one of the reasons why siblings growing up in the same family are so different is genetics: siblings are 50% similar genetically, but this also means that they are 50% different genetically. This is why the NEAD study was embedded in a genetically sensitive design that included identical and nonidentical twins, full siblings, half siblings, and genetically unrelated siblings. First, we used the genetic design simply to ask whether the NEAD measures of family interaction showed genetic influence. We found that genetic factors made a substantial contribution to the interview measures (Plomin, Reiss, Hetherington, & Howe, 1994) as well as to videotaped observations of parent–adolescent interactions (O'Connor, Hetherington, Reiss, & Plomin, 1995). When we analyzed family experiences and adolescent adjustment outcomes using multivariate genetic analysis, we found that nearly all of what looked like nonshared environment was actually genetic (Pike, McGuire, Hetherington, Reiss, & Plomin, 1996). Of the 52 associations between parenting measures and adjustment examined, 44 indicated that genetic influences accounted for more than half of the variance in adolescent outcome. Nonshared environment accounted for less than 5% of the variance. These results suggest that siblings are treated differently because adolescents' genetically influenced patterns of adjustment elicit or evoke different responses from their parents. Differences in parental treatment do not cause the differences in adolescent adjustment by means of nonshared environment.

In summary, what began as a study trying to identify specific sources of nonshared environment ended up as a study showing the pervasive influence of genetic factors in family life. More than a dozen other studies support this conclusion (Plomin, 1994). But what factors are responsible for nonshared environment? Although NEAD could not find specific sources of nonshared environment in the family, behavioral genetic research in most areas of psychology including adjustment consistently shows that most environmental influence operates in a nonshared manner. One possibility is that nonshared environment lies outside the family. A reasonable candidate in adolescence is differential experiences with peers (Harris, 1995), although some evidence suggests substantial genetic influence on choice of peers as well (Plomin, 1994). Although it makes sense to investigate such systematic sources of nonshared environment, we need to keep our minds open to the possibility that chance also contributes to nonshared environment in the sense of idiosyncratic experiences (such as the formative experience when Bill Clinton as an adolescent met John Kennedy) or the subtle interplay of a concatenation of events that might be thought to be chance (Dunn & Plomin, 1990).

Genetic Influence on Measures of the Environment

NEAD is one of many studies that have found genetic influence on measures of the environment (Plomin, 1994). For example, CAP found genetic influence on the most widely used objective measure of the home environment relevant to cognitive development. This measure, called the Home Observation for the Measurement of Environment (HOME), was assessed in home visits when each child was 1 year old and again when each child was 2 years old. The CAP compared similarity on the HOME for nonadoptive siblings who are 50% similar genetically and adoptive siblings who are genetically unrelated. At 1 year, the correlations for nonadoptive and adoptive siblings were .58 and .35, respectively. The results replicated at 2 years when correlations were .57 and .40, respectively. These results suggest that about 40% of the variance of the HOME is genetic in origin.

Genetic influence is not limited to measures of the family environment. In SATSA, for example, we found the first evidence for other measures outside the family, such as life events (Plomin, Lichtenstein, Pedersen, McClearn, & Nesselroade, 1990), social support (Bergeman, Plomin, Pedersen, McClearn, & Nesselroade, 1990), and work environment (Hershberger, Lichtenstein, & Knox, 1994). If environmental measures are influenced by genetic factors and if developmental outcome measures are also influenced by genetic factors, it is possible that the connection between environmental measures and outcome measures is mediated to some extent by genetic factors. CAP was the first study to report genetic influence on the association between measures of family environment and developmental outcomes (Plomin, Loehlin, & DeFries, 1985). The adoption design that includes both nonadoptive and adoptive families makes it possible to compare associations between measures of the family environment and children's developmental outcome when there is a genetic link between the children and their parents (nonadoptive families) and when there is no genetic link (adoptive families). If genetic factors mediate the correlation between a measure of family environment and children's development, we would expect to find that the correlation is greater in nonadoptive families where parents and children are genetically related than in adoptive families where they are not. In CAP, this was the usual finding. For example, the correlation between the HOME and children's IQ at 2 years of age was .42 in nonadoptive families and .27 in adoptive families. The correlation between the HOME and children's language development was .50 in nonadoptive families and .32 in adoptive families. These results suggest that genetic factors account for about half of the correlation between the HOME and these developmental outcomes. Similar results are found longitudinally. For example, the HOME at 2 years correlates with IQ at 7 years of age: .31 in nonadoptive families and .08 in adoptive families (Coon, Fulker, DeFries, & Plomin, 1990).

A more general analytic strategy involves the use of multivariate genetic analysis to analyze the covariance between measures of environment and measure of development (Plomin, 1994). In CAP, multivariate genetic analysis of the covariance between the HOME and IQ at 2 years was conducted using a completely different design, the comparison between nonadoptive and adoptive siblings (Braungart, Fulker, & Plomin, 1992). The same result was found: Genetic factors account for about half of the correlation between the HOME and IQ. Another CAP analysis of this type indicates that genetic influence on the HOME can largely be explained by tester ratings of the children's attention (Saudino & Plomin, 1997).

☐ Back to the Future

A major motivation for writing this chapter is to enlist the aid of the next generation of psychologists to use the theory and methods of behavioral genetics in order to study nature as well as nurture, and especially their interplay, in development. There is much to be done. Behavioral genetics has only scratched the surface of possible applications, even within the domains of cognitive disabilities and abilities, psychopathology, and personality. For cognitive abilities, most genetic research has focused on general cognitive ability and major group factors of specific cognitive abilities. The future of research in this area lies in more fine-grained analyses of cognitive abilities and in the use of information-processing and biological approaches to cognition. For psychopathology, genetic research has just begun to consider disorders other than schizophrenia and the major mood disorders. Little is known as yet about developmental psychopathology. Personality is so complex that it will keep researchers busy for decades, especially as they go beyond self-report questionnaires to use other measures such as observations. A rich territory for future exploration is the links between psychopathology and personality.

Cognitive disabilities and abilities, psychopathology, and personality have been the targets for the vast majority of genetic research in psychology because these areas have traditionally considered individual differences. Three new areas of psychology that are beginning to be explored genetically are psychology and aging, health psychology, and evolutionary psychology. Some of the oldest areas of psychology, perception and learning, for example, have not emphasized individual differences and as a result have yet to be explored systematically from a genetic perspective. Entire disciplines within the social and behavioral sciences, such as economics, education, and sociology, are still essentially untouched by genetic research.

Genetic research in psychology will continue to move beyond simply demonstrating that genetic factors are important for estimating heritabilities. The questions *whether* and *how much* genetic factors affect psychological dimensions and disorders represent important first steps in understanding the origins of individual differences. But these are only first steps. The next steps involve the question *how*, the mechanisms by which genes have their effects. Examples of these directions for genetic research in psychology (developmental genetics, multivariate genetics, genetics of the extremes, nonshared environment, and the interplay between nature and nurture) were described in the previous section. The future will see more research of this type as behavioral genetics continues to go beyond the rudimentary questions of *whether* and *how much* in order to ask the question *how*. Such quantitative genetic research will become increasingly important as it guides molecular genetic research to the most heritable components and constellations throughout development as they interact and correlate with the environment.

Psychology is at the dawn of a new era in which molecular genetic techniques will revolutionize genetic research in psychology by identifying specific genes that contribute to genetic variance for complex dimensions and disorders. The quest is to find not *the* gene for a trait, but the multiple genes that affect the trait as a probabilistic propensity, not as predetermined programming (Plomin, Owen, & McGuffin, 1994). The breathtaking pace of molecular genetics leads me to predict that psychologists will routinely use DNA markers as a tool in their research and clinics in order to identify some of the relevant genetic differences among individuals, which will make it possible to ask more precise questions about how genotypes become phenotypes.

☐ References

Bergeman, C. S., Plomin, R., Pedersen, N. L., McClearn, G. E., & Nesselroade, J. R. (1990). Genetic and environmental influences on social support: The Swedish Adoption/Twin Study of Aging (SATSA). *Journals of Gerontology: Psychological Sciences, 45*, P101–P106.

Braungart, J. M., Fulker, D. W., & Plomin, R. (1992). Genetic influence of the home environment during infancy: A sibling adoption study of the HOME. *Developmental Psychology, 28,* 1048–1055.

Cardon, L. R., & Fulker, D. W. (1993). Genetics of specific cognitive abilities. In R. Plomin & G. E. McClearn (Eds.), *Nature, nurture, and psychology* (pp. 99–120). Washington, DC: American Psychological Association.

Cardon, L. R., Smith, S. D., Fulker, D. W., Kimberling, W. J., Pennington, B. F., & DeFries, J. C. (1994). Quantitative trait locus for reading disability on chromosome 6. *Science, 266,* 276–279.

Chorney, M. J., Chorney, K., Seese, N., Owen, M. J., Daniels, J., McGuffin, P., Thompson, L. A., Detterman, D. K., Benbow, C. P., Lubinski, D., Eley, T. C., & Plomin, R. (1998). A quantitative trait locus (QTL) associated with cognitive ability in children. *Psychological Science, 9,* 1–8.

Coon, H., Fulker, D. W., DeFries, J. C., & Plomin, R. (1990). Home environment and cognitive ability of 7-year-old children in the Colorado Adoption Project: Genetic and environmental etiologies. *Developmental Psychology, 26,* 459–468.

Dale, P. S., Rutter, M., Simonoff, E., Bishop, D. V. M., Eley, T. C., Oliver, B., Price, T. S., Purcell, S., Stevenson, J., & Plomin, R. (1998). *Genetic influence on language delay in 2-year-olds.* Manuscript submitted for publication.

DeFries, J. C., & Fulker, D. W. (1985). Multiple regression analysis of twin data. *Behavior Genetics, 5,* 467–473.

DeFries, J. C., & Fulker, D. W. (1988). Multiple regression analysis of twin data: Etiology of deviant scores versus individual differences. *Acta Geneticae Medicae et Gemellolgiae, 37,* 205–216.

Dunn, J., & Plomin, R. (1990). *Separate lives: Why siblings are so different.* New York: Basic Books.

Eley, T. E., Rutter, M., Simonoff, E., Bishop, D. V. M., Dale, P. S., Oliver, B., Petrill, S. A., Price, T., Purcell, S., Saudino, K. J., Stevenson, J., Taylor, E., & Plomin, R. (1998). *Twin Study of Verbal and Performance Components of Developmental Delay in Two-Year-Olds.* Unpublished manuscript.

Fulker, D. W., Cherny, S. S., & Cardon, L. R. (1993). Continuity and change in cognitive development. In R. Plomin & G. E. McClearn (Eds.), *Nature, nurture, and psychology* (pp. 77–97). Washington, DC: American Psychological Association.

Hamer, D., & Copeland, P. (1998). *Living with our genes.* New York: Doubleday.

Harris, J. R. (1995). Where's the child's environment? A group socialization theory of development. *Psychological Review, 102,* 458–489.

Hershberger, S. L., Lichtenstein, P., & Knox, S. S. (1994). Genetic and environmental influences on perceptions of organizational climate. *Journal of Applied Psychology, 79,* 24–33.

Hetherington, E. M., & Clingempeel, W. G. (1992). Coping with marital transitions: A family systems perspective. *Monographs of the Society for Research in Child Development, 2–3* (Serial No. 227).

McClearn, G. E., Johansson, B., Berg, S., Pedersen, N. L., Ahern, F., Petrill, S. A., & Plomin, R. (1997). Substantial genetic influence on cognitive abilities in twins 80 or more years old. *Science, 276,* 1560–1563.

McGue, M., Bouchard, T. J., Jr., Iacono, W. G., & Lykken, D. T. (1993). Behavioral genetics of cognitive ability: A life-span perspective. In R. Plomin & G. E. McClearn (Eds.), *Nature, nurture, and psychology* (pp. 59–76). Washington, DC: American Psychological Association.

McGuffin, P., Owen, M. J., O'Donovan, M. C., Thapar, A., & Gottesman, I. I. (1994). *Seminars in psychiatric genetics.* London: Gaskell Press.

O'Connor, T. G., Hetherington, E. M., Reiss, D., & Plomin, R. (1995). A twin-sibling study of observed parent-adolescent interactions. *Child Development, 6,* 812–824.

Pedersen, N. L., Plomin, R., & McClearn, G. E. (1994). Is there G beyond g? (Is there genetic influence on specific cognitive abilities independent of genetic influence on general cognitive ability?). *Intelligence, 18,* 133–143.

Pedersen, N. L., Plomin, R., Nesselroade, J. R., & McClearn, G. E. (1992). A quantitative genetic analysis of cognitive abilities during the second half of the life span. *Psychological Science, 3,* 346–353.

Petrill, S. A., Berg, S., Johanson, B., Pedersen, N. L., Ahern, F., Plomin, R., & McClearn, G. E. (1998). The genetic and environmental relationships between general and specific cognitive abilities in twins 80 and older. *Psychological Science, 9,* 183–189.

Pike, A., McGuire, S., Hetherington, E. M., Reiss, D., & Plomin, R. (1996). Family environment and adolescent depressive symptoms and antisocial behavior: A multivariate genetic analysis. *Developmental Psychology, 32,* 590–603.

Plomin, R. (1994). *Genetics and experience: The developmental interplay between nature and nurture.* Newbury Park, CA: Sage.

Plomin, R., Chipuer, H. M., & Neiderhiser, J. M. (1994). Behavioral genetic evidence for the importance of nonshared environment. In E. M. Hetherington, D. Reiss, & R. Plomin (Eds.), *Separate social worlds of siblings: Impact of nonshared environment on development* (pp. 1–31). Hillsdale, NJ: Erlbaum.

Plomin, R., & Daniels, D. (1987). Why are children in the same family so different from each other? *The Behavioral and Brain Sciences, 10,* 1–16.

Plomin, R., DeFries, J. C., McClearn, G. E., & Rutter, M. (1997). *Behavioral genetics* (3rd ed.). New York: W. H. Freeman.

Plomin, R., Fulker, D. W., Corley, R., & DeFries, J. C. (1997). Nature, nurture and cognitive development from 1 to 16 years: A parent-offspring adoption study. *Psychological Science, 8,* 442–447.

Plomin, R., Lichtenstein, P., Pedersen, N. L., McClearn, G. E., & Nesselroade, J. R. (1990). Genetic influence on life events during the last half of the life span. *Psychology and Aging, 5,* 25–30.

Plomin, R., Loehlin, J. C., & DeFries, J. C. (1985). Genetic and environmental components of "environmental" influences. *Developmental Psychology, 21,* 391–402.

Plomin, R., & McClearn, G. E. (Eds.). (1993). *Nature, nurture, and psychology.* Washington, DC: American Psychological Association.

Plomin, R., Owen, M. J., & McGuffin, P. (1994). The genetic basis of complex human behaviors. *Science, 264,* 1733–1739.

Plomin, R., Pedersen, N. L., Lichtenstein, P., & McClearn, G. E. (1994). Variability and stability in cognitive abilities are largely genetic later in life. *Behavior Genetics, 24,* 207–215.

Plomin, R., Reiss, D., Hetherington, E. M., & Howe, G. (1994). Nature and nurture: Genetic influence on measures of the family environment. *Developmental Psychology, 30,* 32–43.

Plomin, R., & Rutter, M. (1998). Child development, molecular genetics, and what to do with genes once they are found. *Child Development, 69,* 1223–1242.

Reiss, D., Neiderhiser, J. M., Hetherington, E. M., & Plomin, R. (in press). *The relationship code: Genetic and social analyses of adolescent development.* Cambridge, MA: Harvard University Press.

Rutter, M., & Plomin, R. (1997). Opportunities for psychiatry from genetic findings. *British Journal of Psychiatry, 171,* 209–219.

Saudino, K. J., & Plomin, R. (1997). Cognitive and temperamental mediators of genetic contributions to the home environment during infancy. *Merrill-Palmer Quarterly, 43,* 1–23.

Wadsworth, S. J. (1994). School achievement. In J. C. DeFries, R. Plomin, & D. W. Fulker (Eds.), *Nature and nurture during middle childhood* (pp. 86–101). Oxford, UK: Blackwell.

James Russell

Playing a Passing Game: Rationalism, Empiricism, and Cognitive Development

☐ Introduction

My brief was to say something about the relation between philosophy and developmental psychology. As this is rather a big undertaking I've limited myself ("limit" is hardly the word) to epistemology. The question of where knowledge comes from, or as philosophers are more likely put it nowadays, how knowledge is "grounded" does, after all, admit developmental answers; and so the question of how the two enterprises are related is a real one. For rationalists,[1] knowledge is grounded by what is inherent in human nature prior to experience, while empiricists say that it is grounded in experience itself. Well, these are the kind of issues that also occupy us, and so our work can sometimes look like philosophy "continued by other means," or at least that is a status to which it might

---

[1] I shall not be presenting the debate in terms of *nativism* versus empiricism. This is because nativism is what is empirically implied by a certain philosophical position (rationalism), rather than itself being a philosophical position. Of itself it has a purely empirical status. My assumption is that if we are interested in a fundamental aspect of human understanding such as rationality and theory of mind, then the debate naturally involves philosophy. If it involves individual differences, it does not. In any event, read "rationalism" as implying "nativism."

aspire. I shall begin by arguing, however, that we often behave like supporters rather than players.

To explain, developmental psychologists usually know which team they support, and, if British, they might tend to think of the history of epistemology in terms of a two-and-a-half-millennia-long soccer match. It is played between Rationality Rovers (ultramarine and white strip, continentals) and Empiricist City (red and yellow strip, mainly home-grown talent with one or two continental signings such as the French lad Gassendi). The styles of play are quite different, with most of the fancy footwork coming from the Rovers. Some of the City have a weakness for toe-poking the ball, as if refuting it.

Plato was an early scorer, after which both teams endured a two-thousand-year-long goal famine until Descartes hammered one in from just outside the six-yard box, swiftly followed by two more from Spinoza and Leibniz. The game then caught fire as retaliation came swiftly from the fresh legs of Locke, Berkeley, and Hume. Things seems to be pretty evenly balanced for a hundred or so years, and the game started to sag. Foggy weather impaired visibility, and during this period Hegel scored a controversial header for the Rovers to even things up. For many years the Rovers had the upper hand, but this was mainly because their nifty passing and obscure tactical maneuvers enabled them to retain possession. The early twentieth century changed all that. The City imported trainers from Vienna, a move which inspired "commitment" among the lads in red and yellow: they went in hard and for a while it seemed the game was all over. But this did not last. Wittgenstein, an unconventional competitor at the best of times, seemed to lose interest in the contest and became the only player in history to send himself off. There was some confusion and a number of City's players seemed to invent their own version of the game, William Webb Ellis-like, and called it "experimental psychology." But the City really seemed to be playing the only game in town, until the early 1960s, that is. As ever, the Americans arrived late to the conflict, but when they did the effect was devastating. Chomksy floated one in from the left wing, and, while the Rovers were recovering, he made a goal for Fodor. Things had not been so nail-biting since the eighteenth century! Then the City started to flag until rejuvenated by connectionist physios wielding not the magic sponge but the magic net. Now all bets are off.

What were developmental psychologists doing meanwhile? They could hardly ignore the game because the philosophers were playing for the intellectual trophies, which they too coveted: accounts of how we come to have a conception of the external world, the self, other minds, rationality, morality. But they had been told that they were not eligible to play because (it was explained to them) the epistemologists on the pitch were contesting issues about what knowledge *is* and how knowledge *is possible,* while, as psychologists, they should really restrict themselves to the more mundane question of how knowledge is *actually acquired.* And so the developmentalists ended up running the supporters club, wore the away-strip to conferences, and played a poorly supported, kick-and-rush version of the game in the local park on Sunday mornings.

Well, this is not even an accurate and a historical burlesque. In the first place the "rationalism-versus-empiricist" conflict is a retrospective idealization of certain nineteenth-century philosophers. A figure like Hume, for example, would have regarded himself as having more in common with certain continental rationalists than with John Locke, and philosophers like Hobbes could have been picked for either side (Woolhouse, 1988). And as I shall be saying later, Chomsky and Fodor do not really belong on this pitch at all. Second, and far more important for our purposes, it neglects the contribution of three figures: Aristotle in ancient world, Kant in the eighteenth century, and Quine in the twentieth. (One could add to the list.) Not only do these thinkers fatally complicate the metaphor, but they were men whose work could inspire a different kind of game: one in which even developmental psychologists might be invited to participate.

To return to the starting point, for the empiricist, knowledge is grounded in perceptual experience such that everything we know is ultimately traceable to what we have experienced. For the rationalist, the fundamental truths are those that constitute the framework of empirical knowledge; and these truths, those of logic and mathematics most especially, cannot be derived from experience. Each view carries different implications both for the philosophy of science and for developmental psychology. In the latter case, if something is derived from experience, then the starting state of the mind can legitimately be thought of in terms of a universal learning machine, something that receives sense impressions (Locke spoke of the mind as being like a "great mirror") and operates on them through all-purpose processes such as association, habit, and the like: raw data plus operations. For the empiricist, the apparently deep truths of logic and mathematics are really uninteresting tautologies, or empty statements that are no more than consequences of initial definitions.

The rationalist will deny all this, saying that such a view finesses the question of how this so-called learning ever gets off the ground. Rationalists have all argued, though in different ways, that acquiring knowledge always presupposes the possession of some prior knowledge. You do not get something for nothing. You cannot grow mental structures out of something whose initial representational format is not appropriately structured. The physical and social world do not contain such things as syllogisms and propositional attitudes directed to contents, and even if they did, how could children understand them unless they had adequately constrained theories about these domains to use for guidance?

Put this way, the debate does indeed have the potential for good end-to-end stuff, and put this way it does indeed suggest that questions about the starting state of the mind (say, domain-general learning capacity versus a honeycomb of purpose-built modules) are going to have to be decided in broad outline by the philosophers. But developmentalists need to move beyond this particular stadium, and they might do so in the company of the philosophers Aristotle, Kant, and Quine.

Aristotle

For Aristotle, rationalism and empiricism (as they came to be called) are each mistaken. His difficulties with the former arose from a denial that there could be a kind of knowledge that was more precise and elaborated than any knowledge that could be demonstrated in experience (and unconscious, into the bargain). He denied that there could be knowledge that did not presuppose certain forms of perceptual experience. Empiricism, on the other hand, assumes it is possible for a creature *with no knowledge at all* to acquire some knowledge, despite the fact that the very idea of knowledge acquisition would seem to imply the possession of prior knowledge to get the process off the ground. Aristotle's attempt to resolve this dilemma can be viewed, according to David Hamlyn (Hamlyn, 1976; and see Russell, 1978), as a kind of "genetic epistemology" in the sense that it attempted the kind of account that Piaget attempted, while not itself being a recognizably Piagetian theory.

What is innate for Aristotle is not mental structure but a potential (*dunamis*) for acquiring knowledge. While his theory has an associationist ring to it, Aristotle's conception of knowledge (scientific and lay) was, as will be seen, rationalist; and he also argued that the broadly associationist processes are not sufficient for knowledge to be acquired. How then does potential come to develop into manifest knowledge? He proposed the mechanism of *epagoge* (meaning literally to "lead on" and normally translated as "induction"). By the process of *epagoge* the mind comes to sort particular instances into general principles aided by the fact that some experiences retain their character through the flux of sensation. His metaphor for this process was that of an army being thrown into chaos after a rout, after which it reforms for defense as one man after another stands firm. Why do some particulars rather than others "stand firm"? Because they are the ones that constantly recur, he answered.

Such ideas did indeed influence what has since become known as associationism (Hartley, 1749), and to the contemporary learning theorist it carries echoes of processes such as perceptual learning and its close relative latent inhibition. It also has to be said that, put as simply as this, it suffers from the shortcomings of any theory of knowledge acquisition that relies heavily on discrimination learning. As Hamlyn (1978, Chapter 2) points out, it ignores the fact that all discrimination is a matter of determining *in virtue of what* a datum has to be discriminated from another datum. Take the case of "red." Could children come to acquire the concept RED by discrimination alone? Hardly, because they would need to know at the outset what to discriminate red things from—from green things for example but not from little things. This does not imply that children must therefore have the innate concept COLOR, but it does suggest that whatever the "potential" is it cannot be a general-purpose discriminator. In any event, given Aristotle's remarks about the inadequacies of what we would now call empiricism, it is likely that he would have shared this skepticism. He did not believe that *epagoge* could lead to true knowledge; all it could achieve was the guiding of the developing mind toward the kind of experiences that could further its development.

The next step requires first saying a little about how Aristotle regarded mature knowledge, before returning to *epagoge* in order to suggest a reading of it that might be more sympathetic to the modern developmentalist. First, far from believing that developed knowledge (*episteme*) is something gained entirely by induction from sensory experience, Aristotle viewed it as a set of necessary truths, arguing that scientific knowledge, and knowledge more generally, is concerned with that which is necessarily the case, and with *epagoge* playing a guiding rather than foundational role in the individual's coming to this view. The truths of science (I shall take that to include the folk science that the child acquires) are not mere listings of phenomena but rather express a system of laws such that if one accepts certain founding principles further truths can be *deduced*. To know about the behavior of objects and of organisms is to be in a position to *explain* phenomena by reference to these principles. This sounds absolutely rationalist but, as Burnyeat (1981) points out, "When Aristotle says that *episteme* is concerned with what cannot be otherwise his claim should not be read . . . as an unexamined legacy of Plato but as a substantial thesis designed to elucidate a current concept of understanding. That understanding is constituted by knowing the explanation of necessary connections in nature" (p. 72).

This has a very modern ring to it. With regard to philosophy (on which I will not dwell) it is the first appearance of the essentialist view of meaning and necessity articulated in this century by Saul Kripke

(1972).[2] To the developmentalist it will recall the currently influential idea that the developing child is a developing "theorist." There are of course both empiricist (Gopnik) and nativist (Fodor) versions of the "theory theory," but what they share is Aristotelian: the view that knowledge in any domain is a matter of knowing principles that govern and unify phenomena. Now back to *epagoge*.

An associationist, discrimination-fueled reading of this principle is not forced upon us. Indeed the idea is better regarded as a theory of how experience can *cause us to move from lower to higher states of knowledge* (see Hamlyn, 1990, Chapter 6). Aristotle (in the *Posterior Analytics* where the discussion of *epagoge* is located) claimed that all learning depends upon prior knowledge, but this does not mean (*pace* Fodor; and see Woodfield, 1987) that all new knowledge *is just the transposition of old knowledge* and thus that everything is somehow there at the beginning. Second, as Hamlyn (1990) writes, it "does not imply that all acquisition of knowledge is the result of learning. Experience can make us see that certain things are so. We may not be able to see them in that way unless we have the concepts which are presupposed in so seeing them. That fact, however, does not go against the idea that we may be *caused* to see them that way" (pp. 118–119, original italics).

What is the cash value of all this for the developmentalist? Here is one cashing at least. There is continuing controversy over how the infant acquires "the object concept." One set of supporters nowadays thinks that such a concept is innately specified, while another thinks it is an emergent property of our developing neural networks. Aristotle cannot be allied with either view. In his terms, one might say that human infants are born with innate predispositions to structure their perceptual inputs along certain lines, but as they gain more acquaintance with objects (e.g., see them falling unsupported, find them resisting their actions) they are caused to abandon primitive conceptions for more elaborated ones. In fact, with direct reference to epagoge, certain kinds of object experience are constantly encountered: that objects are occludable, for example. Such facts "stand firm." And what about the process of "leading on"? It is certainly more than a matter of stimulus generalization.

Take, in illustration, the following idea about object permanence development originally proposed by T. G. R. Bower (1974) and later taken up by Xu and Carey (1996). They remind us that infants must realize that an object's perceptual properties are *noncontingently* related to spa-

---

[2]In Kripke's view a term such as *gold* is taken to be a "rigid designator" of a certain substance with the consequence that "Gold is an element" must be regarded not as a contingent fact but as something that is necessarily true. On this theory of meaning, we cannot say that *it could have turned out that* gold be a compound rather than an element.

tio-temporal facts about it. (Note the echo of Aristotle in the idea that the child must come to acknowledge necessary truths.) For example, they develop the conception that a ball is identified by unique perceptual attributes, not by where it is in space. The crucial experiences that could cause the infant to be led on to this conception from another are not difficult to imagine: seeing which properties are constantly changing while also being changeable by one's own movement (spatio-temporal) and those that are not (color and shape). On such a view one denies both that the object concept is innate (in the sense of being elaborated prior to experience) and that it emerges from experience alone. At each point in development the infant has a conception with built-in obsolescence, but, as he or she develops, progressively more complex forms of experience are needed to render it obsolete and to replace it with another. More generally, the starting potential can only be understood in terms of the experiences that will cause it to become manifest; it is not a set of "rules and representations."

It is in this sense then that pure nativism and pure empiricism are taken to be wrong. Indeed, truly developmental accounts (hence Hamlyn's use of the term "genetic epistemology" as applied to Aristotle's position) are predicated on their being wrong. This bold statement will make a little more sense after the next section.

Kant

Although Kant's *Critique of Pure Reason* (Kemp Smith, 1964) carries not the slightest whiff of Aristotle's developmental style, both philosophers nonetheless shared a common aim: to articulate a view of human knowledge that is neither rationalist nor empiricist. In fact Kant spent most of his career working within the rationalist tradition until reading Hume woke him from what he called his "dogmatic slumbers." But thus awakened he set out to show how empiricism *fails* to account for the objective character of human knowledge. It will be sufficient for me to describe his ideas about causality. Explicitly developmental morals will, again, be drawn when I have done this.

No conception of the objective character of some experiences (e.g., that X must happen whether I experience it or not) and no conception of how we contribute to the nature of our own experiences (e.g., when I do Y my experience must change thus) is possible unless we have an adequate conception of causality. In knowing about objects and about ourselves as perceivers of them we exercise causal notions.

The following is what Hume famously said about how causal concepts are grounded. Because causal notions emanate from the experience of perceiving the constant conjunctions of causes and effects there can be no conception of independent causal necessity beyond the *feeling* of necessity we undergo when we perceive causes of a certain kind preceding effects of a certain kind. The "necessity" of the fact that causes of a certain kind precede effects of a certain kind, or that causes precede effects more generally,[3] is therefore neither an innate idea nor a mind-independent fact about the universe. The idea that causality can be reduced to a cognitive habit of this kind is a psychological thesis, of sorts.

There are clear problems with Hume's thesis. First, it is weak as psychology. This is because it can only support the claim that the experience of the constant conjunction of A then B is one element among others of our causal knowledge: it cannot support the claim that such experiences are *sufficient* for us to make causal judgments. To illustrate, not only is it implausible to say that classically conditioned human subjects judge that the tone (CS) *causes* the puff of wind to the face (UCS), but classical conditioning is one of the phenomena in psychology that yields to an *entirely* subpersonal account. Any reference to concepts of causality is otiose. Second, and more important for our purposes, psychology is not epistemology. Reducing the basic structure of our knowledge to feelings and habits can only erode faith in the very thing that we want to explain, namely, the status of certain kinds of knowledge as *necessary* for objective experience, as sketched above. This was Kant's essential objection to Hume's thesis. He argued that Hume put the cart before the horse insofar as causal concepts are what enable us to conceptualize the event A and the event B in the first place; a conception of causality does not emerge from witnessing their conjunctions.

Kant insisted then that our knowledge of causality cannot be the subjective affair Hume made it. At the same time he did not argue, as would a rationalist, that what we know about causality is something known independently of experience, a format that we apply to our experience but that itself has no experiential taint. For if this were so we could claim access to a world of absolute truths independent of perception; and indeed his worries about this were not dissimilar from Aristotle's. Much of the *Critique* was taken up with saying why we should abandon such claims;

---

[3]Hume describes the fact that causal relations are nothing more than constant conjunctions in a way that reveals a problem with his thesis. Having defined cause as "*an object followed by another, and where all the objects similar to the first are followed by objects similar to the second,*" he goes on to say that "or, in other words, *where if the object had not been, the second never had existed*" (Hume, 1975, section VII, part ii, original italics). However, what is intended as a paraphrase amounts to an admission that causal links are regarded by us as counterfactual (if A had not happened, then B would not have happened), and the counterfactual nature of causal judgments is something that cannot be explained in terms of the experience of constant conjunction.

for it was after all a "critique of pure reason," with "pure" here meaning experience independent. Accordingly, Kant argued that knowledge of causality is something partaking of both experience ("synthetic") and of that which is logically prior to it ("a priori"): it is *synthetic a priori* knowledge. In developmental context, this implies that the process of acquiring concepts of cause and effect is one that cannot be understood in terms of perceptual experience or in terms of innate formats alone.

What can be said about the a priori element? Kant's ideas here were Aristotelian insofar as he believed that all concepts are derived from certain fundamental epistemic "categories," including substance, causality, space, and time. But unlike the rationalist he did not take these to be forms of innate knowledge for reasons given above (what would causal understanding be without causal experience?), although on some readings of Kant (on Piaget's for one!) he did seem to be proposing what one of his commentators dubbed a "crude innatist psychology" (Strawson, 1966, p. 69). But this is a mistake. Sticking with causality, we see that the idea of cause and effect is, like that of the other categories, something that is *presupposed* in the very idea of objective experience. It is, as it were, part of the necessary framework within which all objective experience is undergone. It is not an innate representational format applied to unstructured sensory data. It is *the form that experience has to take* if it is to have an objective character.

We now come to Kant's views about causality, which appear in the Second Analogy section of the *Critique*. Unlike Hume, he did not begin by considering the experience of *two* events: A then B. Rather he begins with the idea of an event per se and with the question of what it takes for a subject to perceive any event at all, in the sense of a mind-independent occurrence in the world. Events, for Kant, are made up of a series of percepts that are undergone in an order over which the subject has no control. And so for an event to be perceived as such the subject must understand that there is something essentially rule bound, he argues, about the way one percept gives rise to the next. His example was that of somebody standing on a river bank and watching a boat sail along. To see this as an event the subject must be, in some sense, recognizing the necessity of the fact that an appearance of the boat in one part of the visual field (e.g., the left) necessarily precedes its appearance in another part (the right). Kant took the objectivity of this sequence to be part and parcel of the fact that it is not *reversible* by the subject and contrasted it with the boat case in which the subject *can* reverse the order in which the percepts arrive. In looking at the front elevation of a house (Kant's example again), one can see the parts of the house in any order one wishes. This is a "subjective" order, and it stands in contrast to the "objective" order experienced in the boat case.

Kant was aiming to prove then in the Second Analogy that "All alterations [changes in perceptual input] take place in conformity with the law of the connection of cause and effect" (Kemp Smith, 1964, p. 22). It seems he used six interweaving arguments to establish this fact, which, if it *is* a fact, would surely constrain theories of the development of causal concepts and of many other concepts besides.

Did he succeed? Almost certainly not. But if the argument fails, why should a developmentalist bother with the Kantian project at all? In a nutshell, because, given the scale of the question, doing the right *kind* of thing and falling short is a major success. But before justifying this view, I need to say why the argument fails.

It contains a non sequitur. Here are two philosophers' comments on it. Bennett (1966) writes that when we look at Kant's attempted proof "[h]ere, even more than usual, respect for Kant's genius requires an irreverent approach to the text" (p. 219). Kant argues, with reference to the objective (boat-sailing) perceptual sequence, that the fact that percepts X-Y could not have occurred in the order Y-X suggests that the causal sequence X-Y was somehow necessary, *that given that X happened, Y had to follow.* This last step is the non sequitur: "The rule which forbids a professor to precede the Vice-Chancellor in a procession does not forbid him to opt out of processing altogether" (p. 221). Strawson meanwhile writes of a "a non sequitur of numbing grossness" (1966, p. 137): "—and here comes the step—to conceive the order of perceptions as necessary is equivalent to conceiving the transition from A to B as *itself* necessary, as falling, that is to say, under a rule or law of causal determination . . . [as if] an event of that type invariably and necessarily follows a condition of that type" (p. 138, original italics).

If a frog leaps from my left hand to my right hand, I will expect that my frog percepts will have a certain trajectory and sequence. But this is not the same as taking this sequence to fall under a rule that is itself necessary. Nothing follows of necessity from "frog at time-one" to "frog at time-two." Flying through the air, anything can happen to the animal. Contingency rules, not necessity.

But there are two kinds of *psychological* readings of the Second Analogy argument available to us (and not psychological in the Humean sense mentioned above). The first is as so-called "transcendental psychology" (the term "transcendental" is Kant's) and the second is as developmental psychology.

Arguments in transcendental psychology take the following form: we know X and this would not be possible unless our experience had form F; therefore, our experience has form F. Back to the Second Analogy. Guyer (1987) argues that what Kant really succeeded in establishing was that unless we applied a concept of causality (which is indissociable from the idea of necessary succession) in our perception of events it would not be possible for us to make sense of the idea of temporal relation. Causal concepts ground temporal concepts; and surely no notion of objecthood and selfhood could emerge without temporal concepts. For reasons that will not detain us, Guyer played down the psychological element in this. Patricia Kitcher (1990), however, in her book on Kant's transcendental psychology, plays it up. What Kant has shown, she argues, is that perception and cognition cannot be successful unless there is the right kind of mutual dependency between temporal and causal concepts. She argues that Kant can, without circularity (see below), accept the converse dependency of causal concepts upon temporal; and she draws out the relevance to contemporary cognitive psychology by reference to Fodor and Bever's (1965) famous "click" experiments on sentential parsing.

But there is certainly no direct relevance to development here. Kitcher writes: "There is no circularity in this analysis [i.e., mutual dependence of the causal and the temporal], however. [This is because] Kant was interested in origins, not development. The claim is not that we must employ causal concepts *before* we can order states of affairs in time but that we can only do one by doing the other, and that `cause' cannot be gotten out of the senses. Although this analysis would put constraints on developmental psychology, it is not itself developmental" (Kitcher, 1990, p. 178, original italics). What are these constraints and what can be made of the Second Analogy that *is* developmental? First, the constraints: If the Kantian view is correct, it puts enormous pressure on modular–nativist theories of development. When suitably spelled out it can, I suggest, render untenable the idea of an innate module for causal judgment. And what is the developmental moral?

As I have argued elsewhere (e.g., Russell, 1996), the contrast Kant draws between subjective (self-determined) sequences and objective (world-determined) ones serves as a foundation for the view that cognitive development is something that can only take place in agents. Again when suitably spelled out, it is the necessary starting point for any theory directed at explaining *the* fundamental process in mental development, which is the development of self–world dualism. The subjective (controllable) sequences are only such in contrast to the objective (uncontrollable); and the objective sequences are only such in contrast to the subjective. What the self achieves is only such in contrast to what the world imposes; and what the world imposes is only such in contrast to what the self achieves. This, for my money, captures the essence of Piagetian theory.

Piaget was an empiricist in the sense that he would have marched behind their banner that *intellectus nihil movet* (the intellect initiates nothing); but he was a rationalist in the sense of assuming that objective knowledge presupposes the existence of the categories. His theory was genuinely developmental in much the same way as Aristotle's. For, although one might fault Piaget for failing to acknowledge the contribution of domain-specific innate potential, he gave a plausible account of how the mind might be "lead on" from a lower cognitive level to a higher one.

Quine

Interdisciplinary workshops for psychologists and philosophers are all the rage these days. They often work well, but they can also be fine examples of "distributed cognition" insofar as the philosophical and the psychological are tightly interwoven within the *group* mind, while each individual mind is computing within a single sealed domain. And more to the present point, some philosophers (not to mention psychologists) are yet to be cured of the view that we are data collectors and nothing more. The convenor (a philosopher) of one such workshop I attended 10 years ago introduced proceedings by saying that the philosophers would discuss the conceptual issues while we, the psychologists, would provide "the facts." In any event, the belief is widely held that philosophical truths are what Kant called "analytic," meaning true a priori and in virtue of the meaning of the terms employed, in contrast to the synthetic truths of psychology that tell us something about the world. But if indeed there *are* synthetic a priori truths, as Kant supposed, then the door is opened onto a kind of cognitive developmental psychology that is interdisciplinary in the true sense: in the sense in which the mind of each of its practitioners is thinking a third kind of thought, in the sense that it is not only the seminar room that is computing the synthetic a priori. And if so, the term "genetic epistemology" ceases to sound like an oxymoron and more like a plausible enterprise.

I mention W. V. O. Quine now because he famously argued against the impermeablity of the analytic–synthetic distinction. Quine listed a number of problems with the distinction as part of a complex argument, and perhaps the most discussed of these is the following. The definition of "analytic" is circular. In explicating the notion "analytic" one gives examples of sentences that are true "by definition," such as "All vertebrates are members of the animal kingdom." Because "vertebrate" means "member of an animal kingdom with a spinal column," we have shown that the sentence is true by virtue of the meaning of the word "vertebrate." Is this sufficient to define a truth as analytic? Not according to Quine, because we only get from "vertebrate" to "member of the animal kingdom with a spinal column" by using the idea of sameness of meaning, and *this notion is no clearer than that of analytic truth itself.* As Quine puts it, sameness of meaning and analytic truth are "members of the same family." And so, because of this interdependence, one cannot establish that a sentence is analytically true without assuming the answer in advance. Consequently, if we cannot define the analytic in a noncircular way we have no warrant for drawing a clean line between the analytic and the synthetic. Everything depends then upon our having a nonquestion-begging criterion for a sentence's expressing an analytic truth.

Quine replaced the picture of two kinds of truth divided by an impermeable barrier with that of a sphere, or circle, at the center of which are those kinds of truth that we take to be unrevisable. At the periphery are truths that we are relaxed about abandoning, with there being no point at which one kind of truth (by definition) becomes another (by fact).

What are the consequences of this picture for human knowledge—scientific and folk? If there are no statements of pure, brute fact (entirely synthetic statements), then the truth of each scientific and everyday statement will inevitably be reliant to some extent upon its conceptual relations with the truths of other statements. That is to say, if empirical statements do not stand heroically alone at the periphery, then they must get whatever truth we give them partly in virtue of how they relate to other statements, whether these be near the core, or near the periphery, or somewhere between, which means that the truth of statements is determined *holistically.* "The totality of our so-called knowledge . . . from the most casual matters of geography and history to the profoundest laws of atomic physics or even of pure mathematics and logic, is a manmade fabric which impinges on experience only along the edges. Or, to change the figure, total science is like a field of force whose boundary conditions are experience." Moreover, a "conflict with experience at the periphery occasions readjustments in the interior of the field" (Quine, 1951, p. 42). Imagine how one single, minute-long act of levitation would impact upon physics, psychology, philosophy, you name it. But more mundanely, consider how what we know about mental development impacts upon philosophical views of the "grounding" of knowledge. If Quine is correct, and of course some deny he is (notably Grice and Strawson, 1956), then the line between transcendental psychology and developmental psychology *simply cannot be drawn.*

☐ Injury Time

I have been trying to articulate the need for a kind of cognitive–developmental psychology that is neither rationalist nor empiricist (in any straightforward sense) and that has both empirical and epistemological aspects. A survey of the present scene suggests that many have already signed up for quite different kinds of enterprise.

Back to the soccer match. On one side of the stadium are those who cheer every time Jerry Fodor touches the ball. I shall first question whether Fodor should really be picked for the Rationalist Rovers at all and then make some comments about the cheering.

Fodor is of course a nativist and so he is committed to an empirical claim commonly made within the rationalist tradition. But the thinker who clearly had the most significant influence on Fodor (apart from Chomksy, not a philosopher, whose references to Descartes and the seventeenth century British Platonists are really window dressing[4]) was *Alan Turing*, someone who would not even be considered for a job as a boot-boy with that team. And there is one thing which sets Fodor in clear opposition to the rationalist mode of thought: his atomism about concepts and how their meaning is fixed. For Fodor (Fodor, 1998, in particular) the meaning of concepts is fixed atomistically and it is fixed "information-ally," by causal inputs from the environment. To say that a concept's meaning is fixed by environmental input is a long way from rationalism, because, for the rationalist, holism is the game plan and the theory of truth in play is a coherence theory not a correspondence theory. (And the converse of this is the holism of the self-styled *empiricist* Quine!) More-over, despite his abhorrence of all things holistic, even Fodor had to admit, in famously postulating the "central systems," that domain-gen-eral cognition (a.k.a. "thinking") is "Quinean" (Fodor, 1983), which, give or take a bit, means holistic. (The question of whether Fodor manages to square this belief with his Turingesque view of mental computation need not detain us.) So what *exactly* is being cheered on?

Now the following remarks about the supporters may seem to have all the subtlety of a late tackle, but I fancy I see Fodor's name is being used to give philosophical underpinning to essentially vacuous developmen-tal claims and in order to justify unconstrained module-making. What meaning, for example, can really be attached to the idea that PRETEND is an item in the toddler's language of thought? And what constrains the christening of new modules, and what possible sense does it make to say that the growth of one module "triggers" another when a module for Fodor, or for anybody indeed, must be "informationally encapsulated"? Sometimes, *sometimes*, module proliferation is what gets done as an alter-native to thinking deeply about mental development. Certainly, for me

---

[4]Chomsky's project is entirely empirical (see Cottingham, 1984). It is not based on philo-sophical ideas about the nature of knowledge. To be a nativist about a certain mental fac-ulty does not amount to rationalism.

at least, The Intention Editor (a submodule of The Will module apparently) and its ilk are horrid pseudopostulates.

On the other side of the stadium we see another set of supporters who look a bit embarrassed about being there. They certainly do not sport red and yellow scarves, but they do allow themselves little smiles of satisfaction when the City scores. These are the connectionists. (Apparently it is possible to be one merely by adopting a certain style of thought [Elman et al., 1996, Chapter 2]. Going anywhere near a computer may not be necessary.) Why are they embarrassed? Because they do not regard themselves *as* empiricists. Rather they take themselves to be *interactionists*, like Piaget (Elman et al., 1996). Paradoxically they too think that the rationalism–empiricism contrast is somewhat misconceived. But they do so for entirely different reasons from the ones I have given. Interactionism for them really refers to what takes place in neural development, while their Piagetian sympathies are so shallow that they have nothing to say about agency and nothing to say about logicomathematical structures. True, when networks use back-propagation algorithms they do something that looks like Piaget's "accommodation." But this is only true at the highest level of metaphor. What they are really doing is instantiating the Rescorla–Wagner rule, and Piaget was not noted for his interest in classical conditioning. Connectionist accounts of mental development, at least as conceived by the authors of Elman et al. (1996), are empiricist. I am not talking about the modelers themselves; I am talking about those who think that cognitive development will yield to thoroughly connectionist account. Such a view is empiricist insofar as it assumes that there is no more in a concept than there is in the experience that gave rise to it (references to "innate" connection weightings for face perception and the like notwithstanding).

The controversy over whether cognition, and thus mental development, can in principle be modeled subsymbolically has been mostly played out over the question of whether networks can model the systematicity of thought[5] (Fodor & Pylyshyn, 1988). It may be that connectionism's problems here are not unique to it (Matthews, 1997), but it

---

[5]The precise definition of this term is itself controversial. This is one way of putting it. If one can *think* that John likes cheese and Mary likes chutney, then one must also be able to think that Mary likes cheese and John likes chutney. Arguments and predicates are freely combinable in thought as they are in language, and having one cognitive capacity entails the ability to exercise an infinity of others (think of Chomsky's remarks on the productivity of syntactic rules). Being systematic and being productive are conceptually related. Prima facie at least, it seems that such a capacity depends upon the computations being done over symbols, over representational states with a *sui generis* character. Connectionist networks, however, do not work by calling up, combining, and embedding representational states with content in this sense, as it done in classical AI. The question is whether this failure is principled.

is interesting to note how *relaxed* developmental connectionists are about shelving the problem. The authors of Elman et al. (1996) simply accept that it cannot be done (p. 103), while a sympathetic philosopher Andy Clark (1993) thinks that systematicity is no more than a criterion of thought *attribution* (Russell, 1996, for commentary). Clark writes, in any event, that the issue can be "bracketed," which is to say "ignored." This does not promise bright prospects for connectionist accounts of cognitive development. Then there is the question of what exactly is being modeled in the connectionist language work. Fodor (1997), I think rightly, points out that what the networks are doing is modeling *correlates* of grammatical classes, not the classes themselves. For example, being preceded by the words "a" and "the" and preceding words that often refer to actions and that take "s" and "ed" suffixes *correlates* with being a noun. But for a net to pick up on these regulaties is not that same as its representing the class "noun" simply because those features are not definitional of that category but are, rather, statistical signals of it in English.

It is also worth wondering whether the sights are not being set far too high. Consider some of the things that networks cannot model. For example, there are as yet no adequate network-style models of (the full complexity) of goal-directed behavior in the laboratory rat (Dickinson & Balleine, 1993). Maybe this will turn out not to be a principled failure. But if it *is* principled it will almost certainly have come about because goals must be represented in a symbollike format; and if this is so it will surely put a warning shot across the bows to those who seek to explain cognitive development in connectionist terms alone, to say the least. More generally, where networks score in psychology is in their modeling of classical conditioning and its cognates, and one of these is categorization. But nobody believes that categories are the same as concepts, that handwriting-recognition programs, for example, have concepts. And while human cognition appears to rest on (among other things) a bedrock of associative processes of which classical conditioning is the paradigm, and while it may even be the case that when humans engage in some forms of causal reasoning (Dickinson & Burke, 1996), they are in fact doing what in rats we would call "backward blocking" (Miller & Matute, 1996); *a bedrock should not be mistaken for an edifice.*

☐ Getting Changed

I have been making two interrelated claims. One is that when faced with questions shading into epistemology (such as about how a potential for knowledge acquisition might be represented in the newborn) developmentalists have tended to side either with what they take to be a glorious tradition (rationalism → nativism → preformed modules) or side with the opposite tradition willy-nilly (Humean empiricism → connectionism). What is wrong in the first place is that the thinker whom the modular nativists take to be the culmination of his tradition, Fodor, is only ambiguously a part of it. The modular nativism that they espouse lacks the philosophical underpinning with which they wish to credit it. What is wrong with the willy-nilly empiricism of the connectionists (remember my target is the kind of claims made in Elman et al., 1996) is that the past two-hundred years have shown us that Humean associationism is a failure, by failing to explain everything from causal judgments, to reasoning, to self-consciousness. But (this is the other claim) the best philosophical ideas about mental development and about the status of developmental science *come from people who worked in neither of these traditions.*

This brings me to the positive and more substantial part of the chapter and the part that is unfortunately more difficult to summarize. From Aristotle we get the thought that knowledge acquisition must be understood as a process of realizing a potential through experience, an inborn potential for judgment whose nature can only be understood by describing a developmental process. Notions like "potential" and ideas about experience "leading on" the child from one conceptual level to another are hard to spell out, but I suggest they are more intellectually enabling than than the confident absolutes we hear from the enthusiasts for innate modules and general-purpose neural networks. From Kant we get the thought that the fundamental cognitive categories (causality, substance, space, time) can be *presupposed* in experience without being innate formats and (via what, to the traditionalist, will surely seem a very idiosyncratic route indeed) considerations in favor of Piaget's idea about the necessary role of agency in development. From Quine we get the idea that there is no principled line to be drawn between empirical and philosophical theses about mental development.

I admit that the prospects for such a different kind of cognitive–developmental psychology—one looking like genetic epistemology[6] though I hope with a nicer name—do look bleak. Will things change? So long as the career structure (Get those data papers out!) of developmental psychology remains as it is and so long as university teaching in psychology remains as it is (as often as not breeding good technicians and poor synthesisers), it will not. But one thing history teaches us is that *you never can tell.*

---

[6]For defenses of the notion of genetic epistomology see Russell (1978, 1979).

☐ References

Bennett, J. (1966). *Kant's analytic.* Cambridge, UK: Cambridge University Press.

Bower, T. G. R. (1974). *Development in infancy.* San Francisco: Freeman.

Burnyeat, M. F. (1981). Aristotle on understanding knowledge. In E. Berti (Ed.), Aristotle on Science: The posterior analytics. Padova, Italy: Antenore.

Clark, A. (1993). *Microcognition.* Cambridge, MA: MIT Press.

Cottingham, J. (1984). *Rationalism.* Chippenham, UK: Thoemmes Press.

Dickinson, A., & Balleine, B. (1993). Actions and responses. In N. Eilan, R. McCarthy, & B. Brewer (Eds.), *Spatial representation: Problems in philosophy and psychology.* Oxford, UK: Blackwell.

Dickinson, A., & Burke, J. (1996). Within-compound associations mediate the retrospective revaluation of causality judgements. *Quarterly Journal of Experimental Psychology, 49B,* 60–80.

Elman, J. L., Bates, E. A., Johnson, M. H., Karmiloff-Smith, A., Parisi, D., & Plunkett, K. (1996). *Rethinking innateness: A connectionist perspective on development.* Cambridge, MA: MIT Press.

Fodor, J. A. (1983). *The modularity of mind.* Cambridge, MA: MIT Press (Bradford Books).

Fodor, J. A. (1997, May 16). Do we have it in us? (Review of Elman, Bates, Johnson, Karmiloff-Smith, Parisi, & Plunkett, 1996). *Times Literary Supplement,* pp. 3–4.

Fodor, J. A. (1998). *Concepts: Where cognitive science went wrong.* Oxford, UK: Oxford University Press.

Fodor, J. A., & Bever, T. G. (1965). The psychological reality of linguistic segments. *Journal of Verbal Learning and Verbal Behavior, 4,* 414–420.

Fodor, J. A., & Pylyshyn, Z. (1988). Connectionism and cognitive architecture. *Cognition, 28,* 3–71.

Grice, H. P., & Strawson, P. F. (1956). In defence of a dogma. *Philosophical Review, 62,* 102–104.

Guyer, P. (1987). *Kant and the claims of knowledge.* Cambridge, UK: Cambridge University Press.

Hamlyn, D. W. (1976). Aristotelian epagoge. *Phronesis, 21,* 167–184.

Hamlyn, D. W. (1978). *Experience and the growth of understanding.* London: Routledge and Kegan Paul.

Hamlyn, D. W. (1990). *In and out of the black box.* Oxford, UK: Blackwell.

Hartley, D. (1749). *Observations on man.* Oxford, UK: Oxford University Press.

Hume, D. (1975). *Enquiring concerning human understanding* (3rd ed.). Oxford, UK: Oxford University Press. (Original work published 1748)

Kemp Smith, N. (1964). *Immanuel Kent's critique of pure reason.* London: Macmillan.

Kitcher, P. (1990). *Kant's transcendental psychology.* Oxford, UK: Oxford University Press.

Kripke, S. (1972). *Naming and necessity.* Oxford, UK: Blackwell.

Matthews, R. J. (1997). Can connectionists explain systematicity? *Mind and Language, 12,* 154–177.

Miller, R. R., & Matute, H. (1996). Biological significance in forward and backward blocking: Resolution of a discrepancy between animal conditioning and human causal judgement. *Journal of Experimental Psychology: General, 125,* 370–386.

Quine, W. V. O. (1951). Two dogmas of empiricsm. In *From a logical point of view.* Cambridge, MA: Harvard University Press.

Russell, J. (1978). *The acquisition of knowledge.* Basingstoke, UK: Macmillan.

Russell, J. (1979). The status of genetic epistomology. *Journal for the Theory of Social Behaviour, 9,* 53–71.

Russell, J. (1996). *Agency: Its role in mental development.* Hove, UK: The Psychology Press.

Strawson, P. F. (1966). *The bounds of sense.* London: Methuen.

Woodfield, A. (1987). On the very idea of acquiring a concept. In J. Russell (Ed.), *Philosophical perspectives on developmental psychology.* Oxford, UK: Blackwell.

Woolhouse, R. S. (1988). *The empiricists.* Oxford, UK: Oxford University Press.

Xu, F., & Carey, S. (1996). Infant's metaphysics: The case of numerical identity. *Cognitive Psychology, 30,* 111–153.

CHAPTER

H. Rudolph Schaffer

Understanding Socialization: From Unidirectional to Bidirectional Conceptions

☐ Introduction

How do children acquire the norms of their society? How, within a relatively short period, do they become capable of sharing the particular sets of habits, beliefs, and values of their caretakers and adopting the standards of behavior to which these individuals conform? The nature of the socialization processes responsible for such changes is a central topic in developmental psychology that is both theoretically intriguing and practically important.

Psychologists have attempted to account for children's socialization in various ways (Schaffer, 1996), but for several decades around the mid-twentieth century one view prevailed above all, the unidirectional approach, so called because it saw this process entirely in terms of what parents (and other caretaking adults) do to children by means of the particular rearing practices they adopt, with no regard for the role children play. The move away from this model and the adoption of an alternate account (a bidirectional one, because of its emphasis on the reciprocity of parental and child influences) represents one of the most profound paradigm shifts we have seen in developmental psychology, and it is the nature of this shift and its implications for the way in which we think about socialization and the relationship between parents and children that I want to describe here.

☐ The Undirectional Approach: Assumptions and Research

There is general agreement that parents play a basic role in children's development, although very much less as to how they do so. One common belief is that this process can be conceived largely in terms of clay molding: The child, it is said, is like an unformed blob of clay at birth that is then molded by mothers, fathers, teachers, etc., into any shape that they arbitrarily decide upon. To understand socialization one must therefore focus on the behavior of caretakers; the child itself is seen as passive, infinitely malleable, and wholly at the mercy of the molding process. Developmental change is thus explained solely in terms of environmental input to the child.

This account was given apparent academic respectability by behaviorism, as first formulated by J. B. Watson. As he once put it, "The behaviorist finds that the human being at birth is a very lowly piece of unformed protoplasm, ready to be shaped by any family in whose care it is first placed" (1928). Subsequently learning theory took this account further by postulating the mechanisms whereby these influences achieve their result: it is the adults' schedules of rewards and punishments, their ways of habit training, and the examples that they model that provide an explanation of the final product (Bijou & Baer, 1962). Socialization, as Bijou (1970) put it, is simply the individual's reinforcement history.

It follows that the research stimulated by this view took as its primary focus the child-rearing activities of parents, as they set about the task of molding their children according to their particular wishes and conceptions. Investigators' interests thus centered on individuals rather than on relationships and on parenting rather than on parent–child interactions. Measures of children's development were obtained separately and regarded as "outcomes," whereas the parents' actions were thought of as the "antecedents" that were directly responsible for these effects. Much of the socialization literature that has accumulated over the last few decades is thus based on correlations between parental and child characteristics, the correlations being interpreted in terms of cause–effect sequences proceeding from parent to child.

There are, however, two problems about this approach. One is that the correlations obtained were often negligible and gave little ground for believing in the all-powerful role of parental influence. Take the classical study by Sears, Maccoby, and Levin (1957), which set out to describe the child-rearing practices of a large sample of American mothers and establish the effects on their children by relating types of child rearing to certain outcome variables selected on the basis of theoretical (mainly Freudian) expectations. As it turned out, however, Sears and his colleagues were markedly unsuccessful in their efforts in demonstrating any association between maternal practices and child outcome variables: only 3% of the variance in the latter, it has been calculated, was accounted for by the former (Yarrow, Campbell, & Burton, 1968). As Maccoby (1992) subsequently put it, so few significant correlations between parental and child measures emerged that virtually nothing could be published relating these two sets of data, and the report became instead a descriptive account of the child-rearing practices of one particular group of American mothers, which is by no means a worthless achievement but not one that the authors had originally set out to obtain.

The second problem about the unidirectional approach concerns the fact that correlation is not causation, which is an elementary point and yet one which, when parent and child measures are at issue, even seasoned investigators still sometimes seem to have difficulty in accepting. There are plenty of examples of associations that even in current literature still tempt writers to put causal interpretations on them: parental punitiveness and child aggressiveness, parental sensitivity and child security, parental pathology and child pathology, and so forth. The use of more neutral terms such as "predicting" hardly disguises the assumptions made, when the direction discussed is invariably from parent to child.

Yet correlations such as those above may be brought about in a great many different ways, and the mere fact of association does not allow one to decide between them. Consider the parent pathology–child pathology link. Children of depressed mothers are themselves at risk for developing some form of psychopathology by a factor of 2 or 3 in comparison with other children (though note the sex-linked nature of the association, according to which it is daughters rather than sons in whom it is found; Boyle & Pickles, 1997). The mechanism behind the association, however, can take many quite different forms: genetic transmission, imitation, disruptive parenting (which in itself refers to a large variety of aspects), intermediate factors such as the parent's unemployment or loss of social contact, marital discord, isolation of the child from favorable social settings such as peer groups, and so on (Dodge, 1990). The fact that characteristics can be transmitted genetically as well as through behavioral interaction is alone of immense significance: as Sandra Scarr (1988) felt impelled to point out, this means that virtually all research on parent–child socialization is uninterpretable because parents provide both genes and environment. To determine either cause or direction of effects as observed in parent–child interaction within biologically related families is therefore impossible. Thus, even in those cases where certain parental and child characteristics have repeatedly been found associated, as in the case of authoritative parenting and child competence, we rarely know how or why this comes about.

What has aroused most interest, however, is the possibility that parent–child correlations may be the result of child influences on parents, i.e., that the cause–effect sequence goes in the opposite direction from that normally assumed. It is this realization that has resulted in such a radical shift in our thinking and research in the socialization area.

☐ A Reinterpretation

For some time there had been various suggestions in the literature that children come into the world with an individuality of their own and that what transpires between parent and child is a function of that as well as of the parent's characteristics. Thomas, Chess, Birch, Hertzig, & Korn, for instance, published their volume *Behavioral Individuality in Early Childhood* in 1963, proposing that inherent temperamental characteristics are operative from birth on and can influence parental-rearing techniques; and in our own early work on mother–infant interaction (Schaffer & Emerson, 1964) we also observed that mothers' behavior was in certain respects driven by the child's individuality and that mutual adaptation to each other's characteristics rather than parental molding was the basis on which the relationship developed. However, it was left to Richard Bell to bring the various isolated findings together and to spell out their implications for our understanding of the socialization process.

Bell's Proposal

In a landmark paper published in 1968, Bell took a new look at the child-rearing literature and, both there and in various subsequent publications (e.g., Bell & Chapman, 1986; Bell & Harper, 1977), proposed that *child effects* (i.e., the influence of child on parent) play as great a part in socialization as do parental influences. Although the number of studies found by Bell that had produced consistent and well-agreed findings for parent–child correlations were in fact relatively small, those that had been established could, he suggested, be just as plausibly interpreted as demonstrating child-to-parent effects as the parent-to-child effects that the prevailing view automatically assumed. Children, that is, by virtue of their individual characteristics, affect how parents behave toward them and in this way help to determine their own upbringing.

Bell bolstered his argument by drawing attention to various findings: the fact, for example, that parents do not behave uniformly to all children in the family; also the observation derived from case studies of abused children that often only one child in a family is selected for such treatment, the choice apparently being based on certain characteristics of that child that the parents found intolerable. As Bell pointed out, findings such as these make it necessary to acknowledge the individuality of children; whatever distinctive behavior tendencies a child brings to the interaction with the parent will play a part in shaping the parent's actions. Fortunately parents do not have rigidly fixed techniques for socializing children; rather, they possess a repertoire from which they select according to each child's nature. Bell, that is, went beyond merely drawing attention to the existence of child effects: he also addressed the issue of bidirectionality as such and did so by proposing a "control theory" to account for the interaction of the two sets of influences. This states that both parent and child have upper and lower tolerance levels for the other's behavior: when the upper limit for one participant is reached, the reaction of the other is to reduce or redirect the partner's excessive behavior; when the lower limit of tolerance is reached, the individual responds with attempts to stimulate the partner into some sort of action. Children as well as parents respond to their partner in this way, thus producing constant reciprocal adaptation to each other's behavior.

Bell's control theory has been applied by various writers to account for the nature of social interaction episodes and found to be of some limited use. His principal contribution, however, remains in drawing attention to the existence of child effects and to the danger of misinterpreting correlations in terms of one particular kind of causal sequence.

The Nature of Child Effects

Since Bell's 1968 paper there has been much discussion about what precisely we mean by child effects and just how they influence the course of parent–child relationships (e.g., Maccoby & Martin, 1983; Russell & Russell, 1992). Attempts to identify them have usually focused on congenital factors, i.e., characteristics that children bring into the world with them that may be of genetic or of prenatal origin and that are relatively fixed and enduring over age. Prominent among these are gender, it being evident that we respond differently to boys and girls from birth or just because they are boys and girls (Golombok & Fivush, 1994); physical attractiveness, which not only in infancy (Langlois, Ritter, Casey, &

Sawin, 1995) but in later childhood too (Elder, Nguyen, & Caspi, 1984) can have marked effects on the kind of relationship established with parents; prematurity, insofar as the disorganized behavior usually found in such infants makes them more difficult to respond to (Eckerman & Oehler, 1992); and above all temperament. Admittedly, there is still no agreement as to the specific constituents of temperament that can be objectively demonstrated; yet Thomas and Chess's (1977) largely intuitively based category of "difficult" temperament has, more than any other inherent child effect, repeatedly been shown to have considerable implications for the quality of the relationship established with parents. A "difficult" infant is, for instance, more likely to experience reduced parental attention, less stimulating contact, more restriction, and more punishment than an "easy" infant (Crockenberg, 1986). The strength of associations reported is by no means always impressive or consistent; other factors such as the parent's tolerance for and subjective interpretation of the child's behavior also play a part. Nevertheless, there is enough evidence to indicate that infants characterized by general irritability, irregularity, and predominantly negative mood tend to have adverse effects on their caretakers, even though specific one-to-one associations can rarely be demonstrated.

Child effects, however, are not confined to static, relatively constant characteristics. The role that developmental change, as an influence in its own right, plays in parent–child interaction must also be recognized. For one thing, the social significance of any given characteristic may well alter with age: impulsiveness at age 10 is no longer the amusing quality that it was at age 2, and the convenient passivity of an infant may manifest itself as the worrying unassertiveness of the school child. What is salient at one age may not be so at another; the changing meaning of particular attributes with development produces different effects on parents at different ages. And for another, as Maccoby (1984) has so convincingly argued, the very nature of development constitutes a force to which parents need to respond: it is not something that they themselves invariably initiate. The fact that children become more emotionally controlled as they grow older, for example, may have little to do with their caretakers' restraining influence, and if some children fail to develop impulse control one cannot automatically attribute it to socializing failure on the part of their parents. Developmental change, as Maccoby pointed out, turns out to be surprisingly independent of the way parents treat children: thus the literature on the development of inhibitory controls over impulsiveness provides few unambiguous indications of any particular kind of input from adults that is related to such development. Not only physical growth, the most obvious example, but also a wide range of psychological developments refer in large part to changes that are biologically programmed rather than brought about by parental action. These changes constitute a powerful thrust that requires continuous adaptation in the way parents respond to their children, and must thus be seen as a dynamic sequence of child effects lying at the very heart of development.

Yet child effects can be said to refer to an even wider range of influences. As analytic studies of parent–child interaction have demonstrated, parental behavior at a given moment of time tends to be a function of all sorts of specific actions emitted by the child. Face-to-face exchanges of mothers and young infants, for instance, undertaken in order to determine who responds to whom, have shown that in many respects it is the infant who drives the interaction by means of glances, vocalizations, movements, and expressions, and even though these may not be used with any intention of affecting the partner they do have just such an effect. The pace of the interaction, its topic, and its emotional tone are thus frequently determined by the infant, with the parent willingly responding to whatever behavior is currently emitted. Again it is apparent that child effects are not confined to some finite group of static characteristics but refer to the whole range of children's interactive behavior.

Let us also bear in mind that children's social interactions are usually observed after they have spent more or less lengthy periods living with others, and how they behave is therefore not merely a matter of congenital factors but also of their past interaction experience. Insofar as such experience has left its mark on the child, parents may well be reacting to characteristics in the child that they themselves have produced but that now in turn influence the nature of their rearing practices. Child effects must therefore be seen as whatever it is children bring to an interaction, whether that is inherent in origin or represents the cumulative consequences of past experience.

☐ From Individuals to Relationship

Accepting the idea of bidirectionality has both practical and theoretical implications. On the practical side, it is clearly unrealistic for parents to be held wholly responsible for their children's characteristics, such as, in particular, their less desirable traits like antisocial tendencies or psychopathological conditions. When, back in 1943, Kanner first described the syndrome of infantile autism, his search for an explanation took him immediately to parental-rearing practices; the result was the proposal that cold, emotionally frozen attitudes toward the child brought about the condition. Automatically attaching blame to parents for their children's deviant behavior may still be common in everyday life; the need to broaden the search for etiological factors, now widely recognized among scientists, is not yet generally accepted.

As to theoretical implications, there have been far-reaching changes in the way we think about parent–child relationships. The change, however, came in stages, for, initially, the concept of bidirectionality merely added another arrow to ways of describing the relationship. Child influences, that is, supplemented parental influences, as though the sum of the two unidirectional forces could adequately describe the relationship. It is only more recently that we have come to accept the idea that relationships are composed of networks of inextricably interwoven forces and that therefore new levels of analysis and new, specifically dyadic concepts are required to do justice to them. The need for such a different orientation becomes evident even when we wish merely to describe the characteristics of the individual participants in the relationship. Individuals' scores derived from a social interaction are often presumed to reflect some within-person trait brought to the encounter and to operate in some constant fashion therein; in fact such scores ought to be seen as a function of the interaction rather than as a purely individual characteristic. A good example is provided by parental sensitivity, which is a highly complex, multilayered concept that manifests itself in diverse ways (Tamis-LeMonda, 1996) but that is generally regarded as an essential prerequisite to various aspects of children's development such as, in particular, the security of attachments. Various measures have been developed that enable one to range parents along this dimension; these tend to reinforce the notion that sensitivity constitutes the "property" of an individual, which can be applied in fixed fashion from one situation to another and from one child to another. This, however, neglects the bidirectional nature of sensitivity: how sensitive a parent is depends also on the *child's* individuality. As has now been repeatedly demonstrated, some children are just more difficult to be sensitive to: if, for instance, their ability to communicate with others and provide them with clear signals is in some way impaired, as has been described for both blind infants (Fraiberg, 1977) and Down's syndrome children (Sorce & Emde, 1982), they become less "readable" and the task of parents accordingly more difficult. Parental sensitivity is therefore a function of the dyad; it is a statement about an interaction and not about an individual, reflecting both the child's skill in signaling and the parent's readiness to respond (van den Boom, 1997).

The shift from individuals to dyads as the unit of analysis in social interaction research is one result of the introduction of child effects into the socialization literature. Instead of making separate statements about each participant and then attempting to interrelate these, concepts have been developed that refer to the interaction per se, concepts such as episodes of maintained engagement (Stern, Beebe, Jaffe, & Bennett, 1977), visual coorientation (Collis & Schaffer, 1975), relationship reciprocity and complementarity (Dunn, 1993), and joint involvement episodes (Schaffer, 1992). In each case one can investigate the structure, function, and developmental course of the concept as such; examining the respective individual contributions made by the participants involves a separate endeavor. One of the earliest but still one of the most influential examples of a dyadic concept is "goodness of fit," the term Thomas and Chess (1977) put forward to describe the circumstances where the demands, expectations, and attitudes of the caretaker match the child's temperamental and other characteristics. Given such a match, optimal development is possible; where poorness of fit occurs, maladaptive functioning may result. The goodness of fit concept has been criticized for its vagueness and for offering few guidelines for detailed investigation. It does, however, have intuitive appeal, and moreover it shows why statements based on the behavior of just one partner often lack predictive power. Take two infants of equally "difficult" temperament: when such an infant is matched with a mother who sees the child's irritability as a challenge and who has the capacity to respond positively, its future development is likely to be very different from that of an infant whose mother, on account of poverty, ill-health, and other such adverse circumstances, is quite unable to take the child's demanding nature in her stride and will therefore respond adversely. However similar the two infants' initial predisposition, their subsequent course is also a function of the parent's ability to adjust to the child's individuality. For predictive purposes it is thus the mutuality of parental and child characteristics that has to be taken into account, and, all in all, goodness of fit has served well in drawing attention to this requirement.

☐ Socialization in an Interactive Context

We now have plenty of evidence to show that a basic mutuality of parent and child exists from birth on, founded on processes of child preadaptation, parental sensitivity, and developing interactive synchrony (Schaffer, 1984). Such mutuality has been demonstrated mainly by observing parents' and children's unstructured interactions as seen, in particular, in free play; there is, however, every reason to believe that the same mutuality prevails in the more structured type of socialization episode, in which parents set out to convey some quite specific aim to their children in the expectation that they will comply with the adult's wishes and adopt them as their own.

Socialization is primarily concerned with the acquisition of standards, the function of which is to inform the child of the dos and don'ts of conduct. Such standards are to be found in all aspects of human activity, ranging from highly specific, concrete behavior patterns such as eating with a spoon and not with fingers to much more encompassing abstract principles like telling the truth and not lying. They generally have both a prescriptive and a proscriptive aspect and are arranged in a hierarchy of psychological complexity that helps to determine their order of acquisition. Standards first become meaningful some time in the latter half of the second year (Kagan, 1981): it is then that children become cognitively capable of comparing the real with the ideal, "how it is" with "how it ought to be," as a result of which they can begin to evaluate their own actions and those of other people, and also the appearance or functioning of physical objects, in the light of particular norms. It is probably no coincidence that just around this age parents begin greatly to increase the pressure they exert on children to conform to adult wishes and requirements. Moreover, by imposing sanctions for violation, they often give these occasions a strong affective coloring: success, and even more so failure, in meeting standards are thus frequently experienced as highly emotional events, and especially so during the acquisition phase.

Parents initiate the setting and communicating of standards; children, however, do not just passively absorb their parents' messages and retain them whole and unchanged. On the contrary, from a very early age on children try actively to interpret and put their own sense on the requirements they are supposed to meet. Acquiring standards is thus far from being a mindless activity: although young children quickly come to realize that they are supposed to share adults' conceptions of what is good and what is bad, they do not automatically adopt their parents' messages but challenge, question, and adapt them to their own mental structures. What is more, they may even deliberately break the rules imposed on them in order to test the limits (Dunn, 1988) and, already from the third year on, they can generate their own standards (Kagan, 1981). As Lawrence and Valsiner (1993) have pointed out, socialization cannot therefore be conceived merely as a process of *transmission*, where one generation simply passes on its own set of values, but needs to be seen in terms of *transformation*, i.e., of culturally provided input incorporated by the child into its own conceptual system.

Differences in standards between parents and children thus need to be recognized as much as similarities. However, if the latter were not greater in extent and more basic in nature, a properly functioning society would not be a possibility, and it is similarities that therefore constitute the starting point for inquiry into how standards come to act as guideposts for children. To conduct such an inquiry we require answers to two key questions: (1) How do parents go about the task of communicating standards so that their children come to share the parents' aims? (2) How do children develop the capacity to adopt standards as their own and internalize them as personal signposts? Let us consider these problems in turn.

Becoming Acquainted With Standards

Research on parental communication of standards shows well how we have moved away from unidirectional to bidirectional thinking. Earlier accounts, influenced by reinforcement concepts, saw parents as "laying down the law" by virtue of their greater power and as enforcing conformity in the context of discipline encounters. More recent work, on the other hand, has placed the whole process in a reciprocal relationship context, stressed the mutual adjustment of parent and child required for successful control–compliance sequences, and treated these encounters more in terms of a joint negotiation process than an adult's arbitrary imposition on an unwilling child victim.

Let us look at some of the findings. Children are more likely to accept their parents' messages when these are delivered in an appropriate emotional climate, against the background of a warm, affectionate relationship, and when a secure attachment to the parents has been established (Londerville & Main, 1981). Compliance is also more likely when the parents sensitively time their demands to take into account the child's focus of attention and ongoing activity, rather than hurl them at the child in a bolt-out-of-the-blue fashion (Schaffer & Crook, 1980). Generally, a history of parental responsiveness to children's needs and wishes increases the children's willingness in turn to comply with the parents' needs and wishes, a condition referred to by Maccoby and Martin (1983) as "reciprocal compliance." In addition, effectiveness is greater if parental messages are made clear and meaningful for the child, the parent having correctly identified the level at which the child is operating and succeeded in diminishing the gap between parental and child schemata (Grusec & Goodnow, 1994). Further, parents are most likely to obtain compliance if they adjust their control techniques to the child's temperamental qualities: a match between temperament and type of technique adopted will facilitate parental socialization; a mismatch, on the other hand, is more likely to be detrimental to these efforts, an example, that is, of "goodness of fit" (Kochanska, 1993).

In short, children are most likely to comply with adult standards when the parents adjust their demands to the child's nature, developmental status, and ongoing activity and interests, and when compliance is not forcibly imposed but jointly constructed by child and parent on the basis of a history of reciprocal interaction. And as Dunn (1988) has shown so vividly, from the age of 2 children are fascinated by the whole subject of rules and sanctions, something they become acquainted with in the familiar, emotional exchanges with family members who clearly and continually articulate these in the course of everyday interactions and at a level that closely matches the child's own changing ability to comprehend, which is a far cry indeed from the punitive climate envisaged by earlier psychoanalytic and behaviorist accounts. Socialization thus occurs in a relationship context; standards are transmitted on the basis of interpersonal processes to which both partners, child as well as parent, make contributions.

Internalizing Standards

The acquisition of standards is generally described as a process that advances from outer to inner regulation. Initially, the standard is external to the child and is conveyed in the course of daily life by the parents, who then take appropriate action to ensure compliance. In due course the child comes to understand that compliance is something desirable. The end point, however, is reached when conforming to the standard has become a spontaneous part of the child's repertoire, i.e., when it is internalized as a means of self-regulation. Admittedly, this account may in some respects be an oversimplification. On the one hand, even young infants are already capable of some measure of self-regulation, as seen, for example, in their ability to control the amount of visual input they receive in face-to-face contact by alternating looking-at and looking-away periods and thus modulating their arousal level (Schaffer, 1984). And on the other hand, as Youniss (1983) has argued, no individual is ever completely free of the requirements of intimate others, and a certain amount of mutual regulation is thus found at every stage of social life. Nevertheless, the progression from outer to inner control does characterize a general drift to be discerned in early development, whereby parents progressively hand over responsibility as the child becomes older and more capable.

As to the processes whereby internalization of standards occurs, we are still largely ignorant despite recent renewed interest in the phenomenon (Grusec & Kuczynski, 1997). One reason concerns the difficulty of finding valid measures for such a subtle phenomenon. The most common means of assessment is by observing a child's willingness to follow parental requests (e.g., not to touch a toy) when the parent is not physically present, or "out-of-sight compliance," as it has been referred to; however, this is a somewhat crude measure with a limited range of applicability. Nevertheless, a few useful findings are available. One is that there appears to be functional continuity between compliance and internalization. The former, that is, is a developmental forerunner of the latter: The more a child has been involved in successful control–compliance sequences, the earlier and the more frequent do signs of an internal conscience regulating the child's behavior become evident (Kochanska, 1993). Another finding refers to the timing of the new capacity: the first indications of consciencelike behavior, such as spontaneous guilt and impulse checking, tend to occur around 2 to 3 years of age; by then the child begins to show that it can carry forward the rules and prohibitions of significant others and to be upset by violation (Emde, Biringen, Clyman, & Oppenheim, 1991). Whatever psychological processes are responsible for the onset of the capacity to internalize, it is at that time that they make their first appearance.

The most important question remaining unanswered, however, is, what are these processes? Some aspect of the capacity for representational thought must be implicated, in that the child draws on past experiences of parental regulation and, being able to "keep these in mind," appropriately applies them to the present situation. What we do not know is the form in which these past experiences are stored. Freud, in his account of superego development, did provide an answer, singling out the harsh, punitive side of the parent as that which the child incorporates and subsequently applies to transgressions; he also provided a rationale for taking such a step, based on the child's need to resolve the conflict between love and hate of the parent. There is, however, little empirical evidence that either force or fear of losing love can account for internalization. In any case, in the wake of attachment theory a rather different view has come to prevail as to what a child internalizes as a result of its involvement in close relationships. Children, as Bowlby (1973) proposed, develop internal working models based on their experiences with attachment figures. However, these reflect the relationship rather than the parent as an individual and, additionally, do not exclusively reflect the punitive, fear-arousing aspects of parenting but present a more positive, all-round picture than the Freudian one. Accounts of working models have, however, been primarily concerned with the security–insecurity aspect of relationships; when it comes to the storing of such specific features as parental standards we remain ignorant as to how these are represented. Are they personalized, as part of the particular parent's identity, or are they in impersonal form, without reference to the originator? Are they context bound, or in generalized, abstract form? Similarly, we do not know in what memory store the parent's messages are retained; the fact that Bowlby timed the onset of working models rather earlier than the age usually given for the beginnings of moral internalization suggests that rather more complex cognitive operations are involved in the latter development. How the emergence of representational thought enables children to keep in mind rules and standards even in the parent's absence; how and in what form these are internalized and retained; under what conditions the parental message becomes decontextualized from its originator and from the situation in which it was first encountered to take the form of abstract knowledge and general principles; whether the parent's verbalizations and the emotions accompanying the message play a part in organizing the child's retention; and generally what role the child's central representation of the parent plays in facilitating self-regulatory capacities—these all remain problems for further investigation. The notion that internalizing is a simple matter of taking in and memorizing parental values wholesale can be discarded. Everything we now know about children indicates that an active process of selecting, interpreting, and adapting in accord with the child's own mental schemas and individuality is likely to be involved. How this is accomplished needs to be addressed empirically.

☐ Conclusions

It is generally agreed that the unidirectional perspective is not an appropriate one for understanding children's socialization and that bidirectional views must prevail. Yet there is still considerable uncertainty as to precisely what bidirectionality actually means. That it involves more than two sets of arrows, one going in each direction between parent and child, is clear. It is also apparent that at its core lies the way in which these two sets of influences mesh, so that for certain purposes they can be treated as one unitary entity. The way in which the process of meshing is to be conceptualized, however, and the language we need to describe the resulting entity, are matters that are still largely unresolved.

What also still needs to be determined is the precise role that parents play in their children's psychological development. That this role is by no means as powerful or as clear-cut as it seemed at one time has gradually become apparent, yet given the ubiquity of parenting it seems ironic that we are still unable to spell out the actual extent of parental influence. No wonder that sharply differing opinions on this subject are to be found, ranging from Scarr's (1992) suggestion that as long as children receive "good enough" parenting their development is determined primarily by inherited characteristics, to Hoffman's (1984) reminder that, whatever the reality of child effects, parents are in a much more powerful position to influence their children than children their parents. Attempts by behavior geneticists to understand the interlocking contributions of inherited and environmental forces are the most likely source of clarity as to the role of parents in their children's lives.

What then has changed as a result of adopting a bidirectional view? Let us briefly mention some of the more prominent points as they apply to the study of social interaction. First, concepts derived from systems analysis have become prevalent: we can no longer think of interactions as chains of alternating elements; more encompassing units need to be adopted. Second, there have been changes in methodology: observational data-gathering techniques need to be such that an eye can be kept on both partners simultaneously, so that their respective contributions can be integrated into one comprehensive stream. Third, a much more positive picture of the parent as socializer has emerged: Freud's stern disciplinarian has given way to a sensitive negotiator, who conveys standards not just in discipline encounters but also by means of play, stories, conversations, and family routines. And, finally, and perhaps most important, there is respect for the child. No one now would dare to support Watson's view of the newborn as a "lowly piece of protoplasm" that only parental treatment can give meaning to; from birth on there is psychological organization and order that are not created by experience, although experience is required to widen their scope. Even the youngest child brings something of its own to all encounters with people and objects that we must acknowledge if we are to understand the nature of these encounters.

☐ References

Bell, R. Q. (1968). A reinterpretation of the direction of effects in studies of socialization. *Psychological Review, 75*, 81–95.

Bell, R. Q., & Chapman, M. (1986). Child effects in studies using experimental or brief longitudinal approaches to socialization. *Developmental Psychology, 22*, 595–603.

Bell, R. Q., & Harper, L. V. (1977). *Child effects on adults.* Hillsdale, NJ: Erlbaum.

Bijou, S. W. (1970). Reinforcement history and socialization. In R. A. Hoppe, G. A. Milton, & E. C. Simmel (Eds.), *Early experiences and the processes of socialization.* New York: Academic Press.

Bijou, S. W., & Baer, D. M. (1962). *Child development.* New York: Appleton-Century-Crofts.

Bowlby, J. (1973). *Attachment and loss. Vol. 2: Separation: Anxiety and anger.* London: Hogarth Press.

Boyle, M. H., & Pickles, A. (1997). Maternal disorder symptoms in children and adolescents. *Journal of Child Psychology and Psychiatry, 38*, 981–992.

Collis, G. M., & Schaffer, H. R. (1975). Synchronization of visual attention in mother-infant pairs. *Journal of Child Psychology and Psychiatry, 16*, 315–320.

Crockenberg, S. B. (1986). Are temperamental differences in babies associated with predictable differences in caregiving? In J. Lerner & R. Lerner (Eds.), *Temperament and social interaction in children*. San Francisco: Jossey-Bass.

Dodge, K. A. (1990). Nature versus nurture in childhood conduct disorder: It is time to ask a different question. *Developmental Psychology, 26*, 698–701.

Dunn, J. (1988). *The beginnings of social understanding*. Oxford, UK: Blackwell.

Dunn, J. (1993). *Young children's close relationships: Beyond attachment*. London: Sage.

Eckerman, C. O., & Oehler, J. M. (1992). Very-low birthweight newborns and parents as early social partners. In S. L. Friedman & M. D. Sigman (Eds.), *The psychological development of low birthweight children*. Norwood, NJ: Ablex.

Elder, G. H., Nguyen, T. V., & Caspi, A. (1984). Linking family hardship to children's lives. *Child Development, 56*, 361–375.

Emde, R. N., Biringen, Z., Clyman, R. B., & Oppenheim, D. (1991). The moral self of infancy: Affective core and procedural knowledge. *Developmental Review, 11*, 251–270.

Fraiberg, S. (1977). *Insights from the blind*. New York: Basic Books.

Golombok, S., & Fivush, R. (1994). *Gender development*. Cambridge, UK: Cambridge University Press.

Grusec, J., & Goodnow, J. (1994). Impact of parental discipline methods on the child's internalization of values: A reconceptualization of current points of view. *Developmental Psychology, 30*, 4–19.

Grusec, J., & Kuczynski, L. (1997). (Eds.). *Parenting and children's internalization of values*. New York: Wiley.

Hoffman, M. L. (1984). Moral development. In M. H. Bornstein & M. E. Lamb (Eds.), *Developmental psychology: An advanced textbook*. Hillsdale, NJ: Erlbaum.

Kagan, J. (1981). *The second year: The emergence of self-awareness*. Cambridge, MA: Harvard University Press.

Kanner, L. (1943). Autistic disturbance of affective contact. *Nervous Child, 2*, 217–250.

Kochanska, G. (1993). Toward a synthesis of parental socialization and child temperament in early development of conscience. *Child Development, 64*, 325–347.

Langlois, J. H., Ritter, J. M., Casey, R. J., & Sawin, D. B. (1995). Infant attractiveness predicts maternal behaviors and attitudes. *Developmental Psychology, 31*, 464–472.

Lawrence, J. A., & Valsiner, J. (1993). Conceptual roots of internalization: From transmission to transformation. *Human Development, 36*, 150–167.

Londerville, S., & Main, M. (1981). Security of attachment, compliance, and maternal training methods in the second year of life. *Developmental Psychology, 17*, 289–299.

Maccoby, E. E. (1984). Socialization and developmental change. *Child Development, 55*, 317–328.

Maccoby, E. E. (1992). The role of parents in the socialization of children: An historical overview. *Developmental Psychology, 28*, 1006–1017.

Maccoby, E., & Martin, J. A. (1983). Socialization in the context of the family: Parent-child interaction. In E. M. Hetherington (Ed.), *Handbook of child psychology* (Vol. 4). New York: Wiley.

Russell, A., & Russell, G. (1992). Child effects in socialization research: Some conceptual and data analysis issues. *Social Development, 1*, 163–184.

Scarr, S. (1988). How genotypes and environments combine: Development and individual differences. In N. Bolger, A. Caspi, G. Downey, & M. Moorehouse (Eds.), *Persons in contexts: Developmental processes*. Cambridge, UK: Cambridge University Press.

Scarr, S. (1992). Developmental theories for the 1990s: Development and individual differences. *Child Development, 63*, 1–19.

Schaffer, H. R. (1984). *The child's entry into a social world*. London: Academic Press.

Schaffer, H. R. (1992). Joint involvement episodes as contexts for cognitive development. In H. McGurk (Ed.), *Childhood social development: Contemporary perspectives.* Hove, UK: Erlbaum.

Schaffer, H. R. (1996). *Social development.* Oxford, UK: Blackwell.

Schaffer, H. R., & Crook, C. K. (1980). Child compliance and maternal control techniques. *Developmental Psychology, 16,* 54–61.

Schaffer, H. R., & Emerson, P. E. (1964). Patterns of response to physical contact in early human development. *Journal of Child Psychology and Psychiatry, 5,* 1–13.

Sears, R. R., Maccoby, E. E., & Levin, H. (1957). *Patterns of child rearing.* Evanston, IL: Row, Peterson.

Sorce, J. F., & Emde, R. N. (1982). The meaning of infant emotional expressions: Regularities in caregiving responses in normal and Down's syndrome infants. *Journal of Child Psychology and Psychiatry, 23,* 145–158.

Stern, D. N., Beebe, B., Jaffe, J., & Bennett, S. (1977). The infant's stimulus world during social interaction. In H. R. Schaffer (Ed.), *Studies in mother-infant interaction.* London: Academic Press.

Tamis-LeMonda, C. S. (1996). Maternal sensitivity: Individual, contextual, and cultural factors in recent conceptualizations. *Early Development and Parenting, 5,* 167–172.

Thomas, A., & Chess, S. (1977). *Temperament and development.* New York: Bremner/Mazel.

Thomas, A., Chess, S., Birch, H. G., Hertzig, M. E., & Korn, S. (1963). *Behavioral individuality in early childhood.* New York: New York University Press.

van den Boom, D. C. (1997). Sensitivity and attachment: Next steps for developmentalists. *Child Development, 64,* 592–594.

Watson, J. B. (1928). *Psychological care of infant and child.* New York: Norton.

Yarrow, M. R., Campbell, J. D., & Burton, R. V. (1968). *Child rearing: An inquiry into research and methods.* San Francisco: Jossey-Bass.

Youniss, J. (1983). Social construction of adolescence by adolescents and parents. In H. D. Grotevant & C. R. Cooper (Eds.), *Adolescent development in the family.* San Francisco: Jossey-Bass.

CHAPTER

Robert J. Sternberg

Looking Back and Looking Forward on Intelligence: Toward a Theory of Successful Intelligence

☐ Introduction

Although many different definitions of intelligence have been proposed over the years (see, e.g., "Intelligence and Its Measurement: A Symposium," 1921; Sternberg & Detterman, 1986), the conventional notion of intelligence is built around a loosely consensual definition of intelligence in terms of generalized adaptation to the environment. Theories of intelligence extend this definition by suggesting that there is a general factor of intelligence, often labeled g, that underlies all adaptive behavior. In many theories, including the theories most widely accepted today (e.g., Carroll, 1993; Gustafsson, 1994; Horn, 1994), other mental abilities are hierarchically nested under this general factor at successively greater levels of specificity. For example, Carroll suggests that three levels can nicely capture the hierarchy of abilities, whereas Cattell (1971) and Vernon (1971) suggested two levels were especially important. In the case

Preparation of this chapter was supported under the Javits Act Program (grant no. R206R50001) as administered by the Office of Educational Research and Improvement, U.S. Department of Education. Grantees undertaking such projects are encouraged to express freely their professional judgment. This article, therefore, does not necessarily represent the position or policies of the Office of Educational Research and Improvement or the U.S. Department of Education, and no official endorsement should be inferred.

289

of Cattell, nested under general ability are fluid abilities of the kind needed to solve abstract reasoning problems such as figural matrices or series completions and crystallized abilities of the kind needed to solve problems of vocabulary and general information. In the case of Vernon, the two levels corresponded to verbal-educational and practical-mechanical (that is, spatial) abilities. These theories and others like them are called into question in this essay.

In this essay I argue that the notion of intelligence as adaptation to the environment and as operationalized in narrowly based intelligence tests is inadequate. Rather I argue for a concept of successful intelligence, according to which intelligence is the ability to achieve success in life, given one's personal standards, within one's sociocultural context. One's ability to achieve success depends on one's capitalizing on one's strengths and correcting or compensating for one's weaknesses through a balance of analytical, creative, and practical abilities in order to adapt to, shape, and select environments.

The remainder of this essay is divided into three main parts. First, I argue that conventional notions of intelligence and its development are, at best, incomplete, and, at worst, wrong. Second, I suggest an alternative notion of successful intelligence that expands upon conventional notions of intelligence. The formulation presented here goes beyond that in previous work (Sternberg, 1997). Finally, I draw some conclusions about the nature of intelligence.

☐ Conventional Notions of Intelligence Are Inadequate

In this section I argue that conventional notions of intelligence are inadequate and certain modern ones also do not pass muster. I explain that intelligence is not a unitary construct, and so theories based on notions of general intelligence, dating back to Spearman (1904) and up to the present (e.g., Brand, 1996; Carroll, 1993; Jensen, 1998), cannot be correct either.

There now has accumulated a substantial body of evidence suggesting that, contrary to conventional notions, intelligence is not a unitary construct. This evidence is a variety of different kinds, most of which suggest that the positive manifold (pattern of positive correlations) among ability tests is not a function of some inherent structure of intellect. Rather, it reflects limitations in the interaction among the kinds of individuals tested, the kinds of tests used in the testing, and the situations in which the individuals are tested.

One kind of evidence suggests the power of situational contexts in testing (see also Ceci, 1996; Gardner, 1983; Lave, 1988; Nuñes, Schliemann, & Carraher, 1993). For example, Carraher, Carraher, and Schliemann (1985) (see also Ceci & Roazzi, 1994; Nuñes, 1994) studied a group of children that is especially relevant for assessing intelligence as adaptation to the environment. The group was of Brazilian street children. Brazilian street children are under great contextual pressure to form a successful street business. If they do not, they risk death at the hands of so-called death squads, which may murder children who, unable to earn money, resort to robbing stores (or who are suspected of resorting to robbing stores). The researchers found that the same children who are able to do the mathematics needed to run their street business are often little able or unable to do school mathematics. In fact, the more abstract and removed from real-world contexts the problems are in their form of presentation, the worse the children do on the problems. These results suggest that differences in context can have a powerful effect on performance.

Such differences are not limited to Brazilian street children. Lave (1988) showed that Berkeley housewives who successfully could do the mathematics needed for comparison shopping in the supermarket were unable to do the same mathematics when they were placed in a classroom and given isomorphic problems presented in an abstract form. In other words, their problem was not at the level of mental processes but at the level of applying the processes in specific environmental contexts.

Ceci and Liker (1986; see also Ceci, 1996) showed that, given tasks relevant to their lives, men would show the same kinds of effects as were shown by women in the Lave studies. These investigators studied men who successfully handicapped horse races. The complexity of their implicit mathematical formulas was unrelated to their IQ. Moreover, despite the complexity of these formulas, the mean IQ among these men was only at roughly the population average or slightly below. Ceci also subsequently found that the skills were really quite specific: The same men did not successfully apply their skills to computations involving securities in the stock market.

In our own research, we have found results consistent with those described above. These results have emanated from studies both in the United States and in other countries. We describe here our international studies because we believe they especially call into question the straightforward interpretation of results from conventional tests of intelligence that suggest the existence of a general factor.

In a study in Usenge, Kenya, near the town of Kisumu, we were interested in school-age children's ability to adapt to their indigenous environment (see Sternberg & Grigorenko, 1997). In collaboration with

Wenzel Geissler, Elena Grigorenko, Kate Nokes, Frederick Okatcha, and Ruth Prince, I was involved in devising a test of indigenous intelligence for adaptation to the environment. The test measured children's informal tacit knowledge for natural herbal medicines that the villagers believe can be used to fight various types of infections. We do not know if all or any of these medicines are actually effective. But from the standpoint of our study, the important thing is that the villagers think they are and therefore that knowledge about them is worth possessing.

We measured the children's ability to identify the medicines, what they are used for, and how they are dosed. Based on work we had done elsewhere, we expected that scores on this test would not correlate with scores on conventional tests of intelligence. In order to test this hypothesis, we also administered to the children the Raven Coloured Progressive Matrices Test, which is a measure of fluid or abstract-reasoning-based abilities, as well as the Mill Hill Vocabulary Scale, which is a measure of crystallized or formal-knowledge-based abilities. In addition, we gave the children a comparable test of vocabulary in their own Duluo language. The Duluo language is spoken in the home, English in the schools.

We did indeed find no correlation between the test of indigenous tacit knowledge and scores on the fluid-ability tests. But to our surprise, we found statistically significant correlations of the tacit-knowledge tests with the tests of crystallized abilities. The correlations, however, were negative. In other words, the higher the children scored on the test of tacit knowledge, the lower they scored, on average, on the tests of crystallized abilities. This surprising result can be interpreted in various ways, but based on the ethnographic observations of the cultural anthropologists on our team, Geissler and Prince, we concluded that a plausible scenario takes into account the expectations of families for their children.

Most families in the village do not particularly value formal Western schooling. There is no reason they should, as their children will for the most part spend their lives farming or engaged in other occupations that make little or no use of Western schooling. These families emphasize teaching their children the indigenous informal knowledge that will lead to successful adaptation in the environments in which they will really live. At the same time, there are some families in the village that have different expectations for their children. They hope that their children eventually may be able to leave the village and to go to a university, perhaps the University of Nairobi. These families tend to emphasize the value of Western education and to devalue indigenous informal knowledge. Thus the families typically value and emphasize one or the other kind of knowledge but not both.

The Kenya study suggests that the identification of a general factor of human intelligence may tell us more about patterns of schooling and especially Western patterns of schooling than it does about the structure of human abilities. In Western schooling, children typically study a variety of subject matters from an early age and thus develop skills in a variety of skill areas. This kind of schooling prepares the children to take a test of intelligence, which typically measures skills in a variety of areas. Often intelligence tests measure skills that children were expected to acquire a few years before taking the intelligence test. But as Rogoff (1990) and others have noted, this pattern of schooling is not universal and has not even been common for much of the history of humankind. Throughout history and in many places still, schooling, especially for boys, takes the form of apprenticeships in which children learn a craft from an early age. They learn what they will need to know in order to succeed in a trade, but not a lot more. They are not simultaneously engaged in tasks that require the development of the particular blend of skills measured by conventional intelligence tests. Hence it is less likely that one would observe a general factor in their scores, much as we discovered in Kenya. Some years back, Vernon (1971) pointed out that the axes of a factor analysis do not necessarily reveal a latent structure of the mind but rather represent a convenient way of characterizing the organization of mental abilities. Vernon believed that there was no one "right" orientation of axes, and indeed, mathematically, an infinite number of orientations of axes can be fit to any solution in an exploratory factor analysis. Vernon's point seems perhaps to have been forgotten or at least ignored by later theorists.

The developing world provides a particularly interesting laboratory for testing theories of intelligence because many of the assumptions that are held as dear in the developed world simply do not apply. A study we have done in Tanzania (see Sternberg & Grigorenko, 1997) points out the risks of giving tests, scoring them, and interpreting the results as measures of some latent intellectual ability or abilities. We administered to young school children in Bagamoyo, Tanzania, tests such as a form-board test and a Twenty Questions Test, which measure the kinds of skills required on conventional tests of intelligence. Of course, we obtained scores that we could analyze and evaluate, ranking the children in terms of their supposed general or other abilities. However, we administered the tests dynamically rather than statically (Feuerstein, 1979; Grigorenko & Sternberg, 1998; Vygotsky, 1978). Dynamic testing is like conventional static testing in that individuals are tested and inferences about their abilities made. But dynamic tests differ in that children are given some kind of feedback in order to help them improve their scores. Vygotsky (1978) suggested that the children's ability to profit from the guided instruction the children received during the testing session could serve as a measure of children's zone of proximal development (ZPD), or the difference between their developed abilities and their latent capacities. In other words, testing and instruction are treated as being of one piece rather than as being distinct processes.

In our assessments, children first were given the ability tests. Then they were given a brief period of instruction in which they were able to learn skills that would potentially enable them to improve their scores. Then they were tested again. Because the instruction for each test lasted only about 15 minutes, one would not expect dramatic gains. Yet, on average, the gains were statistically significant. More importantly, scores on the pretest showed only weak although significant correlations with scores on the posttest. These correlations, at about the .3 level, suggested that when tests are administered statically to children in developing countries, they may be rather unstable and easily subject to influences of training. The reason, of course, is that the children are not accustomed to taking Western-style tests, and so profit quickly even from small amounts of instruction as to what is expected from them. Of course, the more important question is not whether the scores changed or even correlated with each other, but rather how they correlated with other cognitive measures. In other words, which test was a better predictor of transfer to other cognitive performance, the pretest score or the gain from the pretest score to the posttest score? We found the gain score to be the better predictor, by a factor of 4. In other words, any general-factor score, or, really, any other factor score obtained from the pretest, which was equivalent to a typical statically administered test, would be of substantially lower validity than would be a gain score measuring learning at the time of the test as obtained from a dynamically administered test.

If intelligence is not just a single thing that can be measured by a conventional static test of intelligence, what is it? I argue that it comprises three things, each of which is a different aspect of intelligence.

☐ Three Aspects of Intelligence

The intelligence one needs to attain success in life comprises analytical, creative, and practical aspects. According to the proposed theory of human intelligence and its development (Sternberg, 1984, 1985, 1997), a common set of processes underlies these three aspects of intelligence.

Metacomponents, or executive processes, plan what to do, monitor things as they are being done, and evaluate things after they are done. Examples of metacomponents are recognizing the existence of a problem, defining the nature of the problem, deciding on a strategy for solving the problem, monitoring the solution of the problem, and evaluating the solution after the problem is solved. Performance components execute the instructions of the metacomponents. For example, inference is used to decide how two stimuli are related and application is used to apply what one has inferred (Sternberg, 1977). Knowledge-acquisition components are used to learn how to solve problems or simply to acquire declarative knowledge in the first place. For example, selective encoding is used to decide what information is relevant in the context of one's learning and selective comparison is used to bring old information to bear on new problems.

Although the same processes are used for all three aspects of intelligence, these processes are applied to different kinds of tasks and situations depending on whether a given problem requires analytical thinking, creative thinking, practical thinking, or a combination of these kinds of thinking.

Analytical Intelligence

Analytical intelligence is involved when the components of intelligence are applied to analyze, evaluate, judge, or compare and contrast. It typically is involved when components are applied to relatively familiar kinds of problems where the judgments to be made are of an abstract nature.

In some of my early work, I showed how analytical kinds of problems, such as analogies or syllogisms, can be analyzed componentially (Sternberg, 1977, 1983; Sternberg & Gardner, 1983), with response times or error rates decomposed to yield their underlying information-processing components. The goal of this research was to understand the information-processing origins of individual differences in (the analytical aspect of) human intelligence. With componential analysis, one could specify sources of individual differences underlying a factor score such as that for "inductive reasoning." For example, response times on analogies (Sternberg, 1977) and linear syllogisms (Sternberg, 1980) were decomposed into their elementary performance components so that it was possible to specify, in the solving of analogies or other kinds of problems, several sources of important individual or developmental differences:

(1) What performance components are used?
(2) How long does it takes to execute each component?
(3) How susceptible is each component to error?
(4) How are the components combined into strategies?
(5) What are the mental representations upon which the components act?

Studies of reasoning need not use artificial formats. In a more recent study, we looked at predictions for everyday kinds of situations, such as when milk will spoil (Sternberg & Kalmar, 1997). In this study, we looked at both predictions and postdictions (hypotheses about the past where information about the past is unknown) and found that postdictions took longer to make than did predictions.

Research on the components of human intelligence yielded some interesting results. For example, in a study of the development of figural analogical reasoning, we found that although children generally became quicker in information processing with age, not all components were executed more rapidly with age (Sternberg & Rifkin, 1979). The encoding component first showed a decrease in component time with age and then an increase. Apparently, older children realized that their best strategy was to spend more time in encoding the terms of a problem so that they would later be able to spend less time in operating on these encodings. A related finding was that better reasoners tend to spend relatively more time than do poorer reasoners in global, up-front metacomponential planning, when they solve difficult reasoning problems. Poorer reasoners, on the other hand, tend to spend relatively more time in local planning (Sternberg, 1981). Presumably, the better reasoners recognize that it is better to invest more time up front so as to be able to process a problem more efficiently later on. We also found in a study of the development of verbal analogical reasoning that, as children grew older, their strategies shifted so that they relied on word association less and abstract relations more (Sternberg & Nigro, 1980).

Some of our studies concentrated on knowledge-acquisition components rather than on performance components or metacomponents. For example, in one set of studies, we were interested in sources of individual differences in vocabulary (Sternberg & Powell, 1982; Sternberg, Powell, & Kaye, 1982; see also Sternberg, 1987b). We were not content just to write these off as individual differences in declarative knowledge, because we wanted to understand why it was that some people acquired this declarative knowledge and others did not. What we found is that there were multiple sources of individual and developmental differences. The three main sources were in knowledge-acquisition components, use of context clues, and use of mediating variables. For example, in the sentence, "The blen rises in the east and sets in the west," the knowledge-acquisition component of selective comparison is used to relate prior knowledge about a known concept, the sun, to the unknown word (neologism) in the sentence, "blen." Several context cues appear in the sentence, such as the fact that a blen rises, the fact that it sets, and the information about where it rises and sets. A mediating variable is that contextual information can occur after the presentation of the unknown word.

We did research such as that described above because we believed that conventional psychometric research sometimes incorrectly attributed individual and developmental differences. For example, a verbal analogies test that might appear on its surface to measure verbal reasoning might in fact primarily measure vocabulary and general information (Sternberg, 1977). In fact, in some populations, reasoning might hardly be a source of individual or developmental differences at all. And if we then look at the sources of the individual differences in vocabulary, we would need to understand that the differences in knowledge did not come from nowhere: Some children had much more frequent and better opportunities to learn word meanings than did others.

The kinds of analytical skills we studied in this research can be taught. For example, in one study, we tested whether it is possible to teach people better to decontextualize meanings of unknown words presented in context (Sternberg, 1987a). In one study, we gave participants a pretest on their ability to decontextualize word meanings. Then the participants were divided into five conditions, two of which were control conditions that lacked formal instruction. In one condition, participants were not given any instructional treatment. They merely were asked later to take a posttest. In a second condition, they were given practice as an instructional condition, but there was no formal instruction, per se. In a third condition, they were taught knowledge-acquisition component processes that could be used to decontextualize word meanings. In a fourth condition, they were taught to use context cues. In a fifth condition, they were taught to use mediating variables. Participants in all three of the theory-based formal-instructional conditions outperformed participants in the two control conditions, whose performance did not differ. In other words, theory-based instruction was better than no instruction at all or just practice without formal instruction.

Research on the componential bases of intelligence was useful in understanding individual differences in performance on conventional tests of intelligence. But it became increasingly clear to me that this research basically served to partition the variation on conventional tests in a different way, rather than serving to uncover previously untapped sources of variation. Children develop intellectually in ways beyond just what conventional psychometric intelligence tests or even Piagetian tests based on the theory of Piaget (1972) measure. So what might be some of these other sources of variation? Creative intelligence seemed to be one such source of variation, a source that is almost wholly untapped by conventional tests.

Creative Intelligence

Intelligence tests contain a range of problems, some of them more novel than others. In some of our work we have shown that when one goes beyond the range of unconventionality of the tests, one starts to tap sources of individual differences measured little or not at all by the tests. According to the theory of successful intelligence, (creative) intelligence is particularly well measured by problems assessing how well an individual can cope with relative novelty. Thus it is important to include in a battery of test problems that are relatively novel in nature. These problems can be either convergent or divergent in nature.

In work with convergent problems, we presented individuals with novel kinds of reasoning problems that had a single best answer. For example, they might be told that some objects are green and others blue; but still other objects might be grue, meaning green until the year 2000 and blue thereafter, or bleen, meaning blue until the year 2000 and green thereafter. Or they might be told of four kinds of people on the planet Kyron: blens, who are born young and die young; kwefs, who are born old and die old; balts, who are born young and die old; and prosses, who are born old and die young (Sternberg, 1982; Tetewsky & Sternberg, 1986). The individuals' task was to predict future states from past states, given incomplete information. In another set of studies, people were given more conventional kinds of inductive reasoning problems, such as analogies, series completions, and classifications, but were told to solve them. But the problems had premises preceding them that were either conventional (dancers wear shoes) or novel (dancers eat shoes). The participants had to solve the problems as though the counterfactuals were true (Sternberg & Gastel, 1989a, 1989b).

In these studies, we found that correlations with conventional kinds of tests depended on how novel or nonentrenched the conventional tests were. The more novel the items, the higher the correlations of our tests with scores on the conventional tests. We also found that when response times on the relatively novel problems were componentially analyzed, some components better measured the creative aspect of intelligence than did others. For example, in the "grue–bleen" task mentioned above, the information-processing component requiring people to switch from conventional green–blue thinking to grue–bleen thinking and then back to green–blue thinking again was a particularly good measure of the ability to cope with novelty.

In work with divergent reasoning problems having no one best answer, we asked people to create various kinds of products (Lubart & Sternberg, 1995; Sternberg & Lubart, 1991, 1995, 1996) where an infinite variety of responses were possible. Individuals were asked to create products in the realms of writing, art, advertising, and science. In writing, they would be asked to write very short stories for which we would give them a choice of titles, such as "Beyond the Edge" or "The Octopus's Sneakers." In art, they were asked to produce art compositions with titles such as "The Beginning of Time" or "Earth From an Insect's Point of View." In advertising, they were asked to produce advertisements for products such as a brand of bow tie or a brand of doorknob. In science, they were asked to solve problems such as one asking them how people might detect extraterrestrial aliens among us who are seeking to escape detection. Participants created two products in each domain.

We found that creativity is relatively, although not wholly, domain specific. Correlations of ratings of the creative quality of the products across domains were lower than correlations of ratings and generally were at about the .4 level. Thus, there was some degree of relation across domains, at the same time that there was plenty of room for someone to be strong in one or more domains but not in others. More importantly, perhaps, we found, as we had for the convergent problems, a range of correlations with conventional tests of abilities. As was the case for the correlations obtained with convergent problems, correlations were higher to the extent that problems on the conventional tests were nonentrenched. For example, correlations were higher with fluid than with crystallized ability tests, and correlations were higher, the more novel the fluid test was. Even the highest correlations, however, were only at the .5 level, suggesting that tests of creative intelligence tap skills beyond those measured even by relatively novel kinds of items on conventional tests of intelligence.

The work we did on creativity raised a number questions about sources of individual and developmental differences:

(1) To what extent was the thinking of the individual novel or nonentrenched?
(2) What was the quality of the individual's thinking?
(3) To what extent did the thinking of the individual meet the demands of the task?

We also found, though, that creativity, broadly defined, extends beyond the intellectual domain. Sources of individual and developmental differences in creative performance include not only process aspects, but also aspects of knowledge, thinking styles, personality, motivation, and the environmental context in which the individual operates (see Sternberg & Lubart, 1995, for details).

Creative-thinking skills can be taught and we have devised a program for teaching them (Sternberg & Williams, 1996). In some of our work, we divided gifted and nongifted fourth-grade children into experimental and control groups. All children took pretests on insightful thinking. Then some of the children received their regular school instruction, whereas others received instruction on insight skills. After the instruction of whichever kind, all children took a posttest on insight skills. We found that children taught how to solve the insight problems using knowledge-acquisition components gained more from pretest to posttest than did students who were not so taught (Davidson & Sternberg, 1984).

Tests of creative intelligence go beyond tests of analytical intelligence in measuring performance on tasks that require individuals to deal with relatively novel situations. But how about situations that are relatively familiar, but in a practical rather than an academic domain? Can one measure intelligence in the practical domain, and, if so, what is its relation to intelligence in more academic kinds of domains?

Practical Intelligence

Practical intelligence involves individuals applying their abilities to the kinds of problems that confront them in daily life, such as on the job or in the home. Practical intelligence involves applying the components of intelligence to experience so as to (a) adapt to, (b) shape, and (c) select environments. Adaptation is involved when one changes oneself to suit the environment. Shaping is involved when one changes the environment to suit oneself. And selection is involved when one decides to seek out another environment that is a better match to one's needs, abilities, and desires. People differ in their balance of adaptation, shaping, and selection, and in the competence with which they balance among the three possible courses of action.

Much of our work on practical intelligence has centered on the concept of tacit knowledge. We define this construct, for our purposes, as what one needs to know in order to work effectively in an environment that one is not explicitly taught and that often is not even verbalized (Sternberg & Wagner, 1993; Sternberg, Wagner, & Okagaki, 1993; Sternberg, Wagner, Williams, & Horvath, 1995; Wagner & Sternberg, 1986). We represent tacit knowledge in the form of production systems, or sequences of "if–then" statements that describe procedures one follows in various kinds of everyday situations.

We typically have measured tacit knowledge using work-related problems that present problems one might encounter on the job. We have measured tacit knowledge for both children and adults, and among adults, for people in various occupations such as management, sales, academia, and the military. In a typical tacit-knowledge problem, people are asked to read a story about a problem someone faces and to rate, for each statement in a set of statements, how adequate a solution the statement represents. For example, in a paper-and-pencil measure of tacit knowledge for sales, one of the problems deals with sales of photocopy machines. A relatively inexpensive machine is not moving out of the showroom and has become overstocked. The examinee is asked to rate the quality of various solutions for moving the particular model out of the showroom. In a performance-based measure for salespeople, the test-taker makes a phone call to a supposed customer, who is actually the examiner. The test-taker tries to sell advertising space over the phone. The examiner raises various objections to buying the advertising space. The test-taker is evaluated for the quality, rapidity, and fluency of the responses on the telephone.

In our studies, we found that practical intelligence as embodied in tacit knowledge increases with experience, but it is profiting from experience, rather than experience per se, that results in increases in scores. Some people can have been in a job for years and still have acquired relatively little tacit knowledge. We also have found that subscores on tests of tacit knowledge, such as for managing oneself, managing others, and managing tasks, correlate significantly with each other. Moreover, scores on various tests of tacit knowledge, such as for academics and managers, are also correlated fairly substantially (at about the .5 level). However, scores on tacit-knowledge tests do not correlate with scores on conventional tests of intelligence, whether the measures used are single-score measures or multiple-ability batteries. Despite their lack of correlation with conventional measures, the scores on tacit-knowledge tests predict performance on the job as well as or better than do conventional psychometric intelligence tests. In one study done at the Center for Creative Leadership, we further found that scores on our tests of tacit knowledge for management were the best single predictor of performance on a managerial simulation. In a hierarchical regression, scores on conventional tests of intelligence, personality, styles, and interpersonal orientation were entered first, and scores on the test of tacit knowledge were entered last. Scores on the test of tacit knowledge were the single best predictor of managerial simulation score. Moreover, they also contributed significantly to the prediction even after everything else was entered first into the equation. In recent work on military leadership (Hedlund, Sternberg, Horvath, & Dennis, 1998), we found that scores on a test of tacit knowledge for military leadership predicted ratings of leadership effectiveness, whereas scores on a conventional test of intelligence and on our tacit-knowledge test for managers did not significantly predict the ratings of effectiveness.

We have also done studies of social intelligence, which is viewed in the theory of successful intelligence as a part of practical intelligence. In these studies, individuals were presented with photos and were asked to make judgments about the photos. In one kind of photo, they were asked to evaluate whether a male–female couple was a genuine couple (i.e., really involved in a romantic relationship) or a phony couple posed by the experimenters. In another kind of photo, they were asked to indicate which of two individuals was the other's supervisor (Barnes & Sternberg, 1989; Sternberg & Smith, 1985). We found females to be superior to males on these tasks. Scores on the two tasks did not correlate with scores on conventional ability tests, nor did they correlate with each other, suggesting a substantial degree of domain specificity in the task.

Practical-intelligence skills can be taught. We have developed a program for teaching practical intellectual skills, aimed at middle-school students, that explicitly teaches students "practical intelligence for school" in the contexts of doing homework, taking tests, reading, and writing (Williams et al., 1996). We have evaluated the program in a variety of settings (Gardner, Krechevsky, Sternberg, & Okagaki, 1994; Sternberg, Okagaki, & Jackson, 1990) and found that students taught via the program outperform students in control groups that did not receive the instruction.

Combining Analytical, Creative, and Practical Intelligence

The studies described above looked at analytical, creative, and practical intelligence separately. But a full validation of the theory of successful intelligence would require research that looks at all three aspects of intelligence in conjunction. To date, we have done two such sets of studies.

In one set of studies, we explored the question of whether conventional education in school systematically discriminates against children with creative and practical strengths (Sternberg & Clinkenbeard, 1995; Sternberg, Ferrari, Clinkenbeard, & Grigorenko, 1996; Sternberg, Grigorenko, Ferrari, & Clinkenbeard, 1999). Motivating this work was the belief that the systems in schools strongly tend to favor children with strengths in memory and analytical abilities.

We devised a test for high-school students of analytical, creative, and practical abilities that consisted of both multiple-choice and essay items. The multiple-choice items required the three kinds of thinking in three content domains: verbal, quantitative, and figural. Thus there were 9 multiple-choice and 3 essay subtests. The test was administered to 324 children around the United States and in some other countries who were identified by their schools as gifted by any standard whatsoever. Children were selected for a summer program in (college-level) psychology if they fell into one of five ability groupings: high analytical, high creative, high practical, high balanced (high in all three abilities), or low balanced (low in all three abilities). Students who came to Yale were then divided into four instructional groups. Students in all four instructional groups used the same introductory psychology textbook (a preliminary version of Sternberg [1995]) and listened to the same psychology lectures. What differed among them was the type of afternoon discussion section to which they were assigned. They were assigned to an instructional condition that emphasized either memory, analytical, creative, or practical instruction. For example, in the memory condition, they might be asked to describe the main tenets of a major theory of depression. In the analytical condition, they might be asked to compare and contrast two theories of depression. In the creative condition, they might be asked to formulate their own theory of depression. In the practical condition, they might be asked how they could use what they had learned about depression to help a friend who was depressed.

Students in all four instructional conditions were evaluated in terms of their performance on homework, a midterm exam, a final exam, and an independent project. Each type of work was evaluated for memory, analytical, creative, and practical quality. Thus, all students were evaluated in exactly the same way.

Our results suggested the utility of the theory of successful intelligence. First, we observed when the students arrived at Yale that the students in the high creative and high practical groups were much more diverse in terms of racial, ethnic, socioeconomic, and educational backgrounds than were the students in the high-analytical group. In other words, just by expanding the range of abilities we measured, we discovered more intellectual strengths than would have been apparent through a conventional test. Moreover, the kinds of students identified as strong differed in terms of populations from which they were drawn in comparison with students identified as strong solely by analytical measures.

When one does principal-components or principal-factor analysis, one always obtains a general factor if one leaves the solution unrotated. Such a factor is a mathematical property of the algorithm used. But we found the general factor to be very weak, suggesting that the general factor of intelligence is probably relevant only when a fairly narrow range of abilities is measured, as is typically the case with conventional tests. We found that testing format had a large effect on results: Multiple-choice tests tend to correlate with other multiple-choice tests, almost without regard to what they measure. Essay tests show only weak correlations with multiple choice, however. We further found that after we controlled for modality of testing (multiple choice versus essay), the correlations between the analytical, creative, and practical sections were very weak and generally nonsignificant, supporting the relative independence of the various abilities. We found that all three ability tests—analytical, creative, and practical—significantly predicted course performance. When multiple-regression analysis was used, at least two of these ability measures contributed significantly to the prediction of each of the measures of achievement. Perhaps as a reflection of the difficulty of deemphasizing the analytical way of teaching, one of the significant predictors was always the analytical score. (However, in a replication of our study with low-income African-American students from New York, Deborah Coates of the City University of New York found a different pattern of results. Her data indicated that the practical tests were better predictors of course performance than were the analytical measures, suggesting that what ability tests predict depends on population as well as mode of teaching.) Most importantly, there was an aptitude-treatment interaction whereby students who were placed in instructional conditions that better matched their pattern of abilities outperformed students who were mismatched. In other words, when students are taught in a way that fits how they think, they do better in school. Children with creative and practical abilities, who are almost never taught or assessed in a way that matches their pattern of abilities, may be at a disadvantage in course after course, year after year.

In a follow-up study (Sternberg, Torff, & Grigorenko, 1998a, 1998b), we looked at learning of social studies and science by third graders and eighth graders. The third graders were students in a very low income neighborhood in Raleigh, North Carolina. The eighth graders were students who were largely middle to upper-middle class studying in Baltimore, Maryland, and Fresno, California. In this study, students were assigned to one of three instructional conditions. In the first condition, they were taught the course that basically they would have learned had we not intervened. The emphasis in the course was on memory. In a second condition, they were taught in a way that emphasized critical (analytical) thinking. In the third condition, they were taught in a way that emphasized analytical, creative, and practical thinking. All students' performance was assessed for memory learning (through multiple-choice assessments) as well as for analytical, creative, and practical learning (through performance assessments).

As expected, we found that students in the successful-intelligence (analytical, creative, practical) condition outperformed the other students in terms of the performance assessments. One could argue that this result merely reflected the way they were taught. Nevertheless, the result sug-

gested that teaching for these kinds of thinking succeeded. More important, however, was the result that children in the successful–intelligence
condition outperformed the other children even on the multiple-choice
memory tests. In other words, to the extent that one's goal is just to
maximize children's memory for information, teaching for successful intelligence is still superior. It enables children to capitalize on their
strengths and to correct or to compensate for their weaknesses, and it allows children to encode material in a variety of interesting ways.

Thus the results of two sets of studies suggest that the theory of successful intelligence is valid not just in its parts but as a whole. Moreover,
the results suggest that the theory can make a difference not only in laboratory tests, but in school classrooms as well.

☐ Conclusion

The time has come to move beyond conventional theories of intelligence
and its development. In this essay I have provided data suggesting that
conventional theories and tests of intelligence are incomplete. The general factor is an artifact of limitations in populations of individuals tested,
types of materials with which they are tested, and types of methods used
in testing. Indeed, our studies show that even when one wants to predict
school performance, the conventional tests are fairly limited in their predictive validity (Sternberg & Williams, 1997). I have proposed a theory
of successful intelligence and its development that fares well in construct
validations, whether one tests in the laboratory, in schools, or in the
workplace. The greatest obstacle to our moving on is in vested interests,
both in academia and in the world of tests, where testing companies are
doing well financially with existing tests. We now have ways to move
beyond conventional notions of intelligence; we need only the will.

☐ References

Barnes, M. L., & Sternberg, R. J. (1989). Social intelligence and decoding of nonverbal
   cues. *Intelligence, 13,* 263–287.
Brand, C. (1996). *The g factor: General intelligence and its implications.* Chichester, UK: Wiley.
Carraher, T. N., Carraher, D., & Schliemann, A. D. (1985). Mathematics in the streets and
   in schools. *British Journal of Developmental Psychology, 3,* 21–29.
Carroll, J. B. (1993). *Human cognitive abilities: A survey of factor-analytic studies.* New York:
   Cambridge University Press.
Cattell, R. B. (1971). *Abilities: Their structure, growth and action.* Boston: Houghton Mifflin.
Ceci, S. J. (1996). *On intelligence: A bioecological treatise on intellectual development* (expanded
   edition). Cambridge, MA: Harvard University Press.

Ceci, S. J., & Liker, J. (1986). Academic and nonacademic intelligence: An experimental separation. In R. J. Sternberg & R. K. Wagner (Eds.), *Practical intelligence: Nature and origins of competence in the everyday world* (pp. 119–142). New York: Cambridge University Press.

Ceci, S. J., & Roazzi, A. (1994). The effects of context on cognition: postcards from Brazil. In R. J. Sternberg & R. K. Wagner (Eds.), *Mind in context: Interactionist perspectives on human intelligence* (pp. 74–101). New York: Cambridge University Press.

Davidson, J. E., & Sternberg, R. J. (1984). The role of insight in intellectual giftedness. *Gifted Child Quarterly, 28,* 58–64.

Feuerstein, R. (1979). *The dynamic assessment of retarded performers: The learning potential assessment device, theory, instrument, and techniques.* Baltimore, MD: University Park.

Gardner, H. (1983). *Frames of mind: The theory of multiple intelligences.* New York: Basic Books.

Gardner, H., Krechevsky, M., Sternberg, R. J., & Okagaki, L. (1994). Intelligence in context: Enhancing students' practical intelligence for school. In K. McGilly (Ed.), *Classroom lessons: Integrating cognitive theory and classroom practice* (pp. 105–127). Cambridge, MA: Bradford Books.

Grigorenko, E. L., & Sternberg, R. J. (1998). Dynamic assessment. *Psychological Bulletin, 124,* 75–111.

Gustafsson, J. E. (1994). Hierarchical models of intelligence and educational achievement. In A. Demetriou & A. Efklides (Eds.), *Intelligence, mind and reasoning: Structure and development* (pp. 45–73). Amsterdam: North-Holland/Elsevier Science Publishers.

Hedlund, J., Sternberg, R. J., Horvath, J. A., & Dennis, M. (1998, April). The acquisition of tacit knowledge for military leadership: Implications for training. Paper presented at the Society for Industrial and Organizational Psychology Conference, Dallas, TX.

Horn, J. L. (1994). Theory of fluid and crystallized intelligence. In R. J. Sternberg (Ed.), *The encyclopedia of human intelligence* (Vol. 1, pp. 443–451). New York: Macmillan.

Intelligence and its measurement: A symposium. (1921). *Journal of Educational Psychology, 12,* 123–147, 195–216, 271–275.

Jensen, A. R. (1998). *The g factor: The science of mental ability.* Westport, CT: Praeger/Greenwood.

Lave, J. (1988). *Cognition in practice: Mind mathematics and culture in everyday life.* New York: Cambridge University Press.

Lubart, T. I., & Sternberg, R. J. (1995). An investment approach to creativity: Theory and data. In S. M. Smith, T. B. Ward, & R. A. Finke (Eds.), *The creative cognition approach* (pp. 269–302). Cambridge, MA: MIT Press.

Nuñes, T. (1994). Street intelligence. In R. J. Sternberg (Ed.), *Encyclopedia of human intelligence* (Vol. 2, pp. 1045–1049). New York: Macmillan.

Nuñes, T., Schliemann, A. D., & Carraher, D. W. (1993). *Street mathematics and school mathematics.* New York: Cambridge University Press.

Piaget, J. (1972). *The psychology of intelligence.* Totowa, NJ: Littlefield Adams.

Rogoff, B. (1990). *Apprenticeship in thinking: Cognitive development in social context.* New York: Oxford University Press.

Spearman, C. E. (1904). "General intelligence" objectively determined and measured. *American Journal of Psychology, 15,* 201–293.

Sternberg, R. J. (1977). *Intelligence, information processing, and analogical reasoning: The componential analysis of human abilities.* Hillsdale, NJ: Erlbaum.

Sternberg, R. J. (1980). Representation and process in linear syllogistic reasoning. *Journal of Experimental Psychology: General, 109,* 119–159.

Sternberg, R. J. (1981). Intelligence and nonentrenchment. *Journal of Educational Psychology, 73,* 1–16.

Sternberg, R. J. (1982). Natural, unnatural, and supernatural concepts. *Cognitive Psychology, 14,* 451–488.

Sternberg, R. J. (1983). Components of human intelligence. *Cognition, 15,* 1–48.

Sternberg, R. J. (1984). If at first you don't believe, try "tri" again. *Behavioral and Brain Sciences, 7,* 304–315.

Sternberg, R. J. (1985). *Beyond IQ: A triarchic theory of human intelligence.* New York: Cambridge University Press.

Sternberg, R. J. (1987a). Most vocabulary is learned from context. In M. G. McKeown & M. E. Curtis (Eds.), *The nature of vocabulary acquisition* (pp. 89–105). Hillsdale, NJ: Erlbaum.

Sternberg, R. J. (1987b). The psychology of verbal comprehension. In R. Glaser (Ed.), *Advances in instructional psychology* (Vol. 3, pp. 97–151). Hillsdale, NJ: Erlbaum.

Sternberg, R. J. (1995). *In search of the human mind.* Orlando, FL: Harcourt Brace College Publishers.

Sternberg, R. J. (1997). *Successful intelligence.* New York: Plume.

Sternberg, R. J., & Clinkenbeard, P. R. (1995). A triarchic model of identifying, teaching, and assessing gifted children. *Roeper Review, 17,* 255–260.

Sternberg, R. J., & Detterman D. K. (Eds.). (1986). *What is intelligence? Contemporary viewpoints on its nature and definition.* Norwood, NJ: Ablex.

Sternberg, R. J., Ferrari, M., Clinkenbeard, P. R., & Grigorenko, E. L. (1996). Identification, instruction, and assessment of gifted children: A construct validation of a triarchic model. *Gifted Child Quarterly, 40* (3) 129–137.

Sternberg, R. J., & Gardner, M. K. (1983). Unities in inductive reasoning. *Journal of Experimental Psychology: General, 112,* 80–116.

Sternberg, R. J., & Gastel, J. (1989a). Coping with novelty in human intelligence: An empirical investigation. *Intelligence, 13,* 187–197.

Sternberg, R. J., & Gastel, J. (1989b). If dancers ate their shoes: Inductive reasoning with factual and counterfactual premises. *Memory and Cognition, 17,* 1–10.

Sternberg, R. J., & Grigorenko, E. L. (1997, Fall). The cognitive costs of physical and mental ill health: Applying the psychology of the developed world to the problems of the developing world. *Eye on Psi Chi, 2,* 20–27.

Sternberg, R. J., Grigorenko, E. L., Ferrari, M., & Clinkenbeard, P. (1999). A triarchic analysis of an aptitude interaction. *European Journal of Psychological Assessment, 15,* 1–11.

Sternberg, R. J., & Kalmar, D. A. (1997). When will the milk spoil? Everyday induction in human intelligence. *Intelligence, 25,* 185–203.

Sternberg, R. J., & Lubart, T. I. (1991). An investment theory of creativity and its development. *Human Development, 34,* 1–31.

Sternberg, R. J., & Lubart, T. I. (1995). *Defying the crowd: Cultivating creativity in a culture of conformity.* New York: Free Press.

Sternberg, R. J., & Lubart, T. I. (1996). Investing in creativity. *American Psychologist, 51,* 677–688.

Sternberg, R. J., & Nigro, G. (1980). Developmental patterns in the solution of verbal analogies. *Child Development, 51,* 27–38.

Sternberg, R. J., Okagaki, L., & Jackson, A. (1990). Practical intelligence for success in school. *Educational Leadership, 48,* 35–39.

Sternberg, R. J., & Powell, J. S. (1982). Theories of intelligence. In R. J. Sternberg (Ed.), *Handbook of human intelligence* (pp. 975–1005). New York: Cambridge University Press.

Sternberg, R. J., Powell, J. S., & Kaye, D. B. (1982). The nature of verbal comprehension. *Poetics, 11,* 155–187.

Sternberg, R. J., & Rifkin, B. (1979). The development of analogical reasoning processes. *Journal of Experimental Child Psychology, 27,* 195–232.

Sternberg, R. J., & Smith, C. (1985). Social intelligence and decoding skills in nonverbal communication. *Social Cognition, 2,* 168–192.

Sternberg, R. J., Torff, B., & Grigorenko, E. L. (1998a). Teaching for successful intelligence raises school achievement. *Phi Delta Kappan, 79,* 667–669.

Sternberg, R. J., Torff, B., & Grigorenko, E. L. (1998b). Teaching triarchically improves school achievement. *Journal of Educational Psychology, 90,* 374–384.

Sternberg, R. J., & Wagner, R. K. (1993). The g-ocentric view of intelligence and job performance is wrong. *Current Directions in Psychological Science, 2,* 1–4.

Sternberg, R. J., Wagner, R. K., & Okagaki, L. (1993). Practical intelligence: The nature and role of tacit knowledge in work and at school. In H. Reese & J. Puckett (Eds.), *Advances in lifespan development* (pp. 205–227). Hillsdale, NJ: Erlbaum.

Sternberg, R. J., Wagner, R. K., Williams, W. M., & Horvath, J. A. (1995). Testing common sense. *American Psychologist, 50,* 912–927.

Sternberg, R. J., & Williams, W. M. (1996). *How to develop student creativity.* Alexandria, VA: Association for Supervision and Curriculum Development.

Sternberg, R. J., & Williams, W. M. (1997). Does the Graduate Record Examination predict meaningful success in the graduate training of psychologists? A case study. *American Psychologist, 52,* 630–641.

Tetewsky, S. J., & Sternberg, R. J. (1986). Conceptual and lexical determinants of nonentrenched thinking. *Journal of Memory and Language, 25,* 202–225.

Vernon, P. E. (1971). *The structure of human abilities.* London: Methuen.

Vygotsky, L. (1978). *Mind in society: The development of higher order processes.* Cambridge, MA: Harvard University Press.

Wagner, R. K., & Sternberg, R. J. (1986). Tacit knowledge and intelligence in the everyday world. In R. J. Sternberg & R. K. Wagner (Eds.), *Practical intelligence: Nature and origins of competence in the everyday world* (pp. 51–83). New York: Cambridge University Press.

Williams, W. M., Blythe, T., White, N., Li, J., Sternberg, R. J., & Gardner, H. I. (1996). *Practical intelligence for school: A handbook for teachers of grades 5–8.* New York: HarperCollins.

CHAPTER James V. Wertsch

Cognitive Development

☐ Introduction

Reflecting on the study of cognitive development as we near the end of this century naturally leads to questions about how far we have come since 1900. The short answer is that although progress has been uneven and halting it has nevertheless been very impressive. Theoretical and empirical findings from the past one hundred years, especially since World War II, provide us with a much more informed picture of human cognition and its development than was ever before imaginable. (See Case, this volume, for a comprehensive overeiew.)

This progress has been possible because scholars have focused on certain issues and pursued them in detail. Although this strategy has been entirely reasonable and quite productive, it has also involved certain costs in terms of what has been left out of the picture. A useful way to formulate these costs can be found in Kenneth Burke's (1966) account of "terministic screens." In contrast to approaches that focus on the power of insight that theoretical terms bring to an analysis, Burke was often concerned with the limitations and blinders they introduce. He emphasized that: "even if any given terminology is a *reflection* of reality, by its very nature as a terminology it must be a *selection* of reality; and to this extent it must function also as a *deflection* of reality" (1966, p. 45).

The writing of this chapter was supported by the Swedish Collegium for Advanced Study in the Social Sciences, Uppsala, Sweden. The author expresses his appreciation to this organization, where he was a fellow during the 1998 spring semester.

309

Burke's point was not that we should somehow avoid or transcend terministic screens. Indeed, "We *must* use terministic screens, since we can't say anything without the use of terms" (p. 50). Instead, his point was that we need to develop a deeper appreciation of what is neglected and "deflected," as well as "selected" when employing a particular set of terms. This takes on particular importance when considering academic disciplines because being socialized into a discipline means, among other things, becoming fluent in the use of a particular set of terms and hence becoming comfortable with selecting certain aspects of the reality we explore and ignoring others. The result is all too often the development of what Burke called "learned incapacities" that go along with such socialization.

A part of Burke's line of reasoning is that the terms we employ to formulate issues in a discipline emerge for many reasons, some of which have little to do with intellectual merit. To some degree of course the refinement of terms does reflect the beneficial forces of a marketplace of ideas. Terms that are clearly formulated, useful in guiding research, and empirically supported acquire a kind of social capital, and those that fail to meet these tests lose out. However, as a discipline grows and is increasingly shaped by forces such as bureaucratic rationalization (standardized review procedures for professional journals, etc.), terms and associated claims and methods tend to take on a life of their own, a life that often reflects gate keeping processes and other functions involved in reproducing the discipline rather than intellectual merit.

Such observations should in no way be taken to suggest that some kind of conspiracy is involved. At least since the classic writings of Weber (1946), it has been widely recognized that the "iron cage of rationality" is a part of bureaucratic institutions whenever and wherever they arise. By becoming institutionalized a discipline gains a great deal in the way of rationalizing the marketplace of ideas through peer review and so forth, but it does so at the cost of making it quite difficult, especially for junior scholars, to operate outside the boundaries of well-established terministic screens and their associated methods. Disciplines and subdisciplines clearly allow for continuous innovation and growth, but they also tend to impose limits on how much innovation is allowed, or even recognized, when issues are formulated around a particular set of terministic screens.

In what follows, I offer no magic bullets for how to deal with these issues. I don't think there are any, or at least any simple ones. However, I do think that it is possible to take some modest steps toward reflecting on the terministic screens that "constrain" as well as "afford" (Wertsch, 1998) the discourse and thinking of a discipline. Furthermore, I think it is possible to address some of the constraints that terministic screens introduce when trying to build interdisciplinary bridges. In what follows I shall be particularly interested in building bridges that address the relationship between individuals and their social context in the study of cognitive development.

☐ The Terministic Screens of Methodological Individualism

A brief review of the terministic screens we employ in the study of cognitive development provides a useful starting point for what I have to say. In this respect "cognitive development" shares an essential, but little examined, assumption with many other terms from psychology such as "cognition," "perception," "attention," and "memory." What I have in mind is that unless otherwise indicated all of these terms are taken to refer to processes carried out by individuals in isolation. To be sure, interest in topics such as "distributed cognition" (Hutchins, 1991; Salomon, 1993), "collective memory" (Middleton & Edwards, 1990), and "socially shared cognition" (Resnick, Levine, & Teasley, 1991) can be taken to indicate an opposing tendency, but even these terms often leave a commitment to the primacy of the individual in place.

From this perspective it is important to recognize that terms such as "cognition" and "memory" automatically are assumed to apply to processes carried out by the individual unless they are preceded by modifiers such as "socially distributed" or "collective." A perusal of the titles and contents of journals, books, departmental subcommittees, and divisions of professional organizations makes this quite clear. When we buy into the set of assumptions associated with terms such as "cognition," we are giving a sort of analytic primacy to individual over social processes. The implication of having to use modifiers such as "socially distributed" is that cognition in the "real" or "basic" sense is something that goes on "within the skin" or "between the ears" and that socially distributed cognition should be thought of as a sort of artificial or metaphorical extension of its analytically prior conceptual cousin.

The assumptions at work here constitute a form of "methodological individualism." As formulated by Stephen Lukes (1977),

> Methodological individualism . . . is a prescription for explanation, asserting that no purported explanations of social (or individual) phenomena are to count as explanations, or . . . as rock-bottom explanations, unless they are couched wholly in terms of facts about individuals. (p. 180)

In what follows, I shall be examining some of the ways that assumptions and terms associated with methodological individualism constrain us as we seek to understand some of the social dimensions of cognitive development. In pursuing this line of reasoning, it is important to specify what I am *not* saying as well as what I am. Specifically, I am *not* claiming that nothing of interest or importance goes on within individuals. To the contrary, I take it that individual processes are a necessary component in any intelligible account of cognition, memory, and so forth (Wertsch, 1998). Like Hutchins (1995b), I am simply claiming that what goes on within the skin is not *all* that needs to be taken into account in understanding human cognitive functioning. Instead, essential aspects of such functioning can be understood only if we take it to be the case the "mind extends beyond the skin" (Wertsch, 1998).

In my experience the terministic screens that we employ in analyzing cognitive development, at least in the United States, make this claim quite difficult to incorporate into research efforts. The difficulty does not stem from some kind of perverse unwillingness to explore or accept alternative formulations. Indeed, it is often the case that analysts of cognitive development enthusiastically embrace claims about how the mind extends beyond the skin when these claims are explicitly set forth in abstract form. Instead, the difficulty stems from the power of implicit assumptions associated with terministic screens, which make it very hard to put these claims into play and to keep them in play as we go about our research activities.

In this respect, the difficulties we encounter may be compared with those that Michael Reddy (1979) noted we have when we use English to talk about communication. According to him, our habits of thought, in this case shaped by a basic "conduit metaphor" in English, are so entrenched that even when we consciously try to resist them, we soon find ourselves back in their clutches. Reddy observes:

> I do not claim that we cannot think momentarily in terms of another model [than one grounded in the conduit metaphor] of the communication process. I argue, rather, that that thinking will remain brief, isolated, and fragmentary in the face of an entrenched system of opposing attitudes and assumptions. (pp. 297–298)

Similar limitations may be assumed to be associated with terministic screens grounded in methodological individualism that shape our thinking about cognitive development.

Of course the point is not to view the existence and power of terministic screens as a reason to despair. Instead, the point is to become conscious of them, to understand how they both "afford" and "constrain" (Wertsch, 1998) our patterns of thinking and discourse, and to find alternative formulations that make it possible to develop multiple perspectives on complex phenomena. In what follows, I explore these points, beginning with some personal observations about how difficult this can be.

☐ A Personal Journey

My reflections on the terministic screens and assumptions associated with methodological individualism stem from an experience I had early in my career. After obtaining a Ph.D. at the University of Chicago in 1975, I spent a year as a postdoctoral fellow in Moscow working with A. R. Luria, A. N. Leont'ev, D. B. El'konin, V. P. Zinchenko, V. V. Davydov, and others. As preparation for this postdoctoral visit (and many subsequent visits in the years to come) I studied Russian and did a great deal of background reading. Among other places, this showed up in my dissertation on reconstructive memory, where I drew on insights from figures such as L. S. Vygotsky and M. M. Bakhtin.

However, little in all this work prepared me for the conceptual shock that awaited me in Moscow in 1975. I found a great deal that excited, but mostly baffled, me about the way that my colleagues there thought about human consciousness, cognition, cognitive development, and so forth. I soon came to realize that the problem was not language, in the sense of Russian vocabulary and grammar. Although I make no great claims about the strength of my Russian language skills, they were not the seat of the problems that concern me here. I was, however, clearly encountering problems with language in another sense. Namely, I was having a very hard time understanding the conceptual language used to formulate issues in lectures, readings, and discussion.

My initial tendency was to assume that I understood this conceptual language all too well and that what I was hearing was simply a version of what had appeared in the United States some half century or so earlier. This left me with the impression that what I was encountering was a sort of reinvention in the Soviet Union of what had already been done in the United States. After some time, however, it became apparent that this interpretation was inadequate, if not ethnocentric and arrogant. I consistently ran up against the fact that the assumptions and lines of inquiry used by my Soviet colleagues differed in essential respects with mainstream thought in psychology at *any* point in its history in the West. However, the terministic screens that I employed were so grounded in Western ways of seeing that it took me at least half a year of attending lectures and engaging in discussion and reading to begin to fathom this.

What began to dawn on me at that point was that my Russian colleagues were up to something fundamentally different from what I had in mind when approaching issues of cognition and cognitive development. Some of this difference derived from research that was going on at the time I was in Moscow in the mid 1970s, but much of it stemmed from earlier times. A major source of the conceptual difficulty I was having was the seminal work that Vygotsky and his colleagues (especially Leont'ev and Luria) had done in the late 1920s and early 1930s, work that after decades of officially enforced neglect had once again come to dominate much of Soviet psychology in the 1960s and 1970s.

As my understanding of what my colleagues were saying grew deeper I came to recognize that the forces behind my difficulties extended beyond theoretical and methodological orientation. In addition, general cultural differences between the way that a Russian and an American scholar approaches the formulation of human mental processes were involved. I say "Russian," rather than "Soviet" here quite intentionally. My first inclination and the inclination of many others in the 1970s was to attribute the powerful ideas of Vygotsky and his colleagues to the fact that they were trying to develop a Marxist, and more specifically a Soviet Marxist, psychology. In my view there is little doubt that Vygotsky found some of Marx's ideas important and sought to incorporate them into his approach. At the same time, however, there is little, if anything in Vygotsky's writings that is *necessarily* Marxist in my view. In contrast, say, to Leont'ev (1981), who sought to ground his theory of activity in Marx's Sixth Thesis on Feuerbach, the essential theoretical sources for Vygotsky are to be found elsewhere.

In retrospect, then, I see that I came to the discussions in Moscow equipped with terministic screens grounded in methodological individualism. This was by no means a conscious choice; it was not something I had considered as one of several alternatives and decided to accept. Rather, it was just something that I assumed, falsely as it turned out, to be an obvious and natural starting point for the study of human cognition.

The power that these terministic screens had over my thinking was brought home to me by the fact that they continued to have their impact despite the fact that I had spent a good deal of time studying approaches that would seem quite compatible with those outlined by Vygotsky and his colleagues. For example, I had thought a great deal about the ideas of George Herbert Mead (1934), another scholar who is often credited with identifying and criticizing the limitations of methodological individualism (Farr, 1996). Indeed, along with a fellow graduate student, Benjamin Lee, and my dissertation advisor, Carol Feldman, I had offered a seminar on Mead's ideas at the University of Chicago in the early 1970s.

The fact that all of this somehow just did not "take" with me has brought home over the years the power that methodological individualism has over our everyday imagination in the United States, even when we try to struggle against it. In my case, coming to recognize ways in which terministic screens led me to neglect and deflect, as well as select, issues was a slow process. It required being immersed in a different conceptual world for a year as a postdoctoral fellow and continuous effort ever since.

☐ Mind Extends Beyond the Skin

In exploring how mind extends beyond the skin, it is interesting to take note of a useful formulation that can be found in the writings of a scholar best known for his research in neuropsychology, which is a discipline that is usually grounded quite securely in the tenets of methodological individualism. In *Language and Cognition* Luria declared:

> *In order to explain the highly complex forms of human consciousness one must go beyond the human organism. One must seek the origins of conscious activity and "categorical" behavior not in the recesses of the human brain or in the depths of the spirit, but in the external conditions of life. Above all, this means that one must seek these origins in the external processes of social life, in the social and historical forms of human existence.* (1981, p. 25; italics in the original)

Luria's call to go beyond the individual in order to understand individual processes of cognition bears striking parallels to statements made by G. H. Mead, but in Luria's case they grew primarily out of ideas developed by Vygotsky. This is not to suggest that there was no connection between these two traditions. One such connection can be found in the fact that Vygotsky read the works of John Dewey, who was Mead's teacher and colleague, but, more generally, Mead and Vygotsky shared a debt to a common "ancestor," if not the "founder" (Farr, 1996) of a major tradition, namely, Hegel.

For my purposes the crucial point is that there was a strong theoretical assumption on the part of Vygotsky, Luria, and others that basic ties exist between individual mental functioning and social processes. From this perspective there are two related, yet analytically distinct, senses in which mind extends beyond the skin, and exploring these provides a host of important challenges for the study of cognitive development today. In what follows, I shall outline these under the heading of "intermental processes" and "mediated action."

Mind Extends Beyond the Skin I: Intermental Processes

The first sense in which mind extends beyond the skin concerns the fact that mental processes are often carried out on the "intermental," rather than the "intramental" plane. As used here these terms come from Vygotsky's "General Genetic Law of Cultural Development":

> Any function in the child's cultural development appears twice, or on two planes. First it appears on the social plane, and then on the psychological plane. First it appears between people as an interpsychological category, and then within the child as an intrapsychological category. This is equally true with regard to voluntary attention, logical memory, the formation of concepts, and the development of volition. . . . [I]t goes without saying that internalization transforms the process itself and changes its structure and functions. Social relations or relations among people genetically underlie all higher functions and their relationships. (1981b, p. 163)

An essential part of Vygotsky's formulation of the intermental and intramental planes is that he viewed them as being inherently related. Indeed the boundaries between social and individual functioning are quite permeable in his account, and his concern was with ongoing transformations between intermental and intramental processes rather than with any sharp distinctions that can be drawn. From this perspective an element of sociality characterizes even the most private and internal forms of mental functioning.

> [Higher mental functions'] composition, genetic structure, and means of action—in a word, their whole nature—is social. Even when we turn to [internal] mental processes, their nature remains quasi-social. In their own private sphere, human beings retain the functions of social interaction. (Vygotsky, 1981b, p. 164)

This statement does not assume that higher mental functioning in the individual is a direct and simple copy of socially organized processes; the point Vygotsky made in his formulation of the General Genetic Law of Cultural Development about transformations in internalization warns against any such view. Furthermore, it does not assume that nothing of interest goes on in the mind or brain of the individual when participating in intermental functioning. Instead, it simply posits a close connection, grounded in genetic transformations, between the specific strategies and processes of intermental and intramental functioning.

Vygotsky's General Genetic Law of Cultural Development underlies several aspects of his account of human mental functioning. One that has received a great deal of attention in the West is the "zone of proximal development" (e.g., Rogoff & Wertsch, 1984). This is the zone, or distance between the performance level of an apprentice operating independently on the intramental plane and the intermental functioning involving an apprentice and an expert. It has provided the foundation for analyzing adult–child interaction and instruction (Wertsch, 1985), interaction and learning of children with disabilities (Brown & Ferrara, 1985), and many other purposes.

Vygotsky's discussion of intermental processes has also played a role in the recent formulation of ideas about "socially shared cognition" (Resnick et al., 1991), "distributed cognition" (Cole & Engeström, 1993), "collective memory" (Middleton & Edwards, 1990), and other related topics. In several of these cases the discussion does not posit a transition from the social to the individual plane that Vygotsky mentioned in the General Genetic Law of Cultural Development. Instead of speaking of social *origins*, with the assumption that the primary role of intermental functioning is to give rise to intramental functioning, investigators of socially shared cognition are often concerned with human cognitive activity that *remains* on the intermental plane. This is now widely recognized in studies of workplace activities, and it has taken on new importance in educational settings as well with the rise of practices such as "reciprocal teaching" (Palincsar & Brown, 1984) and "communities of learners" (Brown & Campione, 1994).

In analyzing these processes investigators such as Rogoff (1997) have begun to raise a host of interesting questions about how to understand and assess intermental functioning in its own right, for example, without reference to how it may give rise to intramental functioning. This brings with it some interesting new assumptions about how the expression "cognitive development" is to be used. In contrast to the usual assumptions grounded in methodological individualism, the point is that intermental functioning itself may be examined from the perspective of development. From this perspective, it is appropriate to examine the development of cognition *of a group* and not just of the individuals in it. Some dyads and larger groups such as institutions and even entire societies seem to function differently and perhaps at more advanced levels than others. Differences in how "institutions think" (Douglas, 1986) or "societies remember" (Connerton, 1989) have long been recognized by anthropologists, sociologists, and other scholars, but such expressions, let alone the conceptual framework behind them, are quite alien to most studies of cognitive development.

This raises a host of fascinating issues requiring conceptual frameworks that will be quite different from those we currently employ. What does it mean for a group—as a group—to develop cognitively? How can we formulate the processes involved such that they can be studied in some kind of principled way? How would we go about assessing the relative levels of development of groups?

Mind Extends Beyond the Skin II: Mediated Action

The second sense in which mind extends beyond the skin derives from the claim that human action, including mental action, involves the use of "mediational means," or "cultural tools" (terms I shall use interchangeably). From this perspective humans are viewed as fundamentally tool-using animals, where the notion of tool includes semiotic devices as well as instruments such as hammers and saws. In conducting analyses of these issues, it is essential to take into account both cultural tools and the active agents who use them, and in this connection I would propose "mediated action" as a unit of analysis (Wertsch, 1998). Such an approach has a well-established history in the human sciences. For example, Burke (1966) dealt with similar issues in writing about "symbolic action," Dewey (1938; Hickman, 1990) dealt with "instrumental action," and Vygotsky (1981a) did so in his account of phenomena such as the "instrumental act" and "mediation."

Incorporating mediation into an account of human action provides an essential way to avoid some of the problems of methodological individualism. In particular, it provides a way to build a conceptual bridge between sociocultural settings reflecting historical, cultural, and institutional forces, on the one hand, and active agents (individuals or groups), on the other. From this perspective sociocultural settings produce the mediational means that agents employ in carrying out mediated action, and as a result sociocultural settings are "imported" into virtually all areas of human functioning, including mental functioning. Hence it is virtually impossible for us to act in a way that is not socioculturally situated.

In my view the most important point that is missing in many contemporary analyses of cognitive development today is the recognition of how cultural tools shape our action. If one accepts that cultural tools play an essential role in human action, then one is led to recognize that there is an important sense in which such action can never be attributed solely to individuals. Instead, cultural tools make a fundamental contribution to action, even when it is carried out by an individual in physical isolation from others. For example, even for the individual who is solving a mental problem alone, the process remains "quasisocial" in the sense understood by Vygotsky (1981b) because that individual is acting in a sort of collaboration with mediational means.

The defining property of mediated action is the irreducible tension between mediational means, on the one hand, and their use by active agents, on the other. Leaving either of these two elements out of the picture encourages us to engage in a form of reductionism. If our terministic screens lead us to ignore the mediational means, it is all too easy to head down the path of methodological individualism; if we leave out the contribution made by the active agent, we are likely to fall prey to the kind of "oversocialization" that concerned Dewey (1938) and others. In this latter regard it is important to recognize that cultural tools do not mechanistically determine action. Indeed, in and of themselves, cultural tools are powerless. They can only have their impact when actually employed by an individual or individuals. While cultural tools have their "affordances" (Gibson, 1979; Norman, 1988; Still & Costall, 1989), which are likely and strongly suggested uses, even the most sophisticated analysis of the tool in and of itself cannot tell us how it will be used by individuals in the performance of a unique action.

Hence a focus on mediated action requires us to recognize the tension between cultural tools, with all their potential to shape action, on the one hand, and the unique use of these cultural tools, with all its unpredictability and creativity, on the other. This view is generally compatible with several currents of theoretical and empirical research. In studies of the development of language and cognition, for example, Nelson (1996) has outlined a compatible set of claims. Cole (1996) has done a similar thing for cultural psychology. After tracing the historical roots of this "once and future discipline," Cole outlines some illustrations that take the reader far beyond the ordinary confines of cognitive development. Specifically, he notes that an adequate analysis of instruction and cognitive development requires coordination among psychology, anthropology, sociology, and other disciplines.

Similar conclusions emerge when one considers some recent efforts in cognitive science. For example, Rumelhart, Smolensky, McClelland, and Hinton (1986) made the point that much of human cognitive functioning involves a complex combination of processes such as human pattern recognition, on the one hand, and the use of external memory aids such as written numbers, on the other. More recently, Clark (1997) has made similar claims in outlining a set of claims about the philosophical foundations of cognitive science, and empirical findings such as those reported by Hutchins (1995a, 1995b) arrive at similar conclusions about the need to understand human cognitive functioning in terms of agents using cultural tools. In a way that is analogous to those who use terms such as "socially distributed cognition" when examining intermental functioning, Hutchins' studies challenge methodological individualism from the perspective of mediated action. For example, in his account of "how cockpits remember their speeds" (1995b), he points to the need to redefine basic terminology that is usually assumed to refer to mental processes of the individual in isolation (i.e., in isolation from the cultural tools provided by a sociocultural setting).

Thus, recognizing the second sense in which mind extends beyond the skin transforms the study of cognitive development in fundamental ways. By including mediation in the picture the inherent links between cognitive development and the cultural, historical, and institutional settings in which it occurs come into focus in some very promising ways. Furthermore, this has the potential to bring the study of cognitive development into closer, and quite productive, contact with other disciplines such as anthropology and sociology.

☐ Conclusion

I have outlined two sorts of terministic screens that affect our perspective on cognitive development. In my view both cases derive from the methodological individualism that is so pervasive in Western, or at least American, views of the human mind and action. In one case this has led us to draw overly rigid, and hence unproductive, distinctions between intermental and intramental functioning, and in the other it has led us to overlook the ways that we are inherently situated in sociocultural settings by virtue of the cultural tools that shape virtually any action we carry out.

My point in focusing on these terministic screens is not to discount the accomplishments of research in cognitive development over the past century or to suggest that with proper foresight it would have been possible to avoid all the problems it has encountered. As Burke noted, "We *must* use terministic screens, since we can't say anything without the use of terms" (1966, p. 50), so the choice is not one of whether or not to be limited to their constraints in general. Instead, it is choice of *which* terministic screens we choose to use and whether we make conscious efforts to compare the perspectives we derive when using one with others.

In my view the recent rise of studies of the "zone of proximal development" and related intermental phenomena has produced some important new insights into the relationship between social and individual processes. I believe we have further to go, however, when it comes to recognizing the power of mediational means to shape human action. Indeed, I see our continuing resistance to recognizing the power of cultural tools to shape action as one of the most debilitating legacies of methodological individualism in the contemporary study of cognitive development. In seeking to overcome this limitation, the point is not to reject existing perspectives in the hope of creating a new, uncluttered vision.

Rather, the point is to foster research from a variety of perspectives, each empowered and constrained by its own teministic screens, that will allow us to address the complexity we need to recognize as we enter the next century of research on cognitive development.

☐ References

Brown, A. L., & Campione, J. C. (1994). Guided discovery in a community of learners. In K. McGilly (Ed.), *Classroom lessons: Integrating cognitive theory and classroom practice.* Cambridge, MA: MIT Press.

Brown, A. L., & Ferrara, R. A. (1985). Diagnosing zones of proximal development. In J. V. Wertsch, Ed., *Culture, communication, and cognition: Vygotskian perspectives* (pp. 273–305). New York: Cambridge University Press.

Burke, K. (1966). *Language as symbolic action: Essays on life, literature, and method.* Berkeley, CA: University of California Press.

Clark, A. (1997). Connectionism's contribution to the future of cognitive science. In D. M. Johnson & C. E. Erneling (Eds.). *The future of the cognitive revolution.* New York: Oxford University Press.

Cole, M. (1996). *Cultural psychology.* Cambridge, MA: Harvard University Press.

Cole, M., & Engeström, Y. (1993). A cultural-historical interpretation of distributed cognition. In G. Salomon, Ed., *Distributed cognitions: Psychological and educational considerations.* Cambridge, UK: Cambridge University Press.

Connerton, P. (1989). *How societies remember.* Cambridge, UK: Cambridge University Press.

Dewey, J. (1938). *Logic: The theory of inquiry.* New York: Holt, Rinehart and Winston.

Douglas, M. (1986). *How institutions think.* Syracuse, NY: Syracuse University Press.

Farr, R. M. (1996). *The roots of modern social psychology 1872–1954.* London: Blackwell.

Gibson, J. J. (1979). *The ecological approach to visual perception.* Boston: Houghton-Mifflin.

Hickman, L. A. (1990). *John Dewey's pragmatic technology.* Bloomington, IN: Indiana University Press.

Hutchins, E. (1991). The social organization of distributed cognition. In L. B. Resnick, J. M. Levine, & S. D. Teasley (Eds.), *Perspectives on socially shared cognition* (pp. 283–307). Washington, DC: American Psychological Association.

Hutchins, E. (1995a). *Cognition in the wild.* Cambridge, MA: MIT Press.

Hutchins, E. (1995b). How a cockpit remembers its speeds. *Cognitive Science, 19,* 265–288.

Leont'ev, A. N. (1981). The problem of activity in psychology. In J. V. Wertsch, Ed., *The concept of activity in Soviet psychology* (pp. 37–71). Armonk, NY: M. E. Sharpe.

Lukes, S. (1977). Methodological individualism reconsidered. In S. Lukes (Ed.), *Essays in social theory* (pp. 177–186). New York: Columbia University Press.

Luria, A. R. (1981). *Language and cognition,* (J. V. Wertsch, Ed.). New York: Wiley Intersciences.

Mead, G. H. (1934). *Mind, self, and society from the standpoint of a social behaviorist.* Chicago: University of Chicago Press.

Middleton, D., & Edwards, D. (Eds.). (1990). *Collective remembering.* London: Sage.

Nelson, K. (1996). *Language in cognitive development: The emergence of the mediated mind.* New York: Cambridge University Press.

Norman, D. A. (1988). *The psychology of everyday things.* New York: Basic Books.

Palincsar, A. S., & Brown, A. L. (1984). Reciprocal teaching of comprehension-fostering and comprehension-monitoring activities. *Cognition and Instruction, 1,* 117–175.

Reddy, M. J. (1979). The conduit metaphor: A case of frame conflict in our language about language. In A. Ortony (Ed.), *Metaphor and thought.* Cambridge, UK: Cambridge University Press.

Resnick, L. V., Levine, J. M., & Teasley, S. D. (Eds.). (1991). *Perspectives on socially shared cognition.* Washington, DC: American Psychological Association.

Rogoff, B. (1997). Evaluating development in the process of participation: Theory, methods, and practice building on each other. In E. Amsel & A. Renninger, Eds., *Change and development* (pp. 265–285). Hillsdale, NJ: Erlbaum.

Rogoff, B., & Wertsch, J. V. (Ed.). (1984). *Children's learning in the "zone of proximal development,"* no. 23. In *New directions for child development.* San Francisco: Jossey-Bass.

Rumelhart, D. E., Smolensky, P., McClelland, J. L., & Hinton, G. E. (1986). Schemata and sequential thought processes in PDP models. In J. C. McClelland, D. E. Rumelhart, & the PDP Research Group (Eds.), *Parallel distributed processing: Volume 2.* Cambridge, MA: MIT Press.

Salomon, G. (Ed.). (1993). *Distributed cognitions: Psychological and educational implications.* Cambridge, UK: Cambridge University Press.

Still, A., & Costall, A. (1989). Mutual elimination of dualism in Vygotsky and Gibson. *The Quarterly Newsletter of the Laboratory of Comparative Human Cognition, II* (4), 131–136.

Vygotsky, L. S. (1981a). The instrumental method in psychology. In J. V. Wertsch (Ed.), *The concept of activity in Soviet psychology* (pp. 134–143). Armonk, NY: M. E. Sharpe.

Vygotsky, L. S. (1981b). The genesis of higher mental functions. In J. V. Wertsch (Ed.), *The concept of activity in Soviet psychology* (pp. 144–188). Armonk, NY: M. E. Sharpe.

Weber, M. (1946). *From Max Weber: Essays in sociology.* Oxford, UK: Oxford University Press.

Wertsch, J. V. (1985). *Vygotsky and the social formation of mind.* Cambridge, MA: Harvard University Press.

Wertsch, J. V. (1998). *Mind as action.* New York: Oxford University Press.

AUTHOR INDEX

SUBJECT INDEX